Voices of
The Rams

Voices of The Rams

Players, Managers and Supporters Talking About Derby County

IAN HALL

The Breedon Books
Publishing Company
Derby

First published in Great Britain in 2000 by
The Breedon Books Publishing Company Limited
Breedon House, 3 The Parker Centre, Derby, DE21 4SZ.

ISBN 1 85983 167 2

Printed and bound by Butler & Tanner Ltd., Selwood Printing Works,
Caxton Road, Frome, Somerset.

Colour separations and jacket printing by
GreenShires Group Ltd., Leicester.

Contents

Introduction

VOICES OF THE RAMS is not a book about statistics and it certainly does not claim to be a definitive book about the history of Derby County Football Club. These have been already successfully achieved. Rather it is a book about memories. The memories of players, managers and supporters. Its aim is to outline a social history of Derby County for the greater part of the 20th century, as reflected in the words of individuals for whom Derby County played an important part in their lives.

Unlike today, many players who appeared for the Rams through the 1930s to the 1960s were local men who could first be interviewed as supporters themselves. Some recall watching the Rams as schoolboys and then the awesome experience of later playing in the same Derby team as men who they had regarded as their heroes.

The players remember their triumphs and their disasters. And they talk about their teammates and their managers. How hard were George Jobey and Harry Storer? Just what was the Clough magic? Where did Peter Taylor fit in? Who was the best footballer they ever played alongside? And against? And what about that Baseball Ground pitch?

Supporters also recall their favourite players and their most memorable matches, from the pre-war years right up to the move to Pride Park, a ground which is the envy of many Premiership teams. Officials tell the behind-the-scenes story of how Pride Park came about. And earlier, how the Rams almost folded in 1984, their very centenary year.

These memories take the reader on a fascinating walk through Derby County's history as witnessed by those who played and those who watched.

Acknowledgements
Ian Hall would like to express his sincere thanks to all the people – former players, managers, supporters, officials and colleagues in the media – who so willingly gave up their time to talk about Derby County.

Interviewees

Beard	George	Supporter
Bowers	John	Player 1959-65
Brownson	Bill	Supporter
Bullions	Jimmy	Player War years; 1945-47
Buxton	Ian	Player 1959-67; Derbyshire CCC 1959-73
Carlin	Willie	Player 1968-70
Christian	Roy	Supporter; hospital radio broadcaster
Clough	Brian	Manager 1967-73
Davies	Roger	Player 1971-79
Davison	Bobby	Player 1982-87; 1991-92
Dunford	Michael	Assistant secretary; secretary/general manager
Durban	Alan	Player 1963-72
Fearn	Jim	Press officer; communications manager
Flint	Brian	Supporter
Gadsby	Peter	Director, vice-chairman
George	Charlie	Player 1975-81
Gibson	Colin	BBC Radio Derby sports producer
Gretton	Michael	Press steward
Guthrie	Gordon	Player; physiotherapist
Halford	David	Player 1935
Hallam	Ernie	Supporter
Harrison	Reg	Player War years; 1945-54
Hazledine	Don	Player 1952-53
Hazledine	Geoff	Player 1953
Hector	Kevin	Player 1966-81
Hinton	Alan	Player 1967-75
Hopkinson	Mick	Player 1960-67
Hughes	Gordon	Player 1963-67
Jeffries	Alf	Player 1936-38
Knight,	Jeff	Player, War Years
Lawrence	Colin	Supporter
Loring	Keith	Chief executive
Mackay	Dave	Player 1968-70; manager 1973-76
McAndrew	Bob	Player 1963
McClaren	Steve	Player 1985-87; first-team coach 1995-99

McFarland	Roy	Player 1967-83; assistant manager 1984-93; manager 1993-95
McGrath	Paul	Player 1996
McMinn	Ted	Player 1987-92
Mee	Edward 'Ned'	Supporter
Metcalfe	Ron	Player 1966
Millin	Alf	Player 1955
Morris	Johnny	Player 1948-52
Mortimer	Gerald	Derby Evening Telegraph sports writer
Mozley	Bert	Player 1946-54
Newbery	Peter	Player 1958-60
O'Hare	John	Player 1967-73
Parkin	Les	Photographer
Pickering	Lionel	Chairman
Powell	Tommy	Player War years; 1948-61
Powell	Steve	Player 1971-84
Richards	Graham	BBC Radio Derby commentator
Sellors	Graham	Supporter
Smith	Jim	Manager 1995-
Steele	Eric	Player 1984-85; goalkeeping coach
Stimac	Igor	Player 1995-99
Stubley	Tom	Supporter
Sutton	Steve	Player 1984; 1991-96
Tacey	Stan	Supporter
Upton	Frank	Player 1954-66
Wainwright	Bill	Manager, Midland Hotel
Waller	Phil	Player 1961-67
Ward	Tim	Player 1937-50; manager 1962-67
Webb	Stuart	Secretary; chief executive; chairman; director
Webster	Ron	Player 1961-77
Wilkins	Ray	Player 1949-53
Young	Ray	Player 1953-65

Going to the Match

WATCHING professional football usually starts young and for most people interested in football, those early years of 'going to the match' remains a most vivid memory. For supporters who live in and around Derby, walking to the match is normal, but Derby County has always depended for much of its support on people travelling into the city from small towns around the county. For them 'getting to the match' has not always been straightforward.

In the early part of the century, the train was a popular form of transport from places like Ashbourne, Alfreton, Ilkeston and Heanor. Even until the Sixties, Friar Gate Station was a hive of activity on match days. It wasn't until 1913 that buses began to compete with the train, as the Trent Motor Traction Company began to bring people from the county into the centre of town. By 1928, Derby Corporation had purchased its own motor buses in order to to facilitate travel within the town boundaries.

It was the growth of housing estates in the Twenties and Thirties – Littleover, Osmaston Park, Sinfin Lane, Chaddesden, Harvey Road – which stimulated the demand for an improved public transport network within Derby itself. Buses from the Market Place, conveying spectators to the Baseball Ground via Osmaston Road, became a familiar sight on Saturdays. They combined with the Guy trolley-buses, which replaced the electric tramway system after 1932, initially on the Nottingham Road service. Watching a harassed trolley-bus conductor trying to reattach a rooftop conduction arm to the overhead cable with a long swaying pole, became quite a spectator pastime at the bottom of Babington Lane.

Gradually the motor car took over. By the time Derby County took the momentous decision to leave the Baseball Ground for Pride Park, much of the talk centred around car parking provision at the new ground. Nevertheless, an hour before kick-off a steady stream of spectators can be seen heading along Pride Park Way towards a stadium built for the 21st century. It seems to indicate that although many things in football change, some can never be replaced. 'Going to the match' is still a special thrill.

"I went with my Dad"

Jimmy Bullions: I remember going with my Dad to Derby. We went on the train from Chesterfield and walked to the ground. I remember seeing Dai Astley and Charlie Napier. They were inside-forwards. I don't remember who they were playing against. I was about 12 or 13 at the time.

Reg Harrison: I went with my Dad. I was put in the boys' pen and then he'd lift me over and take me to the bottom, under the old scoreboard. We stood right in the corner there, so we could see across the pitch. We walked there, across where Pride Park is built now. I went with my Dad and met my relations when we got there. We usually went to reserve games. That's what blooded us, reserve games, not the first-team games. We went to them on special occasions, Christmas and times like that, to see the first team, but the reserve-team games, that's where I started going, on a Saturday afternoon.

Tommy Powell: Oh. I used to go with my Dad, regularly. My grandad first took me in the stand. That was was a treat, you see. I think it was about 2s 6d or 3s 6d, in the Osmaston Stand. No, my Dad first took me, when you could go on the Popular Side and watch the reserve matches and things like that – and stand there without any problems.

Steve Powell: One of the first games I recall was the Reserves – they played Blackpool – because I think my father actually played then or was due to play, which was 1962. My most vivid memories of going to reserve-team games was watching at the end, the scoreboard at the Osmaston End of the ground, waiting for the first-team scores. The guy used to walk out, the board had A, B, C, D, E, F, G to about P and each letter corresponded to a game, and he'd come and walk out with the individual numbers and put up the half-time scores or in Derby's case, the first team, if they scored. He'd come and change the score and there was always an 'ooh' and 'aah' as he was walking along there, with his numbers.

John Bowers: The first time I went to the Baseball Ground, I went with Richard Hann, Ralph's son. What we used to do was play football for the school in the morning, take a packed lunch and then take it down the Baseball Ground and either Ralph or my Dad, would be at the respective match, either first team or reserve team. We'd be down there, probably about one o'clock, so we'd go up to the billiards room and have our snack and then play snooker until nearer the kick-off. I'd be about 11 or 12 then. I'd just gone to big school. I never went anywhere to matches with my Dad because he was always there first. Most of my time, as a youngster, was spent listening to where Dad had been, like scouting missions and with the team.

Steve Powell: My Dad didn't take me much. When he packed up playing, he had a little bookie's shop down on Abbey Street, but I used to go anyway.

Ernie Hallam: It was the first match of the 1928-29 season when I started watching them. Derby County beat Blackburn 5-1 and I remember the teams of both sides. Funnily enough, I lived in a north-east village of Derbyshire, at Pilsley, but I came to my uncle's and aunt's, who lived in Derby, for my school holidays and my uncle took me to the match. I was keen on Derby, but I'd never seen them. I was 12 years old at the time, but that really whetted my appetite and I saw them again, a couple of weeks later, when we beat Sheffield Wednesday 6-0, so the two results, 5-1 and 6-0, meant I was a real addict of the club from then on. My father only ever went to the Baseball Ground once. I took him, then. That was to see Hughie Gallacher.

Ron Webster: I used to go with my Dad. It was Third Division when I started. Third Division North, that's when I first used to go with my Dad.

Graham Sellors: I think it must have been 1947, '48 or something like that. I can't remember any games in full, I can just remember odd incidents. I went with my mother's family, the whole family. My mother had five sisters and two brothers. They were just Derby County fanatics and so almost all of them, certainly five of them, all went together.

Bill Brownson: The first match that my Dad took me to – I was nine – I think it was Dartford or Aldershot, in the Cup. I think the score was 2-0 and I got the bug and it went from there. I first started watching Derby in 1932. When I went with my Dad originally, I went in the boys' section, just by the terrace on the corner there, at the Normanton End.

Edward 'Ned' Mee: Oh no, my Dad didn't go, he was a Little Eaton man. I was born there. There were seven born there – and three more at Ashbourne. No, I didn't go with my Dad first, I went with my eldest brother. He was about 12 years older than me, mind. His name was Bert. He was ever so keen. I was born in 1906 and I was about six or seven. We used to stand on the 'bobs', what they called 'bobs'. That's Leys' Foundry side. When I went, there were blocks in front of us, concrete blocks, and there were wooden railings set in these blocks to keep folks back. I stood next to these blocks. They put me right at the front because there were my brother and my cousin, three of us.

George Beard: It was the 1926-27 season. Yes, I can remember the match – Bury at Derby. The Derby team was Olney, Cooper, Crilly, McIntyre, Thoms, McLaverty, Thornewell, Gill, Fairclough, Storer and Mee. The Bury team was Richardson, Heap – in a later game Heap died on the field – Adamson, Porter, 'Tiny' Bradshaw, Turner, Robbie, Stage, Bullock, Ball and Amiss. I was 15 or so. I'd come from the Peak District. Father was in the police force, moved up and down the place. We came from New Mills area. My Dad was always talking about Steve Bloomer, the Goodalls and all those, and the goalkeepers Maskrey and Lawrence. My Dad was friendly with Lawrence. I was born in 1910. Yes, I went with my Dad.

Lionel Pickering: Yes I first got involved because my Dad was an ex-miner from Warsop in Nottinghamshire and we used to go to my grandparents there at Christmas. One Boxing Day – I was just 12 because my birthday is in December – my Dad took me to see the old Miners' Welfare football team. When he realised I quite enjoyed watching football – and playing football – he took me at the end of the season to see Derby County play Mansfield Town. It was wartime, Derby won 8-1 and I almost remember the teams to this day. Peter Doherty – we always called him Doh -erty but I understand he always called himself Dock-erty so we'll get it right – he scored three goals and Raich Carter was playing, and it was magical. I was on the corner, the Osmaston corner, underneath the scoreboard.

Ian Buxton: Like most kids I used to stand in the children's corner, which was situated at the left-hand corner of the Normanton End terrace – if you're sitting in the Normanton Stand, underneath it. The first game I remember particularly was when Derby County played Charlton Athletic at Derby after the Cup Final. It was a full house and I went there with my father and we stood at the Osmaston End, upstairs. Standing it was then in the middle tier and there were people climbing everywhere, and my Dad pushed someone out of the way and broke his finger. This is before the match started, and we watched the whole game. I remember at half-time they went round with a massive sheet for people to throw coins in. Whether that was charity or the manager's back pocket, I never found out because I was too young to think about it. But think of that now, how dangerous it would be? They'd be skimming coins all over the place. In those days, it just happened. We went straight from the match to hospital afterwards for my Dad to have his finger set. So that is my first proper memory of going to watch Derby County.

Going to the Match

Ray Young: I went with my father. I didn't go that often. I think the first time I went would be a reserve-team game on the Baseball Ground and Jack Nicholas was playing left-back. What stood out in my mind was that he never, from choice, kicked the ball with his left foot. If he was going to kick it with his left foot, he stopped it and sort of went about four paces back before he kicked it. I think it could have been against Everton Reserves. After that it would be with the Derby Boys, and they took us to the game when Derby played Arsenal and it was the first defeat for Arsenal in about 16 or 17 games. It would be about 1948-49. We were at the Normanton Stand.

Ian Buxton: It was in the days of Woodley and Leuty, Musson, Howe and people like that. I also remember watching them in the Third Division North days, which is a long time afterwards, with Alf Ackerman, Ray Straw and people like that, and Jack Parry even. I was a schoolboy when Jack played for Derby, even though I played with him later on.

Graham Sellors: I went with Mother and my aunties and my uncles, but I didn't go very often with my Dad, although he went on a few occasions. I have a vivid memory of walking out of the ground at the Osmaston End – and this was all brought back to me when I went to collect a season ticket two or three years ago and I had to queue right round on to the Osmaston terrace. There was still a bit of the original terrace in the corner – with those very shallow steps – and I can remember walking out of the ground with my Dad, who had on a mac. Obviously, it was very crowded and I got hold of the belt and walked out of the ground and when I got outside, I looked up and it wasn't my Dad! It was somebody else's mac! I went into a flat panic then, but fortunately he found me.

Michael Dunford: My parents and grandparents all supported Derby County. My father took me to my first game, against Walsall I think it was, 1961. I can't remember the result. We stood in the paddock, in front of what is now the old Main Stand at the Baseball Ground. My father was a policeman in those days and as I got older I had a little more independence and I was allowed to go along on my own.

Mick Hopkinson: The first game I saw on the Baseball Ground was Reds v Whites in a pre-season public practice match. I'd be seven or eight years of age. Always remember that. My mother took me and about three or four others down on the bus. There were buses, and buses, and buses, to get to the ground. It was all worthwhile, when you got there.

Peter Gadsby: We always used to go with my elder brother Michael. No my Dad didn't take us, although he was very much involved in football. He used to drive the van and still had the ticket when they went to Wembley, but I used to work for my Uncle George, delivering milk. That was part of the payment, going to the match.

Mick Hopkinson: I had days off school to go. I particularly remember Bradford Park Avenue, one of Kevin Hector's old clubs. They used to wear multi-coloured shirts, stripes all over. I once had an afternoon off school, got on the bus and there was the teacher, sitting on the bus going to the same match because it was his day off. We sat at the front, getting lower and lower in the seat, from Belper. They were the games I remember most, against Accrington Stanley and Bradford, teams like that.

Roy Christian: I went with an older brother, who was too old to get into the boys' enclosure and we went on the Pop Side. No, we didn't go with my Dad. He played a bit of rugger. He wasn't a soccer enthusiast. He used to watch an occasional match. He'd go to cricket, but he wasn't a football enthusiast. We stood roughly opposite where the players came out.

Brian Flint: The first match was around 1963 against Leeds United. Albert Johanneson, John

Charles – he was a legend, wasn't he? I was only young then. My Mum and Dad took me on the bus from Middleton. I'd got quite bad health then and so it was a matter of when I was well enough to go and the weather was good enough. Then Brian Clough became manager and I sold all my things I didn't want, as a young lad. Also, I took pop bottles back to the beer-offs, what have you, to get three pennies. I bought three season tickets, one for me, one for my Mum and one for my Dad. That was 1967. I've still got the tickets somewhere, upstairs. They were for the Normanton Upper Stand. I bought them, all three and that was it then. My Dad died in 1969, so things altered, but I still kept going.

Colin Gibson: I think it was 1967, sometime around then. The first game was a League Cup semi-final against Leeds United at the Baseball Ground. Derby were in the old Second Division and Leeds were in the First Division, and Derby lost 1-0. Bobby Saxton handled inside the penalty area. I don't know who converted the penalty, but they won 1-0 and Leeds won 3-2 in the second leg at Elland Road, although I think Kevin Hector gave Derby an early lead. That's about all I can remember, apart from the fact that the Baseball Ground was packed and I stood on the boys' end and it cost me about one and six pence. I think I went with a school friend, Paul Fox. He was more into football than I was at that time. The World Cup had been the previous year and that had, I suppose, stoked my interest in football, but he said: "I'm going along to see Derby tonight, do you fancy coming along?" So I thought: "Yes, I've never seen a live football match before, so let's go along." Hooked, from that moment on.

Jim Fearn: It was 1970. Boxing Day. Derby County 4 Manchester United 4. To my shame, I was also a Manchester United fan then. I don't know why. I grew up in Parwich and Matlock and there was no reason for me to support anybody other than Derby. To be fair, after I'd actually been to the game – and I've looked back at my little essay books at Parwich School from that time – it was Hector and O'Hare who caught my imagination. It was a wonderful experience, the snow was on the ground, it was a *Match of the Day* game. I remember everything that happened, the first move, the ball coming out to Willie Morgan down the right wing. I can almost remember every single move in the game. On the videos I can remember thinking: "Well they've cut that bit, moved on to the next bit." It was wonderful to see my local team doing well and almost beating a team which had a forward line of Morgan, Kidd, Charlton, Law and Best. You thought: "Well nothing can beat that." Archie Gemmill played that day and did some wonderful things, skipping over the surface. That changed it for me. I thought it was silly to have a team that could actually draw 4-4 with Manchester United and not support them. So that was the first game and I suppose it has to be all downhill from then, but it was an incredible start.

Steve Sutton: First time? When I got to about eight or nine. My Dad had been a season ticket holder all his life. He came for nearly 60 years. He used to bike from up near Hartington, Warslow, which is the next village along. He used to bike it from Warslow to watch the game, stop here for the weekend with some family and then cycle back Sunday night, to go to work in the quarries Monday morning, which was some feat in those days. It's exactly 27 miles, which is not easy on a push bike. Once I got to eight or nine I used to come to the odd games. We stood on the Pop Side. Then they got the family enclosure. Players? Colin Boulton, Les Green. Always watching the goalkeepers. Then there was Alan Durban, Colin Todd, that era. About 1970 to 1975, I came very, very regularly.

Tom Stubley: The first match? Yes. I can remember two players. One was a bloke named Lawrence who played in goal, and the other one was a little inside-forward called Jimmy Moore. I reckon round about this time I'd be about four or five – about 1920-21 something like that – and I remember my father used to take me to all the reserve games. He wouldn't take me to the first-team games because there were too many people there and in those days, I remember that on the Popular Side it was ashes and the barriers were, in fact, wooden. That's the first match I ever saw.

Gerald Mortimer: The first one I went to was pretty memorable. It was in 1945-46, wartime. They played in the League South and they beat Millwall 8-1 and I thought this was the most enormous fun. Angus Morrison scored three, Carter and Doherty were playing, and Duncan. You know, it was the first time I was introduced to this particular atmosphere of a League football ground and at the age of nine, I was quite captivated by this, and it's an enthusiasm that has never flagged.

Getting there

'Ned' Mee: We went by train from Ashbourne. There were no cars or buses, then. Buses didn't start running till about 1912 or 1913.

Roy Christian: We used to get there not less than an hour before kick-off. I'd be a bit worried we wouldn't get decent places if we were less than an hour before the match started, probably an hour and a half. Quite often we got there before the gates opened. People went on foot or by tram from the Market Place in town, tuppence each way. There used to be a little piece of cardboard stuck in the windows of the trams and it would say: 'Football. Tuppence each way'.

Tom Stubley: Walk. We had to. We're talking about the Baseball Ground now, aren't we? Well, we lived in Leonard Street and we used to go through the Arboretum. In 20 minutes we were on the Baseball Ground.

Tommy Powell: Walk. It used to take us probably half an hour. I used to live at Sherwood Street, the other side of Burton Road, and we'd walk round the back. That was the format, actually, when I started playing for Derby. We always used to report about two in the afternoon, and I think one of the funniest things I can remember about that is when I was coming down Cambridge Street – from the top end – when we played Northampton Town in the Cup. It was the record crowd at the time. It must have been just after two o'clock and a bloke was coming the other way and he said to me: "I wouldn't bother going down, mate. You'll not get in. They've shut the gates!"

Alf Jeffries: I used to walk down. It wasn't far from Crewe Street where I was in the digs with Mrs Smith. Sammy Crooks used to dig there and Tim Ward eventually came to stop there.

Bill Brownson: We went in the car. My father was an auctioneer and valuer. I was born in Littleover and they had a big company called Cumberland & Coates and then they dissolved that. The other partner was my grandfather, who was a right old tyrant, and he wanted to pull out, so my father went on his own and we went to Parwich. We were one of the few who did have a car. I mean, I've never known what it is to be without a car.

Lionel Pickering: We walked, as everybody else did. I suppose some of the older ones would get on their bikes and leave them down somebody's entry. We walked from the Rowditch area. It's a good half an hour walk from the Rowditch. We cut through over Burton Road, down Whittaker Road and through the streets there. Wouldn't dream of getting on a bus to go into town and then go out again. We were just one of a number. I wouldn't say there were massive crowds, but there were lots of times when there were about 18,000 there, at the Baseball Ground or 24,000 or 28,000, and a big match would be 32,000-36,000, say. It varied, but we were there, every home match.

Roy Christian: I was 14, but it wasn't my first League football match. I'd been watching Nottingham Forest – a terrible thing to say – but they were my team because from Riddings, where we lived, although it's in Derbyshire, it was easier to get to Nottingham by rail than Derby. You could get a train from Pye Bridge which was about a mile walk away. You could be on the ground within an hour really, whereas going to Derby meant a change at Ambergate and often a long wait there, so we tended to go to Forest. I think I'd seen probably four or five games at the City Ground and one at Meadow Lane, I think. The first match I ever saw was in 1922, when I was eight.

Ian Buxton: I don't honestly know how we got there. My father had a shoe business. He had a shop, but really he made a living by going to outlying villages like Kirk Ireton, Carsington, Hopton and places and collecting threepence a week off people for repairing shoes. So my father always had some form of transport, mostly an old Morris van or something. I presume we went in that and parked in the side streets by the ground.

Graham Sellors: It was just after the war and petrol was still rationed, and so getting to Derby from Clay Cross, for families like us who didn't have cars, was a bit difficult. There used to be a furniture firm, well it's a carpet firm now, Tommy Nutt's – T. Nutt & Son. Tommy Nutt's brother, Bob Nutt, was a Derby supporter and we used to go in their furniture van. It was all conspiratorial. He used to see my Uncle Arthur up Clay Cross and whisper: "It's all right for Saturday, Arthur." And then we'd all go up to the back of Nutt's shop and get into this furniture van and travel to Derby in it, sitting on bits of furniture, with carpet to cover us up in case the police stopped us and realised it was a non-essential journey. And – with a piano! He used to take a piano every week. He used to drive to his relatives near the Baseball Ground, supposedly delivering this piano to an address in Derby, but really, it just used to keep going up and down the A61, this piano.

Peter Gadsby: We went in my Uncle George's milk van. I can remember about eight of us, all sitting there. We used to move the crates out and we all used to sit there. We used to be dropped off and we would go into the boys' pen. We would go in behind the goal at the Normanton End. We came from Ashbourne. Born in Ashbourne. Family had some milk businesses. Nowadays I see children going to football a lot earlier, but for various reasons – cost, and that, I mean – I never used to go until I was about ten or 12, and that was the first time I can recall going to the Baseball Ground.

George Beard: We went on the bus from Alfreton to Derby. Two shillings return. Two bob return, shilling for me and twopence for a programme. I've still got the programme.

Ray Young: On the trolley bus, for something like twopence or twopence ha'penny return. I lived in Allenton. I'd come from Allenton along the Osmaston Road and I would drop off at Shaftesbury Street.

Roy Christian: The trams went to the end of Shaftesbury Street, I think it is, and you walked from there. The terminus would be just over the railway bridge, just at the end of Litchurch Lane. There was another bus service that turned at what I call the metaphysical island, the one that isn't there – the island painted in the road – that went up Dairyhouse Road. That went to The Vulcan, I think.

Steve Powell: Just walked. We had no transport. My father didn't drive, so we just walked from home, Sunnyhill, which was a 20-25-minute walk. Initially, until I was old enough to drive, I walked as a player. I did get a car, eventually.

Ron Webster: I used to go on the bus. We always went on the bus. I never went to many away matches, though. I used to go to Chesterfield. I used to go by bus to the Baseball Ground. I never used to go to the Reserves, we always used to go to the first-team matches. Just Saturdays we were there. We used to walk up from the bus station, about half an hour's walk.

Michael Dunford: What used to happen was that my father was on point duty at The Vulcan in those days and my mother would take me down and leave me on the corner to meet my father when he came off the duty at three o'clock. If he had to stay on late, then one of the other policemen, who was off duty, would take me to the ground. So invariably I would stand in the paddock, which was very safe – it was only about four or five rows of people and never got too crushed, in the early days anyway.

Tom Stubley: I went to Bemrose School and Derby were playing a cup tie one Wednesday. I think it was Nottingham Forest, but I'm not absolutely sure about that. Anyway, me and a lad named Perkins went and we were at the Osmaston End of the ground and it was crowded to death, this match was, and he broke his leg. I had to go and apologise to the headmaster the following day and got a right royal doing I'll tell you. Perkins was off for about three weeks and I had to take the bullet for both of us.

Colin Gibson: By bus. I can't tell you how much the fare was, but it was from Allenton and you used to get off just before the bridge on Osmaston Road, where the railway lines go underneath. Walked down, walked down Shaftesbury Crescent and, of course, all the houses were there then as well, so you literally walked down in between the houses, into the boys' end, in that nice, tight little corner, and all the boys used to be packed in there. Under the floodlights, of course. It would probably be March time, when semi-finals of League Cups were played. It was terrific.

Signing for Derby County

SIGNING a contract to play for a professional football club is the dream of any youngster from the moment he laces on his first pair of boots. Professional contracts, though, are not given away willy-nilly. 'Signing-on' is the first tangible indication that someone, somewhere, thinks that you have the capability to become a professional footballer. Parents, teachers, scouts, coaches, managers have analysed technical skills, speed, stamina, physical attributes, temperament and the thousand and one bits and pieces which go to make a player. Ultimately, however, it comes down to the basic, all-embracing question: "Can he play?" Whatever that means, professionals know what they mean by it. If the answer is favourable, the formal ceremony follows: "Sign here, young man, on the dotted line..."

It is the beginning of a precarious road. From a young player signing his first-ever contract, to an experienced player putting pen to paper following a complicated transfer, signing-on shapes a destiny.

First impressions

Alan Durban: Tim Ward sent Sammy Crooks to meet me at the station – and he missed me! So my first impression of Derby was on the walk from the station to the Baseball Ground, which isn't the best country walk around. When I got to the Baseball Ground the secretary, Cyril Annable, said: "I'll tell him you're here. Someone should have met you at the station, but someone's missed out." That was Sammy Crooks. I spoke to Tim Ward. I liked him. He obviously knew I played a bit of cricket because I was on the staff at Glamorgan at the time, and he said: "We've got a few cricketers on the staff." I got on with him very well.

John O'Hare: I didn't really know very much about Derby because the North-East is a very parochial place when it comes to football. It was a case of down we come to Derby and see what happens. I mean, I actually signed without ever seeing the place or without ever having ever been to Derby in my life. I remember we drove down, along Siddals Road, to the York Hotel. Not the most impressive part of Derby really. From there to the Baseball Ground. Some of the players were running round there, I remember Reg Mathews was one. I'd never played at the Baseball Ground, no. My wife wasn't too sure about what we'd done at the time, but fortunately it all worked out well.

Alan Durban: I just got a phone call, about a fortnight before pre-season training, to say that they'd agreed a fee with Derby. I was being sold by George Swindin, who'd been a goalkeeper with Arsenal. I hadn't really had a lot of time for his methods and ideas and even at that age,

I'd decided you only need half a brain to be a manager – perhaps I'm reasonably qualified – because here we were, selling three 21-year-olds to buy one 36-year-old. I didn't think that was really logical and as it proved, the three of us that went played loads of League games and John Charles played about 34 or 35 for Cardiff.

Tommy Powell: It was in 1942. Jack 'Nick' came round and said he wanted me to sign pro. Christ, I'd have played for nowt. Same as Reg. Just imagine. In those days, there wasn't a lot of money about anyway, but money wasn't spoken of. It was just the prestige of playing for your club. I mean, to think you'd gone to watch them week after week. And yes, I got my £10 signing on fee. Don't tell the tax man!

Alf Jeffries: In the February, Jobey came up to Bradford City and our manager said to me: "I only want you to do six sprints this morning, Jeff." I said: "Oh. Why's that?" I thought I'd done something wrong, you see. " Oh," he says, "Mr Jobey's coming up from Derby and he wants to sign you on." Just like that, you see. Not: "Do you want to sign on?" Just: "He wants to sign you on." I met Jobey and he had his secretary with him and he said to me: "Are you all right? Are you fit?" I said: "Yes." We did the necessary signing-on, right then.

Frank Upton: Jack Barker. He bought me from Northampton Town. I think Jack Bowers came to watch me one Saturday, that's Johnny Bowers' dad. He came back and gave Jack a good report and he signed me. I was working in the pits at the time, at Nuneaton. I was 17 or 18 and playing with Nuneaton Borough when I got transferred to Northampton. I was playing for Northampton and I think I had a telephone call at the pit where I worked. I was still a part-timer. The call came at the pit and they asked me to go to the phone and I went and answered and, of course, I was over the moon. I was a blacksmith's striker at the time. I thoroughly enjoyed that job, but there was nothing like football.

Ron Webster: It was my schoolteacher – I was reasonably good for local football – and he said: "I'm going to take you to Derby for a trial." You know, I was chuffed. I was about 14, 14½. I was at school you see and I'd just played for Alfreton and District and I happened to play for the county once because I think there were one or two injured. Anyway, the teacher got me a trial and I went just after Christmas and they held them on the Baseball Ground. I had two Sunday matches a fortnight after one another and, after the second one, Johnny McIntyre came in and he said: "I want you to sign on your 15th birthday." I'd only played two matches and I thought that was great. I was chuffed.

Mick Hopkinson: I went for a trial the same day as Ron. I was just 15 and he was 14. His mum and dad were real characters, especially his mum. On the touchline, she called Ron all the names under the sun. We played, me and him, and I think it was about 5-5 or 4-4, something like that and I scored a goal. A tap-in on the goal line.

Steve Powell: Obviously, when you're in the schools football game, lots of clubs come and have a look at you. It was the same for me as anybody else, I suppose. Several scouts from clubs came to watch Derby Boys play, and then they tended to try to get in touch with you to go and have trial games with them. I remember going to Arsenal on a couple of occasions. Chelsea asked me to go down there, but obviously my main thing was to stay in my home town and eventually Derby approached me and I signed for them as a schoolboy when I was, I think, 14. Yes, I played for England Schoolboys for two years, when I was 14 and 15, which was quite unusual at the time. Normally you only played for one year. I was fortunate enough to play two years running. To be honest, there weren't many who went on to make careers out of it. There was a lad called Brian Hornsby, who did quite well at Arsenal and Sheffield

Wednesday. David Price, again was at Arsenal, and went to Crystal Palace later on. The drop-out rate from schoolboy level, to making it as a professional, is very, very high.

Bert Mozley: The manager who signed me was Ted Magner. I'll never forget what he said. We went in the office and while I was signing he said: "Well now, Bert, you're now a professional soccer player and there are thousands of people who'll watch you. You've got the skills, now keep fit," he said. "You tell me another job in this world where you're paid to keep fit."

Johnny Morris: I've always been a fanatic. I've always spoke my mind, you see. I was approached at Manchester United, before I played in the 1948 Cup Final, by a certain person and he gave me a letter with a phone number. It was a year before I rang, but I always knew there was a club there, but I didn't know which club it was. I'd got an idea, though because the person who gave me this letter was an old Derby County player!

Brian Clough: Len Shackleton, who used to play for Sunderland, rang Sam Longson and said: "I've met the best young manager in the Football League. Now I met Sam Longson and his colleagues at a hotel at Scotch Corner. He brought a couple of his colleagues up, Sam Longson did, and he said: "Right, you've got the job, but you've got to come down to a board meeting, so it's confirmed." And that's the end of the boring story.

Ray Young: Stuart McMillan was manager. Sammy Crooks was chief scout and it was Sammy who spent Monday, Tuesday, Wednesday, Thursday, every day and every night of the week, trying to get me to sign amateur forms. I'd had offers to go to a number of clubs but what I said to my father was that I was going to stay and play with my local youth club team and, if I was good enough at 18, I would consider it. He said it was up to me to make my own mind up. In the end I got bloody fed up of Sammy coming round, I suppose.

Don Hazledine: I was a bit disappointed when I first went to Derby. I was only a young lad and, crikey, they were a First Division club. I mean, not a Second or Third, but a First Division club and highly respected throughout the football world and you expect someone to take you aside and point out things, what you're doing wrong, but that didn't happen. Those things seem to have changed, but I enjoyed my football.

Ray Young: There was a Midland Midweek League which was played on Wednesdays or Thursdays on the Baseball Ground. You had the first team and then the Reserves and we played for the Midland Midweek League team and if you played a Villa or West Brom, Birmingham, Notts County, you played on the League grounds. It was superb. We won the Midland Midweek League in the Fifties.

Mick Hopkinson: You know, before I signed for Derby – I always wanted to sign for Derby, they'd just come out of Division Three – I played for West End Boys' Club and Harry Bedford, who was a scout for Arsenal, came to our house about six times. Arsenal, it was. Well, you think: "They're a big club, Arsenal." They wanted me to go down there, on the groundstaff. I couldn't believe it. He was adamant that there was every good chance. I'd no intention of going on Derby's groundstaff because of the money, but to be honest though, there was only one club I wanted to go to.

Ray Young: I played centre-half, but during the first couple of years I played at right-back. I also played at left-back and I played at wing-half, right-half and left-half. Eventually I finished at centre-half. I used to play inside-right at school, to start with.

John Bowers: I used to go along as, I suppose, the boot lad. Getting all the stuff together on and off the first-team coach. I'd be with the third team, so I'd see all the young lads and the older pros recovering from injuries coming back. Playing against all these local clubs, like

Long Eaton and Belper. They used to be needle affairs. When you think of people like Albert Litchfield, at Belper. He used to kick anything above the grass. Even nowadays, although you haven't seen them for such a long time, people come up to you and you think: "Who the hell is that?" Then they'll say: "Do you remember me? I used to play for Belper Town." Or: "I used to play for so and so." It was very bleak at Sinfin and the pitch was as big a mud bath as the Baseball Ground.

Steve Powell: My father played for Derby County for about 20 years. It was my home town and I think most people would prefer to play for their home town club. As I say, I signed schoolboy forms when I was 14. You weren't allowed to actually play for the club until you'd left school. I left school when I had just turned 15 and, funnily enough, I played on a pre-season tour, illegally really I suppose. When I played in Germany I was still, technically, at school, at Bemrose Grammar School. I played on that pre-season tour and I started my apprenticeship the following summer. Brian Clough was the manager and he was the one who signed me on.

Kevin Hector: Jock Buchanan was the manager at Bradford. He'd played for Derby and he called me in and said Derby were interested and would like to talk to me. We went down to Derby on the train, me and Jock Buchanan. I hadn't got a car then. We got off the train at Derby station and went straight to the ground and saw Tim Ward and the directors. We talked for a couple of hours. No, Jock didn't stay in the room. He went out and had a look at the ground where he used to play. There were no agents then!

Steve Powell: Brian Clough came to the school one day, to see the headmaster, Dr Chapman. I knew what he was coming for but hadn't said anything. So everybody was buzzing with: "Oh, Brian Clough's been to the school today." Nobody knew what for – until it came out in the press later! I suppose I was a bit awe-struck, really. You know, he'd come to Derby and taken a team from being a mediocre Second Division side to potential First Division champions, so I suppose I was a bit in awe in one sense and at that age I was very young and naive.

Johnny Morris: Stuart McMillan came up. I said to Stuart: "I want to see a golf course at Derby before I sign." So he came up here and we went back to Derby to look at Kedleston Park and it worked out just like that. It was the best move I ever made.

Kevin Hector: We went back to Bradford on the train. I told them I would think about it and let them know. A day or so later, I was told that Norwich were interested, but by that time I had decided that I was going to Derby. I went back and went on the coach with the team to Northampton. I can't remember whether it was an early-season midweek match or not. I think they won. Anyway, I signed a day or so later.

Gordon Hughes: I'd been at Newcastle about ten years. What it was, why I came down here, I'd had a bad injury, a spinal injury. I had a spinal fusion in my back and I was out about a year and a half.They took a bone out of my hip and fused it into the bottom of my spine. I was in hospital for four months. While I was out they signed Dave Hilley and when I came back, I was in and out of the side, like, but I wasn't quite the same player. Anyway, Bob Ferguson, who was left-back for Derby – he was an ex-Newcastle lad, like – kept coming up and saying: "Why don't you...?" I kept saying: "I'll get back in, I'll get back in." Finally, I was persuaded and I signed on the same day as Alan Durban. At the same table, in the boardroom, that's where we signed. I'd never met Alan before. He came up from Cardiff.

Willie Carlin: On the Monday, the secretary came over – he lived near me – and said: "You're wanted down at the club." So I said to the wife: " No problem, it's about the house." Anyway, when I arrived down at Bramall Lane, the general manager John Harris was there and he says to me: "You can go." I says: "Go where?" He says: "Derby County." I said: "I've come down to buy my house." He said: "You haven't. Brian Clough's in the boardroom. You're going to Derby County." That was the first I knew about it.

Willie Carlin: I went into the boardroom – I can see him now – he had a white polo neck on and a sports jacket, Mr Clough, and as soon as I walked in he said: "Right you little b@!?--, who have you smacked?" I couldn't think and I wondered: "What's he on about?" It wasn't until years later that it came to me. Arthur Rowley had taken over as team manager at Sheffield United and it was an incident at Carlisle after I'd broken my leg and was sitting on the bench for a cup match with Shrewsbury. We had a trainer called Dick Young who was very volatile and Arthur Rowley, who was manager of Shrewsbury, smacked him. So I jumped up and smacked Arthur Rowley. He remembered. You might say he got me back by getting rid of me from Sheffield United.

Roy McFarland: It wasn't, to be quite truthful, really Derby County. It was the personality, it was the selling power, in a sense, of Brian Clough and Peter Taylor. Without doubt, they worked on me. They worked on my Mom. They worked on my Dad and they found, without doubt, the weak link with my father. They chatted to him, talked about the old days, talked about the old players. My Dad, in a sense, was mesmerised, he loved talking football, loved football himself and at the end, I turned round to my father and said that I would like it left it until the following morning. I said that to Clough and Taylor, at the time. They said to me: "We want you to sign now. We want to make a decision now." So I turned round to my father and said: "Dad, what do you think?" He said: "If they want you that badly, son, I'd sign." Within seconds, the papers were there and I signed for Derby County. I knew of Derby County. I knew of the football and the tradition, but I didn't know anything about the club and about the city and anything about it. Without doubt, I signed that day for Brian Clough and Peter Taylor.

Brian Clough: When I signed him, I signed him at where he lived, Birkenhead I think it was, and I chuntered on at him. He came down. He was in bed, actually, and it was only half past nine or ten o'clock. I'd done a deal with Tranmere, so that was all done and dusted and he'd got striped pyjamas on, like the old prisoners used to wear. Do you remember those? Winceyette. So he came down and he didn't know me and I didn't know him, but I'd seen him play against a centre-forward from Hartlepool called Ernie – Ernie what's his name? – Phythian, I think they called him. He never gave him a kick, Roy didn't. He never gave him a smell of the ball at all. So, he comes down in his striped pyjamas, I'm rabbiting on to him and they'd got the biggest log fire you'd ever seen in your life. And his dad said: "You sit there, Brian." So I'm in front of this bloody fire and the sweat is running down my back. So I'm sitting there and the missus is giving me cups of tea that I didn't want, but you know what swung it? I'll swear to you – his Dad said to Roy McFarland: "I want a word with you." Went into the back kitchen, didn't close the door. I'm earwigging and he said: "You sign for Brian." He signed.

Alan Hinton: I signed for Derby County from Nottingham Forest in September, I think, 1967. I knew a long time before I was signing for Derby County because I remember playing cricket in Nottingham and Peter Taylor came to the cricket game. He and I walked round the cricket field after the game and he told me: "We're going to sign you for Derby County, but first of all, we have to sign a centre-half and a centre-forward and, of course, they went off and signed Roy McFarland, which was an unreal signing, and John O'Hare, and then they came and got me. So I think that was three pretty good signings, but what they did was what they told me they were going to do. I knew they were ambitious and wanted to do a good job.

Signing for Derby County

Stuart Webb: Charlie George? Brilliant, Charlie. That was another scene, Charlie coming. I was rung up by a journalist on the night before Charlie was signing for Spurs. The manager of Spurs had organised a press conference and the call was: "Do you know Charlie's available? He's leaving Arsenal and going to Spurs." Dave was in Scotland, so I rang him and he said: "Oh yes. We'll have a bit of that. I fancy him. I'll fly down and set it up. We'll try and meet him in London tomorrow." I'm taking my daughter, Beverley, to school at five to nine on the day, the Thursday, the day of the press conference, and Charlie George rang. "I understand that you want to sign me." I said: "I shouldn't be talking to you, but Dave Mackay's trying to get you and these are the numbers." So that was it. Dave and I were in London that day, that lunchtime. Charlie didn't turn up at the press conference at Tottenham. Dave and I met him at the London Hilton or was it the Carlton Towers? Anyway, we signed him within the hour. Those were the classic situations that you think about. We never set press conferences up. We signed them on the hoof because by the time you set it up, you allow other people to come in. Charlie wanted to come to Derby and he was one of Dave's great signings. He did very well.

Charlie George: Dave Mackay came back off holiday to sign me. We met at the Carlton Towers Hotel. Yes, I signed there and then. It didn't take much time. I didn't want much. Yes, I played against Mackay. Dave was a great player. I tell you, when he tackled you, you knew about it. There was no trouble about signing. Derby were League champions and them wanting to sign me was a recognition that they thought I could play a bit.

Roger Davies: Then I got my chance to come to Derby, just after I'd finished my apprenticeship at work. I didn't know where Derby was in relation to where I came from in Wolverhampton. There were quite a few clubs, apparently, looking at me, but I came over to Derby, the old Baseball Ground, on the night they played Dundee United in the Texaco Cup. The board of Worcester City came with me. There were about five of them.

Bobby Davison: When I signed, Peter Taylor was the manager, with Roy McFarland. I think it came about when I was at Halifax and Roy was at Bradford City. I played against Roy a couple of times and after both games, he asked me if I'd go to Bradford City and obviously our manager at Halifax had seen this happening and wasn't too happy, but a month or so after we'd played Bradford City, Roy had gone to Derby and we'd played down at Wimbledon, won 4-2 and I scored a hat-trick. Arsenal had a scout there and they invited me down to go and play and train with them for a month at Highbury. We got knocked out of the FA Cup on the Saturday, and on the Monday I travelled down to Highbury. I was supposed to stay down a month. I enjoyed it immensely. The only problem was I didn't like travelling in London, to the training ground and to Highbury.

Steve Sutton: I got a phone call – I didn't know Arthur Cox at that stage. I remembered Roy from when I came to Derby on trial and trained a couple of times with the first team. He was a player then and I knew him from that, but really it was a case of Brian Clough coming to me and saying: "Look, Derby are interested. Go and get yourself some games. Go and get fit." I hadn't played for three months because of a back injury.

Bobby Davison: I played against Luton, I think. I trained for a week or so, but Roy and Peter Taylor got wind of this and they approached Halifax and made a bid. Terry Neill, the manager at Arsenal, spoke to me and said: "Look, you're here for a month. You've been here ten days, we'd like to sign you." He said: "Derby County have been in, they've made a bid, but we'll match that, it's just down to you." I had a chat with my wife and we thought maybe Derby would be a better option. Not closer to home particularly, it was more Peter Taylor, not guaranteeing me a first-team place, but he more or less told me: "You've got a better chance of getting in the first team here, than you have at Arsenal." I was 21, 22 then and I thought: "Well, maybe so."

Michael Dunford: I think the first transfer I was involved in must have been Steve Buckley coming in. It wasn't a terribly complicated matter, transferring players. What normally happens is you have a financial agreement which sets out the terms and conditions of the transfer, normally signed by the secretaries of both clubs. Then you have a contract – a blue contract – on which the player agrees to his personal terms. Again, most of those occasions in the late Seventies, early Eighties, were either dealt with by the chairman or the manager, agreeing personal terms with the player. That situation now has tended to change. The forms themselves have changed very little, very little.

Roger Davies: It was like one of those things in the *Sunday People*. 'Roger Davies is being looked at by Man United.' There were all those names about. I didn't take that much notice of it really, as things were going well for me at Worcester City and I was at work. Then, Wednesday morning I got a phone call. It was one of the guys at Worcester City saying: "Derby County want to sign you and we need to go over there tonight, for talks." So I rang my Dad up to get hold of him and he was late getting home from work and didn't know. We met outside The Molineux Arms, actually, and we drove over.

Bobby Davison: From my point of view, I'd played against Derby in a two-legged cup-tie and I'd played at the Baseball Ground and quite enjoyed it, whereas at Arsenal a long way from home, the travelling, maybe not getting straight in the first team. I think Paul Mariner was playing, Kenny Sansom, Graham Rix, all them, so obviously it was going to be very, very difficult.

Frank Upton: I was working at Stanley College, for the sports teacher. I was doing a sports day, as it happens, and who should come walking across but Ted Drake, from Chelsea. He came across and stood in the middle of the sports field that day and we talked about me going to Chelsea. So I said: "Yes I'll come down and have a look." So I finished up at Chelsea, which was brilliant. I learned more football at Chelsea than anywhere. The quality of the players there...well, no disrespect to the lads at Derby. Ted Drake brought me down there, and then Tommy Docherty took over.

Ted McMinn: I was over there in Seville. I was over there for a year after leaving Glasgow Rangers. Jock Wallace was the manager over there and Jock had phoned me up after two successful games in Europe for Rangers, which were televised live in Spain, to go across there, which was great. I think the experience over there made me a better player, playing abroad against your Barcelonas, Real Madrids, people like that. You see them on Sky every Saturday now, crowds of 80,000, 90,000.

Eric Steele: Basically, I was at Watford for five years under Graham Taylor and I'd spent the last 15 months at reserve level because Taylor had made the decision to play Sherwood. I got involved in the FA Cup run of '84 when they got to the Final at Wembley and lost to Everton 2-0. I was involved in that up to the quarter-final stage, but he left me out. Obviously I knew then, as it happens in football, there was a preference. Graham Taylor had a preference for another goalkeeper and it was time for me to leave. He offered me terms to stay and, in all fairness, I waited only three weeks and spoke to about four clubs, one of which was Derby.

Ted McMinn: Then Jock got the sack and more or less worked as an agent to get me back to Britain, and the only two clubs were Derby and Newcastle. I was all for going to Newcastle, where Willie McFaul was manager – I promised Willie I'd go to him – and then Mr Webb came across, flew over to Seville, and I spoke to the gaffer, Mr Cox. He was exactly the same sort of manager as Jock Wallace and said: "Listen, we want you here." It wasn't money. It was: "We want you to play for Derby County. We want you. Just sign the form and get over here."

Eric Steele: I got a phone call from Arthur Cox to my in-laws in Newcastle. Somehow, I don't know how, he'd got the number and he spoke to my parents. I was up there having a week's break and I spoke to him. He'd just come down himself from Newcastle. I came to the Baseball Ground, had two meetings because he was obviously looking at other goalkeepers as well, which was understandable. He was looking to rebuild.

Steve Sutton: I came here on trial many times, in the holidays and whatever, and Steve Cherry was here. He's 18 months older than me and he'd just been taken on and they were looking to me to be a first-year apprentice. At that stage, 1975, Derby were League champions. Nottingham Forest were in the old Second Division. I'd been across and obviously knew all about Brian Clough from his Derby days and we were very impressed with what he had to say, but I genuinely felt I had a better chance at Forest. I was overawed by the place at Derby because they were League champions and they were my heroes. I thought: "Well, I've got no chance of getting a game there at all." Steve Cherry, I thought, was brilliant at that age and so I went to Forest, played in a couple of 'A' team games and enjoyed it. I thought: "I stand a chance here." John Middleton was in goals. No disrespect to John, but I was thinking: "In two or three years' time, Forest in the First Division. I've got a chance."

Getting paid

Johnny Morris: I'd played for Bolton Wanderers, as an amateur, at 15½ because their lads were called up into the militia. A lad called Bert Whalley and I went as guests to Bolton and when we'd finished the game, the secretary there gave us an envelope with about seven quid in it! You felt like a millionaire, didn't you? It was only £8, full-time, before the war.

Alf Jeffries: I saw him just before he died. I went down to see him and whether it was right or wrong I don't know, but Jack Barker told me that he was never on top money. I couldn't imagine that being right. I couldn't imagine that. Whether Jobey had wangled it...? Of course, they used to try it on. They tried it on all the time, but Jack said he was never on top money. I couldn't imagine it – Jack Barker!

Tom Stubley: He told me exactly the same story. I think Ben Hall will tell you exactly the same story as well. When Jack lived in Henry Street with his wife, and they were on their own living there, I used to go to see Jack once a fortnight because he'd been a good old scout as far as I was concerned. I don't know whether it was his mind or what, but we had the same two stories week after week. No matter, whatever, it would always come round to one story about Mr Rous – Stanley Rous – and the other that he was never on top money at Derby.

Johnny Morris: Before I was getting to 17, which was when you could sign pro, I was called back from Bolton to United. Travelling with them at Bolton and playing occasionally, I used to get half a crown! (13p).

Ray Young: I went to Derby when I was 15 and you couldn't sign professional until you were 17. I signed part-time when I was 17. I played in the 'A' team. Up until then I used to get my bus fare. Actually, I got 5s (25p). It only cost me 6d (3p) and I got 5s. So I was quite well off.

Tommy Powell: In those days, we got paid out of the 'gate'. I think it was about 30 bob [£1.50] or something like that. After the war, I don't know whether it was £10 and £8 or £8 and £6.

£10 in the winter and £8 in the summer. If you weren't playing you got £1 retainer. I didn't play much while I was in the Forces. The most I ever got was £25. It went up to £25 just as I finished!

Alf Jeffries: We used to get paid on a Friday, but before we got paid we did some sprints and then we used to go up in the billiards room. Jimmy Hagan was a dab hand at that game. He was a cracking lad was Jimmy.

Johnny Morris: We weren't treated very well at United. I don't mean illegal payments. We'd won the Cup and we went on a summer tour of Southern Ireland. Johnny Carey was a Southern Irish lad. All the lads were grumbling and, being the youngest, I was a listener. I had to sit and listen, else I'd have got a good hiding off somebody, Allen Chilton probably, although we were all best of pals. Him being a senior player, he used to lay the law down a bit if anyone said something out of turn. We went to Dublin and it was legal for the club to pay us £2 expenses and during that ten days, we had six meetings to get the two quid. This was Matt Busby. Don't forget, I'm talking about Matt when he was a 'rookie' manager then.

Ray Young: When I got to 17, I had a chance to follow Sammy Crooks to Shrewsbury, but because I was signed on amateur forms at Derby, they said that they'd got a hold on me. I was actually offered something in my back pocket to go to Shrewsbury. A couple of hundred, which was big money in those days.

Frank Upton: When I came to Derby I was on £5 and £6, I think. You know, £6 in the playing season and £5 in the summer, as a part-timer. No, we didn't get any extra for playing in the team. We got a bonus, that was all, if we won or drew.

Ian Buxton: I remember signing for Harry Storer. I signed for £5 a week basic wage, £7 in the Reserves and £10 if I played in the first team. Not £10 on top of the £5, £10 total. So I played in the Second Division for £10 a week. I don't think it was £10 a match even, it was £10 a week. So if I played Wednesday and Saturday in the first team, it was still £10.

Roger Davies: I think at the time it was a record transfer fee for a non-League player, £14,000 from Worcester City. I'd only played seven games for them, actually, and Peter Taylor had been to watch me play a few times. I did well when I went there. I think I scored seven goals in three games for Worcester City. It was the first time I'd ever been paid for playing football, for Worcester City. I thought it was you play football for enjoyment and someone starts paying you for it, I thought it was absolutely brilliant, getting money for playing football.

Alan Durban: I think I'd gone from something like £12 and £10, to something like £20 and £18, which was a monstrous rise for me at that stage. I said yes within, probably, an hour, jumped back on the train, went back to my Mum and Dad. Funny, isn't it? I mean, nowadays they're on mobile phones, asking advice from all quarters, but there I was, just 21 years old. I just got on the train and went to Derby. Went in the office for an hour, decided in my own mind: "Yeah, I think it will be good for me." And left.

Kevin Hector: I think the £2 win bonuses were fixed by the League, but we had a crowd bonus scheme at Bradford where we got so much over a gate of 5,000. The best thing was that I got ten per cent of the transfer fee, about £4,000, which was quite a lot of money then. It meant I was able to buy my house.

Ray Young: While I was in the army my Derby contract was £1 a week retainer but £6 when playing in any team, whether it was the Colts, the 'A' team, the Reserves or the first team. Apparently it was the maximum they could pay you when doing National Service. If I didn't play I got £1 a week. So because I was injured and only getting £1 a week, I was still coming home every week and I was going to the games, but I didn't show my face. I used to go in through the players' entrance and then go and stand on the Pop Side. I did that for probably, I don't know, about two months – until Harry Storer got to know about it. He rang the major up at camp and gave him a rollicking and said I'd got to show my face. The major told him: "If you're only going to pay him £1 a week, I don't blame the lad for not coming to see you." I enjoyed it more standing among the crowd than standing in the players' pen or sitting in B Stand. Some of the comments were superb. I used to think a lot of the true supporters came from out of Derby, from outlying districts.

Frank Upton: Most I got was 30 quid a week. Thirty quid a week, when I went to Chelsea. I was only on, most probably, £18 and £20, at Derby.

Willie Carlin: If you weren't in the team, you got no appearance money, you got no League position money, no points money. All you got was a basic, which was nothing really. So you had to play and you had to get out on that field. At Derby I was on £40 a week basic. It's changed dramatically now. It's gone the other way completely.

Roger Davies: I remember – my Dad still goes on about it now – Brian was in there and he said: "We've done the deal and everything. Have you sorted out your personal terms, whatever?" Well there were no agents or anything and I was 21 years old. In fact I wasn't even 21 and coming raw from non-League football. He said: "Have you sorted out what's happening?" I said: "Not really." "Well," he said. "You need to get some money from them for coming." I think I'd agreed something like £1,000 tax free, whatever. So he said: "I'll tell them you haven't signed yet." He said: "I'll tell them you haven't signed yet because you need to sort out that." I had, but he said: "No. I'll tell them you haven't signed yet and you can sort out the deal with Worcester." We sorted out £1,000 cash, no tax. Anyway, when they paid me, they'd taxed it. They still fiddled me – and they got £14,000 out of the deal.

Steve Powell: My first wage was as an apprentice. I think we went up to £6, from 15 to 16; £7 from 16 to 17; £10 from 18 to 19. My first professional wage was £45 per week, which is slightly different to what they're earning nowadays, but I'm not envious of that. I was so happy to play football and good luck to them, the money they get the players and the money they earn nowadays. It's a short career and there's a lot of pressure on them. So as I say, good luck to them.

Roger Davies: When I first came, I was getting £40 a week. I was coming into the Reserves. It was £40 and there would be appearance money if you moved on, but my first season was in the reserve side.

Michael Dunford: I remember back in the early Seventies, when we had the first three players at Derby who went on to £100 per week. And bear in mind that Johnny Haynes, at Fulham, had gone on to £100 per week in the mid-Sixties. Kevin Hector, John O'Hare, Roy McFarland, I think in 1970-71, went over the £100 a week threshold. Amazing. Now you try to put a value on those players nowadays and their personal terms!

Waiting for the retained list

Tommy Powell: You always had to wait for the retained list coming out. The old saying was: "Start playing well in February." We only had one-year contracts, of course. That made a difference. If you know your money is there for five years, you've got it whether you play good or bad. It's guaranteed for five years. Well, I mean!

Geoff Hazledine: It was one-year contracts and all that, as you know. At the end of the season it was a question of whether you were retained or not. One year some us held out over the pay because they'd asked us to take a £1 drop in wages. Then we heard that Bert Mozley and one or two others were getting the same money they'd received the previous year. So a few of us held out. There was Norman Neilson, there was Glyn Davies, and the outcome was that they wouldn't put me on the transfer list, they retained me. So I was in a sort of limbo. Once they put you on the transfer list, then you could sign for a non-League club, but until that happened, you couldn't go anywhere. You couldn't kick a ball for anyone and it was a desperate state of affairs for me. They didn't put me on the transfer list for ages, but eventually they did.

Michael Dunford: The system was completely different then, in the Sixties and Seventies. Come the end of April, when the retained list went up, players were hoping they were going to get offered a contract. Now, the mentality is completely different. With Bosman, the top 15 per cent to 20 per cent of players are going to earn an absolute fortune, but I do honestly think that the moderate players, the middle of the road players, are going to suffer long-term because there are going to be an awful lot out of work. Clubs will just not be able to afford to pay them. We may go back to the problems we had in the mid-Sixties.

Debut Days

ALL players remember their debuts. "It doesn't matter which club you play for – Real Madrid, Rochdale or Blidworth Miners' Welfare," said Sam Weaver, the Newcastle, Chelsea and England wing-half of the Thirties, who was the original long throw-in exponent. "There's only one team to play in – and that's the first team!" When they sign professional forms the big ambition of all players is to be selected for the first team. If the first team happens to play at Old Trafford, Anfield, Highbury or any of the other major grounds in the country, so much the better. All players, like supporters, have favourite grounds.

My first game

Tommy Powell (debut aged 16): It was Christmas Day. It was only against an RAF side. I was at the Firs Estate Youth Club the night before and Jack Nick came in and said: "You're playing tomorrow. You'd better get off home." Not that I'd have been doing anything anyway. I said: "You're joking aren't you?" And he said: "No. Jimmy Hagan can't get." So I was bunged in with Jack Bowers and all them, at the Baseball Ground. It was Christmas Day morning. It was only a friendly, really, but there were 10,000 there. I've still got the cutting out of the paper because I started to keep a scrapbook for a few months then, but I got fed up with it.

Alf Jeffries (signed from Bradford City, February 1937): Jobey said: "What I want you to do now, is go down to your digs, tell your landlady what's happening and you're off. Then come down to the station and we'll go on from there to Derby. Bring your boots with you. Tell your landlady you'll be coming back tonight. You can stop until Friday, get your things sorted out and then come back to Derby." This was the Monday. Well, I did all this. When he also said: "I want you to play on Wednesday," I thought: "Smashing. Reserve match." I told the landlady I'd been transferred and I went and sat down, in the digs, to read the paper. I turned to the sports page and there it hit me. Just like someone had hit me on the head. 'Arsenal's team to play at Derby on Wednesday'. Well. I started fluttering then. I mean, they were big noises in those days, as were Derby, of course. Like Sunderland and those people. Arsenal were the big noises then. Well, apparently, Sammy, who was the right winger then – Sammy Crooks – he was having leg trouble. Though it wasn't an injury so much as the fact his wife was expecting and he was having a reaction. Isn't that strange? Mind you, Sammy was full of those tricks.

Bert Mozley: In 1946 I was playing for Shelton United, back of the pub there. I was playing inside-left. Jack Bowers came and saw me up there and he got hold of me and said: "I think you'd be better in defence." So he put me to right-back and I played in the 'A' team. Then I played in the reserve team. Jack Nicholas was right-back and he got the 'flu and they put me in. Jack never got back in and he never spoke to me for two months. No because he couldn't get back in the team and I stayed in the team until 1955.

Alf Jeffries: I didn't know what I was walking on. Honest, I didn't. Those couple of days went so quick. Because there were no floodlights then, so it was played in the afternoon. In the

Arsenal side there was Leslie Compton at full-back. The outside-right they had was Alf Kirchen.

Ray Young: I played against Doncaster, away. That would be Easter Monday 1954, same year as I went in the Forces to do my National Service.

Don Hazledine: At Bolton – Nat Lofthouse was playing. I also remember playing against Wolves, against Billy Wright.

Peter Newbery: It was against Sunderland in 1958. Charlie Hurley was at centre-half for them. Storer told me to knock him around, sort him out. He said he liked to play on the ball and I'd soon unsettle him. Well, not only was he a big guy, he was also a good player. We were beaten 3-0. I remember it very well.

Ron Webster: Bury, away. A fellow called Jackson was leading goalscorer at that time and they said to me: "He's mustard." Luckily – well, I don't know about luckily – I had a good game against him and he never scored, but we drew two-each. I played like the old wing-half kind of thing of that time, but I was, like, marking him. I can't remember who was in the team, Geoff Barrowcliffe perhaps. I've got the programme upstairs somewhere.

John O'Hare: Charlton, at home. It was the first game of the season, 1967. No, I didn't know any of the players. Yes, we won 3-2. Yes, I scored. I remember Ronnie Webster stuck me through, inside-right position. You always remember the first game when you score a goal. I'd had a groin injury pre-season and I wasn't at my fittest. I was maybe a bit short. I did okay without playing particularly well. I did okay and scoring a goal helped a little bit.

Mick Hopkinson: When I made my debut, at home to Plymouth, they had a lad playing – I thought of this when Derby played Plymouth in the Cup – a midfielder called Johnny Williams. Best attacking wing-half at the time. He never bothered defending, just attacked. I finished up marking him all the match. Ralph Hann was shouting to Barry Hutchinson: "He's only a young lad, only 18 making his debut, give him a bit of a hand, Barry." Hutch just said: "I prefer to play in their half." In those days, you came back with your midfielder, wing-half or inside-forward. That's how the marking was or should have been!

Ian Buxton: Home, Ipswich. No idea who told me. No, I can't remember how I got to know I was playing. We won 3-0 at Derby – and I scored two – but I can't remember how I was told I was playing or anything about it.

Phil Waller: Preston, at Preston. I think someone was injured on a Tuesday or Wednesday or something.

John Bowers: My debut was at Huddersfield. It was my birthday. Denis Law was playing and then he was signed by Manchester City straight after. We drew 2-2 and the nice thing about it was although I was absolutely as nervous as hell, everybody was great and I had loads of telegrams. I don't know whether people send telegrams these days, they probably have faxes, but I had loads of telegrams from all over the place and that gave me a bit of confidence.

Steve Powell: (debut aged 16) I made my first-team debut in the old Texaco Cup against Stoke on a Wednesday night and then on the following Saturday I was substitute against Arsenal, which was my League debut. I came on for about the last 15 minutes and then I played a full game against Nottingham Forest the Saturday after that. How old? I was just turned 16. I don't remember an awful lot about it, no. I do remember a bit about the Liverpool game later in the season.

Roger Davies: The second season, I went on loan to Preston. That was for a few games. That was before I'd made my League debut for Derby. I went up there, to Preston. We played QPR on a Saturday and we drew. We went up to Burnley and got stuffed about six, I think. I went to see Brian Clough and asked him if I could come back because I thought our reserve side was better than Preston's first team, at the time. He brought me back. He let me come back. I made my debut in the Texaco Cup Final, against Aidrie, and I managed to score in that. Even then it probably wasn't the biggest crowd, but for somebody who'd played at the lower levels, coming to that, it was tremendous. My League debut for Derby was Man City, away. We lost 4-0. I think it was 4-0, but running out at Maine Road, with a crowd like that...well.

Charlie George: Debut in the Charity Shield. Then we played at Sheffield United. Draw, 1-1. I scored the goal. Home debut? Was it QPR? Well, they were a useful side at the time and these things happen in football. We must have been on the piss the night before – no, I don't really mean that. I suppose it was a bit strange losing like that, 5-1, but you get strange results like that even today, don't you?

"Once, I played for Derby County."

Geoff Hazledine: That's right, I played at Oldham. The situation was that I could play anywhere and sometimes it works for you and sometimes it could work against you. I played at Oldham, on the left wing, but I went to Derby as a centre-forward. Jack Barker was manager. He called me into the office – Friday morning I think it was – and he said: "Now then. You've been playing well in all positions. I want to put the pressure on Cec Law because he's not playing well. Could you play outside-left?" So I said: "Well, I've never played outside-left for the club and I wouldn't particularly care to play outside-left, but to get in the first team I'll play outside-left." So he picked me in the team.

Bob McAndrew: It was at the Baseball Ground in April 1964, against Swindon. We won 3-0 and I thought I had a good game. I thought I was in then, until the end of the season. Three games left...I thought: "This is it. This is my chance." It wasn't to be. How can you explain it from my point of view? Win 3-0, have quite a good game and finish up being left out the next week?

Ron Metcalfe: It was against Plymouth. It was the last game of the season, in 1967. It was at home, we drew 1-1. I got a seven in *The People*. Actually, I had a decent game. Derek Draper, he scored our goal. I was 18. I played on the left wing. It was at a time when Tim Ward had just got sacked. The team sheet went up, like it does every Friday after training and I went to have a look, expecting to be in the Reserves, and there I was, on the first-team sheet. I can remember the exact words I said, I probably said them a little bit big-headedly. I can remember saying: "It's about bloody time."

Alf Millin: It was against Bradford City at Valley Parade. In the books it's got Scunthorpe and that's wrong. Bradford City, away. We lost 2-1. Ray Straw scored in the first five minutes and we thought we were on to a good thing, but after that they were all over us and we never did anything after that.

Geoff Hazledine: It was a game that was a non-event. It seemed to be all midfield. I had one chance. Hit the post. It never seemed to get going.

Bob McAndrew: Tim Ward was the manager. No, he hadn't got the sack then. I got the sack before Tim did. I think he got the sack for sacking me!

Alf Millin: I was in the Forces at the time and I managed to get off, midweek, to play for the Reserves. From there they just sent me a card, like, through the post. Through the post to where I was stationed, down London. Harry Storer was the manager. I was outside-left. There was

Albert Mays, Paddy Ryan was behind me...Geoff Barrowcliffe...Keith Savin left-back...I think McDonnell was playing centre-half...Jock Buchanan.

Ron Metcalfe: Colin Boulton was in goals. Alan Durban played, Eddie Thomas played. The crowd was 11,000 something. The pitch was quite hard and no grass on it. I remember two particularly good runs I had that finished up with shots. It was literally the last game before Cloughie took over. Then when Cloughie came he bought Alan Hinton – and that was that.

Bob McAndrew: A lot of the times it used to be that you were dragged off the Reserves' coach and told you were going to play – "Bobby Ferguson's injured," and all the rest of it. Get taken to the dressing-room, Bobby shakes my hand and all the rest of it. He goes into the medical room limping. Comes out running like a two-year-old! That happened on numerous occasions, but, on this occasion, I was picked. He was injured, I was in the side and I thoroughly enjoyed it. Other players? Ray Young, 'Barra'. Reg Matthews, Jack Parry, Ron Webster, Bill Curry.

Geoff Hazledine: I naturally presumed, taking into consideration we'd got a draw away from home, that I'd be in again. Most decidedly. I didn't think I'd played particularly well, but I thought for my first game, I hadn't done bad. The added fact that we'd got a goalless draw, I thought: "Well, I'm automatic for next week." Friday morning the team sheet went up and I just couldn't believe what I was seeing. He'd put Cec back in, you see. I was so disappointed. I just wanted to get away from the ground as quickly as possible.

Bob McAndrew: I was gutted. The position being the end of the season, three games to go and a victory. Played well. Just left out. No I didn't go to see him. I just accepted it. I was only a part-timer and, I suppose, you've got to be grateful for what you've got. People say: "You only played once for Derby County." Yes, but that was one game – and I was at Derby County from the age of 15 until I was 22 or something like that. So I had seven or eight years. It was absolutely wonderful.

Alf Millin: I was looking forward to playing the next week, but I never got a card or anything. They never said I wouldn't be playing or anything. They never said I would be playing either. As I say, I was stationed down London, so I didn't hear anything. I think there was a midweek match, see, but I never got asked to play. Oh yes, I was pleased to play, but disappointed I didn't get to play the next match. I know I hardly had a kick, kind of thing, but they were all over us after the first five minutes. I think when we went to Bradford, we were top and they were second. Eventually we finished second, behind Grimsby. After the Forces, I was back on the staff for another 12 months. June 1956 I think my contract ran out.

Ron Metcalfe: I always look back and think, as a kid, I was always expected and going to be a professional footballer. I played for the town and the county and I always classed it as a failure in my life I wasn't more successful. My Dad played professional as well and we look at it now okay, but at the time, I looked on it as a big failure. I personally classed it as a big failure, anyway. It's probably only the last four or five years that I've started to talk about it. I've never really talked about it before. To be fair, over the last few years – and I think it's a lot to do with the fact that I have been going to one or two of the Derby County Former Players' 'do's' – I have changed my attitude a little bit, but for a long time, it was a sort of, taboo subject. I didn't want to talk about it. It was a sort of failure.

Geoff Hazledine: I'm very proud of it, my one appearance. I love the club very much.

The First 50 Years

DERBY County Football Club was established in 1884 and was one of the 12 founder members of the Football League in 1888. The club was quickly successful and during the 1890s finished three times in the top three positions in the First Division. Two successive FA Cup Finals were also reached, but both were lost – one against Nottingham Forest (1898) – before Derby County reached the FA Cup Final again, in 1903. This time they were beaten 6-0 by Bury, which is still a record defeat in a Cup Final.

A first relegation was suffered in 1907, before the club regained its position in the First Division in 1912, only to be relegated again to the Second Division, in 1914. Only one season passed before they were promoted again, this time as champions, before League football was suspended in 1915 because of World War One.

The club's most famous player in those early times was Steve Bloomer. He made 525 appearances and scored 332 goals between 1892 and 1914. Some claim that he was Derby County's greatest ever player and he is certainly the only one to have had a commemorative monument erected to him. This was unveiled in 1996 and stands proudly in Lock Up Yard off the Cornmarket, in the centre of town. It is a constant reminder to passers-by of the place of football in the city's history and also the place in history of one of Derby's favourite sons. In his later years, Bloomer worked at the Baseball Ground on general maintenance and some people featured in this chapter knew him. One or two even saw him play.

Relegation from Division One was the club's fate in 1921, but promotion was achieved in 1926, after which Derby County finished outside the top ten in the First Division on only three occasions, before the outbreak of World War Two in 1939. The Thirties were heady days, as under the astute managership of George Jobey, Derby County challenged for the Division One championship on several occasions and were recognised as one of the top clubs in the country. On opposition grounds they set several attendance records. In 1934, the legendary Hughie Gallacher became the 400th player to play for Derby County.

Steve Bloomer

'Ned' Mee: I thought he was very good, I did. I saw him in one incident. He ran through three or four players and put it in the net. Fans, spectators, used to shout at him for not parting with it. Oh aye. He was a very popular player. He took all the penalties, Steve Bloomer did. He was good, all right.

Ernie Hallam: I knew him quite well because I lived in Great Northern Road for a time and Steve was at the Great Northern pub in Junction Street, just off Great Northern Road. His sister kept it, Hettie. Of course, his grandson, Steve Richards, went to school with my younger brother. They were good friends of ours. Steve Bloomer worked on the ground as a sort of groundsman, but I once saw him actually play, in so much as when I first came to Derby, the first game of a season was a walking match between railway veterans or something. I can't remember much about it, but Steve Bloomer was in the opposite side. A walking match. An opener to the season. Railway Veterans v an ex-Derby side, I suppose.

Tommy Powell: I never met Steve. I say I never met him, but one day – I used to go as a kid – you know how you stand outside the ground and pass your book in to the bus for them to sign and, one day, a bloke said to me: "Never mind them, you want to go and get his autograph, over there." And I said: "Whose that?" And he said: "Steve Bloomer." I've still got it. He signed it for me and I thought: "Well, fantastic." As a kid you don't realise.

The Twenties and Thirties

George Beard: I watched them regularly from 1926. Stood on the terrace under the main stand. They turned out right by the netting at the back of the goal. They came out there. The dressing-rooms must have been behind the stand at that end. If I remember rightly, that stand was a great big thing, arced over like half a barrel and I remember, early season, when somebody took a terrific shot, a Jack Stamps type of free-kick and it hit the underside of the stand and everything shuddered and a lot of dust came down. I remember that as well as anything. Tremendous laughter. I saw the 'greats' in that season. Aston Villa. I saw Charlie Buchan and the Arsenal team, with a lot of 'B's' in it – Brain, Blyth, Buchan. They'd about five or six 'B's', Butler, Baker. That season I saw a lot of stars. I couldn't wait to get on the ground. Tottenham. Grimsdell, Fanny Walden. Jimmy Dimmock was a real sprightly winger.

Roy Christian: I first watched Derby County in 1928, last Saturday in August, I think. I happen to know because it was the same day that Ernie Hallam watched the same match. That was his first match, too, and it was Derby County v Blackburn Rovers and Derby won 5-1, but Jock Hutton, who was a Scottish international right-back, a hefty bloke, a great big bloke, had his leg broken by Jackie Whitehouse, who was a rather notorious character. He was carried off, of course, and there were no substitutes in those days. They had ten men for most of the game, so it wasn't really quite as easy as that.

George Beard: Always near the top, but never there. Nearest we came was not long before the war. I think we were leading with two or three points. Everton were our rivals and we drew at Everton, 2-2. You played them alternate days at Christmas. Then we won at Derby, 2-1, so it gave us a good lead. Then, we went and lost to Brentford at home! Two successive matches at home – I think the other might have been Birmingham – but we claimed that the Birmingham bloke had fouled our goalkeeper, Jack Kirby. Knocked him over the goal-line.

Roy Christian: We had a good all-round side. Of course, we had Jack Barker, who was a great centre-half. He was a tough bloke. He was hopeless as a manager, but he was a good footballer. We had Jackie Bowers, who popped in a lot of goals. In fact, he developed into a very good centre-forward. He was very raw when he started, but he was always a goalscorer and he improved as a player.

Dave Halford: We had a saloon on the train. Oh yes, a reserved saloon. It used to be hooked up to the train at Derby and taken off when we got back.

Hughie Gallacher

Bill Brownson: Oh yes, I can remember him. I can remember when they had six international forwards and one had to play in the Reserves each week. Gallacher, Bowers, Crooks, Dally Duncan, Napier and the Scotsman, Boyd.

Tom Stubley: I thought Hughie Gallacher was one of the best centre-forwards I ever saw playing and I remember Tom Cooper, in one of the papers, saying that Hughie Gallacher was by far and away the best centre-forward he ever played against. When he left Derby he went to Notts County and Syd Arkle and I – Syd was the bandleader in Derby – we went to see him play and Notts County were playing Cardiff City and they'd got a lad at outside-right called Tex Ricards. Everybody was shouting: "Come on Tex." Hughie Gallacher was made skipper for the day and they were given a free-kick outside the penalty box. Hughie decided to take it and he ran up to the ball and stopped and all their players went to one side and he shoved it in the net on the other side. One of the best goals I've ever seen and it was pure kid'em, pure kid'em.

Dave Halford: Gallacher used to show us all these tricks, you see. He used to sit on the ball. Have you ever seen them do that? When a centre used to come over, Gallacher used to go like this – bend his knees like that – and trap it with his backside. He taught us loads of tricks did Gallacher. Oh, he were great.

'Ned' Mee: I can remember him well. He were very 'dirty', mind you, but he were good.

Tom Stubley: Tommy Eggleston played with Derby and Tom told us that he was one of the few players in the old days – and you'd know more of this than I do – when you've got reserve dressing-rooms and first-team dressing-rooms. And Tom told us Hughie was one of the very few players who'd take them, the Reserves, out on the pitch and show them how to play 'dirty' – and how to get out of it.

Tommy Powell: I saw Hughie Gallacher play. Tremendous. No bigger than two penn'orth of chips, but he could make a ball talk. Back to the goal, I mean, he used to be so cheeky. He'd back-heel them here and there. They almost fielded an all-Scots forward line. There was Jimmy Boyd, Charlie Napier, Hughie Gallacher and Dally Duncan. Then Dave McCulloch came later. Hughie was probably more skilful than John O'Hare, but John was the ideal centre-forward.

Ernie Hallam: Oh, tremendous. I mean, his skill was outstanding. He was only small, but the outstanding thing in that particular game was that Liverpool had a giant centre-half called 'Tiny' Bradshaw and Hughie Gallacher caught him off balance and knocked him over. Of course, that was a great laugh.

Reg Harrison: I saw Hughie about twice, I think it was.

George Beard: Magnificent – and he wasn't at his best. He could play a ball on this green carpet here and still beat two or three chaps with his neat little trickery. I remember him scoring two against Blackburn Rovers from nearly under the bar, quick turns and a flick of the foot. Little chap, but stocky. Went back to a meagre job on the shipbuilding line. Something went wrong and he put his head on a railway line, committed suicide. What a sad thing.

Alf Jeffries: I saw Hughie at his best, at Newcastle. I was a schoolboy then and my Dad took me to the first professional match I ever saw because we lived in South Durham near Bishop Auckland. For a treat, he took me to Newcastle and Hughie was centre-forward. Aah, he was brilliant. They used to kick him to pieces you know. Oh, aye, they kicked him all over the bloody show. The team they played was Leicester City and I was struck by the brilliant blue shirts they had. Then I saw Hughie when he'd finished, more or less, when he was at Notts County. He scored with a backheel. Brilliant. He was old then, but brilliant. A fool to himself though.

Sammy and Dally

Reg Harrison: My fellows were Sammy and Dally. Being wingers they were closer to me. I mean, Cooper and Collins were playing in those days, Jack Barker. They were a good side in those days. They were about ten points clear one year – at Christmas – and never won the League!

Roy Christian: My real favourites were the wingers, particularly Sammy because I knew him personally very well. He was a very nice chap. I played for Littleover at cricket, in fact I was captain a season or two before the war and Sammy was one of our stalwarts. He wasn't a good cricketer, in fact, he wasn't really interested in the game, but he was a natural ball player and couldn't play any game badly. He was a very good golfer, I believe. He'd always score a few runs and try to bowl very fast. A lot of bad stuff, but the odd wicket with the odd good ball and he was very good in the field because he was so nippy.

Alf Jeffries: He was a good golfer, Sammy. He must have been down to about four, must have been. He was a big pal of mine. He and I were great friends because he comes from Durham, same as me. Him, and Harry Elliott of course, had the sports shop. When Sammy used to go up to Durham to see his mother, it was me who used to drive his car. I'll never forget it because it was a Standard Flying 12 and the number was DNU 995. That's ages ago, isn't it, the old Derby number?

Roy Christian: Sammy sometimes gave me a lift – he only lived in Blagreaves Lane and we lived in the village then. And he'd say: "Oh, I've got a pair of boots in the back of the car." He'd say: "I never go without a pair of boots and if I see some young lads playing on the rec, I'll go and play with them." He'd say: "I can always pass on a few tips and they sometimes pass on a few to me!" Amazing, isn't it? He was an amazing chap, Sammy. Everyone loved Sammy and his great use to us was that he was the only one in the team with a car, I think, in those days. It meant he always carried the bag so he was sure of a place. He was a nice bloke and he was a generous chap. He had about six sisters and I think he supported them, apart from his parents.

Tommy Powell: Ah, Sammy. Brilliant. When I first went to Derby, Sammy used to play. I'm not kidding, if he went towards the full-back and pushed it inside, all I had to do was scoop it back and Sam was gone. Quick. You knew what he wanted you to do, straightaway. He was a lovely bloke. He was a brilliant crosser of the ball.

Alf Jeffries: Sammy was like a little 'lop'. He used to be in and out and all over the place. He was a great friend of mine and we both played the same position, you see. When I made my debut, Sammy sat beside me and tried to buck me up kind of thing. He was very good was Sam, very quick. Yes, he could dribble, too.

Roy Christian: Sammy was a good player. His centring was so accurate. He'd cut in more than most wingers did in those days, I think, but he was very adaptable and he would have adapted to the modern game. Dally Duncan was the complete opposite. He was the introvert, whereas Sammy was the extrovert. Nice chap was Duncan, but a different type. You wouldn't get him mixing so much, but get him on his own and he'd talk to me about Aberdeen and what a wonderful city it was and all the rest of it. A very pleasant bloke, but very quiet and not bubbly, like Sammy.

'Ned' Mee: Sammy were good, but to be candid, there was 'Spud' Murphy before him and Georgie Thornewell. Duncan was Sammy's mate on the other wing, wasn't he? I mean, I don't think there were a deal in them, in playing. Georgie Thornewell kept the White Hart in Duffield and I went working at Duffield in the building trade for a chap named Bates. He was on the board at Derby County, Bates was.

George Beard: Oh. Sammy was brilliant. Fast. I've seen him at Derby, sort of near the centre flag. A ball's come along to him and some tough merchant – and there were some tough merchants, Wilf Copping, Collier of Sheffield Wednesday – has come along and I've seen him slip the ball past him and run round the other side and away.

Ernie Hallam: Ah, lovely man, Sammy. I've seen Sammy come inside-right from outside-right and turn the game round for us in the Thirties. Lovely, enthusiastic fellow, Sammy. Very quick. You could picture Sammy breasting his way past on the outside. A lot of wingers are a bit dodgy about going on the outside, at pace, but Sammy used to breast by them.

Roy Christian: I think he would have adapted very well to the modern game because the thing about Sammy that always struck me was that if we were winning with say ten minutes to go, he'd be strolling about on the wing and waiting for the ball. If we were losing 1-0 or 2-0, you'd see him at left full-back and up in the attack and centre-half and he never stopped. I mean, no match was ever lost to Sammy, until the referee blew his final whistle. Tremendous energy and determination to win. Very clean player, but he said the only time he was ever cautioned by the referee – they didn't have 'bookings' in those days – was against Richardson of West Brom. Derby got a corner and Sammy said: "No ref, I touched it. It touched my boot." And the referee cautioned him for dissent!

Tommy Powell: Dally was clever with it, but he wasn't the forceful type. You wouldn't see him go and knock a full-back over or anything like that, but he'd got a lot of skill had Dally. I think one of Dally's favourites was if he was on the wing and anyone hit it over, Dally could take it in his stride with his right foot and cross it with his left. He was so graceful. A bit similar to Alan Hinton, but more graceful.

George Beard: Very tricky. Dribble. Mostly left foot. Quite fast.

Tommy Powell: When they talk these days about free-kicks, well, these balls now are bendy-bendies, aren't they? Dally could bend the heavy ball. He scored direct from a corner, against Sunderland I think, with one of them, if I remember rightly. Yes, outside of his foot.

Ernie Hallam: Wonderful player, Dally. I once read that 'Dally' was actually 'Dolly' in Scotland. I don't know just what inference you get from that, but Dally had a wonderful trick and I've never seen it done quite the same since. Dally was all left foot and he would get the ball inside his left foot and turn away from his man and go right round with the man following him round and he'd be clear on the outside, all with the left foot. His real quality was that he was able to swerve the ball with the outside of the foot.

Roy Christian: Wonderful left foot. Wonderful dribbler. It's something that has almost gone out now, isn't it. Compared to Sammy, he looked big, but he wasn't really. He was broader. I would think he was about 5ft 9ins, 5ft 10ins, something like that, whereas Sammy was 5ft 6ins. Less of a winger's build than Sammy, but Dally scored some good goals. They were mostly from the wing, he very rarely cut in, but he could swerve the ball, which not many people could do in those days.

Alf Jeffries: Lovely footballer was Dally. Tight as a duck's bottom. Wouldn't give anything away. Wouldn't give a thing away. I don't suppose he ever gave a penny for a flag. He finished up on the south coast at Brighton, in a hotel. He died down there. Good footballer, mind.

David Halford

Tommy Powell: Yes, he was a tall, gangly bloke and I can remember a match – I think it was 1935-36. It was when King George died, I think. Anyway, they played Forest at Derby in a cup match and I've got a photo somewhere. My grandad took me and I was only, what nine or ten and I can remember them standing all-round the centre-circle with black armbands on. Yes, I saw him quite a few times when he played at Derby.

Dave Halford: Here, look at this here. This is the day King George V died. We stood round the centre-circle. It was against Nottingham Forest. That's Sammy Crooks there, on the photo. He's just turned away.

Jack Nicholas

Alf Jeffries: I reckon that the luckiest bloke who ever put a pair of football boots on at Derby was Jack Nicholas. I never reckoned him as a footballer. Well, he wasn't a footballer. The crowd used to get at him: "Go on Jack. Kick it anywhere." And he would kick it over the stand, if it would please them. He wasn't the same man when he went away. I always reckoned he was dead lucky. He was. He managed, though. He carried on all them games and played in the Cup Final and was captain, wasn't he?

Tommy Cooper

Ernie Hallam: He was perhaps my all-time favourite. Captained England, as well as Derby County.

'Ned' Mee: There were some good full-backs. There were Chandler, Jack Howe, there were some really good full-backs. They had one from Port Vale. His name were Cooper, Tommy Cooper. Whaa...aat, he was a good one, he was.

Jack Bowers

'Ned' Mee: Jack Bowers were the best centre-forward I've ever seen. I wouldn't condemn who's it? The postman fellow, Kevin Hector? He was a good one, wasn't he? But Jack Bowers were the best centre-forward. Once, I remember, he scored four goals in about 15 minutes. He got hurt against Wolves, with the railings. Because they were just iron railings, spiked, and he did a fish dive and he hit his head on these railings. He were out many a while. He were a very good header of the ball.

Tommy Powell: Jack was a tremendous player. I've seen him dive down here in a load of boots. Jack was two-footed as well. His left foot clog was his best, but even so.

'Ned' Mee: I saw Jack Bowers score a goal from 30 yards, and I'll tell you who were in goal. We were playing Birmingham and Hibbs were in goal. Jack Bowers were good.

Jack Howe

Tommy Powell: I think one of the best two-footed players was Jack Howe. I didn't know which was his best foot. Jack would take dead-ball kicks either foot, it didn't make any difference. He was brilliant, Jack was.

Ralph Hann

Alf Jeffries: Ralph Hann was a good wing-half. Tough was Ralph. He was another Durham bloke.

Peter Ramage

Tommy Powell: I'll tell you another bloke that I never mentioned in the forward line and my uncle always used to say to me: "He's the best player Derby's got." When I signed for Derby, there was a trial and there was about 16 there and I signed amateur – we got £10 for signing-on. It was about 1942 when I signed and we started playing matches in a local league against local sides and that. The fellow who was in charge of us then was Peter Ramage. "Cor!" I said to my uncle afterwards, "I take it all back." I said: "He makes the ball talk. He never gives it you if you're in trouble." I said: "He's absolutely brilliant." Dally Duncan always said to me: "I wouldn't have got a cap without Peter." That's praise and he was a lovely bloke as well.

George Beard: Peter was brilliant. Not a goalscorer though. He was a plier of passes, when we had what we don't have now, wingers.

Johnnie McIntyre

'Ned' Mee: He were good, John. Not very big, but he were stout. He took some shifting off that ball, I'll tell you. He did.

The Reserves

Tim Ward: Bill Bromage was reserve-team trainer and there was a pal of George Jobey's who went away with us and who reported back to Jobey. No directors ever went with us. Jimmy McIntyre looked after the Colts team.

Reg Harrison: You could have anyone playing in the Reserves, really. There was no first-team squad in those days. I can't understand it now. If a fellow out of the reserve side played wing-half, he went in the first side as a wing-half, if anyone got hurt. They didn't jockey players about so much.

Tim Ward: One day, we were playing against Manchester City Reserves, just before Christmas 1937. They had just signed a lad from Oldham for about £7,000. His name was Hannigan or Hannaway, something like that. I was changing next to Freddie Jessop, who was playing centre-half. Jessop had been at Derby some time and was a hard player. This day we were talking about Manchester City's new player. "It's a lot of money to pay," somebody said. "Aye," said Freddie Jessop. "We'll have to get rid of him early doors. We'll have to get the chopper out on him." I carried on changing. We'd been playing about 20 minutes and this player went into a tackle with Jessop. He was carried off on a stretcher. I didn't really see what happened.

Others

Tommy Powell: They talk about hard hitters of a ball. There used to be a fellow called Eric Brook, who played for Manchester City. He could hit a ball. Eric Houghton, who used to play for Aston Villa. God, he could really thump them. I saw Tommy Lawton, when he first played for Everton. Tommy was tremendous in the air. I saw Tommy play quite a few times.

'Ned' Mee: Ben Olney, a big chap. He could pick the ball up with one hand, he could. He was best goalkeeper I saw.

Ernie Hallam: I saw Sammy Crooks play for England at Wembley about 1936 and McCulloch, who was with Hearts, was centre-forward for Scotland. We'd got Tommy Cooper for England, who was opposite Dally Duncan for Scotland. Dave McCulloch came to Derby, from Brentford. Jack Barker was centre-half and we'd a really good showing. We drew 1-1. Tommy Walker was the outstanding player for Scotland.

Tommy Powell: I mean, you'd got Jack 'Nick' one side and a fellow named 'Iky' Keen used to play. 'Iky' was up and down, 'Iky' was. Tommy Cooper and Georgie Collin were the full-backs. Jack Kirby was in goals and then Ken Scattergood. Frank Boulton came later on, from Arsenal. Of course, your forward line, looking from the right, you'd got Crookie, Jimmy Boyd, Ronnie Dix, Dai Astley, Charlie Napier, Jimmy Hagan, Jack Bowers, Dave McCulloch, Hughie Gallacher, Dally. All those. It's hard to compare eras. Probably the measure of fitness wasn't what it is now, but, for me, there's no substitute for skill, is there? They always had 11 players who were top class.

Dave Halford: Arthur Groves was a good player. They got him from Blackburn Rovers. His lad, John, played in the Cup Final, for Luton, when Forest beat them. When I came to Derby there were so many pros on the books.

Tommy Powell: They had such as Jimmy Hagan. I mean, Jimmy was an absolutely brilliant youngster, but couldn't get in the side because you'd got players like Astley, Dix, Napier and people like that.

Alf Jeffries: Jimmy Hagan was a brilliant player. He could control the game. He had a funny sort of humour, absolutely dry. When we were both at Derby, he said to me one weekend: "I want you to come out with me tomorrow." He says: "I've got to meet a girl and she's got a pal. I want you to take the pal." So I says: "Fair enough." I can't remember what the picture house was called, it was opposite the Midland Drapery, where the crossroads is. Well his girl happened to be Iris, and he went with her until he married her. The other one, well I only took her out this once. But she was a livewire was Iris. She was a Derby girl, of course.

'Ned' Mee: Harry Bedford? He come from Blackpool, him and Georgie Mee. No, George wasn't my brother. I wish he had been. After he retired, he got on the front at Blackpool, singing, didn't he? I used to go to Blackpool once a year, when I was fit. He were a winger. Outside-left.

Crowds

Ernie Hallam: Derby was never a hugely supported team at that time. We had the odd big gate, but if you got 20,000, you did well, really. The average wasn't great at all. They were always an attraction away, though. I knew people in London, if Derby were playing – whether it was at Arsenal, Chelsea, Charlton, whoever – they would go to watch Derby play. They were a big attraction.

Roy Christian: A man used to come round the ground with a little blackboard over his shoulder saying 'Late changes'. The players weren't numbered in those days. 'Outside-left for Derby – Harry Mann instead of Georgie Mee.' Just plain shirts. It must have been terrible doing a commentary in those days. Celtic used to have numbers only on their shorts, didn't they?

In digs

Alf Jeffries: I was in digs with Jack Nicholas' mother. It was one of the streets near the Cavendish, near to Crewe Street because I finished up in Crewe Street. There was Jack Nicholas, Ken Scattergood, Jack Howe and somebody else. All in the same digs.

On tour

Dave Halford: They took this party to Germany because Derby were such a good team they thought they were the best club to send to Germany. So I was lucky enough to go. I was only about 19. We went on the boat from Dover to Ostend. We played four matches, Frankfurt, Cologne, Düsseldorf and Dortmund. I only played in one, that was the last one, Dortmund. When I played we drew 1-1, but oh, they didn't half give us a hard time. They were good players, oh aye. Big crowds.

Dave Halford: They were preparing for war, oh yes. If you said: "Good morning." They'd say: "Heil Hitler." Wherever you went, if you went in a pub, they didn't say: "Good evening." No. "Heil Hitler." Lots of troops, everywhere. Tommy Cooper and Sammy had to come back to play for England and so Georgie Collins was captain.

Mr Jobey

Roy Christian: I met him after he'd finished with football or after football finished with him because he was thrown out. I used to meet him at Meadow Lane and places like that. I was doing a few reports for *Sport in the Midlands*, as it was then, under David Coleman, actually. I remember Barney Bamford, nice chap, it was a slippery day and his car went into a ditch. I could hear him explaining and apologising and David Coleman said: "The listener doesn't want to hear about your /@!|$* exploits. Get on and tell us what happened."

Alf Jeffries: I'll tell you one thing. They used to say all kind of things about him, but he knew football did Jobey and he knew the players, oh aye. He used to drink port wine and could get a bit tipsy. He smoked corona cigars, too.

'Ned' Mee: When Napier were bought, I was in the pub just below the Legion and Jobey came in this pub and he was just on his way to buy Napier.

Roy Christian: I got on quite well with him. He knew his football. He was a strong, tough sort of character. He didn't have any nonsense from the players. He was only a 'name' because of his managerial skills. He was never much of a player.

Alf Jeffries: Now you talk about Jobey. Now Ike Keen was a lightweight really, but he was a good half-back. He'd opened up a tea business called 'Rington's' or 'Errington's' or something like that. Errington was his first name, of course. He was a gambler and he used to go to the dogs at Derby, Long Eaton, Nottingham and places like that. Sammy used to go to the dogs as well. Anyway, Ike used to put his hand in the till. Of course, if he won, he never put it back and Jobey rescued him twice from the income tax man. You have to talk as you find and I always found Jobey very good.

Chairmen

Roy Christian: Well, they had several. Ossie Jackson – O.J. Jackson – who was a builder, Derwent Builders. There was Ben Robshaw, who was a rag and bone merchant – in a big way. Bendle-Moore, I think, was the chairman as well. Now he was the coroner. I think he was chairman, he may have been vice-chairman. Jackson and Robshaw were the two I remember most.

Leaving...

Alf Jeffries: I left because I had no sense. That's why. They just came and asked me to go to Sheffield United, that was it. I don't know why I left. Mind, I've told people since then: "If I'd realised what was going to happen, I'd never have gone." The point was, Jimmy Hagan and me, we played the right wing in the Reserves, mostly. You see, Jimmy couldn't get into the side and Jobey, at times before I went, used to play him on the right wing. This wasn't right because Jimmy was a good footballer. He was an inside-forward good and proper was Jimmy. He got transferred to Sheffield United in the 1938-39 season and they didn't win the League, but they were promoted to the First Division. I went there in the summer of 1939.

In Wartime

THE football played during World War Two is often overlooked, but quite a lot took place. Some of the representative service teams were of international quality. Many footballers became physical training instructors in the armed services.

Naturally, the quality of football at home declined, as clubs were forced to field scratch teams, but supporters were sometimes rewarded with the surprise appearance of an established star, who was passing through the locality on military duties. Other well established stars were occasionally transferred to a local army or air force placement. Two of the greatest names in Derby's history, Raich Carter and Peter Doherty, first came together at an RAF camp near Loughborough.

Some players, who did not serve in the forces because they were employed in industries considered crucial to the national war effort, for example coal mining, made a considerable number of appearances for their local clubs during the war. Unfortunately for them, the record books refer only to matches played in peacetime and so their first-team appearances are recorded as being many less than would possibly have been the case in normal times. Jack Stamps, for instance, first played for Derby in 1938-39 and by the time he made his last appearance in 1953-54 he had totalled 262 games and 126 goals. But what would those figures had been had he not lost seven entire League seasons to the war?

Spectators watched matches as and when they could.

The day war broke out

Roy Christian: I saw a bit. Not much at Derby because I wasn't here very much. Of course, they packed up immediately war broke out. September 1939. The last match was on the Saturday before war broke out on the Sunday. We beat Aston Villa 1-0. I think Jack Nicholas with a penalty scored the only goal. Then there was nothing here until 1942, 1943, something like that. I used to see quite a bit at Fratton Park, Portsmouth, and The Dell, Southampton. Oh, and Hibernian. I became a supporter of Hibernian. Twice I was doing courses in minesweeping at the training place up there, by the Forth Bridge. It was easy to nip into Edinburgh and watch Hibs. Hearts never seemed to be at home when I was in harbour.

Tommy Powell: I played quite a bit during the war. I scored four against Villa – no it wasn't, it was against Birmingham at Villa Park. We won 5-1. I was 17 then and I scored four. Gil Merrick was in goal for them. I was working at E. W. Bliss down on City Road. Of course, during the war we were only playing for a few bob per match.

Reg Harrison: When war broke out Derby packed up and all those players from Derby County came into the Derby Senior League. Jack 'Nick' played for us at Derby Corinthians. Sammy Crooks, Dally Duncan and Ralph Hann played with Wiresheds, that was the Carriage and Wagon Works. 'Leuts' played with Royces. There were one or two more played with Royces

'Young Nipper', the boxer Eric Dalby. Good players. The best team in the league was the Royal Engineers, stationed down on Siddals Road. It was a full professional side and the captain of the team was Warney Cresswell, who'd played for England in the Twenties. Sam Bartram played for – it was the Bloomberries they called them – for an Air Force team. They played on the old Tigers' rugby ground. The garage and part of Alvaston Lake is there now. They were all in the league. I think that's what did us good. You went to Holbrook. A chap named Webster played, inside-forward. He played with Chesterfield. Chick Musson, Jackie Parr. They were all on Derby's books. That's when Chick hit me. I got this ball and I beat this fellow. I took it past him and Chick's coming behind him and he hit me, bang, straight down the middle. Holbrook. Syd Ottewall. He was there.

Ernie Hallam: I saw all the wartime games at the Baseball Ground aye. Yes, you never knew who you were watching. Almost anybody could turn up and get a game sometimes. I mean, there were players like Arnie Grace, Slackie from Holbrook. They all played fairly regular. Kinnerley and people like that, who played in the Derby and District League. They got the odd game.

Reg Harrison: I signed amateur before I went in the army. It'd be 1941. They signed them on because they could retain a player as an amateur then. Another one McMillan signed on the same day from Corinthians was Frank Watson. He was a centre-half and he kept Leuty out of the representative side. He didn't keep him out altogether, but Frank played centre-half and Leuty had to play right-half. He was a good player, Frank Watson.

Colleagues and opponents

Tommy Powell: We used to play against Stoke who had Frankie Bowyer, the Mountfords, Frankie Soo and Neil Franklin. We got to know them quite well, actually. We had quite few games with them because they had that Northern League then, you see. When they talk about appearances, we made a hell of a lot of appearances during the war. I've said to people, that's false, the appearances for League matches. These were League matches, but during the war. I remember Charlie Williams, the comedian, playing for Doncaster Rovers against us. I played in that match when we beat Villa 6-0 in the Midland Cup. Peter Doherty scored five. We had a chap called Clarrie Jordan play centre-forward that day. He went to Sheffield Wednesday. I also played for Lincoln and Forest. I also played for Chesterfield once, with 'Spider' Linacre, who played for Middlesbrough.

Johnny Morris: I spent four and a half years in the army from 18 years old. I'd already played for United in 1941. I guested at Charlton early on in the war, when I was about 17. Playing with United, we used to have seven or eight guesting. I think it made us mature quicker. You had to adapt your game, you see.

Dave Halford: I played a bit for Queen's Park Rangers. Len Goulden played. Right at the start of the war, I played for Oldham. I was 31 when I finished in the army. Of course, the war took the best years.

Reg Harrison: While I was in the army I was asked to play for Sheffield United, Charlton, Notts County. People would ask: "Are you signed on with anybody?" I'd say: "Amateur." "Oh that's nothing," they'd say and it was nothing, to them. "Do you want to come down...?" Later on, when I went professional with Derby, they got me with Hartlepools. They'd got some good players, like Chilton from Manchester United.

Alf Jeffries: When I got called up I went across to the Pompey ground because I was stationed at Gosport, the other side. I was training at the ground and there was old Jack Tinn, the manager with the lucky Cup Final spats, and I says: "Is it all right to train with the club, Mr Tinn?" And he said: "Yes, who are you?" So I told him and he said: "Aye, carry on." Well, the following week, he was all over me because he'd contacted people and found out who I was and, of course, we were guest players at times and I guested for them and played outside-left. That was the time they had a very good team. I forget who the bloke was behind me at left-half. He was a Scot and he was a tough bugger. One match we played, he was shouting like hell, up and down the wing, shouting at me. Anyway, at half-time I says: "What's wrong with you then? What's all this shouting at me?" He said: "I'm not shouting at you. I'm shouting at these other buggers for not taking up the ball from you."

Roy Christian: The second-in-command at our base was a Lieutenant Black and we got a bit of a football team going amongst the ships and I said: "Do you play football by any chance?" He said: "No, I'm not very interested in the game." Then one day, I was walking with him on the quay and there were some lads kicking a ball about and it came our way and this chap Black just sort of put his foot on the ball; instant control, ball absolutely dead, a brilliant piece of trapping. I said: "I thought you told me you didn't play football. It looks to me as though you're pretty good." He said: "Well, I do play as a matter of fact, but it's my living and I don't want to risk an injury by playing in a scratch match of no importance." He said: "It's the only thing I can do in civvy street." I said: "Who do you play for?" and he said: "Kilmarnock." I said: "And Scotland...?" and he said: "That's right. I've played a bit for Scotland." He was the inside-right for the Scottish international team, the current Scotland inside-right. I'd no idea at all.

Tommy Powell: They were both at Loughborough, Raich Carter and Peter Doherty, and the fellow who used to bring them – who used to come in the dressing-room – was Dan Maskell of tennis fame. He was their squadron leader, Dan was. Yes, he was a nice bloke as well and he used to come with them every week. Great players, different styles. Raich, I mean, anywhere from 30 yards the goalkeeper had to watch out. Pin-point passes. A bit 'sergeant majorish' Raich was, but he was OK. Peter was a different kettle of fish altogether. Peter was up and down, up and down, and if anything went wrong on the pitch it was always: "I'll help you out son, I'll help you out."

Stan Tacey: I knew a local lad who played centre-forward, Smith from Draycott. He played one or two matches, in between Carter and Doherty, and I said: "What was it like playing in between Carter and Doherty?" And he said: "Well, I remember Raich coming up to me, before I went on the pitch. It was my first match and he said: "Lad, I'll apologise now for anything I might say to you during the match. I can't control myself during the game, so I'm apologising now, first."

Reg Harrison: I'd just come home on leave and went up training and he called me in the office, Stuart McMillan. He said: "They tell me you're playing outside-right at Hartlepools." I said: "Yes." He said: "We're looking for an outside-right to take Sammy's place. Will you play on Saturday?" I said: "Yes." There was Raich, Dave McCulloch, Peter and Dally. All internationals they were and I played on the wing and stayed there. First match was as a winger. Home, against Brentford. Dave McCulloch came from Brentford by the way.

The Day Derby Won the Cup

THE 1946 FA Cup Final victory over Charlton Athletic is one of the great moments in Derby County's history. It is significant for two reasons. It was the first FA Cup Final after World War Two, which signalled to the nation that the country was, at last, able to resume its collective business without hindrance. It was also the first major trophy that Derby County had won. In three previous FA Cup Finals, they had been defeated, but by winning the 1946 Cup Final, the club reaffirmed its position in English football. It compensated, in some way, for not winning the championship, after some near misses in the Thirties. So near and yet, so far.

After all the horrors and self-denial of warfare, the 1946 Cup Final brought an early smile back to the Derby and Derbyshire public. Many people, however, who would dearly have liked to have attended that Wembley occasion were otherwise engaged, still caught up in the aftermath of war. Others simply could not obtain a ticket. For the lucky ones, it was a day they will never forget.

Early rounds

Tommy Powell: It was quite strange really. I went into the army to do my National Service in November 1945 and when Derby won the Cup they played Luton in one of the early rounds. I was doing my sapper's course at Preston. Derby sent a telegram to see if I could play midweek in the second leg, but the army wouldn't let me off. We had some match, up there at Preston. They wouldn't let me go, otherwise I'd have been part of that Cup run.

Roy Christian: I did go to one of the earlier rounds, at The Hawthorns, West Brom. We won 3-1, I think. Peter Doherty had a marvellous game in a snowstorm. I was in Flushing and I'd got a couple of little vessels, motor launches really, fitted out for minesweeping. We'd been sweeping the Vesa in Germany and we were supposed to come back through the Dutch waterways. The thing was that if I got blown up, they'd have had to sweep the canals you see, but if I didn't get blown up, there was no need. They didn't tell me until afterwards! They'd saved a huge amount of money and I didn't get blown up, but they said we weren't sufficiently seaworthy; weren't built for seagoing. They were Broads craft really, I suppose. They said we'd got to wait for a tank landing craft. Well this tank landing craft duly arrived, a sub-lieutenant in command. Well, the weather was too bad and he wouldn't sail, you see, for two or three days. Finally, I said to him, I think it was the Thursday: "I think we shall have to go today. I've got some important business on Saturday." I didn't tell him it was at The Hawthorns, of course. He said: "Well, you're senior to me. You'll have to make the decision." I said: "All right, we'll sail." So we did. We had one or two anxious moments, but we got through to Sheerness,

Queenborough, eventually. That was the last thing I did in the navy and I came up on the Friday and got to the match on the Saturday. It was a very good game. It was worth it, but I don't know what view the Admiralty would have taken if I'd have sunk both ships – but it was important to get to the match.

Lionel Pickering: I went to Sheffield for the semi-final, but I didn't actually see the game because I was so small. We got there two hours before kick-off – my Dad took me everywhere – and stood on the Kop, a massive Kop at Hillsborough, before it was developed as it is today. There were 75,000 people there and we got behind one of the barriers and, of course, it was such packed crowd, there were people standing in front of me. We should have taken an orange box, like some dads used to think about. Anyway, we'd never been in a crowd like that before and all I saw was the ball when it was in the air. I couldn't even see the goalposts or anything. I don't know, I think that may have influenced my Dad, about getting me down to Wembley because I was then about 14 and a small 14 at that. I grew a little bit more after that, when I was about 17, actually, but I was quite a small 14-year-old and I always believed that he couldn't get me a ticket.

Some were lucky...

Ernie Hallam: I was, aye. Oooohh, aye. Funnily, Reg Harrison got my my ticket. I used to live next door but one to Reg at that time and he married a girl who lived a couple of doors away from me. Next door but one, the other way, was my good friend who was married to the sister of Reg's wife. We went everywhere together that year. I had to work nights in order to go to away games and all that sort of thing – to pull the matches in – but Reg got us our tickets for the Cup Final.

Bill Brownson: No I didn't go, I was in Egypt when the Cup Final was on. I was trying to listen to a radio. That was a great pity. I couldn't hear much at all, to tell you the truth.

Ernie Hallam: They were 10s 6d [53p] seats, which were where the players' wives sat. Reg had got us good seats. We were just in front of the Royal Box. The seats were just below, to the left. I didn't know anything about the argument regarding the seats, at the time.

Lionel Pickering: It was a few years afterwards, actually – my Dad's been dead now for about five years; he died aged 92 – and I only found out the story when I got involved with Derby County this time, on the board. Angus Morrison and one or two of the players like Reg Harrison and Jimmy Bullions, who both played in the Cup Final – and Angus would have played, but of course, Jack Stamps took his place instead. Angus played in some of the earlier games and he was a very good centre-forward, but of course, on the day, Jack took all the glory, scored two goals, two great goals, and we won 4-1. Anyway, my Dad happened to say when he met Angus: "Do you remember selling me a Cup Final ticket?" So Angus said: "Yes I do. As a matter of fact, it was on the railway station. Do you remember we were going somewhere or other?" In those days, the players travelled on the train, same as the fans. Anyway, they were all hanging around, waiting for the train to come and Angus said: "Yes, I've got one. I've got a ten and sixpenny one." It was a guinea in those days for a good seat and 10s 6d for the players' tickets. There was a bit of a kerfuffle about that too, wives had not been put in the proper side of the ground and there was quite a story there. Anyway, good old Angus said: "Yes, I've got one and here it is. It's ten and six pence." My Dad paid him 10s 6d. He didn't pay a pound. He didn't pay a fiver. Ten shillings and sixpence.

Ernie Hallam: We went down by coach and we had the top of the coach open. 'Charabancs' they called them. Coming back, we thought we owned the world. We sat on the top, waving the rattles. There was no hooliganism. Going down, we were shouting: "We're up for the Cup." Oh tremendous.

Roy Christian: I didn't go. I couldn't get a ticket. I was on demob leave, but I hadn't actually been demobbed and I wasn't back in Derby early enough to get a ticket, so I didn't go. Great pity.

Lionel Pickering: Then my Dad had second thoughts. He'd got a ticket and there were five or six of them going down there. He always told me he didn't get me a ticket, but Angus Morrison did, in fact, provide a ticket. My Dad got cold feet because in those days it was about 100,000 at Wembley, mostly standing up, and I don't think he was sure whether he could protect me properly. It had been a bit of a frightening experience at Hillsborough. Of course, Angus still comes to the games. All the three players from those days come to the games and it's a thrill for me, as an old football fan, to see some of my heroes and think that I can help them by having them into the directors' box. We managed to get them introduced to the Queen even and they were all thrilled with that.

Stan Tacey: I did three years in India and I got back on the Thursday before the Cup Final and my wife greeted me with the words: "My Dad's got you a ticket for the Cup Final." I never asked how he got it. It was only a 3s 6d [18p] standing ticket. One ticket. He'd got one for himself. I think it was 30s [£1.50] as it was in those days – and he was sitting up somewhere near the Queen!

Tommy Powell: No, I didn't go. Being in the army I couldn't get off, actually. In fact, I was coming home on leave halfway through the afternoon and I remember asking a bloke at Kettering – I had to change a Kettering – and he told me what the score was at the time and what was happening. Jack Parr got me a couple of tickets. Jack had broken his arm and couldn't play and so my uncle and my aunt went with the tickets.

Jimmy Bullions: As you know, there was all the palaver about us being given cheap tickets for our wives. Carter and them said that the tickets we got were for seats out in the open – I think they was 10s the tickets in those days – and they didn't want the wives getting wet if it rained. Of course, it was my mother in my case, although I had my aunties who came down from Scotland, but I always remember, we got the better tickets eventually, seeing as the players were going on strike and such. They were adamant about it. As you know, I was the youngest player and I never had any say in such things. When you've got personalities like Carter, they dominate things and young players like myself and Reg, well... There was Stampie and Jack Howe and they said to Jack 'Nick': "We're not having this."

Jimmy Bullions: Anyway, we got these complimentary tickets. They were 42s [£2.10] each and I gave mine to my mother. They were on the opposite side to the Royal Box. My two aunties and my dad, also my pals from Shuttleworth – who I'd once let down some years before – they all went down by bus to Wembley. We got another 50 tickets you see and 30 went to all my pals, who worked at the pit at Oxcroft Colliery and played with me for Shuttleworth Juniors. We paid for those tickets, but I never charged them. They were 10s [50p] each. I can't remember what we got for complimentaries. I think we only had that one, that 42s one. Anyway, it turned out that my aunties and my dad were sat right alongside the Royal Box and I was able to speak to them as we went up the stairs for the Cup. It backfired, didn't it because my mother, with her 42s ticket, never saw the Queen and the King and that, only from the opposite side of the ground. The wives, too, would be all sat with my mother like. Forty-two shilling seats was a lot of money in those days. Here was my Aunt Jessie and my Aunt Meg on the cheaper tickets, and my dad and all my pals from Shuttleworth.

Ernie Hallam: They supposedly laid the 'Gypsy's Curse' by winning, of course. The funny thing was – about the curse, you know – was that it was a gypsy who was the groundsman. Mallender. Old Mallender. When the club turfed these gypsies off, they supposedly laid a curse on and a lot's been made of it since, but for years after, one of the gypsies was the groundsman – Old Mallender. Anyway, we went and crossed somebody's palm and had it laid before the Cup Final, but, oh, it was a marvellous day. Funnily enough, people today ask me: "How do you think they'll do? What's the score today, Ernie? What do you think?" And I always say: "Sorry, I don't know. I never predict!" And I don't, but in those days, I'd worked myself up into a pitch, so I knew, I knew. I really and truly, honestly believed, that we'd enough quality, skill and endeavour, with Carter and Doherty, to win. It could overcome bad luck and all sorts of things and I was so confident. It was unbelievable and it was borne out on the day.

Stan Tacey: I went with my father-in-law and when we got to Wembley I said to him: "I've never been here before. I better go in to make sure I can see." So I went into Wembley and the first time you go there it's overwhelming, really. There were all the paddocks separated and when I got in, there was hardly anybody there. So I went and leaned on one of the balustrades viewing the empty ground, and a fellow from Bemrose's, who I hadn't seen for six years, suddenly appeared.

The day

Stan Tacey: I can't remember the weather much. It didn't rain. It was warm.

Jimmy Bullions: It was a really hot day. Very hot, in fact.

Ernie Hallam: It was a warm day, it was. It was, as I remember it.

Reg Harrison: Oh, beautiful, warm. A no-coat day. Beautiful pitch. Dave Willis went down before and put our studs in, an-inch long, and he was asked then: "What are you doing that for? I think it was 'Leut' who asked him: "What are you doing that for?" He said: "I've been here before." I don't know whether he had, but he was right because the grass was quite long and it gave us a better grip.

The captain

Jimmy Bullions: Jack was a smashing fellow to get on with. He was stern and all the rest of it. In fact when I went from Chesterfield to Derby, he didn't speak to me for quite some time. I went to play right-half and Jack had been kind of running Derby. After the war started they'd got no manager until Ted Magner came. Jack felt I was going to shove him out, but they moved him to right-back and it wasn't until he'd played right-back for a bit that he started talking to me.

Status

Jimmy Bullions: There was a great divide between playing as a reserve and then going into the first team and these players had been playing with Derby before the war. So on many things, Raich Carter and Jack Stamps, Jack Howe, they all had plenty to say. Not Peter Doherty though. Peter thought about it before he shouted his mouth off.

Preparation

Reg Harrison: We went on the Friday the week before. Played Charlton on the Saturday the week before, but we took players out. Peter and Raich didn't play. I played inside-forward, Sammy played outside me, and I think Angus Morrison played centre-forward. Jack Stamps played inside-left, and Dally was on the other wing.

Reg Harrison: On the day, it was just normal for us. We were sleeping four in a room and there was a lot of ribbing the night before. Four in a room. Big room though. There was Angus, myself, Jimmy and Chick.

The match

Jimmy Bullions: I had to mark this big fellow, Don Welsh. He was big. He was a sergeant major or something, in the army. He was a big, powerful fellow and the other inside-forward was 'Sailor' Brown and he was small and quick. He'd got this rolling gait, that's why they called him 'Sailor'. I marked Welsh, except at corner- kicks. We'd played them in a match the week before, at Charlton. Carter and Doherty and one or two others didn't play, but I played in that game at The Valley. Anyway, going back to Wembley, my job, of course, was to make sure I cut Welsh out. I'll always remember, Jack Nicholas saying to me: "At corner-kicks, I'm going to watch Welsh." Jack was a big bustler. He said: "You take Duffy, if he's not taking the corner on that side. Or one of the other players." Well, that took a lot of pressure off me because Welsh was big and strong and good in the air and it was a bit of a worry.

1–0

Jimmy Bullions: When we scored, I thought "Hey, this is great." Then we gave this silly free-kick away. I can't remember who gave it away. I hope it wasn't me.

Own goal: 1–1

Jimmy Bullions: We all lined up and I remember Turner taking this shot and I can't remember which leg it hit, but it deflected the ball and put Vic Woodley out of it.

Ball burst

Jimmy Bullions: I can't remember whether it was towards the end of 90 minutes or at the start of extra-time. I was behind Jack Stamps, right behind him, and he volleyed this ball and from where I was it looked a goal all the way. I thought: "By, this is going in." Jack loved to volley them you know. They'd go over the top and all over, but he loved to volley the ball. Anyway, he really hit this one and then, in it's path, it went ...phut. Do you know, I've never seen any films or anything, pictures whatever, of the ball actually bursting.

Stan Tacey: Jack Stamps fired in the shot and it looked a goal all the way. It was just before the end of ordinary time. He fired in this shot, it looked like a goal all the way and then it went pheeewwww... Sam Bartram caught it – and the ball was flat. I thought: "What's the referee going to do now?" He gave a bounce-up from where the shot was taken, not from where Bartram caught it.

Jimmy Bullions: Then Sam Bartram did something really good. If it had been me, I'd have been holding the ball up and saying: "Eh, ref. Ball's burst." I reckon Sam threw it to be out of the danger area. I had a feeling it was quick thinking really. A bounce-up with a new ball, where he'd caught it? That would have been dangerous. I was right behind it and it just went like a balloon and zig-zagged, but Bartram got it and threw it away then.

Stan Tacey: I came back on the train. I arranged to meet my father-in-law somewhere and we came back on the train.

Man of the match?

Ernie Hallam: A bit difficult for me to say. Young Reg played wide on the right. He didn't let us down at all, he played well he did, but it was a tragedy for Sammy. Man of the Match? Tell you who I was disappointed with on the day, Dally Duncan. Old 'Nick' was brilliant. Couldn't kick with his left foot but he had a great game in his own particular, rough way. Leuty? Carter? I wouldn't like to say who was Man of the Match. Probably didn't look for Man of the Match in those days.

Jimmy Bullions: I would think Carter would be Man of the Match. Raich was never one for the occasion to overawe him. He responded to the occasion. He still wanted the ball, all through the game. I mean, Jack Stamps never had a kick for the first 90 minutes. He'd been completely out of it with Oakes and them round him.

Stan Tacey: I should say Jackie Stamps. He scored the goals didn't he? He could have had a hat-trick in the final seconds because Bartram brought off a terrific save from him again.

Extra-time

Jimmy Bullions: When we started off the extra-time, they seemed deflated somehow. I don't know why. I know it was a warm day, but I've seen loads of Cup Finals and been to them and I've seen them get cramp and the rest of it, yet I can't remember the match ever stopping for that and it was a hot day. I know, perhaps, they run a lot quicker than we did, but I don't really know.

Reg Harrison: What a relief when we'd finished. That we'd won. I can't remember too much about it, really.

'Stampie'

Jimmy Bullions: Well Jack – he was the perfect foil for the others. Derby, just now, they could do with a Jack Stamps coming in from corner-kicks. For me, Jack was a worker. He never gave in. He fought and that, but he wasn't in Lawton's class. Or the best centre-forwards. He was a power man for years, right until he died, really. He was a bustler and got his backside going. Jack was like me, he liked it when it was sludgy. Heavy grounds suited Jack. He was strong and ploughed through it. The Baseball Ground was just a treat for us.

Johnny Morris: He was like a cart-horse really. Don't forget, we used to play on really heavy, muddy grounds.

Stan Tacey: I don't think there's one like him in present-day football. He was always there when he was wanted. Big fellow. I should say he was six foot. There was only one Stamps. Oh no, no, he wasn't a good footballer. He was an opportunist, always there in the middle. He took the weight off the rest of the forwards.

Bill Brownson: Jack Stamps was probably the most underrated player – underrated centre-forward – that I know because believe me, you weren't a mug to play between Doherty and Carter. People have said that he was the weak link. He wasn't. He got some goals for those people. I can remember us beating Manchester City 6-0 and he let fly from just outside the penalty area and it hit the crossbar. It was still wagging for about five minutes. By God, he could hit a ball.

Tommy Powell: Jack used to hold it: "You'll not get round me." He was a gentle giant, really.

Ernie Hallam: I hardly like saying, – it's my humble opinion and I might be hopelessly wrong – but I think he's been more revered in history since he finished playing than he ever was while he was playing. I mean, he did a great job in the Cup Final and you can't take that away from him. He was 100 per cent honest, but I don't think he was a great player at all.

Don Hazledine: He was always very friendly and helpful because you didn't really, going there as a youngster, you never got a lot of help. I don't think he'd stand out in present day football, but the Baseball Ground suited him. I don't think it would've suited Baiano!

Note: *Perhaps the final verdict on Jack Stamps should be left to one of the most talented players in Derby County's history. Raich Carter is on record as saying that Jack Stamps was hugely underrated and a fine footballer who'd played many games as an inside-forward although everyone remembered him, unfairly in Carter's opinion, only as a 'battering-ram' centre-forward.*

Raich and Peter

Ernie Hallam: Incomparable. I still hark back to them as a yardstick – Raich and Peter. So different and yet both had the same properties, wanting to win, score goals. Peter, a 'prince of players'. Raich, who's really got the will to win. He's got the skill; he's got a terrific shot, right or left foot; and he could hold people off while he got his shot in. Did he know his own worth? He did, he did, by God, he did. I've heard Tim Ward say: "He didn't train too hard." Tim used to say that Raich would say: "Just a couple of laps round the pitch will do me this morning." I don't think the manager argued with him because he was always fit on the day. Always fit on the day.

Jimmy Bullions: I was lucky because I usually had Raich Carter in front of me, who always wanted the ball. There was no hiding with Raich. He wanted the ball and, as you know, he wanted to throw it in as well. I didn't throw it in much because he always wanted to take them. He wanted to take corner-kicks, everything. He wanted to run the game and when you've got good players like him and Doherty, it makes it a lot easier. A tremendously lot easier, really because I've played in sides when you've got the ball and you look up and everyone is stood next to the full-backs and one thing and another and you're left there on your own, with nobody to find.

Tommy Powell: Raich would shout at people. He had tremendous presence about him. I saw him play for Sunderland before the war. I can remember seeing Peter score, when Man City beat Derby 7-1 at Derby, and I saw Peter back-heel one from nearly the edge of the box! I thought: "Christ, what a player!" To think you're ever going to play with them later on, well! Because I used to get the lads later on and say to them: "To think I queued for your blessed autographs outside the ground."

Reg Harrison: We all had tracksuits after the war and Raich had taken his home to have a number put on it, to identify it. It came back and across the front was 'Snowy' and on the back it was 'Maestro Moan A Lot'. He was the boss on the field and he ruled it, but off the field, although he'd got this air about him, he could stand a joke even if it was against him.

'Ned' Mee: Raich Carter were good – and Doherty. I mean, Peter Doherty could turn round on sixpence. He were a good player. I'm not saying he were the best of two. I think Carter just had the edge over him, I do. Different styles, them two. They came as guest players to start with, during the war.

Tommy Powell: Peter used to just roll penalties in the corner. Goalkeepers never had any chance at all. He used to just stick them away. He always went to the 'keeper's right. They were tremendous to watch, the two of them playing together. Of course, they'd got a good foil in big Stampie.

Reg Harrison: You take Georgie Best and Bobby Charlton. Totally different. They were the only two you could compare. One was a passer, the other was a dribbler. Peter was a dribbler, Raich was a passer and it was just that they slotted in and worked together. I think Peter was better than Best because he hit a lot of legs, Peter didn't.

Roy Christian: Raich Carter was a great player. Among the very best I've seen. He was everything really. In those days players were usually either what we called schemers or they were goalscorers, but Raich was both. He could play any sort – he was very adaptable – he could play any sort of game. He refereed as well! I saw him when he was player-manager of Hull in a match at Doncaster. Somebody handled the ball, Carter was actually being tackled when it happened. Carter picked the ball up, put it down, took the free-kick and the referee never blew at all. The referee looked a bit puzzled but: "It's Mr Carter." The referee was probably younger than Carter anyway.

Johnny Morris: The best inside-forward I ever saw was Peter Doherty. The difference between him and Raich Carter was that Raich was a ten-minute player. He played in bursts. He looked good for ten minutes and then you'd not see him for 20. During that ten minutes he was a good player, but Peter was going all the time. He was as tough as steel as well. I played against him at Huddersfield. At times, he was beating four or five men. We beat 'em 6-5. When you think about it, it's bad defence on both sides, but the crowd thought it the best game they'd ever seen.

Reg Harrison: Nobody was fitter than Peter. He used to go out on the field in training and just run with the ball. You never saw him doing what we did. Never, ever saw him do the sprinting that we did. It was his balance, his swerve.

Roy Christian: He was a commanding presence on the field, Raich Carter. He looked a bit like a general in a footballing sense. A great shot he'd got. A bit like Bobby Charlton. I mean, he'd take aim from well outside the penalty area and the ball would go in, just as Bobby Charlton used to do, later on.

Lionel Pickering: Peter Doherty? He was something special. He was a schoolboy's hero. He was captain of Ireland. He was like a nice George Best. I've seen him dribble round six or seven people and then pass it back to his goalkeeper because he started on the centre-circle on a mazy run forward and after the ball was lost, he'd finish up getting back into his own penalty area in time and passing it back to the goalkeeper. In that time he's dribbled round six or seven players. I saw him when he scored his five goals against Villa. They stupidly tried to play the offside trap and he just dribbled through and he finished up with the last goal dribbling round the goalkeeper or putting it through his legs.

Roy Christian: Doherty was quite a different player. He could have dribbled the football-round this room and you wouldn't have worried about anything being smashed. He had amazing control of the ball. He and Alex James of Arsenal were probably the best controllers of the ball I ever saw, just as Hoddle was the best passer of the ball I've ever seen. Wonderful passer, wasn't he?

Lionel Pickering: Peter Doherty was a pure showman – and he was brave as well. In the semi-final replay at Maine Road there was a 50-50 ball between him and their full-back, Duckhouse, right on the edge of the penalty area. They both got laid out and the ball finished in the back of the net. Duckhouse broke his leg in the collision. Doherty had got there just that fraction before Duckhouse and the ball was in the back of the net and we finished up winning and getting to Wembley. So he wasn't just a showman.

George Beard: Words defy you, don't they, absolutely? Carter and Doherty, that first season after the war. I was demobbed in May 1945 and we had two little nippers, a boy of three and a little girl 12 months old, and we went into Derby with the wife and they went off shopping and I nipped off to the Baseball Ground. Doherty was a spring-heeled Jack. Lively, feet twitching. He used to do little tricks with the ball before the game. Lightning, when he set off. Took some catching. Raich was ponderous, a bit ponderous, if you might call it that. Oh, yes, they were great and the rest of that season was a joy to me. Wonderful.

Chick Musson

Tommy Powell: In those days it was different. Take Chick Musson. He'd never be on the park now and Chick wasn't a dirty player. He was straightforward, but they wouldn't have had it these days. Died at 35. Like Lee Leuty.

Bert Mozley: If he were playing nowadays, he'd have a red card every game. He wouldn't be playing. He'd be suspended the rest of his life. Yet Chick was an honest, fair tackler.

Johnny Morris: Oh, he was like a lion. He was stocky, five-eight, five-nine. Like a lion.

Ernie Hallam: Came from Holbrook St Michael's, Chick did. Aye, he was hard, Chick. Got his nose down and did the job. Not a lot of finesse. When he jumped up, he was shorter than when he stood straight; he used to tuck his head like, but he was a hard man and would give his lot – 100 per cent endeavour type of player, which complemented some of the class that won the Cup.

Roy Christian: I first met Chick Musson when he was about 15 and I was keeping goal for Derby St John's. I didn't usually keep goal, but the regular goalkeeper was away. It was 1-1 and the ref gave them a penalty. Chick Musson was probably the youngest player on the field, but he was a big strong lad. He looked just about like he did later on and he shot almost straight at me. I got my hands to it, but it nearly broke my wrists. The ball still went in. He had a kick like a mule and he was a strong lad. When he tackled, he tackled, but he wasn't dirty. He wasn't one of those malicious people. He was a good reliable wing-half. I think he'd have been all right in the modern game, he'd have done quite well. I suppose midfield players have to be more mobile now, they cover a wider area than the old wing-half.

Ray Young: A great fellow. A hard man, really hard, but great. Not big, but solid. Just solid, one of these that you could hit him, but it was just like hitting a brick wall.

Years later...

Lionel Pickering: The introduction of the Cup Final players to the Queen was off the cuff. We'd been told what we had to do and as we were walking back to the players' entrance – through which the Queen was going back out to the car – I said to her: "I suppose you do remember the first Cup Final you saw? You'd been in the army and you'd be 19 and it was 1946. I should imagine that was the first Cup Final you saw?" She said: "Yes, it was." So I said: "That was Derby County and there are two of the players who met your father and were given the medals, they're here today and they're sitting to the left of where you're going." I said: "If you're not in a desperate hurry to go, they'd be delighted to meet you." She said:

"Oh, that's all right." That's about all I can really remember of about 20 minutes or half an hour with the Queen. I haven't got a clue what we spoke about, but she was very good. We left the red carpet that was laid down and burrowed through the photographers, who were all around. They panned out and let us through and the Queen and the Duke spoke to the players – Jim Bullions and Reg Harrison who both played in the Final, and Angus Morrison who'd played in some of the earlier games in the run – and I think it was Jim Bullions who pulled out a photograph of the King presenting him with the medal. I didn't actually see it, but I saw him showing the Queen the photograph.

The Roaring Forties

IN the years after World War Two, interest and enthusiasm for attending football matches had never been higher, nor would it ever be again. In 1948-49 attendances stood at a massive 41.2 million, but had declined to 17.8 million in 1984-85. Post-war austerity, epitomised by ration books and queues, was lightened by the thought of the match at the weekend. Local communities identified strongly with their 'own' team, local rivalries were intense, 'derby' matches fierce. Football clubs and their supporters tended to be insular and parochial in outlook, reflecting the protective mood of a nation following the ravages of war.

Football on an *ad hoc* basis had taken place throughout the war period, but now people were ready for the real thing and Derby County's victory in the 1946 Cup Final had whetted appetites. Under a rigid maximum wage structure, the top clubs employed huge professional staffs, often more than 50, sometimes more than 60 players. Competition for places? You bet.

Ray Young: Huge staffs. There would have been probably enough professionals for four sides. To me, when I first signed, it was like going and doing an apprenticeship through work. You went through the teams. You started in the fourth team, then eventually the third team and then the Reserves and the first team. And really, you weren't usually considered for the first team until you were 20 years of age.

1948 FA Cup semi-final: Derby County 1 Manchester United 3

Reg Harrison: I think we were well beaten. They were a good side. And 3-1 is a good beating. I'd say they were well worth it.

Johnny Morris: Of course, I was with United then. Stan Pearson got all three goals, a hat-trick. We were the better side. It was played at Sheffield Wednesday's ground, at Hillsborough. Somebody said to me after the game: "How much money were you on?" Of course, we got nothing extra at United, but what I'm sure he meant was Derby were on some extra. They were well known for 'perks' at that time.

Other matches

Tommy Powell: We got through to the sixth round two years on the trot after I came out of the Forces. It was 1948-49 and 1949-50 and we got beat 2-1 each time. First, against

Portsmouth, it was 1-1 with about three minutes to go and Ike Clarke got away from Leon Leuty – the only time he got away – and he scored the winner. The following year we lost to Everton at Derby. I'd scored and we were winning 1-0 with about ten minutes to go when Eddie Wainwright scored direct from a corner and then Harry Catterick got the winner. It was the only time in football I ever felt like crying. Wembley was unique in those days. You didn't get non-League clubs going. It would have been a thrill.

Johnny Morris: I think Ben Robshaw, the chairman, got suspended over so-called illegal payments. A pity that because there was so much going on at the time. I thought Ben Robshaw was a great lad, it was such a pity. I'm sure that's what killed him really because he'd given his life to Derby. He was a good friend, actually, until he died. Derby were bigger than Manchester United in those days.

Johnny Morris and Billy Steel

Bill Brownson: I won't say they never played well together, but what they didn't do was get on well. They shouldn't really have been in the same team. They were great footballers, great footballers. It was probably just one of those things that didn't happen. Billy Steel was one of the finest inside-forwards we've seen at Derby, including Doherty and Carter.

Tommy Powell: I went over to Germany in the Forces and played against Billy Steel the week before he signed for Derby. He came over with Scotland. They played a BAOR [British Army of the Rhine] team over there. One of our players was Eddie Baily of Spurs. I think Derby signed Steel for about £15,000 the week after.

Reg Harrison: Johnny Morris was a good passer of the ball. He was a good player, but he hung on, sometimes, too long. You'd make two or three moves, go one way and you wouldn't get the ball, go the other way and you wouldn't get the ball. You'd think: "Oh, where can I go?" Then it comes and you perhaps don't want it then. He was a good player, though, there's no doubt about that.

Don Hazledine: They paid £25,000 for Johnny Morris, a British record. He wasn't too pleased with me because eventually he wasn't in favour and they put me in. So he wasn't too happy with me, but it wasn't my fault. He left for Leicester shortly afterwards.

Roy Christian: John Morris was a good footballer. I did know Morris a bit. He said that his job – with all the clubs he'd been – was when they took a corner, because he was small, his job was to stand by the goalkeeper and punch him in the ribs. I said: "Didn't referees pick you up?" He said: "Only about twice." Johnny Morris was streetwise, very much so. Politically, very left wing. Footballers aren't usually politically inclined, but Johnny Morris was very strong left wing. He was an amusing chap, really. Nice fellow.

Don Hazledine: He was a useful player, oh yes. Typical inside-forward. He'd got a lot of skills, same as Shackleton, but I don't think he would give you 100 per cent in present-day football because he wouldn't get back enough. Good passer.

Tim Ward: Billy Steel started the downhill run at Derby County and I don't mean that because of his playing ability, but because of other things that happened. When players such as Raich and Leon Leuty found out what was happening and the way Billy was being treated, naturally, everybody was upset. I was probably one of the few people who wasn't worried. I'd come back from the war and a lot of my friends hadn't. It didn't affect me that way, but I can see Raich's point of view. A great player, Raich, probably one of the greatest ever and Billy appearing on the scene, suddenly writing articles for newspapers and getting paid for it, driving about in a new car and those sort of things, well, Raich didn't think much to it. In those days, of course, players didn't go in cars. They were very lucky if they got a lift off someone in a car, but Billy got everything and, unfortunately, Billy only played when Billy felt like it.

Roy Christian: I think Billy Steel was very temperamental. He was good on his day, but he wasn't always on his day. It struck me that he was a bit lazy. I think he boozed quite a lot, but he really got his reputation on the strength of one brilliant international match, against England I think. He never quite lived up to it at Derby. There was an odd game or two when he played like it. Charlie Napier was a bit the same.

Johnny Morris: Well, he was a typical Scottish player. Yes, a dribbler. He used to run himself into the ground. He was the type of player you can't play with. They had one at Liverpool, McManaman. Nice lad, Billy, but football? I remember playing against Sunderland. Shackleton was a good player and he was playing for them. We were losing 2-0 at half-time and Billy came in moaning and I said: "It's your fault. It's no good you running back like that." All he was doing was hindering the defence. "Let your defenders defend," I told him. They used to clap him for chasing back. Anyway, he sulked a bit, but I'll tell you what, we beat them 3-2. Billy played more up front, rather than chasing back so much.

Reg Harrison: Good on the ball, but as Frank Broome once said: "I get that ball and the only ball I can give is back to Billy Steel." He ran it at him, gave him the ball and then Frank would look at him and think: "Well, it's got to go back there." I never thought he was very good for the club, his attitude. Sometimes he wouldn't play.

Bert Mozley

Johnny Morris: He was a good player – until he played with England! He started to play the way Walter Winterbottom started England playing. He used to stand behind the centre-half. I lived here near Manchester for six months before I went down. I still trained at United and travelled down and stayed at Bert's on the Friday night. He was a big pal of mine was Bert. I mean, he was a good player because I played with him for the Football League against the Scottish League and Irish League, but as soon as he played for England, he started playing as a cover centre-half. His winger was free, you see.

Graham Sellors: I can still see certain incidents, although I can't remember the games. I can remember players and things happening. I can remember Bert Mozley scoring, I think this was 1949. I don't know that, I looked it up. I can remember him scoring against Birmingham City, Gilbert Merrick was in goal. It seemed to me, although it probably wasn't – 1949, I'd be eight – it seemed to me as though he'd shot from about the halfway line and right out on the wing where a full-back might be, and Merrick was an England goalkeeper, of course. Straight in the top corner. I remember that.

Bert Mozley: I went to St Paul's until I was 14. Then I left school and I started at Rolls-Royce. There was a St Paul's Church School soccer team, with 17 and 18-year-olds, and I got picked to play with them and I was thrilled to bits. It was on Darley Fields – we lived just across from Darley Fields. I was ready in my white shorts and red and white squares top and I went on the field an hour before they even started to shoot in and I was shooting in and a ball came across and it was a bit far for me. I reached to kick it and – what I know now – pulled a big groin muscle. I couldn't play, that first game. I went home crying – and I never kicked a ball again until I was 18 years old.

Reg Harrison: St Paul's first. When you left school it was hard to get a game because there was just the Sunday School League; the intermediate division and the Under-19s. One was Under-17s and one was Under-19s. I didn't get a game straightaway and then a chap who lived round our way, he got injured and he came to see if I'd play for St Paul's. I was 14 and he wanted me to play for St Paul's, in the Sunday School League. I went and played the game that day and he never got back. The funny thing about it was that on the same day that I was to play for St Paul's, Bert Mozley was going to play – and he pulled a muscle, kicking in! We'd known each other ever since we were kids. We used to go down Chester Green. Play our street versus your street. Well, he pulled a muscle and I don't think he played again until he played with Shelton United, I think it was.

Tim Ward

Ray Young: Tim was there then, Tim Ward. He was just the opposite to Chick. He was a gentleman footballer really.

Johnny Morris: Nicey, nicey player, Tim. Nice enough player. He wasn't a good reader of the game though. He used to take throw-ins and throw it down the bloody wing all the time, every time, every time. We used to run in, free towards him for the ball, never got it. Ask Reggie, struggling to try to head it and there's a bloody six-foot full-back behind him.

Alf Jeffries: Nice player. He was sort of a reserved kind of player. He was a gentleman. He knew when to tackle and when not to tackle, that was the beauty of it with a bloke like that. Nice man, good to play with, he was.

Others

Tommy Powell: Crookie was a scout then and he said: "If you see anything in the army Tom, let me know." Anyway, I played against Dougie Taft. I said: "The lad's got a lot of ability." Dougie looked quite useful, so he came over and didn't do bad, but I said: "We've got a goalkeeper playing for the BAOR who's the best I've seen since Frank Swift." They didn't do anything about it and next I knew he'd played for Scotland against England at Wembley – Jimmy Cowan.

Stanley Matthews

Bert Mozley: Stan Matthews. He would come up to you and he only had one trick anyway and everybody knew it, but they couldn't stop him. He was so quick off the mark. A defender, if he thought: "The thing's mine. He's come too close, I've got him," well, he'd lift his foot to get it – and Stan's gone. That's one guy out of the game, you see, it makes an open space. I never actually played directly against him because he played right wing and I played right-back, but you watched him, shuffling up, pin-toed and they thought they'd got him: "He's a little bit too close this time." Then he'd gone, he'd gone. Like a flash.

Tommy Lawton

Bert Mozley: I played against Tommy at Highbury. England Under-21s against an Old England team and I think we won 3-1. Tommy played then. He was getting towards the end like, but you could tell his class. In the air he was just like climbing a ladder. Stan Matthews was playing right wing and Roger Byrne, from Manchester United, played left-back. He died in the Munich disaster. Stan showed him how a right winger should play. It was the day before the Cup Final.

Crowds

Ernie Hallam: Massive crowds. Oh, aye. Everybody was dying to get back to the game, weren't they?

Graham Sellors: Lots of things stood out. There was the whole thing of getting dressed up and getting there because they used to wear black and white hats, black and white scarves. My mother used to make black and white golliwogs to pin on our lapels. I wasn't big enough to see over the wall at the back of the Osmaston End, so we presumably used to have to get there early because we used to have to take a stool and I used to stand on the stool. We always stood at the Osmaston End, behind the goal. Directly behind the goal.

Johnny Morris: I think while I was there the record crowd was 32,000. About that. They were standing on each other's heads with 32,000. It was regular, quite regular that we had big crowds away too.

Bert Mozley: Oh, the crowds were big, weren't they? We got bigger crowds than they do now, even with the big grounds. We were getting 25,000 or 26,000 then at home and away matches, 80,000 at Chelsea. We had so many people at Queen's Park Rangers one time that they put kitchen chairs round the ground for people to sit on. I bet they wasn't more than two or three feet, from the touchline.

"I cracked Scoular"

Johnny Morris: Aye, I cracked Scoular. Referee was a lad that had only one arm, Alf Bond. Scoular had clogged Tommy or Reg. He clogged one of them. We'd ten men and he went after the other lad, which was Reg or Tommy, I forget which way it was. Well, I've got it and I'm going away with the ball and he comes behind me and tries to clog me. So I turned round and clonked him. I wasn't sent off, I walked off. Even Alf Bond, the referee, didn't know what had happened. The League had an enquiry. They gave me a week's suspension. They didn't fine me. We went down to Portsmouth later that season. Stuart McMillan said: "They're playing Scoular centre-half. Do you want to play centre-forward?" I said: "Aye, I'll play centre-forward." Anyway, when we got down there and got to the ground, Scoular was outside, waiting. He said: "I'll give you some tickets. Complimentaries." We couldn't get any, it wasn't that easy. In the game he kept saying: "It's your ball. You have it." That's during the game. He wasn't the hard man we thought he was.

Travelling away

Reg Harrison: Coach. By bus really. It was a bus taken out of service, 644 the number was. We travelled to London by train. Most of it was by coach, though. No tables or anything like that. Harry Ellis was the driver. He was the regular one. The non-drinkers – Tommy didn't drink, I didn't, Jack Parr didn't – we used to stop on the bus with Harry when the others went for a drink. We used to get off to have a meal, but If we were stopping just for a drink, we'd sit with Harry and he'd come out with all these rhymes. "There was an old woman..." You couldn't repeat them and I couldn't remember them, but he'd come out with them for hour after hour, week after week, but he kept us entertained. He was a good driver.

Bert Mozley: Train to London or Southampton. Otherwise we went by bus. Derby Trent bus. We had a big white bus and the same driver. He was always telling jokes. Harry...Harry, I forget his second name, but he was the same driver all the while. We used to catch the one o'clock train to London on Friday afternoon, go to one of the best shows on Friday night, play Saturday and come back that night.

Injuries and Equipment

"A PLAYER who's not fit is no use to anyone," said Raich Carter. Being injured is an occupational hazard for footballers, which some accept more than others. "You can play if you're not fit, but you can't play well," said Denis Law. Modern medicine has transformed the treatment of players and, with it, attitudes towards playing with injuries. The long-term consequences of playing with an injury are less for modern players than for those of years ago. High wages and long contracts have made it less of a necessity to play with injury, but it still hurts, sometimes.

"…a thing about crutches"

Brian Clough: I'd got a thing about crutches. People who came in on crutches, that's who had to get out. They used to come in. Bad news for me, crutches. I'd say: "You're no good to me. Get out." I was rude and ignorant and arrogant, as I am now, but I couldn't stand crutches. Players played because they wanted to, though.

Gordon Guthrie: Brian used to like them out there. I think, the type of man he was – and the great manager he was – I think he instilled this in them, that they wanted to play. They knew that if they'd got a little niggle, it could be strapped up and they could get through the game and, if they could do themselves justice, they'd play. Really, if you were injured, it was like having the scarlet fever with Brian. At the time, we hadn't got a very big squad when we won that first championship. I think it was something he instilled in them because he was that type of man, wasn't he? He loved to win and I think when Brian saw them playing, it gave him a bit of a lift because he always remembers having his career cut short with a very, very bad injury.

Willie Carlin: Jack Burkitt, our old trainer, told me the story when they were down at Lilleshall and Tommy Docherty was there and the Sheffield United staff were having a go at Docherty, saying he was a conman and everything. So Docherty says to the Sheffield people: "I'm a conman? How about you?" He said: "You've just sold one of the original seven dwarfs to Derby County for £67,000. And he's a cripple." It never sunk in with me. That's what it was, arthritis in the hip. They knew, Cloughie and Taylor. They sold me on when I was 30 years old, getting on for 31, and £40,000 for a cripple wasn't bad money.

Arthur Hobson

Reg Harrison: First full season training, after the war, I pulled a muscle, a kicking muscle. They mucked about with me really and in the end I went to Arthur Hobson. First, though, Derby took me to Stoke, with Jack 'Nick'. He'd pulled a muscle at the back and this fellow, well it was a joke to me. He got this muscle and was shaking his shoulders and he said: "You've got two muscles crossed." I thought: "Blimey, how do you get muscles crossed?" He was a joke. He gave me this stuff and Dave Willis put it on under a heat lamp and it blistered me, all over my thigh. My Dad was working with Arthur at Combustion and Arthur said: "Send him to me." Anyway, they mucked me about all August and I thought: "I'm having no more of this." So I went to see Arthur. He had me fit in a fortnight...I was playing in a fortnight.

John Bowers: The main thing I remember about Arthur was that he was very quick witted and he had no time for 'nancy boys'. He was a hard man. If you weren't injured before you got on the table, you were certainly injured afterwards. Even tough guys like Frank Upton used to wince a bit!

Ron Webster: Arthur Hobson was trainer of the 'A' team. Old Arthur. He used to like me though, I was all right. I was all right with Arthur. He was a bit hard. I used to get injured a bit at that time. That was my worst period really, 18 to 20, I was out two years then. I broke my collar-bone, first match of the season. Well I cracked it and then played again in the Reserves and I broke it then. First match back in pre-season we played Stoke and I broke my ankle, first match back. Soon as I got right, about Christmas time, I twisted my knee. Knee ligaments and I was out about two seasons and they used to say I was injury prone, like, but then, after that, I had a good run actually.

Serious stuff

Alf Jeffries: It was the last match of the season. The ball, it dropped between him and me and I thought: "Here we go, I'm going to have a real good lunge at this and I'm going to miss the ball and kick him." Well, he was just as wise as me. He's got half forward and as I've gone through, I've belted my leg, you see, and I've felt something go in my knee. I thought: "Serves you right for trying to kick somebody, trying to get your own back." I ran about and that was all right, but when I came to touch the ball it was terrible. I thought: 'Well, if I say anything to Jobey about this, I'll be here all summer." Because I was single and everything and I was going back home to Durham through the summer, I thought: "I better keep my mouth shut." So I did.

Gordon Guthrie: Knee injury. At West Brom. Bit of play in front of us and I've got the ball and I've turned back to roll it to Terry Adlington. And that one foot's stuck and I've gone right round and over. I've gone down and Jack Bowers has come on to me. Of course, I'm trying to get up and I'll always remember him because he smacked me. Crack! He said: "Lie still." You know what Jack was like. So I'm lying there and he's manoeuvring it about and all of a sudden – I'll always remember it – there's a terrific crack. It sounded terrific to me. It went crack, just like that. I said: "Bloody hell, Jack." "That's all right," he says. "Stand up." So I stood up, like, and I was a bit shaky. There was about four minutes to go. We were drawing and we had no subs, of course. So I said: "I'll go and stand on the wing." So I've gone to stand on the wing. Next thing, Adlington's thrown the ball out to me again, hasn't he? I've tried to control it and, of course, I've gone down again and then I was off. That resulted in a cruciate ligament and a lateral cartilage and they couldn't repair them then. I tried again at Bolton, about 15 months later. It was sludgy and down I went again. That was it.

Alf Jeffries: After that summer, I was training and doing everything, but then we went up to the training ground one day and, of course, they'd all done the pre-season training and got fit you see and I thought: "I've got to be crafty here." We kicked the balls about a bit and, of course, when it came to me, I kicked it with my left foot, you see. I was keeping my eye on Jobey. He was with one of the trainers on the other side and it came to me again and I hit it with my right foot, just as Jobey was looking across. He shouted: "Jeffries. What's wrong with you?" I said: "I've twisted my knee, Mr Jobey." "Oh, right. Off you go, back to the ground." I went back to the ground and it wasn't getting any better and this was going on for weeks. Anyway, they decided to send me up to Belper with Ken Scattergood, to see the bone setter, old what's-his-name. What the hell's his name? He'd got a great reputation in this country because he'd treated Prince Obelensky, the Russian prince who'd been at Cambridge and played for England at rugby.

Ron Webster: Just hot and cold really. Hot and cold water, to get the swelling down and then Jack Bowers' thumb rubbing. It was just, like, thumb treatment, rubbing on it. Hot and cold for a week, in that old bathroom. It used to be freezing. Luckily, I was all right.

Alf Jeffries: Unfortunately for Ken Scattergood every time he dived, he put his shoulder out which was bad for a goalkeeper, of course. We went up to Belper and sat down on this couch and this chap said to me: "What's wrong with you then?" I said: "I've hurt my right knee, behind here." "Well," he said. "Did you know your back cartilage is out?" He said: "Shall I pull it back?" I thought: "Blimey, here we go." Anyway, I said: "Yes, please." So he put his fingers in and worked around a bit and then he said: "That's it. It's back now." I said: "Is that it?" And he said: "Yeah, it's back. Tell Mr Jobey you've got to ride a bicycle round the track to strengthen it." Well, when I got back, Jobey said: "How did you go on, Jeffries?" I said: "Mr Blount says – yes, that was his name, Mr Blount – Mr Blount says I've put my back cartilage out, Mr Jobey, and he's put it back. He also says I've got to tell you that I've got to ride a bicycle round the ground to strengthen it." Well. Out came the language then. I can tell you, I never rode any bikes round. I was round the track all right – running.

Mick Hopkinson: I always remember playing at Coventry, in the George Curtis- Jimmy Hill days. I got kicked in the face, enough to knock me out. It was the first time on a football field I'd been knocked out. I then looked up and Ralph's over the top of me with the old sponge, rubbing my face down and I'd burst a blood vessel behind my eye. Already, while I was coming to, I couldn't see out of my eye. I thought my eye was closing up, but it was wide open, it was just the internal bleeding. Well, he's sponging my face away, Ralph, and he's saying to Jack Parry: "Come on Jack, now, get it out to the wing." And he's sponging my face down and he's no idea what injury I'd got and he's sending messages out to other players: "Pick up so and so. Do this, do that." Now, whenever I see players go down on a football field, the attention they get is absolutely superb. Four people out there looking after them, everybody's concerned, but in my day the trainer used to run on to pass on messages from the manager. I finished up in hospital for two weeks. If you get a blow on the head now, you can't even play for two weeks.

Peter Newbery: The worst injury I ever had was when I was playing against Bury Reserves and the former Derby player Norman Nielson was playing left-back. I played on the wing that day and I cut across him and he whacked me with his knee into the front of the thigh and I was out of the game for five or six months. That was the worst injury.

Frank Upton: Not many injuries, not really. I had an operation on my knee, just for exploration and that, but nothing really, other than cartilages and general. I think there was once, when I had a bad one. We were playing Portsmouth down at Fratton Park, I was going for this ball down the line like, inexperience and everything else: "I'm going to win this ball." Jimmy Dickinson put his foot over the top of it and done my ankle. I was out for about four weeks, five weeks, I think. I always remember Tommy Powell coming up to him and having a right go at Dickinson.

Gordon Guthrie: I'd always been interested in that side while Jack and Ralph were here, whenever I'd finished training or anything. And I used to come down on Sunday mornings and I used to walk into the treatment room and watch them and listen to them. Of course, if you remember, we used to have Sammy Crooks here then and Sammy used to tell a million stories on a Sunday. Ralph was first-team and Jack was second-team trainer and they were really very knowledgeable about the game and injuries, especially Jack. Even though they'd had no formal training, they were very knowledgeable. I just used to sit there and watch them.They took me under their wing really as regards that.

Peter Newbery: Well, Ralph Hann and Jack Bowers, I'm quite sure, were very clued up with the ways and means of injuries at the time. I know they used to go on courses. Yes, I think they were very good in the way we had injuries treated.

Alf Jeffries: Hot water, cold water. Same with the ankles. You know in those days we were all putting our ankles out. I did it three times. Your ankle came up and you were off for weeks. And you used to sit there on the edge of the slipper baths, hot and cold. Hot to get the circulation, cold to deaden it. I used to reckon the cold was a bloody sight worse than the hot. Talk about Chinese torture.

Kevin Hector: Prehistoric. Hot and cold. Remember, we only used about 14 players when we won the League. Yes, I played when I wasn't fit. Cloughie used to say: "If you don't play well, I'll take the blame." It took the pressure off a bit, but he was really talking you into playing. I get a bit of trouble with my ankles sometimes, but fortunately I've kept free of long-term injuries.

Gordon Guthrie: Dave Mackay came in here in the treatment room once, with a medial ligament strain. Although I say it myself, some people would have been out three weeks. He came in and sat on the bed and I says: "You're not going to play for two weeks." And he said: "I'll play Saturday." He played Saturday, with the old strapping round it, which really didn't do it any good, but psychologically for him, it did. He never missed a game. That was the spirit and the type of man he was. Pain didn't apply to him.

Mick Hopkinson: There used to be two big baths in the changing room and Frank Upton and myself used to fill them up with cold water. Into the hot bath – big bath – straight out, into the cold bath, and Frank and myself used to see who could stop in it the longest. Players would tiptoe through hoping you'd not notice them. By the time you jumped out of the cold bath, you were glowing. People were sneaking through and you'd get a bucket. Into a bath with a bucket, all over the player. There'd be more fights go off in there than, well, anywhere.

Gordon Guthrie: I went back to the railway. Then one morning I got a phone call from Sammy. They had four junior teams here then, one in the Derby and District League. There was also a local team called Roe Farm and it was always us and them for top of the League. Anyway, out of the blue, Sammy's rung and said: "We're looking for somebody to look after the juniors. Are you interested, do you fancy it?" And so I said : "Yeah, I'll come along." So I came along and that was it. That was the beginning really. Tim was here then, but he was only here a few more months before Brian came.

Frank Upton: Well there is no comparison with what happens today, but it doesn't matter what kind of injury you have, it's got a certain time to get right but I do think the machines and such they have today does bring it forward more.

Gordon Guthrie: It wasn't long after that, that Jack had a bit of a heart attack. Then he had a more serious one and finished up, unfortunately, in a wheelchair. In between times I'd been to Lilleshall and done all these courses and everything. FA Treatment of Injury courses and things and I'd more less put them aside. Anyway, Brian came down and he said: "Unfortunately, Jack's not going to come back any more, so the job's yours. You're the only one qualified." So from then on the coaching went less and the injuries went more. Jimmy Gordon came then.

Steve Powell: Again, a lot less scientific than today. I mean, most injuries were, like, rub a bit of Vaseline on and get back out there. Or, in the later days, to be honest, put a needle in it and get out there. I think that's pretty general that even nowadays a lot of players go out that aren't 100 per cent fit, but it's just the nature of the game. If you wanted to be 100 per cent fit every time you turned out you wouldn't complete more than ten or 12 games a season. I mean, we always used to say that once pre-season had gone and you started playing, you were never really 100 per cent fit until the following pre-season. I think probably in any sport, people play with injuries.

Gordon Guthrie: A lot of the machines are more complicated nowadays and are supposed to do a better job, but the principles are still the same. I think there's a lot to be said for the old principles where it was contrast bathing – hot and cold. Hot water in the bath, cold hose pipe or in the bucket. It's just the same as when they say: "Put the ice on immediately."

Peter Gadsby: I did enjoy my football. I was always regarded as being rather cocky and I think that affected me. I broke my leg in three places. I was 14 then. I remember the first time, it was someone called Johnson. He was a good centre-half and I was a bit cocky. I went passed him once and he said: "You won't go again." And I didn't. That meant 18 months in plaster and when I go down to Derby County now and see the physiotherapy and what happens – how they recover so fast – I recall 18 months, 18 months in plaster.

Gordon Guthrie: I think they sometimes get them back quicker from injuries now, although, as you well know, everyone is different in their healing. Some heal quick, some are very slow healers. Psychologically, you get a certain type of player who wants to get back and then the other who says: "Will it be right. Is it all right?" Iffing and butting. So it's all in the make-up of the player really. Everybody's different.

Gordon Guthrie: I'd have to say Martin Taylor, at Southend, was the worst injury I had to deal with. A broken leg. It looked as though the forward was going to get hurt. Next thing, they've clashed and Martin's gone down, the ball's gone away from him and he's kind of got half up to get out for a corner, then he's laid down. When we got on to him, you could see straight away. It was a compound fracture. It had broken the skin, but it hadn't come through. It was just starting but it was a bad one. It was broken in more than one place. He did well to get over that, but he worked tremendously hard.

Boots, boots, boots...

Alf Jeffries: You had boots one size less than your ordinary shoe. I took seven and had a six boot. I mean, you wore them without any socks on, straight into a bucket of water. Oh, aye, I've had plenty of them, blisters. Those boots fitted you like a glove eventually, but you could hardly tie the laces up when you started on the original job. And you used to use two or three pairs of boots a season.

Johnny Morris: A pair of boots used to last us five or six years. The older they got, the better they were. Arthur was the cobbler, I remember him.

Ray Young: When I first joined Derby the two trainers were Jack Poole and Jack Bowers and at kitting out they asked me what size shoe I took. I said: "Nine." They said: "Right. Seven and a half football boots." I couldn't believe it. I was actually given a pair of seven and a half football boots up to the ankle with hard heels and hard toes. I said: "I can't get them on." They said: "Put plenty of powder on your feet and put the boots on and go and stand in the bath." So I was there standing in water. I always lost my toe nails, every year, until Dennis Woodhead came along. He always took a size and a half bigger! "I've never had any problems with my feet," he said. He used to wear two pairs of socks.

Peter Newbery: I can remember the way we used to break the boots in. We'd probably buy a pair a size smaller than you really needed and then wear them in with bare feet and use them in the shooting box. Black toe nails, sore heels. That's the way it was done then.

Frank Upton: Oh yeah. I always used to have leather studs and I used to like them knocked in with the nails. Then we couldn't get any of them and we went on to screw-ins, didn't we? The boots you got in those days, you knew as soon as you put them on all your nails were going to come off because we got black toe nails. Smaller sizes, that's right, which I think is a bit of a myth, but the boots were quite good. Nowadays they stick them straight on and go and play in them. Take them out the box and play in them, which is entirely different.

Ian Buxton: Boots? I remember you used to go down to Field Sports to get them. You didn't go down for a pair of Adidas or whatever, you weren't sponsored by anybody. I went down for a pair that fitted and if they were £2 10s, you had those. You had to break them in, in those days. They were hard leather. You had to break all sorts of shoes in then. No. I didn't suffer particularly on hard grounds. I think everybody in those days got blisters because the soles weren't soft like they are today, so if you played in the spring on a bone hard pitch, I think everybody suffered from blisters.

Don Hazledine: I remember they were called McGregor. I used to take a size seven, but I used to start off with a five and a half, put Vaseline on them and train in them. They used to mould round your feet.

Alf Jeffries: I never had them, but there were spikes there, if you wanted them. Some players used them. You've got to have a bit of knowledge of how to run with spikes because you can easily turn you ankle over and you can do other damage.

Frank Upton: Yes, I remember the rubber-soled boots coming in. I wasn't a great lover of them because I liked to have a bit of firmness under my feet, being a big lad. I think the rubber soles used to give a bit and I didn't think for the big lads, well for me anyway, I wasn't really comfortable with them. I'd sooner have my ordinary stud boots, but with rubber studs put in. I used to change them that way.

Ian Buxton: Shin-pads were the old five-cane jobs. They stuck out and made it look as if your legs were made of muscles, but they weren't. The socks were heavy and the shorts! Everybody wore short shorts eventually, but if your shorts weren't short, to stay in fashion, you had to roll them up at the waistband, do you remember? You got people like Albert Quixall who had them rolled up round up round his waist so they were like briefs. If ever you see old film on television now, that's the first thing that strikes you of football 30 years or so ago, the shortness of the shorts. It looks ridiculous doesn't it? Just the same as it looked ridiculous when the long shorts came in 15 years ago.

Mac the cobbler

Ray Young: Superb, yes, Mac. They used to have studs where you could build them up, so you could have them longer. Did you ever have them where they had taken half of them off and put screws in – and taken the heads off? We actually played in one match where on an icy ground we were like ballerinas. If we'd had an inspection, we'd all have got done. Mac, the cobbler. Oh. He used to come down Tuesday nights and Thursday nights and, I think, on Fridays and, of course, on Saturday.

Peter Newbery: Mac? Yes, I remember him well. Again, he came on Tuesday and Thursday nights when we trained and he used to do all the boots. Fred Cooke was the groundsman, of course. When you had to decide what studs to wear you obviously checked the pitch out and either peeled off a layer of leather or stuck another one on, but yes, the nails used to come through.

Gordon Guthrie: I don't think I knew his last name, but he'd been here years and years. He was a legend because the players entrusted him with their boots. He was unique really because he could do stitching – anything and everything. He used to have a portable stitching machine. Really, no job was impossible for him when it came to repairing boots.

Icy grounds

Gordon Guthrie: Just a little bit of nail, sticking out because there was no being checked by the referee in those days.

Technology for goalkeepers

Eric Steele: Changes? Just a bit! Gloves for a start. Technology has aided goalkeepers. I mean, even since from when I was playing here, when I see them get kitted out to train in with pads on the hips, pads on the arms. I mean, we used to put tuba grip, Gordon Guthrie with cotton wool and tuba grip. We used to have elbow pads from cycle shops. The equipment they have now is frightening. When I first went to Newcastle, Gordon Marshall was in goal and it was spit on the hands or if it was raining it was green gloves or you'd go to Dunn & Co in Newcastle – Gordon Marshall used to go to Dunn & Co – and buy string gloves, the sort that you'd wear to church on Sunday. You look at what they have now. They have a range of wet, dry, semi-wet, semi-dry. Frightening, the technology that you have. People say that goalkeepers nowadays punch a ball further. They should, the padding they've got on those fingers. That's come a long way, but it had to because the ball's changed and that's the biggest difference.

The ball is different to deal with because the coating now lasts much longer. In the past, the outer coating split, was scratched, gained moisture, and in the last half-hour would be really heavy. Nowadays the makers can guarantee that the ball keeps its shape, doesn't lose its skin, for the 90 minutes. So at the end of a game the ball's as light as when you started.

Decline and Fall

IF THE immediate post-war years saw a boom in football attendances, the Fifties saw a decline. By 1956, attendances had fallen to 33.31 million, seven million below the post-war peak, as other leisure pursuits rose in popularity.

England entered the World Cup for the first time in 1950 and promptly suffered a humiliating 1-0 defeat at the hands of the United States in Belo Horizonte. The notion that English football was invincible received another blow when Hungary won 6-3 at Wembley in 1953. Puskas, Koscis, Czibor and Hidegkuti opened people's eyes to 'football dressed in new colours not seen in this country before', as Geoffrey Green of *The Times* described it.

Despite this, English football did broaden its horizons. The European Cup was established for the 1955-56 season. English champions, Chelsea, did not enter when the Football League persuaded them that the new competition would 'interfere with home commitments'. The following year, the 'Busby Babes' of Manchester United did take up the quest for European glory. The following season United again went into Europe, only to perish in the snow, at Munich, in February 1958. A nation mourned.

In the same year, a 17-year-old called Edson Arantes do Nascimento scored two goals for Brazil against Sweden in the World Cup Final in Stockholm. The second goal, in particular, was a marvellous example of precocious skill. Pelé had arrived.

Meanwhile, Real Madrid established a stranglehold on the European Cup. They won it in the first five years of its existence, led by Argentinean Alfredo di Stefano, Frenchman Raymond Kopa, Hungarian Ferenc Puskas and Uruguayan Jose Santamaria. Signs of things to come?

At home, the white ball was introduced in 1951, floodlights became widespread during the decade – they were installed at the Baseball Ground in 1953. Television, in flickering black and white, discovered football could hold an audience enthralled, as under the Molineux floodlights, Wolverhampton Wanderers pounded visiting European teams like Honved and Moscow Spartak to restore English pride. Nearer to home, after being a major First Division club for more than 20 seasons (1926-27 to 1952-53), Derby County fell into the Third Division North. Promotion under manager Harry Storer, in 1957, saw them back in the Second Division at the end of the decade.

Bill Brownson: I think a lot of that probably went back to Ben Robshaw. We've always had problems at board level, haven't we? It doesn't matter whether we've had good blokes, bad blokes, we've always had problems up there. There's always been somebody who wanted to upset the apple cart. They've never been stable and that was the trouble. If Derby had been stable at boardroom level, I think they'd have been one of the biggest clubs in the country now.

Ernie Hallam: After we lost Carter and Doherty it started going down and it just continued. Of course, we signed Johnny Morris and Billy Steel, but they went and I remember saying to my brother: "If we're not careful, this team's going to be relegated." He couldn't believe it. Unfortunately we did, didn't we?

Johnny Morris: I left because I knew they were going down and they did, that season. Told McMillan. I asked for a transfer. Harry Storer contacted me later on. Asked me to go back. I was 33 or something then. I kept the newsagent's business in Derby all the time I was at Leicester. Five or six years. I used to love Derby. I loved the club, really. Why didn't I go back? I don't know.

Stuart McMillan

Johnny Morris: Stuart, as I've said before, was the best manager I've played for – until he started talking football! For the first three years, I never heard him talk football and we were doing well, but of course he sold Leon Leuty to Bradford and he relied on Ken Oliver. You remember Ken? Not quite good enough. Not for the First Division. Smashing lad, though, a real 100 per center.

Ernie Hallam: I never came into contact with him personally, but I think he was a lucky manager, really. I mean, Ted Magner was the man who was in control of the team until a few weeks before the Final.

Reg Harrison: He was a gentleman, but he wasn't a good manager. He didn't come in and take charge. He wasn't 'the boss', if you follow me.

Ray Young: He had a twitch in his nose. Somebody said it was a whisky twitch because he drank a bottle of whisky a day. It used to move. Most of the time when I was in his office I couldn't take my eyes of the nose twitching. It was most peculiar and somebody said he thought it was a whisky twitch, sort of thing. You never saw him all that much really. In fact I think later, when Harry Storer was the manager, I saw more of him, but then I never really managed to get a word in.

Don Hazledine: He was the old fashioned type, wasn't he? Old fashioned, like you can imagine the director type. Like at Arsenal, with Allison and people like that. I think he used to be on the drink quite a lot because he always had one of those red noses, you know? He was always dressed up, very dapper. Never saw him in a tracksuit. He seemed very old anyway. Maybe he wasn't so old, but he had his hair flat back, with a parting down the middle, and he looked to me to be between 55-60, but maybe he wasn't as old as that.

Jack Barker

Reg Harrison: Jack wasn't a good manager but I liked him. He was a rough sort of fellow and a blunt sort of fellow and no tact at all, but I liked him.

Frank Upton: Jack Barker was only there 12 months. He seemed a nice bloke. I'm only a baby in the game at the time, but he seemed a big, strong, sturdy man. When he spoke, like, you listened. He was one of those type of blokes that had a presence about him, very much so. He'd come out with a tracksuit on, but he never did any coaching or anything.

Derby County 1 Boston United 6

Ian Buxton: I remember very clearly the Boston United FA Cup match in 1955. I saw that one. I couldn't believe it, I just couldn't believe it. I remember Boston attacked and scored and there was a bit of nothing play, then Boston attacked and scored again and it was a Hazledine or somebody else, who'd been at Derby. It was an unbelievable game, unbelievable.

Reg Harrison: That was great. I'd seen Albert Mays on the day of the second-round draw, on the Monday. I was going towards Babington Lane and he was coming the other way. He'd been up the snooker hall and he saw me and said: "Have you seen the draw? We'll thrash you." I just grinned.

Ray Wilkins: It was on Saturday, 10 December 1955. A dull day. It didn't rain, but the pitch was quite heavy, as always. There was a good crowd as I remember, something over 23,000, I think.

Don Hazledine: As you know at the Baseball Ground, it wasn't anything special, but personally, I didn't find it too heavy on the day. It wasn't noticeably heavy. As I remember it, the day was fine. It was a good day, overcast, a December day.

Geoff Hazledine: Everyone from Boston was there so the ovation both teams got was kind of equal. It was a home game for Derby, but it was a home game for us too, because we'd nearly as much experience of the Baseball Ground as they had. It was really like two Derby County teams playing each other. It was most wonderful and most odd because we all knew each other, which is an odd situation really.

Ray Wilkins: I think we went straight to the ground, Reg and me, with us living in Derby. No, no, we went to the Midland. We met at the Midland, had lunch there. Met the team at the Midland. Occasionally, if we were travelling away, we met and had a bit of lunch, on special occasions.

Don Hazledine: I lived in Boston so I travelled with the main party on the bus.

Ray Wilkins: Ray Middleton's team talks were never much. Ray was more inclined to be famous after the match, when, if we had lost, he would sit in the corner, covered in mud and he'd still be sitting like that when we'd all showered and were going home. He was like that, but he was quite a good manager. He encouraged individuality a little bit. He was a Justice of the Peace and he spoke quite a lot. He was a local preacher as well and spent quite some time at various chapels and churches. He asked me once or twice to read lessons and that. He was quite a character, really.

Don Hazledine: We were in the Midland League. We had a good side. We were full of confidence. Ray Middleton was player-manager. Ray never used to burden us with too many tactics. To be quite honest and fair to him, I don't think he could anyway. He was a goalkeeper after all, wasn't he?

Ray Wilkins: There were seven on the books, actually, who'd played for Derby County, but only six played on the day. The one who was missing was Steve Wheatley. Those who played were Ray Middleton, Reg, myself, Don and Geoff Hazledine and Dave Miller. Dave was with Derby at one time, but I didn't remember him, he was before my time at Derby.

Don Hazledine: We had Dave Miller, of course. He was a very good player who'd been on Middlesbrough's and Wolves' books. He was the old fashioned type of centre-half, big fellow, very tough, great in the air. He could direct it to a player, not just boot it out of the way. Reg Harrison was there, of course, on the wing. He always used to make space. You could find him blindfolded. He was really, really good at that, making space.

Geoff Hazledine: Ray and I played up front. 'Midd' was the manager, but Dave Miller, who played centre-half, was a really inspirational figure. He played at Derby and we didn't know that until we were talking to Reg Harrison recently. He said it was a pity he didn't have more time to settle when he was with Derby, but Don and I never realised he'd played at Derby. He was a superb player for us.

Ray Wilkins: No, no. We weren't confident before the match. A couple of weeks before, Ray Middleton took us to watch Derby play because we hadn't a match that day. I remember the radio man came to interview him afterwards, as he sat in the stand. I always remember the reporter saying: "What sort of chance do you think you've got?" Ray – and this is what I say, he was quite a character – said: "Oh we've no chance. They'll slaughter us. They'll be far too good for us." Of course, they were third then in the Third Division North and we were in the Midland League. That was Ray. It's not what we really thought, of course. We were more confident than that.

Reg Harrison: We thought we could beat them. Ray 'Midd' took them all, the lads from Boston, to watch Derby play. Freddy Tunstall – he used to be with Sheffield United – and it must have been the following Saturday, he said: "Oh, we can beat them. The two wing-halves will go storming forward." That was Paddy Ryan and Albert Mays, and he said: "The centre-half stays back and if we get into that gap, between the two of them and go at him..." I thought Freddie was quite clever upstairs.

Don Hazledine: I suppose Derby must have taken us lightly. They didn't realise our true potential. Like I say, we had some good players and they were being well paid. I think they were talking about, if we won, we'd get a bonus of £4. It doesn't seem a lot now, but it was then. We had a chairman, who was a real director type. Malkinson, his name was. He loved being a director, big cigar and everything, but he was very, very good. A very likable man.

Ray Wilkins: I played centre-forward. You don't forget the goals you scored or some you missed, of course. The first was some sort of a knock-in, really. Reg had a shot that was passing across the goal. It was a knock-in. For the second, the cuttings say: "He dribbled the ball away from the advancing Webster, before sidefooting into the net." Well, actually, it was quite a goal this was because I got the ball in my own half, in the centre-circle. I gave it to Reg – laid it off to Reg – and turned inside. A couple came at us and we played a one-two and found ourselves with no one in front of us and about 40 yards to go for the goal. We ran almost shoulder to shoulder towards Terry Webster. Just before we got there, we parted and Reg went with the ball and, of course, Terry went across to him, a couple of yards to the left and I just had to put it in again. So they weren't great goals, but they were goals you remember, obviously because of the match.

Geoff Hazledine: Well. I scored a hat-trick, as you know, and basically they were all from a decent distance. There was one from 20 yards, one from 25 yards and the other from about ten yards. I think the goalkeeper was Terry Webster. Yes, Terry Webster I think it was.

Don Hazledine: Ray Wilkins was very steady. Wasn't spectacular, but very steady. Quite good in the air, used to get up well. They were all easy to play with. The whole team was easy to play with. We were confident, but not over confident. We were quite assured, really. Like I say, we didn't go in a lot for complicated tactics. We didn't go in for saying: "Watch him and look out for him." We never bothered. That wasn't just for Derby, it was for all the teams we played, like Peterborough, for example. We just took them on. We had this spirit and confidence, you see.

Reg Harrison: This centre-half – Martin McDonnell – Ray was coming off him and balls were played in short and he didn't know what to do. We played quite well.

Geoff Hazledine: With having a lot of old lads who were playing at Boston, it was like, shall we say, a return of the Derby lads, a reunion. It was such a wonderful occasion. Superb, when we heard the draw. Superb. You see, the thing was that we, at Boston, felt we could take on any side. I mean, even when we played Tottenham and we lost 4-0, the accolades that poured on us after the game were unbelievable.

Ray Wilkins: Our only aim was to go to the Baseball Ground and play football and get rid of this myth that non-League was just bang, bang and up the field. That was our objective, whatever was said before the game. "Let's play football," is what we said. If we're going to lose, we'd let the crowd go away thinking: "Well, they played a reasonable game of football."

Geoff Hazledine: The thing was, we had such power. When we were playing in the Midland League, teams, if they got away with a 3-0 thrashing, they thought they'd played well. We were so confident, you see. We blended well. 'Midd', although he was the manager, never actually gave us any coaching or tuition. He just used to let us go out and play our own game. Dave Miller was a kind of motivator, he and Tommy Lowther. Tommy always had a lot to say, psyching us up before the game, but Reg was a cooling influence. They were the three most experienced players in the team and the combination of those blended into a perfect ingredient, with all the youngsters in the mix kind of thing.

Don Hazledine: At Boston we were getting very good gates. We averaged around 8,000. You must remember we were better off than many players in the League at that time. I had quite a number of offers to go back into the League, but it wouldn't have paid me. When the maximum wage was £14, I was on a good wage at Boston, I'd got a job and a car and was living in bungalow, rent free, in Boston. I mean, someone coming along and offering me £14 a week, well, that was no good. I was settled there, family and everything, so I wasn't going to move for that. Jesse Pye, he went to Wisbech. They had three internationals there. Bobby Langton was one, who used to play at Bolton. They weren't paying them peanuts, were they?

Geoff Hazledine: We were paid a lot more than the Derby lads. I mean, the maximum you could earn then was, I think, £20 and £17. It might have been less. When I went to Boston I had offers to stay in the League, but the money they offered me surpassed that by far, well it was double the League money. The top money you got in the First Division then or in any team, was £20 and £17. That was the maximum. Totalling up all the little perks, I was on over £50 per week.

Ray Wilkins: The crowd gave us a tremendous reception coming off. They really did, I must admit. Of course, there were a lot of Boston people there, but I mean, the whole crowd gave us a great reception. We went back to the Midland and had a meal there. The next match was a bit different. We won 3-1, away at Grantham. The next cup round was away, at Tottenham. That was a remarkable day. We played on a pitch that was twice as bad as the Baseball Ground ever was. They'd quite a good side too. Reynolds in goal. Norman and Hopkins at full-back. Blanchflower, Clarke and Marchi; Brookes, Duquemin, Smith and George Robb. Robb was the amateur international, but he'd signed pro then. I was at college with him.

Don Hazledine: There were no extreme celebrations. We all went our different ways, you see. I think Geoff, with him getting a hat-trick, he got on the television news and that. They were interviewed, him and Ray. No, we didn't do anything special, really.

Geoff Hazledine: With knowing all the lads we said after the game, that the Boston lads would stay over and we'd all meet at the Trocadero, the dance hall, as it was, but Ray 'Midd' and I went to Birmingham, to be on television. I've still got the fee that I got from that, £5. I also made a broadcast on radio and I got £3 3s.

Characters and players

Ray Young: Albert Mays lived in Alvaston. If I hadn't been playing, but watching the game, Albert always wanted me to go his way home, which meant going into town and then from town all the way round London Road. All I'd get from Albert was: "How did I play? How did I play?" He'd then tell you every good pass he'd made in that 90 minutes. It was amazing. He could remember everything good he'd done in 90 minutes. He didn't remember the rest. Albert was already at Derby when I went there.

John Bowers: Albert Mays I always thought was very, very moody. Again, though, a good player.

Peter Newbery: We had some fine players. Obviously I remember Tommy Powell very well. I remember with great affection, Jesse Pye, who was not only a good player, but really a nice man as well and very encouraging. Very few of the pros were encouraging, so far as the youngsters were concerned. Whether they felt you were threat to their place I really don't know, but Jesse was a great guy. I remember him very well indeed. Ray Middleton was a nice fellow. Jack Parry? Well Jack was a funny man, wasn't he? He and Dennis Woodhead. They were real comedians and we had many laughs. Yes Jack – and he was a good player, as was Dennis Woodhead. I think Dennis had played his best times at Sheffield Wednesday, but he was still a good player at Derby.

Frank Upton: Geoff Barrowcliffe, Terry Webster, Keith Savin, Tommy, a good friend Tommy. Ray Straw eventually came into it. Glyn Davies. Yes, Reg Ryan came and he was like the old head of the side. He was a good player, Paddy, was and he wanted the ball. He was a good skipper. He talked to people, he helped you, he talked to you. He did both. He could shout, but he mainly talked, softly to you.

Ray Young: 1951 was when I signed professional. I played with Bert Mozley, Jackie Stamps, Chick Musson. I think Johnny Morris was still there. Ray Middleton. There was Les Mynard, Hughie McLaren. Of course, Reggie Harrison was still there. Albert Mays. Then in the Reserves you had Colin Bell, Colin Walker, the Hazledine lads were there, Don and Geoff. Derby were in the First Division when I signed on, but went down in 1953.

Geoff Hazledine: The age gap was such a contrast. Chick was finishing. Stampie was finishing. Jack Lee was finishing and all those people that were 'over the top'. When you got into the first team, you weren't being blended into the first team gradually, you were expected to be in it straight away.

Peter Newbery: I think the best times for me were undoubtedly with Jack Barker. He signed me from school and I enjoyed those early days. I became a little bit disillusioned with the professional game in Harry Storer's time, possibly because I was part-time anyway.

Part-timers

Ray Young: I worked for Ford & Weston, as an apprentice plumber, purely because Ossie Jackson owned Ford & Weston and he was also chairman of the football club. It meant I could have time off and they paid me for it.

Gordon Guthrie: There was Jack Bowers and Ralph Hann, the trainers. Ralph used to take the

Tuesday nights and Jack used to take the Thursdays. We didn't used to like the Thursdays very much because that was most physical, but we got used to it – eventually. Jack was more into the sprints and everything on a Thursday nights. All the players, such as myself, used to come about five o'clock and used to leave, about what? Towards eight o'clock. I worked at the railway.

Ian Buxton: It entailed arriving there as near to six o'clock as you could, after work. Train for an hour and a half, hour and three-quarters, and then go home for your tea – and that was two nights a week, Tuesday night and Thursday night.

Frank Upton: I went part-time at Derby because I didn't want to go in the Forces to do my National Service. So I worked at Denby Loco. I worked in the blacksmith's shop there and I used to have to get up at five in the morning. I used to live at the hostel. Remember it? I lived there and I used to have to get up at five, walk into town, catch a bus, go to work, come back – I used to leave work about half three – catch a bus straight down to the Baseball Ground and do my training. Yes, Tuesday and Thursday nights. I thoroughly enjoyed it. I was a bit shattered when I got home though.

Ray Wilkins: Yes, I went to Boston as a part-timer and I was at Derby as a part-timer too. Tuesday and Thursday nights. They contacted me at Loughborough, at college. They kept pestering me to sign full-time, but in those days it wasn't worth it. You'd got to weigh up the future. It was difficult because once you'd started teaching in those days, it's not like today. You'd got a grant for a start, from the government. That was okay, provided you didn't leave the profession straight away and then, if you did, you had to pay it back. Also, if you went out of teaching, within two or three years of training, quite a lot of questions were asked as to why? You were blacklisted in other words.

Ian Buxton: In those days, part-time was fairly normal and there were quite a lot of part-timers around the country, not just at Derby County. We had people who played regularly in the first team that were part-time. I played regularly for a couple of seasons and we had people like Les Moore, who was a part-timer, training on Tuesday and Thursday nights. John Bowers, for instance, who played quite lot of first-team games, as well. Peter Newbery, John Richmond and people played odd games, Bobby McAndrew, but all clubs then had part-time professionals. It wouldn't be entertained now at all, but it was for then, normal.

Frank Upton: Gordon Guthrie was a part-timer, John Richmond came later, the Hazledines. There were a few others. The training was done at the Baseball Ground, round the track or up at Sinfin. Mainly, we trained at the Baseball Ground. On the dark nights, with the floodlights on.

Peter Newbery: The team sheet was posted on a Friday morning at the ground. Some of us were normally training at the ground on Friday. We'd wait after training for the team to go up, so either you were in the first team or sometimes playing at Potton United in the thirds.

Ray Young: We had the small gym. We could use the track, but if it was really bad we'd use the stand. We'd run along 'B' Stand, 'A' Stand and down and up the steps and round Osmaston Stand back down. We'd have a run or we'd use the pub car park on the corner. We used to use that. They'd got a couple of lights up there. After being a part-timer, I did two years National Service and from then on I did 12 years full-time football at Derby.

Gordon Guthrie: We always trained at the Baseball Ground. What is now the office was the gymnasium and we also had what was known as a shooting box, which is long time gone. There was the car park behind the Baseball Hotel, which had a couple of temporary floodlights and we used to switch them on and play five-a-sides on the asphalt. We used to have a medicine ball in a circle for one goal and a medicine ball at the other end. You could never get us out of there.

Bob McAndrew: We trained Tuesdays and Thursdays. We used to go straight down from work. Of course, we had the pre-season and what have you. I was working at the railway as an apprentice. I think we had to get there about quarter to six. Jack Bowers and Ralph Hann were the trainers.

Ian Buxton: In those days the trainers were Ralph Hann and Gordon Guthrie and Jack Bowers who also did a bit of the training. Gordon Guthrie was a part-time player then, but when he gave up playing, he went on the staff almost straight away.

Bob McAndrew: Gordon Guthrie, Johnny Bowers, Peter Hawley and Pete Newbery. We used to go round the track together. Circuits under the Osmaston Stand, with the weights and all the rest of it. If it was very inclement, we used to do a turn up and down the stairs all the way around the ground, on the stands. No ball work at all sometimes. Crab football in the gym. We sometimes never saw a ball until Saturday. We were certainly fit, though.

Part-time v full-time

Gordon Hughes: When I first started at Newcastle, at 18, I was part-time, serving my time as an engineer. Tuesday and Thursday night training. I was in the first team at Newcastle. I was lucky, there were a few injuries originally, so I got straight in the side. People have asked that question about part-timers and full-timers and I must be honest and say, as far as I was concerned, there wasn't any difference whatsoever. All right, it may have been youth. I was fit and I used to work pretty hard, but I say to this day that there wasn't any difference, really.

John Bowers: I think they might put up with it now, but not at a high level. Take the Premiership, there's no reason to be part-time now. Not even the First Division, but when you get down to the Second or Third Divisions – and high level non-League sides – that's where you find the part-timers.

Gordon Guthrie and Sir Stanley Matthews

Ian Buxton: Oh yes,Guth was a player in those days and, of course, his chief claim to fame was playing against Stanley Matthews. Matthews played for Blackpool Reserves against Derby Reserves. I didn't play in that match.

Gordon Guthrie: I think he had been out with some sort of injury for quite a while and they'd got an important League game the following week, so he'd decided to play. In that game, if you remember, we scored three goals and the blooming referee disallowed two of them. I'll tell you who put three of them in the net – Gordon Brown. We came away with a point, so I must have done a reasonable job.

Harry Storer

HARRY Storer became manager of Derby County in the close season of 1955. He succeeded Rams legend Jack Barker, but he was no stranger to the club and no stranger to Derbyshire. He was one of only ten players in the 20th century, to play professionally at football and cricket for Derby County and Derbyshire and his combined total of 576 appearances for the two clubs puts him at the head of that list.

A tough tackling wing-half in the Twenties, he won two England caps at football and he was a member of the Derbyshire team that won the County Cricket Championship in 1936. Will Taylor, who was secretary of the cricket club for more than 50 years, rated Harry Storer as the best batsman Derbyshire ever had, but by the time the cricket county championship was won – the Rams finished second in the First Division in the same year – Storer had moved on to become manager of Coventry City. He was appointed in 1931 and won promotion from the old Third Division South in 1935-36 and is the only man ever to be a county cricketer, whilst also being a football club manager in the Football League.

Storer came from a sporting family. In the 19th century, his uncle William also played for Derby County and Derbyshire and won England caps at cricket, whilst his father Harry senior, who was born in Ripley, played in goal for Woolwich Arsenal and Liverpool. A larger than life figure with a famously square jaw, Harry Storer knew a lot about sport and a lot about people. He knew a lot about many things and loved an argument about everything from literature to religion, in spite of being an avowed atheist. He was blunt of speech and upset many people with his penchant for calling a spade a shovel. He detested coaching theory and after listening impatiently to some technical breakdown of a player's strengths and weaknesses, his words were invariably: "Yes. I know all that, but can he play?" He liked players with what he called heart and his defenders usually took few prisoners, but he did appreciate skilful players in forward positions. On Derby County trips to the North-East, the young Brian Clough was a regular visitor to the team's hotel where he listened and learned a lot from Harry Storer. In many ways, Storer was Brian Clough's early mentor. Like all 'characters', the stories about Harry Storer – and his dog, Bill – are legion.

Harry Storer

'Ned' Mee: I saw Harry Storer play. He was all right and was very good at times, but he got that bit of, well, he was a bit 'dirty'. Yes he was. He'd kick a chap up in the air, and think nothing about it.

Ernie Hallam: Harry, aye. Loved Harry. I saw Harry play, of course. In 1928, he was playing. Yes, he was a hard man. He was a hard man as a manager, wasn't he? Let rip, wouldn't he? Even the girls at the *Telegraph* used to tell me that he'd ring up and wouldn't be long at coming out with a mouthful but, I mean, he was a great man wasn't he, Harry, in sport, cricket, football, management?

Tommy Powell: I always got on well with him, actually. I felt I could talk to him. I felt that I could shout at him, really. I'll never forget, once. He came in the dressing-room at half-time when we was in the Third Division North and he had a fag on and I said: "Hey, can't you see that notice?" "Oh, I'm sorry Tom," he said and put it out. That's how he was. I just felt as though I could talk to him. He used to say, when we were waiting for the coach and we'd got a rough match on: "How many hearts have we got here today?" He let you express yourself. I remember seeing him play cricket for Derbyshire too.

Ernie Hallam: In fact, he probably arrested what could have been a long, long period in the lower divisions for Derby County. He came with his knowledge. He'd been at Burnley, at Coventry as manager, and Birmingham. He brought in Paddy Ryan, who did a great job. He brought in the centre-half, Martin McDonnell. He was a hard man as well, but he did a job at that level. I mean, Paddy had a bit of polish and I thought they were the real reasons we did well and the others linked in.

Gerald Mortimer: He bought some experienced old dogs, didn't he, to come and play for him? I think he failed to carry it on in the Second Division, for one reason or another.

Tommy Powell: He bought Martin McDonnell, who wasn't the most skilful, but by Christ, he stopped them. He bought Paddy Ryan. Paddy could spray it about. He bought 'Woody', Dennis Woodhead. He was another one. He bought Roy Martin from Birmingham. He bought little Georgie Darwin. He liked forwards who could play, but he liked defenders who could defend.

Gordon Guthrie: I was a full-back. Full-backs had to tackle then. If you played for Mr Storer and you couldn't win the ball – and you were a defender – you weren't here long.

Bill Brownson: I thought he did very well for us. He got us out of the Third Division, didn't he? He was good. He sorted one or two out. He bought McDonnell.

Ray Young: Harry came when I was doing my National Service. I didn't really meet him until I'd done my National Service. I played over 30 games in 1954-55 and he came that summer.

Alf Millin: He was a good bloke. He told you what he thought about you, but if you said anything wrong, that was it...he didn't like it.

Ian Buxton: As cricketers, we all got on quite well with Harry because if ever you talked to Harry, if you remember, he always turned the subject to cricket and got on about how to play off-spinners on a turning wicket.

Frank Upton: Harry was a different bloke to Jack Barker. I'd have run through a brick wall – every manager I'd run through a brick wall for because that's the way I am – but Harry! He'd bought me once, when I was playing with Nuneaton. He was manager at Coventry and he'd come across and seen me at Nuneaton and went back to the directors for their agreement – this is what he told me, anyway. He says: "I've bought you once and I got the sack over it, virtually." He says: "I paid £1,000 for you, from Nuneaton. I went back to the board and said:

'I've just given my word to Nuneaton Borough that we'll buy this lad'." Anyway, he says: "I left Coventry a bit after that because they wouldn't honour my word." That was my first introduction to him.

Ron Webster: I thought he was great. Fair. You know, before I got my debut they were struggling, you see, and were near the bottom and he was trying everybody and I went in to see him on the Monday. I think they had lost the week before and I said: "How is it you've not given me a chance, Mr Storer?" He said: "Well, do you think you're good enough?" I said: "Yes, I'm better than these you've been playing." So, on the next Saturday, I was in! He said: "I'll give you a chance." I was in and I stayed in for a while, like to the end of one season and then the season after. That's when the injuries started. I'd be about 17 or 18.

Ian Buxton: When I signed, Harry said: "Look, son. When you get to be regular in the Reserves, we'll give you a rise." So I played in the first team and scored two on my debut against Ipswich, so I thought: "Eh up, I'm in for a rise here." So on the Tuesday night I was waiting around for Harry to come down to training and I went knocking on his door. I went in there and came out with a flea in my ear thinking I was lucky to be a professional and getting paid for doing anything at all. I'd just played in the first team on the Saturday and scored two, but I certainly didn't get a rise. That was Harry.

Frank Upton: He was honest. He was knowledgeable about the game. A different kettle of fish to Jack Barker, but I didn't know Jack much because he was only there 12 months and you don't get to talk to managers much in 12 months. Harry Storer was a character. He used to tell me tales. I used to love listening to him, sitting listening to him on away trips, by train. He liked an argument, but he knew his football. He knew what he wanted and that's probably why he was successful in the game as long as he was. Not really a tactician, no. Managers didn't go in for much of that, not in those days. I think he just left it to Jack and Ralph to do the training. He used to pick the teams. He used to come up to Sinfin, with Charlie Elliott the cricketer, who used to be his henchman or whatever, and his dog, of course. They always used to be around.

Gerald Mortimer: I met him two or three times. I pestered old Wilf Shaw, who used to write for the *Telegraph*, to meet Harry. Wilf used to write the football and cricket. I found Harry fascinating. I think he made a virtue of being blunt and outspoken – and rude, but I always found him worth listening to. In a way, he was an earlier Clough, wasn't he?

Ray Young: I never managed to get a word in. I mean, I've been in there, in the office, on a Friday. I've been wanting a move and gone in to say my piece and I've come out – having walked over his dog, who was blind – and come out again thinking: "Why did I go in there?" I'd never managed to get a word in!

Gerald Mortimer: He used to say some controversial things on *Sport in the Midlands*, when more people listened to radio, when television wasn't God. He was quite a figure in his way, Harry, I think. Of the ones before, I don't think Stuart McMillan was ever a manager. Or Jack Barker, who was obviously a great player, although I never saw him play. I did meet him once and found him fascinating to talk to, but I think he was a disaster as a manager and I know he found the board very tedious. That situation had to go on through Storer and Tim Ward and, to an extent, Brian Clough really. I remember Harry sort of leaving instructions that if Fred Walters came and put any flowers on his grave to: "Chuck them in the @!?--- bin!"

Frank Upton: Yes, I had some run-ins with Storer, one or two. More when I'd been there a while. I was the skipper and I think when you're skipper, it gives you a little more leeway and

I think you've got to think a little bit more about the players and your job as a skipper.

Gordon Guthrie: I sometimes wonder what he would have said had he seen the sign in the treatment room now, about not having a mobile phone working. Then, we were lucky to have a bike. Now everyone's got one, like a car. Its just progress, I suppose.

Phil Waller: Well, his bark was worse than his bite towards the end, wasn't it? He had a lot to say about everything, didn't he, Harry? He had a view about everything. Politics. Everything.

Frank Upton: There was one incident when he came up to my house and he was going to sue me for this and sue me for that because I did something – so he said – to get him out of the game. What happened was, I was asked a question by the hierarchy, who said to me: "What do you think?" We weren't doing very well at that time. We'd had a bad start and they asked me the question. "Well," I said, "As far as I'm concerned, it's football and that's the way it goes." I said: "With me being skipper, you're asking me a question, so I will ask the players how they feel." So that's what I did. Then one player said to me: "I don't think you should be doing this, Frank." So straightaway, I went to the person who'd asked me to do it and I said: "No. It's not the right thing to be done, after thinking about it." And that was that.

Most probably two years later or something like that, Harry came knocking at my door at twelve o'clock at night, with a friend. He's fuming. It was in the summer and he'd been down to the cricket ground watching Derbyshire play and he'd come across one of the players and the player must have mentioned it to him. He came up that night and mentioned the player's name, that he'd been talking to and so on. I said: "That's right. I was asked, as I told you, and that was the end of it." He said: "I'm going to sue you for libel." I told him to piss off out of the house, in a few short words. I told his friend to go as well. Anyway, that wasn't the end of it. He came back about a week later, with his solicitor.

By this time I was fuming because as far as I was concerned, I hadn't done anything wrong. Anyway, he came back, with his solicitor. He knocked at the door, you know how he was, straight John Bull, bolshie like. So I said: "What do you want, Harry?" He says: "Can I come in? Bring my friend?" I says: "You can can come in, but your friend's not coming in." He says: "Why not, he came in the last time?" I said: "That's nothing to do with you. Do you want to come in or not?" We had a bit of an argument, like, on the doorstep. He came in and, in the end, I just told him what to do. It never had any effect on the football. I think Harry was the type of bloke, if you were good enough for your place, you kept it. The game's about football, anyway, isn't it?

Peter Newbery: I remember Eric Kitchen, the coach driver, very well. Yes, very well indeed. He used to get some stick from Harry Storer, when he wasn't driving quick enough. Then again, Eric did drive very quickly anyway. He was a good driver and would take a few risks to get us there, but he was never quick enough for Harry Storer. He was good man, Eric, but he was never quick enough for Harry.

For some they were the best years

At the end of season 1954-55, Derby County slipped into the Third Division North. They finished runners-up to Grimsby Town in 1956, but only one team was promoted in those days. The following season, Derby County were champions. The average home attendance was 19,609 and centre-forward Ray Straw scored 37 League goals in 44 games.

Tommy Powell: We loved it, we loved it. We had a grand team. 'Strawie' was as soft as muck, a lovely lad and 'Barra' and Glyn Davies. Everybody got this feeling when they went to the ground, that they were going to see four or five goals. That's how we were. If we didn't score two or three, we'd had a bad game. We were just different class, really. It was nice to be able to go and play your football.

Graham Sellors: I saw a lot of that period ...a lot of Reg Ryan and Jack Parry, Martin McDonnell, I associated him with Norman Nielson. Were they similar sorts of players? A bit.

Tommy Powell: I remember when we first went in the Third Division we played Mansfield on a Saturday night and we got around 24,000 there then. It was some gate. We went up the following season.

Frank Upton: I didn't play a lot of games in that season though because I was in the Forces. I went in the Forces and I was glad I did, now. I was stationed at Lichfield. I got it sorted out where they got me a home station like, so that every week I was off I came back for football. I played more football in the RAF than anything really, for the RAF side, for the group sides, all those kind of things.

Graham Sellors: We usually stood at the Osmaston End, although I was in the stand when Derby beat Chesterfield 7-1 on Easter Monday – they'd drawn 2-2 at Chesterfield on Good Friday and it snowed. On the Monday, Ray Straw scored three. Hutchinson scored for Chesterfield with a penalty, didn't he? Hit Terry Webster's hands and sort of spun him round. He wasn't very big, Terry Webster.

Tommy Powell: People still say to me now: "I did enjoy that Third Division North." I mean, two years running we scored well over 100 goals in the season. Football's a lot about opinions, but something I don't agree with a lot of people is when they talk about 'clean sheets'. It's all right having a 'clean sheet', but if you don't score in the other end, you're going to win nothing, especially these days of three points and one. It was bad enough when it was two points and one, but if you don't score goals you'll win nothing.

Gerald Mortimer: The two Third North seasons I didn't see a lot of because I was in the Army, but they were fun seasons because they scored a lot of goals and it was everybody's Cup-tie against Derby County. They got 110 and 111 goals, I think, in the two seasons.

Graham Sellors: It was a big social thing wasn't it, going to football matches? I remember the talking about football matches, the leg pulling about football matches, as much as I remember the football matches themselves. There was a bloke who was courting my aunt – it was a long-term courtship and so he was called 'uncle' – who was a Manchester United supporter and he used to pull my leg terribly. He bet me that Liverpool would beat Derby in the Cup sixth round, in the late Forties. They won 1-0 and he burnt the score on to my sledge: 'Liverpool 1 Derby 0'. I was about seven and I can remember crying when I saw it.

Tommy Powell: They said that Northampton Cup match was a record and that the gate was over 38,000. When Derby played Middlesbrough in 1997 and got knocked out of the Cup, I stood outside the ground, where we usually stand talking. I said to my mate: "I can't believe this. It's the sixth round of the FA Cup and there's no atmosphere, no atmosphere at all. Years ago this would have been alive. There'd have been rosettes on, rattles going and all that." I said: "Another thing. I can't believe that there's a Cup-tie on this week. People used to talk about it for the whole week before." You'd get on the ground and the atmosphere would be electric for a Cup match.

Tommy Powell: Crowds could mix then, of course. You didn't get any trouble at all, but it was tremendous. People are frightened to wear rosettes now. I remember one of the big firms said to me once: "You know, Tom, when Derby's doing well, the lads come to work and can't wait for the next Saturday, but they work like hell. It's unbelievable," he said. "If Derby's doing well, you don't have to watch them. They just want to get the work done and get ready for the weekend." In those times you had to be there early to get on the ground at all.

Players and characters

Frank Upton: Paddy Ryan was a good player. I remember him playing one training day, at Sinfin. He'd just come and, you know me, I'm an honest 90-minute player and if the ball was there, I was always going in to get it. It was a sticky morning, a lot of dew on the ground. Paddy came from West Brom, who'd just won the Cup, and he was the big 'I am' with his chest stuck out . Somebody played him a ball and, of course, I just go in to win the ball and I slipped and caught his ankle. He screamed. Then he had a go at Harry Storer. He said: "What the bloody hell have we got here? I'm trying to play football." I just says: "The ball's there to be won." It was only because of the dew on the floor that I slipped.

Frank Upton: He always had a go at me, Paddy. He always used to say to me: "Stroke the ball to me, don't blast it. Stroke it." I think that's where I got my name 'Stroker' from.

Ray Young: Dennis Woodhead was a real character. And he used to do a lot of fishing.

Tommy Powell: Oh yes, he was a good player, 'Woodie'. I played against 'Woodie' when he was with Sheffield Wednesday and he was always a good player, but when he came to Derby ...well. There weren't many bookings in those days, but I always remember, he fouled Peter Russell at Notts County. The ref came across and got me instead and 'Woodie' was laughing like hell. When we came out after half-time, the ref apologised to me, realising that he'd made a mistake.

Graham Sellors: I remember Tommy Powell from those days. Straw and Powell. Ryan and Woodhead. I remember Woodhead at Chesterfield, letting the ball run under his foot. All wingers did that at some point or other, didn't they? Letting the ball run under their foot and out of play. He was entertaining wasn't he, Woodhead?

Frank Upton: Brilliant. Yeah, I mean, Tommy Powell, he'd got virtually everything one wanted. Sometimes he wasn't the bravest, but that wasn't one of his strengths. His strengths were his ability on the ball, his crossing, his passing. He was a gentleman, really. You could always find him with the ball. You always knew, you didn't have to look up because he was there. A diagonal ball was made for Tommy. He was unbelievable at bringing it down. They go on today about doing this and doing that, but some of the things Tommy did, like when he pulled it down and that, they'd be over the moon nowadays because you've only got to turn on the ball and someone will say: "Brilliant." Or a 30-yarder, 40-yard pass: "Brilliant, brilliant." Tommy used to do that all the while.

Ian Buxton: Yes, good player Tommy Powell. Yes, I played with Tommy. He was like Tim Ward in training. Tim used to train with us at night and you used to drift into a position, knowing you'd get the ball from Tim. Tommy was the same. I was up front, of course, and if there was space out right, I knew the ball would come. I didn't need to look at him. You didn't have to think: "I wonder if he's noticed me?" You just knew it was going to come. He was a very good player, Tommy.

Ian Buxton: Geoff Barrowcliffe was just a 'come day, go day' chap. He just got on with it. Never won at cards in his life, Geoff. He used to go home with more money than he came, but he never won at cards – so he said! He was a good player. I saw him play as a centre-forward. Yes, I played with him, but not when he played at centre-forward. I was in the stand that day. It was in the Third Division, before I was there.

Ian Buxton: I think Glyn Davies was captain of the club under Storer. I've seen Glyn once a twice. He retired back to South Wales into the sports trade. I met him at one or two trade fairs. He was a hard man in the Storer mould. I remember his battle with a chap from Southampton.

John Bowers: Jack Parry. Good player, good shot. A comic. He'd have you absolutely in stitches in the dressing-room, before you went out. In a reserve match, up at Manchester United, Barry Hutchinson got a bad cut over his eye. Dad went on and Jack was in the Reserves for some reason and as Dad ran on Jack's saying: "Quick, quick, it's his ankle," because all this blood's streaming down his face.

Ron Webster: I used to like Jack Parry. The first season Derby went down, Jack got injured against Grimsby and we just missed out on promotion.

The DeGruchy tackle

Tommy Powell: That was the first year in the Third North and we would have gone up if Jack hadn't been injured and missed the rest of the season. Of course, Jack was scoring goals right left and centre, but DeGruchy did Jack and we got beat 3-1. There were 33,000 there that day.

Ron Webster: Yes, I was there, at back of the goals. DeGruchy did him. They missed out that season but next season they were up. Soon after that, I joined them.

Ernie Hallam: I don't think there was a person on the ground who didn't think it was a bad tackle. It was at the Ossie End, if I remember rightly. I wouldn't argue too hard on that, but I think, well facing from the Ossie End, it would be on the left-hand side. It was, really, a dirty tackle. They were a hard side at the time. Funnily enough, they were one of Harry's teams. He played for Grimsby, didn't he?

Mick Hopkinson: Do you know, reading *The Trader* last week, they were talking about hard men and going down the list, at the bottom, was Ray DeGruchy. Now he did Jack Parry's back and every time I see Jack I think of that and I'm sure he suffered in later years with his back. People remember those things, don't they?

The Early Sixties

THE early Sixties was a period of change in football. The maximum wage was abolished in 1961, after the Professional Footballers' Association led by Jimmy Hill, threatened to bring its members out on strike. The stipulated maximum weekly wage any player could be paid was £20 in the season and £17 in the close season – and some were even paid the minimum rate of £8 per week. Bonus payments were strictly controlled and even if his club won the League title, the FA Cup and even the European Cup, the maximum a player could legally earn was £1,500.

Two years later came a decisive High Court judgement in the George Eastham versus Newcastle United case, in which Mr Justice Wilberforce declared the retain-and-transfer system to be an unfair restriction of trade. Henceforth players were free to negotiate their own wages and length of contract. It was the start of the road which led to the Bosman ruling.

Later in the decade, Johnny Haynes became the first player to be paid £100 per week, while lower down the scale, groundstaff boys became apprentices and saw their wages rise from £3 12s 0d (£3.60p) to £5 per week.

In 1961, Tottenham Hotspur won the League championship and the FA Cup and so became the first team in the 20th century to do the 'double', Dave Mackay, one of Spurs' all-time 'greats', was a major factor in that 'double' team. In 1968 he surprised the football world by joining Derby County.

In 1963, George Best, aged 17, made his debut for Manchester United. A sign perhaps, that a new, more modern era of football was dawning. In 1965, as if to signify the end of the old order, Stanley Matthews played his final First Division match, for Stoke City v Fulham. He was aged 50! He regretted later that he didn't carry on for another couple years. He was knighted in the New Year's Honours List.

In 1965, substitutes were allowed for the first time, one per team and then only for an injured player. On a memorable day at Wembley in 1966, England won the World Cup by beating West Germany 4-2, after extra-time.

At the start of the decade, Derby County, managed by Harry Storer, were an average Second Division team. Liverpool, Leeds United, Lincoln City and Scunthorpe United were all in the same division, but the Bill Shankly influence was just beginning and the Merseysiders gained promotion in 1962. Leeds, under Don Revie, followed in 1964. By the time the 'Swinging Sixties' came to an end, the Rams, too, were in the top flight and heading for glory under Brian Clough. First, though, in October 1961, there was a game against Liverpool...

Over the wall at the Baseball Ground

Gordon Guthrie: I can remember a game against Liverpool. Ron Yeats put Bill Curry – where it says Burton Glass, I can see it now – over those little railings straight on to the top of the crowd. Bill was in full flight and Yeats hit him and he's gone over into the crowd like that and the spectators just got him and pushed him back on to the field. I'll always remember that.

Michael Dunford: Bill Curry, I think I'm right in saying, had just come out of National Service in the early Sixties. He'd been at Newcastle and Brighton and he'd had one or two tussles with Ron Yeats and Charlie Hurley and people like that. Pop Side? I remember that. That's when we had the small railings in front, quite dangerous really. There was always the story that Stanley Matthews wouldn't play at the Baseball Ground, for that very reason. Too close to the side and the railings put him off!

Ray Young: Through the railings. In fact his leg went through, I think. Bill was a lucky lad.

Mick Hopkinson: The crowd got a bit frantic then. I can remember Jack Parry grabbing hold of me and saying: "Get off. Let's get off." This was at full-time.

Hoppy's goal

Mick Hopkinson: The famous goal. The famous one. Left foot. A surprise indeed, but the thing is, if I had to tell you the truth, I never saw it because I collided with Bill Curry. I did. I reckon it must have been from 80 yards! I think, I think I must have been 18 years old and you know what you're like when you're 18, anything outside the box, you are going to have a blast at. Probably a more thoughtful player might have thought: "Bring it down, play it out to the wing." But I was forced upon it because Bill and I was going for the same ball. I'm sure it was Bill and not a Liverpool defender. I was going to hit it as soon as it came out of the box. Wherever it came to me, I was going to hit it – and I did.

Ray Young: Oh yes. Left foot. That was in the same match as Curry went through the railings, wasn't it? I can still see it now. Hoppy can probably see it too. Further out and quicker! We won 2-0.

Mick Hopkinson: The goal was scored, as you come out of the tunnel, on the right- hand side, where the boys' pen used to be. The Normanton End. In those days we didn't go charging around, saluting the crowd and what have you. You felt a bit embarrassed, really, that you'd created a problem for somebody. Do you know, I can always remember Roger Hunt. He came to me after the match. There was some trouble in the crowd that day and they was all trying to get off the ground and I can remember him coming up to my and saying: "You'll never score another goal like that, if you live to be 100." Well, I don't think I ever did score again, did I? [*In fact Mick Hopkinson scored another five goals for Derby County*]

Frank Upton: I've heard about it. Hoppy was in and out of the side then. He came into the side when I virtually left. Like Phil Waller came into the side, too, for the first time anyway.

Mick Hopkinson: Shankly was the Liverpool manager and he collared me after the game, but he was just a face then. Obviously a legend now, but just a face then, wasn't he? A Second Division manager. You know, even when I walk about now, the older supporters always want to talk about that goal. Anyone would think I never played another game for Derby. I played about 130 matches!

"...and I nearly signed for Liverpool"

Frank Upton: I loved Liverpool. You know, like, you can go into some matches and you have good games and it's then your ground, isn't it? Liverpool always used to be a favourite. I always used to have a good game there, always. The crowd used to get on to me because I was playing against Hunt and these people – St John, Yeats – and so at that ground I used to perform, tremendous. Most probably that's why Shanks wanted to buy me. He came down late one night with his chairman to buy me. Harry Storer came to the house and brought him up. You know Shanks. He came into the house. "I want to sign you, son," he says. "I think you're a good player. I'm building a team and you're one of the ones I want." He said: "I've got a big fellow to go alongside you." That was Yeats, you see. I said: "Okay Bill. I'd love to come up and have a look round." So we went up on the Saturday morning. He showed us all around and we went into a restaurant and I had milk to drink. He said: "Do you just drink milk, son? That's good." I'd have signed there and then, but Joy said: "Let's go back and think about it." Then my daughter took ill on the Saturday night. She went into intensive care and so I rang him on the Monday and said: "Look Bill, my daughter's took ill and is in intensive care and I don't want to sign anything until she's clear." Shanks, being the man he was, said: 'Well, son, I'm sorry but I can't wait." Everything had to be done then. He said: "I can't wait. I wish you all the very best, but I'll have to look elsewhere." I'd have been a Liverpool player when they were starting to build their side, but Shankly went and bought Willie Stevenson instead.

On the groundstaff

Ron Webster: When I was 15, I went on a school outing to Wales and Derby phoned up wanting to know where I was because I hadn't signed. Eventually I signed schoolboy forms. I went to Butterley first, for six months, standing by a machine. I didn't think much to that. It was the groundstaff for me, not apprentice. Me, Phil Waller and, I think, Hoppy, went that year. We were all there together. We cleaned boots. I used to have to clean and iron the snooker table in the top room above the gym, in the afternoons. Jack Bowers made me do that. Of course, I did a bit of practising too. We trained every morning. Sometimes with the first team, sometimes with the Reserves. They had four teams then and the Central Alliance team were all pros, like Brian Daykin and them, because we had quite a big staff. The Central Alliance teams we played against were older pros. For a season I played in the 'A' team, in the Central Alliance, at Sinfin. After that I played in the Reserves and didn't go back to the 'A' much after that.

Mick Hopkinson: No, I wasn't actually on the groundstaff. I was a miner. Harry Storer wanted me to go on the groundstaff. Offered me £2 6s 0d – that was a week! £2 6s 0d a week and I was getting about £9 down the pit and I'd no intention of coming out of the pit for that. There was Phil Waller, Ronnie Webster and a lad called Barry Hardy. They were the three groundstaff lads to start with.

Positions and players

Ron Webster: Jack Bowers used to come in and say: "You've just not got that bit of..." I used to like Jack. He used to talk to me anyway and help me. "You're just lacking that extra skill around the box and whatever, but you're good at defending." "In the end," he said, "you'll come to full-back." Then, when Cloughie came, he put me there anyway. I was happy to go to full-back really because I liked defending. In my mind, I was a good defender. I filled the little gaps in and whatever, but I was limited. You know the wing-backs today? I don't think I'd be able to do that properly, you know because I wouldn't be good enough when I got round their box. Round their box I wasn't very good. I was good at getting it and giving it to players who could do it.

Mick Hopkinson: I think a lot of Second and First Division clubs were like that, attacking, with wingers. The emphasis was more on forward play, wasn't it? The midfield players were more conscious of going forward than defending. The worst player for that, that I ever played with, was Barry Hutchinson. Barry would never come back in his own half, if he could help it.

Peter Gadsby: My brother Michael, who is a little bit older than me, played for Notts County, then he played for Hartlepool and York City. He was always the goalkeeper and I went with him. My recollections were being put down at the front behind the goal and one of the early people I used to relate to – and also being a goalscorer, which I wanted to be – was Bill Curry. I had this affection for Bill Curry. Barrel-chested – I can still see him – charging through the mud and knocking them in. I always wanted to be Bill Curry. Michael was the goalkeeper and he wanted to be Reg Matthews. He was hard, Reg Matthews. You could see that when he played. Bony.

Michael Dunford: Well, the first players I can really remember were Bill Curry and Reg Matthews, England goalkeeper. Super player, Reg. I mean, brave, daft. Too daft really. So brave it was untrue. I can remember a game against Preston and Alex Dawson, who was a bit of a bulldozer himself, was playing for them. Reg would come out, one hand for the ball and one hand for the oncoming centre-forward, and both clattered into each other. He came to Derby with a superb reputation at Coventry and Chelsea and was an England international. We didn't see too many internationals in those days.

Willie Carlin: I'd played at the Baseball Ground and been chased off the pitch by Matthews because it was the first time ever I went to the corner flag and kept the ball in the corner and we finished up winning 1-0 on a Wednesday night. Reg came over and said: "If I'd have got you, I'd have kicked you over the stand." I said: "Reg. There's the money, in the back pocket. There's the bonus." He chased me off the pitch.

Gordon Guthrie: He was a fantastic 'keeper. Athletic. He was one of the worst, really, for being nervous. Yet when he got out on the pitch, he never showed he was nervous, did he?

Ray Young: Reg Matthews? I mean, Reg always used to have a cigarette before the game. Most goalkeepers smoked. Nerves I suppose. Ray Middleton did, Ray chain-smoked I think. Colin Boulton smoked. I don't know about Adlington. I know the Ox [*Ken Oxford*] did. We used to say: "He always had a fall of soot through the year."

Graham Sellors: I don't remember a lot of finesse about Glyn Davies and Frank Upton. He was like a tank, wasn't he, Upton?

Peter Gadsby: I always recall Gordon Hughes. He used to go down the right side – if you'd opened the doors he'd have run out – and he used to put those crosses in and Bill Curry used to love that. There was an Ashbourne lad playing as well, on the fringes, a lad called Mick Williamson. A left winger and Ashbourne didn't often get players at Derby and it was always the sort of thing you looked out for. Those were my early days watching Derby County.

Football – and cricket?

Ian Buxton: No, I don't think it's possible any more. When we did it, we finished cricket at the end of August or first week in September, and football didn't start until end of August anyway. Also, the Cup Final was always the last week in April, to start with. Then it became the first week in May and the League had finished the week before the Final. The first thing that happened was that football invented the League Cup, which extended the season a bit, and cricket got the Sunday League, which extended the cricket season to fit it in. So both seasons overlapped more than they did when we played both.

Ian Buxton: It was the structure which changed, not the ability to do both or the fitness. I think they would say now that you couldn't do both because you wouldn't have sufficient rest periods. That's what I keep hearing about cricket now – you've got to have quality rest periods, rather than practice periods. Hmmm. No, I think people would have the ability, but the changeover periods are always difficult and you'd be missing most of the pre-season and so you'd be struggling in games to start with, but two games a week is the best pre-season you can have and within a fortnight you'd be all right, I think.

Ian Buxton: I've played cricket in a match finishing on a Friday, and Second Division football, as it was then, at Crystal Palace on the Saturday. I may have done a couple of days' pre-season or something before. I got away with it as well, but I don't think you could do that today, but on the other hand the cricket season goes on too long. People like Ted Hemsley and Chris Balderstone, who played on after us, didn't do the two sports equally. They were both footballers, who played cricket for Worcestershire or Leicestershire, when they were available. Many people played second-team cricket. Alan Durban, for example. If he'd had the chance to play both equally, he might have been a county cricketer, I don't know, but he was a footballer who was available to play cricket for two months in the summer. Difficult.

Under Tim Ward

Alan Durban: The funny thing is, you'd have thought we wanted defenders the goals that we'd let in, but Tim went and bought Kevin. Tim was a creative player himself and he wanted a nice 'slide-rule pass' team, wanted goalscorers, and if you look, we bought very few defenders. He kept buying creative players, rather than others.

Alan Durban: How did I come to Derby? Cardiff put everybody on the transfer list. They needed £30,000 in a hurry, to buy John Charles back from Roma. He'd gone from Juventus to Roma and they put everybody on the transfer list, except a 34-year-old, Ivor Allchurch. Three 21-year-olds got sold. I'd an opportunity to go to Hull, who were then owned by the Hoveringham Gravel Company. The chairman was Harold Needler. He'd put some money in there. They were a reasonable side, a Second Division side then, but I didn't really fancy it. It wasn't a club with a lot of tradition and I wasn't desperate to leave Cardiff because I'd got about 90 appearances in, in about four years, which wasn't bad considering I didn't do an apprenticeship. I'd come straight in from grammar school, you see. So I went to Derby where Tim Ward was manager and once you got into that Baseball Ground... It's got a tradition that even Cardiff didn't have and, although I'd played 90 games at Cardiff, no one ever stopped me to talk about football there because the place was so rugby orientated.

Alan Durban: We're talking about 18 years or so after after the 1946 Cup Final, but I felt that there was goodwill still around Derby County, even then. It had been the peak spectator period in the late Forties and the fact that we'd won the FA Cup straight after the war meant that the goodwill had stayed within Derby County, even though we'd sometimes see attendances down to 9,000-10,000. I did feel there was a lot of goodwill and if I'm really truthful, I've always thought that Derby is a very, very closely-knit town. It's very compact and most of it still had a fair amount of goodwill towards their football club.

Ron Webster: I thought he was good, Tim Ward. He did quite well. A lot of young players came through. Hoppy, me, Saxton, John Richardson, Phil Waller, Peter Daniel, whatever. And he signed Kevin, didn't he? That gave the club a lift, when he signed Kevin.

Alan Durban: The big thing for me, of course, was the signing of Eddie Thomas because, all of a sudden, we played either side of Ian Buxton, and Ian could get hold of it. Very similar to John O'Hare in terms of being terrific with his back to goal. I mean, I had two years where I scored over 20 goals which for someone with no pace, well. If we could have defended, we might have won something. Jack Parry was an attacker as well. I enjoyed it. It was all new for me and it was fresh, although the pitch got to be a bit of a problem from Christmas onwards. I wasn't the strongest runner and physically wasn't that strong, but goalscoring. If you have half a dozen bad games, but knock two or three goals in during that time, people don't think of leaving you out of the side, do they?

Ernie Hallam: He was frustrated for such a long while trying to sign Kevin Hector, wasn't he? While the fee went up from £15,000 to about £40,000 odd. Always wanted him from the day he saw him. I've heard him talk about it. He got Eddie Thomas on the cheap. Durban. He got plenty of good players in.

Alan Durban: I liked him. I took an instant liking to him and he'd obviously remembered my debut about three years earlier, at the Baseball Ground. That was my first match for Cardiff and we'd beaten Derby 2-1. I did okay, for a debut. He'd obviously remembered that and that's where it came from.

Ian Buxton: I remember a match at Birmingham under Tim Ward and we actually drew 5-5! Fancy playing away from home and drawing five-each. I can't tell you what was said to the defence afterwards, by the forwards. Like all matches like that, you get in the dressing-room and...! We should have been euphoric because we were 5-3 down with five minutes to play and ended up five-each, but you go in and sit down and suddenly somebody says: "What the @$!?--- hell were you doing, you defence?" You know, what happens next, everyone's at it, but it's a strange game isn't it, five-each?

Kevin Hector: I thought they were a decent side. There were a lot of young players coming though. Tim Ward did well like that, with the younger players. Bad results went against him, though, and I didn't know anything about the politics of it. Perhaps he should have had another year because things were just beginning to take shape really.

Alan Durban: I thought Tim was a good judge of a player and was a fairly decent judge of who would fit into a team. Of the £10,000 signings, there weren't many bad ones! We got our money's worth out of Bobby Ferguson, who came about the same time as me. Eddie Thomas was a terrific buy for less than £10,000. Gordon Hughes did a good job. I can't remember us buying a lot who failed really. Most of the lads were actually there when I got there – Phil Waller, Hoppy, Richo, Ronnie Webster, Bobby Saxton. Bob Stephenson didn't stay very long He played cricket for Derbyshire and then went down to Hampshire. We had some fairly decent youngsters as well.

Ian Buxton: Didn't we lose 5-4 in the League Cup at Chester? It was one of Eddie Thomas's first games. Every time they scored, the ball kept coming back and Eddie kept muttering: "What's this? Is this normal?" To lose 5-4 to a team from a lower division as well – he didn't know what was happening.

Gordon Hughes: Tim signed Kevin Hector. Tim signed Eddie Thomas. Eddie scored about 20 goals in about 24 games when he first came. I think Tim hadn't the finance. Certainly he didn't have the money that Cloughie had.

Ian Buxton: Good finisher. He was very calm in front of goal, Eddie. He had a good record at Derby.

Alan Durban: My wife and Tim's wife got on reasonably well. We had mutual friends in Bill Whitehall, the garage owner, and quite often, we would go out with them socially. That's unheard of now, isn't it? I never thought anything of it at the time and Tim dropped me like everybody else. I got dropped. I'm not saying regularly, but I got left out of the side. Tim advised me where to go and get a car. I got my signing-on fee and I got friendly with Bill and, of course, Bill was a friend, so he used to invite us and we had a lot in common with him, like a great interest in cricket.

Michael Dunford: No, I don't think he did have a fair deal. I know Sammy Crooks was instrumental in Kevin coming as well, but I don't think Tim got much credit for an awful lot of things that he did. I mean Tim, in fairness, brought in people like Colin Boulton, who was a police cadet in Cheltenham and, again, those people – that type of player – gave the club good service. Bobby Saxton, your Phil Wallers and people like that. I think he brought Frank Upton back from Chelsea. And, of course, he signed Eddie Thomas, Alan Durban – and, as we've just said, Kevin Hector...

Kevin Hector

WHEN asked about winning golf 'majors', the great golfers look back at shots in particular rounds that were crucially important moments in winning a tournament, which may have shaped their lives and destinies. Football clubs, too, have defining moments in their histories. Some of those moments can be argued about, but most supporters would agree that the signing of Kevin Hector was such a moment in the story of Derby County.

Ernie Hallam: The crowd loved him, didn't they love him? He scored goals and they always love a goalscorer. He made an impact almost immediately and it all stemmed from being able to score goals. It was a natural part of his play, you know; ride tackles and get his shot in. They used to talk about these big, burly centre-forwards you've got to have in attack, but Kevin wasn't big and burly. He was faster than people realised, but his balance, well. He seemed to ride the tackles. They never seemed to hit him.

Alan Durban: In his first game, I got three goals – and didn't get a mention! £40,000? I don't think we'd paid more than £12,000 for anybody up until then. There was also that television programme at the time, called *United*. Zak somebody was in it, the star player. Kevin soon picked up that nickname.

Gordon Hughes: Yes, Zak the King. I thought Kevin was a great lad, a nice lad, a quite lad. Not a prima donna, which I seem to feel there are more and more of in the game now. He was a good, good striker, Kevin Hector. He had the speed, he nearly always hit the target and he could take men on in the last third of the pitch. In today's game, I'm crying out for our midfield players to go into the space and go past people or even wingers to take men on and get to the byline, but it seems to me that doesn't happen. But Kevin, I mean, his record proves it. His goalscoring for Derby was phenomenal.

Mick Hopkinson: He always blamed me for calling him that, for starting the name off. But there was a programme on television at the time called *United*. It was about a star player, Zak Bishop, arriving and it just fell in at the same time that Kevin come to Derby. I walked in one morning and said: "How you going on Zak?" He'd never heard it before. I don't think Kevin bothered much with television, but Zak was the figurehead for *United*, this programme on television. It happened just the same at Derby.

Bill Brownson: Tim Ward signed him and shortly afterwards, Tim was gone. Cloughie came and he had something of the basis of a promotion team with Kevin Hector.

Mick Hopkinson: What did he come for, £40,000, was it? I mean, I think Tim had to mortgage the club for that, didn't he? That, for me, was the starting point. If you can think of a starting point, that was it because all of a sudden Derby were spending big money and getting value for money. No club will ever get the same value for money in a player as Derby did with Kevin. I don't think him and John O'Hare hardly missed a game for about four seasons. You know, you hear talk about hard players, but these players were playing with injuries. They weren't fit all the time.

Kevin Hector

Brian Clough: You know who signed Kevin Hector? Sam Longson. I think Tim Ward actually signed him when they eventually got him, but Sam Longson set it up. It was a good signing – until I dropped him! Charming young man and a good player. Pace, ability to put the ball in the net, occasionally. Do you know that's the hardest thing in football? I watched two matches last night and they were missing them all over the bloody place. They couldn't even hit the target. Somebody once criticised me – and rightly so – by saying: "He only gets his goals inside, five, six seven, eight, nine yards. That's where he scores them." That's where you get them. In there. When I played in my testimonial, at Sunderland, my first touch was about four yards out and I tucked it past the goalkeeper. I heard the crowd go... oooooohhhh. There was 32,000 there. You get the goals, in the box.

Roy McFarland: We had people who could deliver the ball and we had people who could put the ball on the spot, but you still need to be there to put it in. The hardest shot in football, the hardest pass in football, is putting the ball in the back of the net, no matter what anybody says. Cloughie always said that – and would still say that – and Hector was always there to put the ball in the back of the net. In the 1972 team I scored quite a few goals; Alan Durban could score goals, Alan Hinton could score goals. We'd get the odd goal from midfield, maybe not, and although John O'Hare was not prolific, he'd come in with just enough to keep us going, but the one who really stuck the ball in the back of the net was Kevin.

Alan Durban: I don't know whether Sam was chairman or Sydney Bradley was still chairman, but that was the first significant move which had an impact on what happened in the next seven or eight years.

Gordon Hughes: He was the first big signing there and what a signing he proved to be, didn't he? They'd been slumbering, like, a long while, Derby, and he was the first signing that was going to take the club up. Tim signed Kevin Hector, of course.

Kevin Hector: Well, I'd been at Bradford for three and a half, four years or so and there'd been talk of transfers and that, but I think the money Bradford wanted put people off. £35,000, £40,000. Malcolm Allison had rung me up a couple of times and said he wanted me to go there, to Manchester City, so I knew they were interested, but then that fell through. I think they signed Colin Bell, from Bury. I thought there was a good chance of going to Manchester City and I was thinking of that, although Bradford Park Avenue was a good club with a decent ground then. Good playing surface and the dressing-rooms in that cottage in the corner.

Roy McFarland: He was tremendous and people would look back and say: "Yes, but there was a lot of question marks against Kevin Hector." But when you look at the videos and think back – and I do think back, often – I say: "What a great and prolific goalscorer he was." Kevin virtually never got injured as such and what he did have was the great skill of riding tackles. When people did hit him, he could ride them. This was Bestie's gift, George Best. You can speak about all sorts and we talk about the hard men in football, let's say Tommy Smith and whoever, who could hit you, but Best had the ability of riding them. Kevin not so much, but Kevin had that similar balance that when people hit him – and people knocked him at times – he didn't go down, kept his balance. Great balance, great balance on his left foot, on his right foot. It's unfair to try to describe Kevin as being a George Best. He wasn't, but Kevin had great balance and the best thing was that when he got there, he always poked it, put it past the goalkeeper. His record at that time was second to none. A great goalscorer.

Ron Webster: He always looked a good player, didn't he? For me he did. He was like a Rolls-Royce is to a normal car. He just seemed to have that a bit extra, Kevin. I thought over ten years: "What a player." He was magic. To think he only got a couple of caps... at that time there was nobody playing better than him for ten years. I mean, with the goals he got and all that. He always used to show defenders the ball and nip them by. He never got injured, did he? If you look through his career, there weren't many injuries. He used to ride the tackles. I thought he should have had a lot more caps.

Alan Durban: I always thought Kevin was an unglamorous player, but so effective. You need to do your apprenticeship in games. Kevin had done that at Bradford.

Ernie Hallam: Well he was that natural, that he was better than anyone realised, I think. Kevin was such a natural. Nobody ever knocked him about. He wasn't big or heavy, but he'd drive, he'd such a centre of balance he could ride tackles. It all looked easy to him. You never saw him do anything really spectacular. He was a natural. An ordinary lad in his attitude. In fact, he was good for the team at the time because we had a few personalities, but Kevin did his job and he'd go out and have a drink and all that sort of thing, but he had his own quite little manner with him.

Kevin Hector: Derby was a big club for me. I think the supporters were expecting a big type of centre-forward and when I turned up, they must have wondered what was happening. Derby were quite a big side, with some tall players and having scored 44 goals the season before, I think people expected a big, battering-ram type of centre-forward. I always knew I could score goals and the supporters were brilliant.

Steve Powell: Another great player. Great goalscorer, but also a very, very good dribbler. Always very sharp, always kept himself in good condition. Even now, when you see him now, apart from a few grey hairs, he doesn't look much different to what he did 20 years ago. Tremendous balance. Tremendous balance.

Kevin Hector: Sam Longson asked me if I had a girlfriend. They wondered if I was a kind of 'Jack the Lad'. I said: "Yes, I have a girlfriend and we're getting married in October." I don't know why we got married in October. I think it might have been because it was better for tax purposes. A lot clubs made players get married out of the football season. I can't remember if it was in the contract, but there was an agreement that I should miss a match, to get married. I missed the Rotherham match in October. It was the best thing I ever did.

Brian Clough: I tried to sign Ken Wagstaff. No, not to swap Hector. Hull City wouldn't sell, though.

Roy McFarland: The stories that were rife at the time and maybe still talked about now, were that Brian and Peter were always trying to replace Kevin. Always trying to get a better goalscorer. Well, they tried to replace him, but at the finish, they couldn't and that's a credit to Kevin and a credit, in a sense, to his record. I mean, nobody really came up trumps to fill his boots. Kevin wasn't, maybe, the most demonstrative person. He was quite quiet and reserved, until you got him in a corner and maybe got a few drinks down him. Then he'd open up a little bit, but his humour was very dry. He didn't say much overall, though.

Kevin Hector: I used to prefer defenders to come tight, then I could turn past them easier. Peter Storey at Arsenal was a difficult player to play against. He wasn't a household name, but he was difficult. Norman Hunter, of course, and Phil Beal of Tottenham, again, not a big name but he marked tight.

Roy McFarland: Like I say, when I was a kid, I was loud, I was noisy and I'd say things and speak my mind. The majority of the players did. Like when you're in the dressing-room with Mackay, who everybody idolised and who was a legend; and Willie Carlin, who would never keep his trap shut and would say what he felt; with Alan Hinton, Alan always said his piece; Alan Durban was very diplomatic. There were, maybe, quite a few generals in our team, with opinions and who knew a lot about football. I would like to think that I learned very quickly about the game and with their help as well, but I thought: "I'm not going to sit back and just listen to what they say, I'm always going to put in my two penn'orth." Kevin never did. Kevin was always reserved and didn't say much and when you turned round to Kevin and said: "What do you think, Kev?" He'd say: "Well, I'm not particularly bothered, actually. As long as I can get a pint on a Saturday night, I'm quite happy." And that was Kevin's attitude.

Jim Fearn: My favourite player was always Kevin Hector. I don't see any reason to change that. Having spoken to him a few times – and Kevin's very reticent about coming, as you know – he doesn't quite live up to what I expected him to be. You expect somebody who's that incredibly confident on a football pitch to be the same sort of person off it. Kevin isn't. That's not taking away anything that he is at all. In fact, he's probably happier keeping his head down, but I used to love watching him play. I used to love watching him come out to the wings and find some green patches at the Baseball Ground and I remember one particular night match when he skinned the United right-back – I think it was Jimmy Nichol – just for fun almost. He kept showing him the ball and kept going past. We always think of Kevin down the middle, but he could do almost anything with his balance and everything else.

Michael Dunford: Kevin had silky skills. I mean, he would get the ball on the halfway line and he'd attack people. He'd run at people and I think the season before he joined us in September 1966, he'd scored, 44 goals for Bradford, I think. He was playing along with Bobby Ham and Jim Fryatt in those days, at Bradford.

Alan Durban: The other important thing was that he could perform outstandingly on any going. When he was running on heavy grounds, his feet were that quick, they only touched the surface. He never looked heavy. When Archie, who was exactly the same, came they could run over the top of it. It didn't matter how heavy it was. We're talking about us others being six inches down, while those two ran on the top.

Willie Carlin: Kevin was great to play with. Wonderful balance, wonderful speed, eye for a goal. I just wished – and I mean this sincerely – I wished he'd had more aggression. If he'd had aggression, he'd have been an England international many times. He was – how can I say? – so quiet, so unassuming. Put it this way, if he'd had my character, he'd have been a hell of a player. This is what McFarland had, McFarland had aggression, but Kevin let his game do his talking and that was it. He was a hell of a nice lad, but hard to communicate with, very hard.

Michael Dunford: Derby paid £38,000, which was a tremendous amount of money, just after the time when the board had been criticised for a lack of ambition. I think there were two critical points whilst I was at Derby. One was the appointment of Brian Clough, but before that, when Kevin was with us. I did think then, that it signalled that Derby County had some form of ambition, which previously hadn't been there.

Ernie Hallam: Funny thing he didn't lose much through injury. I can never remember him having a serious one. Of course, he must have played with injury. I mean, any pro's got to be a bit harder than you think, but you'd hardly think he'd been a pro, really. He never lost time through injury and, as you say, you don't play up front without getting a few knocks, do you?

Gordon Hughes: He was like all strikers, he was selfish. There was nobody more selfish than Brian Clough, though. I remember him saying to me: "When I was in the box and I could get the ball, I'd push anybody out of the way to score. It was my job to score." I think all good strikers have to have that. Kevin wasn't as selfish as Clough, but if the ball was there to be put in the net, he'd run in front of you to get it. That's how it should be because he always hit the target. The likes of us weren't so good in front of goal. That's their job. Our job was to make the goals, but Kevin was selfish in the way he should be and all strikers should be like that.

Alan Durban: Kevin was one of the first centre-forwards or strikers, who I'd played with, that was very happy to be wide. It's a thing everybody tells strikers now: "Just fan off. Just drop off him. Get wide." If you look, he was one of the very first who often found himself in that outside-right position and on the Baseball Ground, you didn't have to have particularly good control at that time because it was so heavy. Once he started running with it, Cloughie saw this straightaway and thought "I must get somebody on the other side, just balance it up." In a way we almost played with a left winger and a sort of right winger. Kevin very rarely found himself on the left- hand side. If you look at his goals, very few came on the left-hand side.

Michael Dunford: From my point of view, Kevin was the first 'hero' that Derby County had. That never changed, even when I went to work for the club. The prospect of being in the same room as Kevin Hector, Roy McFarland and Dave Mackay was a tremendous feeling for me.

Mick Hopkinson: He liked a pint, but he was a terrific athlete. A fit lad. Looked after himself. He's 55, 56 now, still playing. He's kept it going. He was the start of everything at Derby, for me. No one had ever heard of Kevin Hector before. He was always going to get a few goals, obviously. He'd got goals at Bradford, but he'd got a lot more to it than just scoring goals. He'd score 20 to 25 goals a season and he'd make 25 a season too. That was his ability. All of a sudden people were seeing a young kid ghosting past players and they responded. The emphasis, in my opinion, at that time when Zak first came, was more for attacking. That's why the team got 80 goals for and 80 against, but he didn't look out of place then as a young kid – and he didn't look out of place with the Mackays and McFarlands.

Stuart Webb: Liked him. Thought he was good. I didn't think he got the recognition he should have done. He was a great club player. I didn't think he got the international recognition, but he was a class act wasn't he? Just stuck the ball in the net. He kept himself fit and even when he was injured, he turned out and did the business. He and John O'Hare were a great partnership. To see him skipping through the middle there, just a little jink – and it was in the back of the net. A very class act. He was a great signing by Tim Ward.

Gordon Guthrie: He had a great career, Kevin. He trained hard and well. Most of them did. That's why they played so many matches.

Mick Hopkinson: The crowd took to him straight away. If you had a popularity poll of players, right from when I first started, Kevin Hector would be in the first three. As a club player – and he didn't get many international caps – there was no player better thought of, but it's still goalscorers isn't it? Lads who plod along at full-back or centre-half – unless you're a McFarland – they're taken for granted, aren't they? But someone who could stick the ball in the back of the net, well...

Kevin Hector: Best goal? Cardiff, away. Most of my goals were scored close in, but this one was way out. Nearly 40 yards and I caught it just right. I scored a hat-trick for Derby in that match. It was the second goal. I can't remember the other two. The Benfica goal was a good one. Many people thought I'd mis-hit it. Left foot. Great night.

Roy McFarland: The majority of good players in a football team are also usually the loudest in the dressing-room because they know who they are. It's like a pecking order most times when you go in a dressing-room. You know that as well as anybody, the better players are usually the loudest. They're the ones who shout their mouths off and dictate and say those things. Kevin was a good player, but never demonstrative and would never outwardly say things. Like I say, obviously we've had many good nights out together and yet even when you got Kevin a little bit tipsy, he wouldn't really say much, but when he said something, everybody listened because they knew it was important – and it was!

A Man Called Clough

BRIAN Clough joined Derby County on 15 May 1967. "I think we started Clough on £5,000 a year and he asked for £2,500 for Peter," said Sam Longson, chairman of Derby County, in *The Derby County Story*. Glory years followed. Rams supporters – and players – who were lucky enough to be around at the time experienced a thrilling roller-coaster football ride, which became etched in the memory. The compact Baseball Ground bulged at the seams; the highest attendance was a record 41,826 and in one season, 1969-70, the average gate was 35,000! Can you imagine it?

Derby County became big news, the old press box overflowed. Clough, the Pied Piper, played the tune as from the lower reaches of the old Second Division, Derby County rocketed to the Football League championship in 1972 and on into Europe. Tragically, by October 1973 the train had come off the rails. Clough and Taylor left. Suddenly.

In due course, after his achievements at Nottingham Forest, Clough became recognised as one of the great managers in English football. Interestingly, since those magical days with the Rams, Brian Clough has always lived in Derby.

Brian Flint: There seemed an enthusiasm, a buzz. Whether it was because I was at an impressionable age 13 or 14, 15 at the time, I don't know, but everything seemed so up key and expectations and confidence so high.

Gerald Mortimer: Exciting days indeed, but like all exciting days, at the time you don't quite appreciate them as much as you should. It was a first for all of us really. I mean, obviously, it was a first for Brian and Peter because they were not that long out of Hartlepool United, and it was a first for Derby County, which had always rather fancied itself as a big club, but had never quite cut the mustard, as you might say.

Tommy Powell: I met Cloughie before he ever came to Derby. Obviously, I played against him, but in Harry Storer's day, whenever we went to Middlesbrough and we went to the hotel, who should be waiting there but Brian, Peter Taylor and Lindy Delapenha. I think Cloughie doted on Harry. He thought the world of him. I think he learned a lot from Harry.

Phil Waller: I think he learned from Harry Storer. Certainly in terms of the way he operated. When we used play in the North-East, he always came if we stayed Friday nights or whatever. He always came to listen to Harry.

Stuart Webb: No, no. I hadn't met him before. I'd read about him because he'd come into the game and obviously made a big impression. Got Derby up and all the rest of it. I just thought very eccentric, extremely talented and yes, good to be around and I could see what he was doing. Motivating people and all of that and a successful manager. He was a charmer. If he wanted you, he'd charm you from the trees. It was a charm exercise but you could see how he was doing his job because he was highly successful. He was bringing in quality players and all the things that were happening were exciting. His media exposure; how he was playing the game; how he was doing it all was quite fascinating for me to see and I thought: "Blimey, this is the place to be."

John O'Hare: I always thought he'd be a successful guy, I really did. He'd done quite a good job at Hartlepool and he had that self-belief, whatever you call it. That arrogance, self-belief. He really thought he was going to be a good manager – and I did as well!

Phil Waller: I can remember where we were when they appointed him. We were at the airport, going on a close season tour to East Germany I think. Sam, no, Jack Bowers was in charge. It must have been Heathrow. I remember Sam saying he'd been appointed.

Ron Metcalfe: I was there nearly a year with Cloughie. We went on tour to Germany and Sam Longson announced it on tour, that Cloughie was coming.

Michael Dunford: He was a strange man in as much that he was very unpredictable. He would be very strict on discipline with the players and, indeed, the staff, but he had a kind streak in him as well.

Gordon Hughes: Me, being up the North-East, heard plenty of rumours. I think I'm right in saying that Clough came down, probably about a fortnight before he eventually did take over at Derby. He didn't exactly interview people, but he talked to a lot of the staff. Not as a prospective manager, just as an interested party. Then, you know what he did? He sacked nearly everybody, apart from Gordon Guthrie. Everybody. Ralph Hann, the physiotherapist – if he said anything I don't know – but Ralph went immediately and the whole staff went, apart from Gordon.

Kevin Hector: I remember him coming. Everyone was sitting around in the home dressing-room, for what seemed like forever. Then the door opened and in he came. I'll always remember the first thing he said. He said: "Are you still playing Reg?" That was the first thing he said, to Reg Matthews: "You still playing Reg?" And we were all frightened to death.

Ron Webster: We didn't know what to expect. We were all in the first-team dressing-room and he just came in, him and Peter Taylor. He seemed to lift everybody, the first day. He didn't say anything individually to me, but you just sat up. It's hard to explain. We didn't do very well, first season. I think we finished third or fourth, from bottom. You had that feeling, though, that something was going to happen. Something different to what had been there.

Ron Metcalfe: When we got back from Germany, we all went to a meeting with Cloughie. He came into the dressing-room and introduced himself. He made a big fuss of Reg Matthews. He obviously knew him from way back and I remember the words he said: "It's been a long season. Go away and have a good holiday. See you in July."

Brian Clough: I bowled in like a bull at a gate. In those days, chairmen and vice-chairmen sat back and didn't do that much. They'd put nothing in. Sam Longson used to brag that he'd got nine shares – at a pound each! He used to brag about it. He used to tell everybody. Then I went to work for him, but I took the bull by the horns, to run the club the way I wanted it run.

Ron Webster: I think I was 24 or something like that, when he came. Nobody knew him, no.

I can remember one of the first things he said was: "If you don't want to get into the First Division, we don't need you." I thought: "Eh, up!" It was something new and I thought it was great. It lifted me a bit. "If you're good enough, we're up there," he said.

Alan Durban: None of us met him until pre-season training. We came in and he kept us waiting, as usual.

Phil Waller: He made us all wait. He saw us each individually. He sent a telegram while we were out in Germany saying such and such. We all sat in the dressing-room. He was late coming, as he always was. We got there for nine or whatever it was. He got there for 11. He piled in two hours late. He'd only set off from Middlesbrough when we were in the dressing-room. He gave us the bit that he'd never seen us play and he wanted to see us on an individual basis.

Ian Buxton: Cloughie came at the end of a season. I'd been retained, but I was playing cricket, so always I'd negotiated with the manager to do what pre-season training I could. If there was no cricket, I trained, but under Cloughie the first thing that happened was I got a letter saying 'Pre-season. Report so and so'. So I filed that away, sort of thing. We were playing at Worcester on the first day that pre-season training took place and we were fielding. I came off at lunch time and the Worcestershire secretary told me there was a message for me: "Would you phone Brian Clough, please?"

Kevin Hector: He interviewed a lot of players separately. I went into the office and he said to me: "I've been trying for three years to get you to Hartlepool. I'm glad you're here. Now get out." I was very pleased.

Ian Buxton: So I phoned Brian Clough and he said: "What the **** are you doing? Where are you?" I said: "You know very well where I am. I'm at Worcester." He said: "What are you doing there?" I said: "Come off it. I'm playing cricket, as you well know. I was offered a contract by Derby County, knowing that I was also a cricketer." That was my side of it, but Cloughie said that from the day they reported back for training, I was a footballer. So, obviously, we agreed to differ. I was 29, so I had two or three years at football left, but much longer at cricket, if I wanted to. I agreed to meet him at the ground the following Wednesday.

Ron Metcalfe: I knew him before because I was an amateur at Sunderland. I signed for Sunderland when I was 15 or so and he was youth team coach, so I was aware of him. I got my release from Sunderland and Derby signed me pro. Alan Brown was Sunderland manager and they tried to get me to stay, so I had experience of Cloughie then. He was just very brash. No, he didn't remember me.

Alan Durban: I think he saw everybody together and if I remember rightly, he told us to come back in the afternoon. By then, he had split the staff a little bit. I think most of the senior pros and potential first-team players came back, as a squad in the afternoon, when he had another chat with us.

Ron Metcalfe: I can remember coming back and Cloughie split the dressing-rooms for training. It had never happened before. He had the reserves and the apprentices in the away dressing-rooms and I can remember coming back and being disappointed that I was in the away dressing-room. I obviously didn't fit into his plans.

Phil Waller: He said he'd give me a chance, although he said: "I've never seen you play." We were in dispute over two quid, I think. I think we played at Buxton in a testimonial game after the end of the season and Sam had agreed to give us an extra two quid. Cloughie said he wanted to see everybody, individually. I think he started about eleven o'clock and finished about eleven at night. It was one of those jobs. I think I went in about four o'clock. He gave it the 'never seen you play' bit and 'give it three months to see the salary situation'. I think, obviously, he had seen us play, really.

Ian Buxton: So I went down there, to the ground. No sign of Cloughie. We were playing at Derby on that Wednesday, so I'd arranged to meet him at nine o'clock. Cloughie wasn't there. So I waited as long as possible and then I had to get to the County Ground, so I missed him. We didn't get off to an auspicious start and Clough, in the end, gave me an ultimatum that I gave up cricket, otherwise he'd sign somebody else and I was not guaranteed ever to play in his first team again. So I said: "Well, I'm sorry. The club offered me a contract knowing that I was a cricketer and I can't accept that. I'm a cricketer as well." We agreed to differ and, in fact, we did quite well that year and I stayed with cricket perhaps a week longer than normal. Had one or two phone calls from the football club and I said: "Well, if we lose this match I'll be back at training next Wednesday." He said: "The next thing you'll be telling me is that if you haven't had cornflakes for breakfast, you won't be coming in training."

John O'Hare: When I signed I remember him saying: "We'll pass Sunderland. They'll be on the way down and we'll be on the way up." I don't think it happened exactly like that, but when we did go up, they went down the following year. I think we played them one season in the First Division. He wasn't very far out in his prophecy.

Ian Buxton: Anyway, on the August Bank Holiday Monday night I was in the first team at Rotherham – after he'd said I'd never play in his first team again. We won 3-1 and I scored. Looking back, that was quite clever because to sell me he had probably to say I was a valuable member of his first-team squad, so he got £10,000 for me whereas, in those days, I was only going to be playing football for two more years at most. I was worth £2,000 probably – and he got ten! I got on with him really. He was as straight with as you could expect a manager to be. Straighter than most managers, in those circumstances. I've a lot of time for Cloughie.

Tommy Powell: You've got to hand it to him. He signed some class players at reasonable prices. When you come to think how he signed Dave Mackay, Colin Todd, Roy McFarland, David Nish, Alan Hinton, John O'Hare...well!

Dave Mackay: I met him sitting on the corner of the park, at White Hart Lane. All the rest of the team were training down at Cheshunt, which is the training ground, so there's only Brian and myself, right in the corner of the park, sat down there. We had a half-hour chat and he convinced me, as he convinces most people, as you know. Well, he said, I'd play at the back and I thought: "Well it's easy to play at the back. It's an easy game there." If you want to be a footballer, be a sweeper.

Colin Lawrence: I first met him in Ferrers Way, where he lived. I knew a lot about him because a pal of mine, Gordon Turner, used to play for Luton when they were in the First Division. In fact he used to come round to our club when he had just got into the sports outfitting business, selling us kit. We got to know each other quite well. We used to talk about Brian because Gordon played for the Football League and the FA and he came back once and said: "I've been up to Newcastle – just outside – and I met Brian Clough; we all met in the hotel after training. We got the cards out and the waiter came in and wanted to clear the table. Brian said: 'You're not clearing that table, young man, not while we're playing cards.' I just couldn't believe it because he'd only be a young lad. He'd be about 22, 23, and coming from him! Alan A'Court from Liverpool was there and a few others, more experienced."

Kevin Hector: He knew from his days at Hartlepool what he wanted. He had a lot of contacts and he knew who he wanted. McFarland at Tranmere, me when I was at Bradford, Gemmill at Preston, McGovern at Hartlepool, O'Hare at Sunderland. He knew from his days at Hartlepool, all those players.

Colin Lawrence: I came to live up here in 1961. Gordon Turner was godfather to my youngest lad and, consequently, he used to come up at a weekend or if they were playing a match up here at Sheffield, for instance. I lived then in Bardon Drive, just round the corner from Brian. I used to see him then when he first came into Ferrers Way and he used to be up in the morning. I'd be just going off and there would be Brian, in the front, in the kitchen, having a wash. Typical. He'd wave, I'd wave and then we began to see each other casually.

Phil Waller: Generally, it was a bit of a fear scenario. I mean, there weren't many senior players there. There were some one-club players who were very inexperienced in terms of the world. He'd got Hughesie, Eddie, but he got the real senior players out of the club within a couple of months. They were just unloaded after that pre-season tour. He got them unloaded within two months.

John O'Hare: He always said he'd bring players in. Two or three days after I signed, he signed Roy McFarland. It didn't take him long. Alan Hinton came not long after that. Players came and players went.

Gordon Guthrie: They had character. As Mr Storer used to say: "If you've no character, you'll never make a player." I think that is what Brian and Peter looked for in players, before they ever signed them. When you go through the people they did sign, they all had it. I always quote John McGovern. I mean, he came from Hartlepool – and I hope he won't mind me saying it – but he looked like Bambi on strings, didn't he, the way he used to run and everything? Once he got in the team, though, he did the simple thing. He could get the ball and pass it and I've heard Brian say to him: "That's all I want you to do. Pass it to a white shirt." He had a great engine, John. He could go for 190 minutes and never tire, but he just did what he was good at.

Stuart Webb: Who was the first signing I was concerned with? Archie Gemmill, I think, at Preston. Because I was there, I obviously knew what was going on and Everton were also after Archie Gemmill. I said to Peter Taylor: "You want to look at Archie Gemmill, good little player." "Yeah," he said. "We've looked at him. We're not so bothered, really." That was how he put it: "We'll keep an eye on him." So I went home that next weekend and somebody at the club said that Everton were signing him the next Monday. So when I got back, I told Peter and Brian. The mood changed a bit because Everton were in. So they went to have a look and it was all happening. Then Brian and I went up and we signed him more or less overnight. Brian stayed at Archie's house in Lytham and that was it. That was a little help from myself in knowing what was happening at Deepdale.

Colin Lawrence: Gordon would come up, on a Sunday, and he'd say: "You know, I'd love to go round and see him." So I said: 'Well, why don't you?' He said: "No, Sunday's his day off. I want to give him a break." By that time it had been diagnosed that Gordon had got Motor Neurone Disease.

Stuart Webb: It wasn't really a smooth signing, not really because we went up and saw Alan Ball senior, who was the manager of Preston, and he had his son, young Alan, with him. We walked into this pub – in Bolton where they lived – and it was like: "What's happening?" Archie admired Alan Ball because he was the international and we thought: "There's something wrong here. They're trying to take him to Everton." Then, the next day, we went to Deepdale and I knew my way around the back corridors, obviously. We got Archie to sign and you need the third signature – which is the secretary of the selling club – and as we went out through one side, Alan Ball and Harry Catterick were coming round the other side. It was quite unbelievable how it happened. We got in the car park, waved and off we went. Archie was on his way.

Lionel Pickering: Brian was always on the television, wasn't he? "I won't have this player if he crawled up the motorway on his hands and knees," he'd say. He'd always got plenty to say. Big mouth or big head, he was a personality and he proved us all wrong. I mean, anybody who criticised him had egg on his face because he got them promotion from the Second Division and so on.

Colin Lawrence: I was going off to Bristol one morning and Brian was just coming back along Ferrers Way, having taken his two boys to school. He use to take his kids everywhere with him. I stopped, wound the window down. He'd just got his pale blue Rover 2000, he hadn't got his silver Mercedes then. I said: "I've just been talking about you, this weekend." He said: "What about?" I said: "Well, with a pal you used to play with, Gordon Turner." "Oh," he said. "Tell him if he doesn't come round to see me, I'll break his neck. I'll bloody well break his neck, if he don't come round and see me." Anyway, the next time Gordon came up, I sent him round. So he asked Gordon: "What's happened to your pal I saw on Ferrers Way?" So Gordon said: "Oh, he's at home." Brian said: "Tell him I'll break his neck if he doesn't come round next time." From there, it sort of developed.

Dave Mackay: We went to St Johnstone. That was our first game and we lost 1-0. Even going up on the coach and that, I'm looking at John Robson and I think: "Well, he's got to be a left winger." I didn't want to say: "Eh, where do you play, son?" So I just left it at that. I was trying to build in my own mind what the team would be, so when the team was picked, I'd know who everybody was.

Lionel Pickering: We used to put all the Clough jokes in the *Derby Trader's* 'Town Talk' column ...we used to put those in there and take the mickey out of him. I don't know, he just took offence. I know one of the times he banned me – one of the two times – one of the girls in our office said: "Guess whose been to see my parent's house at Littleover?" I said: "Oh, who's that then?" She said: "Cloughie." So I remember the intro was: 'Hold your breath Littleover, Cloughie's looking for a house in your area'. He saw that as private. That's his private life. It was innocent stuff, of course. He had been looking, actually, it was just a pure fluke about the house in Littleover. He didn't go there anyway, he went to Quarndon, but he was very sensitive and he was quick to ban people in those days. I think there was a bloke named Jarratt that got banned – from *The Mail* – as well. It's ridiculous really.

Colin Lawrence: He looked after Gordon Turner when Gordon came up. By that time Gordon couldn't move. Brian used to have the commissionaire at the Baseball Ground arrange for two chaps to help Gordon up into the directors' box. Brian had been at home, his mother had died and he came back – we were playing a Yugoslav team in the European Cup – and I thought to have all that, he'd lost his mother, he'd got the match, but he still had time to talk to Gordon and make sure his wants were cared for and I thought: "By, that's the measure of a man. That is the measure of the man."

Ron Webster: I think most of the signings turned out as good signings, near enough. There was one though, Arthur Stewart, from Ireland. They said he was a sweeper – I think it was – and he was in front of midfield and the forwards most of the time! A lot of them were good signings, though. Although, at the time they didn't look good signings, did they? When you first saw John, he didn't look anything did he? But I think John O'Hare was a magic player.

Alan Durban: No, no, I didn't take to Cloughie straightaway. No, he was a pain in the arse, a pain in the arse. Because he stopped us playing golf and things, all of a sudden. Peter Daniel was always going back to work on the farm; Webber was always going back farming; me and Saxo used to spend a bit of time in the betting shop and so on – we all had other interests. I think that the other interests, at times, overtook our jobs. At the time we didn't realise it, but then all of a sudden, he came in and very, very quickly changed our thinking, so that we were focussed completely on the job. If I remember rightly, we went on tour to Germany. I think that was his first move – to arrange this trip. I know there was certainly an argument among the players about our spending money. I think he told us there was no spending money. In the end, I think we went without spending money.

Colin Lawrence: We used to meet at Kedleston, the Broadway Hotel, Sunday mornings, chatting. David Cox came. And at the Midland Hotel for matches. Dave Mackay stayed there. I used to sit up at the Ossie End and we'd leave five or ten minutes before the end, to get back to the business, the papers. But Brian was always on the phone: "Come on. Where are we going, where are we going?" That was it. Michael Keeling was a good pal of his – he was on the board – and looked after his administration, but we used to circulate together. Michael had a heart of gold. We used to get on quite well.

Ernie Hallam: He was a king to me, Brian was. It was him who actually started me working for the club apart from the supporters' end. I used to take a big case, with all the souvenirs, on the trains. I used to run the Ramaways at that time and it was Brian who got me involved. In fact, he's made me squirm Brian has. When the train came back – sometimes they'd travel with us, you know – they always went in the Midland Hotel, with Bill Wainwright. Cloughie was very well in with Bill. He always went in there and the players and them were having a drink, and me and the guy who helped me, Steve, we used to pop in for a drink and Cloughie's shouting: "Come on in Ernie." I'd have my bloody case there and he'd shout: "This bloody lad does more for me than any of you buggers. Works harder than you." Made me cringe, but that was Cloughie wasn't it? He was a king to me, Brian was.

Graham Richards: The all-time best manager of my era, I think you'd argue that Busby was that. I'd have to agree on logic and history Busby was, but the man that I knew from my period – of people that I've met – Clough, without a doubt. Don't ask me the easy question: 'Why?' I'm not sure I'll ever come up with a satisfactory answer.

What was the secret?

Brian Clough: You've got to have a passion to run a football club. I've come in here – not this particular house – when I was broke and very brave. I've gone in there, house dark, Barbara with three children under three, and I've just flopped on the bed and gone to sleep because I was so tired. I'd been at work since half past eight and I'd done all my jobs at the Baseball Ground for example and then gone on to watch a match. They don't do it now.

Kevin Hector: He was confident about football. He knew what he wanted and he was able to get the best out of players. He could always get the best out of players and players stuck together with him, but there was a little bit of fear there as well, which isn't a bad thing with players.

Gordon Hughes: The question about Brian Clough – it must have been asked scores of times – is how did he get the success he had? And I've talked to players like John O'Hare, who played with him a long time, John McGovern, who he brought down from Hartlepools. They all seem to come to the conclusion that he ruled – not ruled – but he got the best out of players and it was, like, this fear thing. He got players who hadn't done so well at previous clubs, like Alan Hinton, John Robertson, the centre-half Kenny Burns. He seemed to mould them. This is your last chance, kind of thing.

Willie Carlin: What Brian Clough did was he bought players who could play and see things on the pitch.

Gordon Guthrie: He didn't expect them to do things they couldn't do. He had specialists like Alan Hinton. If he saw anybody else going to take a corner, he used to say, even in training: "Eh, leave that to Alan Hinton, the specialist who knows what he's doing. You do what you can do."

Steve Powell: I think the key was he got the best players he could and fitted them to the pattern that suited the players he'd got available. That was his success. I think he also got players in, who had a lot of pride in how they played and wanted to win at all costs really. That was another one of his successful ploys.

John Robson: Honesty.

Roy McFarland: It was almost like being back at school. I was very hot headed as a youngster. I'd fight the world, I'd scrap and kicked everybody and I realised that there were different ways to win a football match, and Mackay and Cloughie and Taylor, they taught me how to deal with people and taught me how to be with people because you cannot win football matches individually. You've got to win it as a team. It takes all sorts to get a group of players together and that was Cloughie's strength. He knew how to get the best out of people, but he knew how to blend them. He knew how to get them to mix together and how that group of players needs to be effective and that's how we were a successful team.

Gordon Guthrie: Another thing Brian used to emphasise: "If you can't pass, son, you can't play." When you think about it, it's simple, but it's right.

Steve Sutton: Someone asked me a question at a coaching course: "Write down the most influential person in your life and why." I wrote his name down, but I couldn't put down, in words, what it was about him. Was he a motivator? Certainly. Was he a tactician, was he this, was he that, was he the other? He was everything – but you never saw it as such. He never said: "Right, we're going to play 4-2-4 and that's how we're going to play." He would suggest something and really, at Forest in those days, we just got on with it. "Lads, go out and enjoy yourselves," he'd say. He would spit the dummy out occasionally – and quite rightly so when you look back – but what had he got and how did he do it? I don't know. A total enigma.

Gordon Hughes: Clough was the first manager, on a Friday night, that ever said to me: "Go and have a pint." Some players didn't want a pint, but you could go to the bar, have a pint and a chat after your meal on a Friday night for relaxation. Then off to bed.

Alan Durban: I don't know whether he started working straightaway at the spirit that evolved, but I think he sorted out straightaway who was with him and who was against. I found it very difficult to adjust because I liked my time planned, if I wanted to play a bit of golf or a bit of tennis, but I did quite a lot away from the ground. I didn't really waste my time. I used to get some eggs off Brian Daykin and I had a little egg round on a Thursday and Friday afternoon, but all of a sudden, he might say: "We're back this afternoon." It did mess us about something awful but all he was trying to do was to get us focussed, to see that the football was fairly important. With due respect to Tim, this type of management was entirely different.

You'll know from your playing days that we did exactly the same every day. Thursday mornings, we used to train half-an-hour extra because there was a board meeting and we were trying to impress upon the directors that we were working hard. Not with him.

Gordon Hughes: Do you know what? Obviously Brian Clough was probably one of the biggest names in football and his record is marvellous, but when Brian Clough came to Derby you know, I remember we used to go down to Colwick Woods in Nottingham pre-season training and Brian Clough wasn't the confident chap then. He was the one who got the likes of myself – who was what you can call a senior professional – and he used to say: "Do you think the training's all right Gordon? Are you enjoying the training? Do you think we're doing this right?" He was feeling his way all the time and I can remember those days. Initially, from Hartlepool, he hadn't so much experience you see and he was only a young chap through having to finish with his bad injury, but he felt his way and he did lean on the more senior pros. He sorted the wheat from the chaff and that was his gift. He did that, but he wasn't always the sort of know-all brash chap originally.

Alan Durban: We didn't have a particularly good first season. I remember one of the Easter games being asked to be skipper the side for some reason. Someone must have been injured. We had a lot of injuries at first and, had we not won at home, there was every chance we could have been relegated. So many people were coming and going. He actually brought quite a lot of people into the side that first year, one or two who made no impact whatsoever.

Ernie Hallam: He didn't suffer fools gladly. He didn't suffer intelligent people gladly at times, but he knew what he wanted and he'd supreme confidence in his own ability. It was a natural feeling I think, with him. He didn't have to adopt a stance. He was a natural.

Graham Richards: He won the European Cup twice, with a club that's not in a European 'league' at all. He got Derby to the semi-finals. He picked up two League championships and he made so many careers from bread and butter players, who went on to have a real part in the game's history and the medals to prove it. Yet when they came to Clough or Clough got hold of them first, they were non-events really and there were so many of them. That's the greatest thing you can say of a manager, that he 'made' careers. He got brilliant players who played for him brilliantly, but he made careers as well. His secret was that he seemed to have no secret! It was his strong personality; his unorthodox approach; his sense of timing; his force of personality; and he was a disciplinarian in the old fashioned sense. Do you remember him speaking to Trevor Francis on national television saying: "Take your hands out of your pockets,"? Somehow that's a management technique and, maybe, that's the quintessential part of his.

Brian Clough: I'm in contact with people. Working at a football club is not just working there, it's throughout the community. It's going to charity shows, doing presentations. It's being likable, abrasive, whatever.

Was it all calculated?

Brian Clough: No, no. That was just me. That was just me. Conceited, arrogant, er... generous. I'm still that now.

Bobby Saxton's handball

Brian Clough: Sacked him. He gave a penalty away. Handball. He could have headed it. He said: "I know you're going to sack me." I said: "Yeah, you're right." He handled it. He just went up, like that, bobbed it down. Ref? Pen. In the net. Whether we won or not, I don't know, but I was only interested in one thing. Winning. Wasn't interested in nothing else.

Colin Gibson: It was against Leeds in the League Cup semi-final. It would be a 7.30pm kick-off. Football matches kicked-off at proper times in those days, not 7.45pm I don't remember much about getting there or anything leading up to the game. I just remember the game and I clearly remember that handball by Bobby Saxton because it was at the Normanton End, where the boys' pen was.

Bobby Saxton: Once Cloughie came in the dressing-room before the game, that was it. No one was allowed in and no one was to knock on the door. Anyone knocking on the door, chairman, anybody, was likely to get blasted. This particular match, I was just bending down tying my bootlaces and a knock came on the door. We all looked at each other and waited for the explosion. The door opened slightly and this voice said: "I haven't got the tickets..." It was my dad! He was down for the match. I think it was the first time he'd been and he'd gone to the wrong window and that. I thought: "Christ. What's going to happen now?" Anyway, Cloughie went to the door, saw this chap there and went out into the corridor. I was shaking like a leaf, I can tell you. All the lads were smirking and grinning. Cloughie came back and I kept pretending to tie my boots with my head down. He came over and I thought: "This is it." He put his hand on my shoulder: "Don't worry," he said, "I've seen to the old man. I've fixed him up with a couple of tickets in the directors' box." Well, I felt ten feet tall. What a relief. I went out and was ready to kick anything that moved. Brilliant. That was Cloughie.

Chairmen and directors

Brian Clough: I didn't used to sit in the directors' box. I was never a directors' man. I got close to some chairmen. I got close to Stuart Dryden at Nottingham Forest, but I was never a chairman's man. I was my own man. It was miles apart, being a director and a chairman, to a manager. All I was interested in was winning things.

Board meetings

Stuart Webb: He came in when he wanted. He didn't come in many times. It was quite funny really. No, he just used to breeze in, when he wanted to, with his tracksuit on. He'd always have the position that the board were there and the shareholders were there, but really – he was the club. His players were the club. I remember one Annual General Meeting – the shareholders always go to those for the manager's talk. The business of the AGM goes away in five minutes, but then it's the manager and the questions. On this occasion there was a packed audience and the board were saying: "He's not coming, he's not coming." Panic! Sam Longson's saying: "I don't think he's coming." Anyway, he sent somebody – I think it was Mike Keeling – in with a tape recorder. When it was the manager's time to speak, it was played: "Gentlemen, I am down at Bisham Abbey with the most important people at this club. That's not the chairman, Mr Longson – and not you shareholders." That was how it was.

Tactics

Willie Carlin: He never said anything really. Its amazing, actually. If you go over the records of Derby County when we played, we never practised any dead-ball situations, but when you look at it, the free-kicks, the goals we scored from them and everything...

Steve Powell: Sometimes he didn't need to say an awful lot to get his point over. A a lot depended on the situation at the time. You know, whether we were playing well or badly, whether it was half-time, full-time, but he didn't waste any words. He got straight to the point and people knew exactly where they stood and what was expected of them.

Roger Davies: My first season I played in the Reserves and we played Bolton. We were 1-0 down after 30 seconds and we actually won the game 5-1 and I remember I was just going over the halfway line – probably received it in my own half – and I saw the goalie off the line and I chipped him. It must have been 40 yards at least, over the top of him. Alan Boswell it was, in goal. Brian came in after and he said to me: "I dreamed I scored a goal like that once." People like that saying such things to you, it builds your confidence, your ego up.

Willie Carlin: What he did was this. He bought players and allowed them to play. Obviously he kept them in check. If you got a bit big headed, he'd knock you down and if you were down, he lifted you. He just bought me and said: "Go out and play." So what really happened was that Dave Mackay, he took the back four and I sort of, took midfield and up front. That's how we worked it. As it was, we had the blend. There was Dave and myself as I've said and then we had a lot of young lads, you know: John O'Hare, Kevin Hector, John Robson, John McGovern. So there was a good blend there and Dave at the back, with his experience, was fantastic for them – and Roy McFarland.

Roger Davies: We played at Scarborough in a reserve match and I wasn't having the best of games. It was coming up and not sticking. It was one of those games. I was losing it and it was going away and he was shouting. Anyway, I came off. It was only the reserve side we were playing and he suddenly said: "When the trainer brought you off, I lost interest in the game." He said the game had 'gone' because it wasn't the same anymore. You know, he really knew how to build up your confidence. He'd also have a go, of course, but you took whatever he said as gospel because he knew really what he was talking about.

Brian Clough: When we played Benfica in the European Cup I sat in the directors' box at Derby next to a guy called Sir Stanley Rous and I was doing the coaching bit, shouting. I think we finished up winning 3-0 and Sir Stanley Rous said to me: "Brian, why are you shouting? You're winning." Well I just ignored that and then he said: "I was in London last night and we had no rain." He said: "That pitch out there is six inches deep in rain." What he didn't know was that I'd been up all night watering the pitch. The second the Portuguese lads walked on the pitch – they were all in flannels and beautiful suits, suede shoes and all that – they took one look and they went back in, quick. Well, we murdered them.

Willie Carlin: You'd come in on a Monday thinking you'd got a week's training down at the Baseball Ground. You'd walk in on Monday, get changed, you'd have the paper, waiting to go training and he'd come in say: "Right. Pack your bags, we're off to Guernsey." Or: "We're off to Bisham Abbey." You'd say: "Eh? The wife's got to go to the doctor's." Or something like that. He'd say: "Do you want your cards? Do you want to be a milkman?" In the end my wife had a bag permanently packed. It's true, what I'm telling you. You know, my wife told me that in nine months once, we were away four months. You know, a week here, a week there, but the secret was that Cloughie never came on those trips. You were away to relax. They, Brian and Peter, were great at getting you to relax.

Peter Taylor

Colin Lawrence: I got to know Peter quite well. I like to think that I am one of the few, really. In some ways then you were a Peter Taylor pal or you were a Brian Clough pal. I was a friend of Brian's, but I always got on well with both of them, Peter as well. Completely different personalities, completely. Always a job to get the cash out of Peter like, but he was always very good and I always got on very well.

Brian Clough: Taylor always thought to do the job successfully was a two-man job. Peter took a lot of weight off my shoulders. I did most of the work! He was brilliant, at his job. John O'Hare? He'd never seen him play. He'd never seen Colin Todd play either. He had seen John McGovern, when we were at Hartlepools.

Roger Davies: He came to watch me at Barnet. Flat cap and all that, standing behind the goal. He left at half-time and apparently bumped into a scout from another club – I've forgotten his name – and Peter said: "Oh, I've seen him, don't bother." I signed a few days later! He was always reminiscing: "Do you remember that time?" I was playing in the Reserves and we used to train with the first team and I was playing against Roy. It was only at the Municipal, on the all-weather, but I kicked him accidentally and I apologised: "Sorry, Roy." Later, Peter said to Roy: "Does he still say 'sorry' to you? Remember that day when he said 'sorry' to you?" And to me: "Do you remember that?"

Ian Buxton: He was a strange man and I never felt at ease with Peter Taylor. He was the soft man to Cloughie's hard man and they played one off against the other, but I'm not sure how much that was an act and how much it was natural. Put it this way: I felt that Cloughie was straight. If I wanted a straight answer to a straight question, I could go and sit down with Cloughie and ask him something and, if I didn't believe him, I could say: "Come on, tell me the truth." And I think he would have done. With Taylor, I could never, ever believe what he told me. It may have been true, but it didn't sound right to me sometimes, coming from him.

Brian Clough: Peter Taylor couldn't get into League management without me. He was manager at Burton Albion and he couldn't get in without me. Anyway, I got him to Hartlepools. He was good at picking good players, which is the most important thing. Frank Clark has just got the sack. He couldn't pick his nose.

Steve Powell: Taylor was more of a straight man really. Clough would come in and, maybe, give us a rollicking and then he'd sort of calm things down, but together, as a pair, they were obviously very successful.

Colin Lawrence: He always held that Brian was number one. He always held to that, even when they went into the offices at Forest. Peter had a smaller office.

Clough and Taylor

Ernie Hallam: His initial alliance with Peter worked wonderfully because they knew how to play one against the other. It was a great partnership. It was a tragedy how it went wrong, wasn't it?

Colin Lawrence: It was always what I would call a 'professional within the game' relationship. Outside of football, there was no interest, no They'd meet up occasionally, that's all. On holidays they might meet up, occasionally. Peter was always very good with the children, with Brian's children. He'd play for hours with young Nigel. He could always flick a coin and make it come out of the joints of his hand and say: "What's that Nigel?" Nigel would look away there would be a two bob piece or something. Very good, very good. A dry sense of humour, Peter had.

Alan Durban: One of the things that they did, which a lot of managers really ought to be more aware of, is they did check on people's character, very much so.

Gerald Mortimer: I got on famously with them really. I spent hours sitting around waiting for Clough, but it was usually worth it. In fact I wish, looking back, I'd been more experienced. I could have made more of it, I think. I was just happy to sit listening to him and I think, perhaps, I should have written a bit more than I did sometimes. I think they were tremendous. I think we had the best of them. I always felt that the way they left Derby soured Brian particularly, in relationships with directors and, possibly, media. I don't know. That developed over years, but I'm sure we had the best of them.

Willie Carlin: Peter's function was to take us away. I maintain – it's my own theory – that if you had too much of Cloughie, you'd finish up belting him because he was always pushing, pushing, pushing. On the other side, if you had too much of Taylor, he was too easy. What they had between them was timing. They knew when to take us away and when we needed pushing. When we needed a break, we went with Taylor and when we needed pushing, we went with Cloughie. That was the secret.

Roger Davies: It was the way they used to act together. I mean, until you've been with them, it's hard to explain to people because they were always bouncing things off one another. "What do you think?" "He hasn't played well today, has he?" "What do you think, Brian?" "Are we going to...?"

Alan Hinton: Emphasising strengths? Oh, absolutely. He did it with me. I was known as a player who didn't go and win the ball. I was pretty frail in the tackle. Even now, I'm 57 years of age, nearly 58, but I don't have any knee problems! I don't have any ankle problems either and my poor dear friend John O'Hare, who's got all sorts of ankle problems and the difficulty he has is probably created by the fact that I used to give him difficult balls to control, and Alan Durban did and everybody did, and John used to hold it up and get kicked from behind all the time. That's when referees didn't penalise that kind of situation like they do today. I was not known for tackling and winning the ball, but the day it stopped – the players of Derby County saying he doesn't win the ball and all this stuff – was when Peter Taylor made a speech and Cloughie made a speech also, talking about courage. They said: "Courage isn't just tackling and winning the ball. Courage is when Alan goes down the wing and full-backs are sticking the cleats up and he crosses the ball in and doesn't care about getting his leg broken, when they're all trying to get at him. That's courage."

Roger Davies: They were always bouncing things off one another and you wondered which one was going to say something next. Like if we were waiting to go down, when pay time had come. You'd be sitting down in the dressing-room waiting for your turn in the office and you'd sit there getting everything just right. It was long before agents. I'd never done anything like it before and you'd be thinking things like: "What do I say? What do I do?" You know: "Well, I've had a good season and..." You'd walk in and Peter would say: "We're just thinking whether to give you a drop in wages or not." Everything in your mind would go out the window then. They were brilliant. They would bounce things off one another and they were very, very effective at it.

Alan Hinton: I thought they were miles ahead of their years at the time and, certainly, it made me feel a very special player because they used to say: "Get the ball out to Alan. He'll show you what to do with it." They made me feel like a king, when previous managers hadn't. Whether I was good enough to have their support I don't know, but I certainly felt better for it and, as a consequence, all my coaching experiences have been developed on the positive rather than the negative. That was what they were very, very good at. Strengths were the most important thing to them and they'd blow away the weaknesses.

Colin Lawrence: Brian could always go to Peter and ask about something or other, but at the end of the day, Brian – he always said – picked the team. He might have had a chat with Peter, but his decision was what mattered.

Roger Davies: Did Brian have the last word? I think he did. Overall, when push came to shove, Brian was the one, but Pete was brilliant. To play for Brian Clough was absolutely brilliant. Him and Peter Taylor, together. Brilliant.

The break up

Colin Lawrence: That was always the saddest thing. A few years ago, I was aiming to tempt Brian to get them to meet up and get back together again. It was always something that I feel sorry for, that I failed. I didn't manage it.

Alan Hinton: You know, that's been the tragedy for all of the players who played for Derby in their best times, if you like, but we do remember Clough and Taylor. They were both different, but very much a partnership and it was particularly sad when that fell apart and a lot of anger came into it. In the end we're all going to die and Peter, of course, died far too young and Brian's not in the game any more and is fighting his own personal battles. I understand it's going pretty good right now, so I hope that's the case. But you've got to do what you've got to do when you're going through the game, but for me, there was nothing like Clough and Taylor. They were absolutely brilliant together. Got us playing. Their biggest strength was player identification and Peter was superb at that and Cloughie supported him and Peter supported Cloughie. We went and won championships and it was a particular great time for all of us involved.

Would Clough have been successful today?

Gordon Hughes: I think he would have had problems. Clough could really be very abrasive to people. All right, the maximum wage came off in 1962 and that was when he was finding his feet. I don't think he would have been able to get away with his way of handling the lads. I don't think they would have stood for it today. I think the game's changing that way. A lot of them are millionaires. I'm not saying the dedication is not there, but they don't seem to be as... You see, they complain about pressure. I can't understand what they mean, pressure.

Graham Richards: I think he was lucky, but I think all great men are lucky and, once again, we're back to fortune favouring the brave. He must have been a great tactician, but the players who played for him say that isn't the case. He had an excellent, beyond excellent, an absolutely supreme assistant in Peter Taylor, who was a totally different sort of man and combined together they were like eggs and bacon – very much better together than they are apart. For me he will remain, without a doubt, the supreme manager of my era.

Back to the Top

SOME people will argue that the team that won promotion to the First Division in 1969, was a better team than either of the two championship winning sides. Whether or not that is true, the winning of the Second Division championship was tangible and living proof of success that Derby County supporters had craved for since the 1946 FA Cup triumph. Dave Mackay shared the Footballer of the Year trophy with Tony Book of Manchester City. Bobby Robson was sacked as manager of Fulham and was succeeded by Johnny Haynes. Haynes packed in the job after four games.

Leeds United won the First Division championship for the first time in their history, Liverpool were runners-up, whilst Manchester City beat Leicester City 1-0 in the FA Cup Final. Leicester were also relegated to the Second Division.

1969 was also notable for the maiden flight of Concorde and the first voyage of the QE2. Meanwhile, Derby County had some fine players...

John O'Hare

Brian Clough: He had the biggest heart – I'd been with him at Sunderland – in England. The least pace and took the most kicks. Now, John O'Hare's got bad ankles because he took kicks. The secret with his success was (a) the size of his heart and (b) he had his back to everybody. He would have the ball any time and they'd be coming into him every time. That's why I signed him. He never let it run away. He took the knocks. He had a little spell there, at inside-forward for Sunderland, but he didn't play there mainly. I don't think Sunderland knew his best position.

John O'Hare: I knew Brian Clough from Sunderland. After he was injured, he took over as youth-team coach and I was in the youth team there. Ian McColl was manager. He was a Scottish guy, who came from the same place as me in Scotland, the next village, yes, but I didn't get on very well with him. I'd been put on the transfer list for disciplinary reasons, actually. A journalist had written an article after I'd spoken to the newspapers about not being happy and them bringing older players in and things like that. Obviously I'd been speaking out of turn and that's why he put me on the transfer list basically. I didn't ask to go on, no. No, he put me on.

Ron Webster: Well, in my position at that time, right-back, I didn't have a right winger, so the only player really I could see when I looked up was John O'Hare. Alan Durban was the wing-half, so down my side there wasn't much defensive play, was there? John O'Hare was always there. Whenever I got it, I could always hit John O'Hare, no matter what. He just seemed to be there and if you hit him a bad ball he'd get to it, he'd get it down and whatever and they'd feed off him, wouldn't they? He was a good target man, John. If he'd been a left-footed player, I'd have been struggling, wouldn't I? There'd have been nobody there. If he'd been a left-footed player, they'd have had to play with a right winger, with Alan Hinton being on the other side. He was a good player though, John O'Hare.

Back to the Top

John O'Hare: A journalist in the North-East called Doug Weatherall rang me up. He was quite pally with Cloughie. He called me and basically arranged for them to come and see me. So he and Pete came to see me and I remember it was a Sunday because you couldn't sign players on a Sunday in those days. I didn't know that, I didn't have a clue about that, but it was actually a Sunday evening they came, him and Pete. To be quite honest, it didn't take that long. Although I didn't want to leave Sunderland, it was a case of having to leave really.

Tommy Powell: I mean, defenders in trouble could always play it up to John and his arms went out. When I've run teams I've said: "Look, just put your arms out here. I don't want to see defenders come in front of you to take the ball. You're not giving a foul or anything, but defenders can't get by you." John was tremendous.

Kevin Hector: If the ball went there, it stuck. I used to drop off defenders and go a bit wide and they didn't quite know whether to come or stay. He was strong and held the ball so well and they couldn't knock him off it. If he'd had my pace, he'd have been some player.

Dave Mackay: He could hold it up. Great holding-up player. You could knock it up to him and know he was going to hold it, wait for support from Kevin Hector and Alan Durban.

Gordon Hughes: When Derby did well with Kevin Hector and John O'Hare up front, I thought they had the perfect partnership for that era. What they used to do, you know – and I remember them putting it into practice during the game – was if you were at full-back, you hit the ball 40 yards up, in a line. If you were in the centre-half position, you hit the ball 40 yards, in a line. Wherever you were in the pitch the same, right? John O'Hare used to stand in line and Kevin Hector was never more than ten yards away from him. Of course, John was probably one of the best target men there's been. You could drive a ball from 20 yards at John and it was down and laying it off. He used to pull it down or flick it on and Hector was in. That's what it was. They never stood more than ten yards apart, Hector and O'Hare. They used to drive the ball, as I say, from anywhere and they were always in the vicinity. They knew it was coming on the head or lower, and you could hear it blind because John O'Hare used to stand there you see and Hector used to pick up John O'Hare's pieces. I used to try that, when I used to coach but it didn't work. There wasn't a John O'Hare, you see! It used to be bouncing off chests and going away. You've got to have the right chap to do it and I thought he was a great target man, John O'Hare.

Willie Carlin: John O'Hare was never appreciated at Derby until he left because they were brought up on Jackie Stamps and Bill Curry and people like that, the old fashioned centre-forward. When John came along, they couldn't understand it. It wasn't until he went that they realised what they had. John was tremendous. If we were in trouble...there was a lad called John Robson at left-back, only 18 or 19 then, and if ever he was in trouble he used to hit it blind up the line because he knew John was there. John would kill it dead and let us get up to him. If the ball's played up to him and he holds it, it gives us – the midfield players – time to get out. If the midfield gets out, the back four gets out and you're coming on to the ball. That was the beauty of John – and Mark Hughes. He's been a revelation hasn't he?

Steve Powell: John O'Hare was a fantastic front player. You knew, as a midfield player, that whenever you got the ball you could almost knock it blind up front and John would be somewhere along the line, holding it up and bringing other players into play. I mean, I think he was very, very underrated at Derby.

Dave Mackay

Bill Brownson: There again, Cloughie brought him to Derby. It was a fantastic achievement to get Dave Mackay here. It was probably one of the biggest turning points for Derby County.

Lionel Pickering: I came back in 1966. I was here when he signed Dave Mackay. That was a bit like Igor Stimac, wasn't it? There were some good players around him, but it was a big name, Dave Mackay, coming on the scene.

Dave Mackay: The reason I left Tottenham Hotspur – and I only left on the last day of the season – was that we played Manchester City at home, with Francis Lee, Summerbee, Colin Bell, and they played us off the park. We had been beaten at White Hart Lane before – not very often – but we had never been played off the park. I thought: "Eh. It's time to pack in, really. I've had a good time at Tottenham and I don't want to start another season if this is going to happen because nobody's ever done it to us." So I thought: "Well, it's time for Dave Mackay to go." So I went and knocked on Bill Nick's door and said: "Hey, Bill, I've had enough. I think it's time for me to leave."

Brian Clough: David Mackay was one of the top three signings that I made. Roy McFarland was the best one I ever signed. David Mackay came and he sat in my office, which was a big office, too. It was a boardroom, it wasn't really my office, but David Mackay was incredible. He taught my lads in the shooting box. With him living in the Midland Hotel, he was up and about before you and I. He used to get to the ground early. In those days, I used to get to the ground reasonably early and David would be there, in his gear and I'd got my sons with me because I took them everywhere. He'd say: "Right. Let's get in the shooting box." I genuinely believe that David Mackay taught my son, Nigel, how to score goals because in the shooting box at Derby we had the equivalent to a dart board, with squares on it. David could plonk it anywhere. His favourite phrase was: "Don't bother moving." He used to shout that: "Don't bother moving, I'll plonk it." Nice man, nice man.

Dave Mackay: I was going back to Hearts, as player-manager. I went up there. Everything was checked out and Brian knew about this. When I came back from Hearts I was almost, about 75 per cent certain, but the thing that stopped me going back was that I was going to play. When I left Hearts I was 11st 4lbs; coming back, 13st and 33 years old, slowing all the time. I finally thought: "Well, I'm not going to play in Edinburgh. I left there as a hero and I'm not going back for them to say: "Hey, here's grandad. You said he was a super athlete and look at him now, he's fat." So no way was I going to play for Hearts. I knew I could still play, but not at the Tottenham level. I thought: "I'm past that now, so I'll do something else."

Ron Webster: I thought Dave was brilliant. His first match – I can remember it now – he was in the box and it was all crowded and it came to him and he stopped it. You know, I thought: "Get the...!" And he just back-heeled it to Les Green! I thought: "What a bloody class player." I thought he was great, Dave, I did. It made you ooze with confidence playing with Dave. You did his running a bit but he was there and he was hard. Hard man, Dave. In training and everything, he was, I thought, brilliant. Yes, he'd got a lot of skill for saying that he'd only got his left foot, brilliant. He was good at the time, just to lift you. He was always there. He used to chip the ball on to the crossbar. Just practice chipping and hitting the crossbar.

Dave Mackay: I flew up to Edinburgh to see the Hearts chairman and, more or less, everything was arranged. I didn't want to give up playing, but I didn't want to play for Hearts. If it had been me finished completely, I'd have been back at Hearts because that's my favourite club, Heart of Midlothian.

Back to the Top

Brian Flint: My biggest buzz – and I still get hairs at the back of my neck prickling – was when I was delivering night papers and the first one down John Street, I picked it out and looked at the back page and it said: 'Rams sign Dave Mackay.' That was it. If I see him today, I still get those prickles. Nobody else, nobody else, just him. We've often tried to work out what the equivalent of the Dave Mackay signing would be now. We can't work one out. It was just... well, he was a legend, wasn't he? After that, good players, very good players came, but not the same. The impact wasn't the same. He was Dave Mackay.

Roy McFarland: I was fortunate when I played for England in that I played with five players who'd won the World Cup: Gordon Banks in goal; I played alongside Bobby Moore; I had Martin Peters and Alan Ball in midfield; and Geoff Hurst up front. Players who'd won the World Cup and it was great playing with what I'd call great players. Certainly in one or two cases, certainly with Bobby Moore, world class, but I was also fortunate to learn my trade alongside Mackay. I would genuinely say the best player I ever played with – and I played alongside Colin Todd and me and Toddy had a great understanding, great partnership – was Dave Mackay. He was a legend. Special, different, still one of the team, though. Make no mistake, Mackay was still one of the team, but he was special and he was different. He had this great ability; he had this great left foot; he had this great attitude.

Dave Mackay: He contacted me by telephone. He knew I was on offer, he knew that. He rang me up at the tie shop – Dave Mackay Club Ties – and more or less stressed that he'd love me to come to Derby. I thought: "Well, I'm going down a division, but..." You know Brian, he sells everyone a good line.

Kevin Hector: There was speculation about, but we thought: "No, no chance. Not Mackay." He was a legend at Tottenham, wasn't he? When he came, we couldn't believe it. Changing in the same dressing-room as Dave Mackay! It was like having a player-manager, really. In training, everything, he was competitive. Great skill, left foot tremendous.

Gerald Mortimer: I remember reading about them signing Dave Mackay and I thought: "I'll believe that when I see him running out." Even when it had been confirmed, I thought: "Hmm..., until I see him run out...." I mean, this was the guy that all the Spurs double team will tell you was the biggest influence of the lot and was worth 'two to us' and so on. I mean, he was a legendary player, a legendary player. He was wonderful as a player and he wasn't a bad manager either.

Willie Carlin: At the time, he wasn't the best player I ever played with. The best player I ever played with was Roy McFarland, but my only regret in football was that I didn't play with Dave Mackay when he was 26 or 27. He must have been awesome because when I first met him he was what, 34? So he was past his best. At the time he was tremendous, but what a player he must have been at 26. He must have been unbelievable. Oh yes, he must have been.

Roy McFarland: I remember playing at Palace. It was in our promotion year and I was suffering with a very, very bad groin injury, which I'd struggled, maybe, for about six or seven games. I just felt I couldn't go on in this match and I kicked the ball and collapsed. Jimmy Gordon ran on and got the sponge and stuck it where most players don't like it and I said: "Jim, I can't go on...I just can't walk, I can't kick the ball, I can't walk." And Mackay stood over me and he said: "Get up, you coward." Those were his words and I saw the red mist and I wanted to get up and punch him, but he sparked something in me and I got through the game. I got up and I said: "I'll show you. I'll get through this game." That was Mackay.

Dave Mackay: I was brought up to be a real grafter. In the old days, it was your two inside-forwards and two wing-halves. No one else worked really. Left-back never went over the halfway line and the outside-left, outside-right, only had one half of the pitch to play in. They had it easy then, but your grafters were two wing-halves and two inside-forwards. So I thought: "Eh, I'll have some of this, playing at the back." The Second Division, to me, honestly, was so simple and so easy that I just couldn't believe it. I'd tried to get out of the First Division and I thought the Second Division was so easy I couldn't believe it, but then we were promoted and I was popped back into the First Division and we finished fourth in the first season, which was great. I could do the job in the First Division at the back with Derby, but I couldn't have done that at Tottenham.

Steve Powell: I didn't play an actual game with him for Derby, but I played with them when I was a schoolboy, in the school holidays and he used to join in the training. I played with him on the training ground, both with and against him, and I actually played against him when he played at Swindon, when he was player-manager there, in a testimonial game. He was tremendous and, I mean, a great person and an absolutely fantastic player. You know, even when he came to Derby as a manager, he'd join in five-a-sides and he was still a tremendous player. As I say, he had fantastic ability, but he'd got this sort of aura about him and a tremendous will to win. I'll never forget five-a-sides, they sometimes used to go on until three o'clock in the afternoon, until he was on the winning side. Then, the minute he was one goal ahead that was it, it was over.

Brian Flint: He looked ten feet tall on the pitch. His leadership, his tackling, his passing. He'd lift his foot to kick the ball, centre-forward would turn away and he'd let it run through to Les Green. It was just so different. We'd never seen it, you see.

Roy McFarland: As a young player, I was very demanding and very impetuous. I was very loud both on the training ground and loud on the football pitch and a good friend, who is next door to us here – Alan Hinton – eventually he and I roomed together for many, many years in those lovely days – and Ally used to jump out the way now and again. He won't mind me saying that, but he was careful, that's probably the best way to say it and I used to go berserk when players shirked tackles or got out the way. Mackay pulled me to one side in a quiet moment in the game and he said: "Hey, keep your trap shut. What he does for the team, you cannot do. You cannot produce what he can. Let him get on with it. Let him do what he can do. You've got to accept that he can't do those things." It wasn't until three or four games later that I realised what Dave was on about and what Cloughie was talking about and all these things. It was almost like being at football college.

Dave Mackay: I played against Brian Clough for the Under-23s and I always remember he had a big black eye. Someone must have done him on the Saturday. He had a big black eye. 1-1 was the score, but nothing really happened in the game, nothing that would have said he's a great player or anything that he would think that I was a great player. My contact with him was minimal. I'd never spoken to the guy. Maybe called him a few names, perhaps.

Willie Carlin: He used to get very annoyed when people compared him with Blanchflower. They used to say Blanchflower was all artistic, the ball player, and Dave was the cruncher. He used to get annoyed. I can tell you, honestly, Dave Mackay could do anything with a ball and I mean anything. He was terrific with a ball, do anything, but the papers, as usual, categorise players. In training he used to have a saying. If you were passing a ball over 30 or 40 yards, Dave would strike it and he'd shout: "Don't move." You didn't have to, he was just spot on. Don't you think, though, that left-footed players have a wonderful flow? I don't know what it is, but they seem to have that grace and flow into it. It's the same with kiddies, how they stroke the ball, so graceful.

Dave Mackay: I could remember the previous season they'd played Leeds United, I don't know whether it was in the League Cup or something. The game was at Derby and this was the first time I knew some of the names in the team. Alan Hinton I knew, Alan Durban I knew because they had been bigger names and older players, but the majority of the players, your McFarlands and people like that, Robson, Webster, who had been there a long time, I didn't really know these players at all.

Gordon Guthrie: On a Friday, Dave sometimes wouldn't like to touch a ball. He'd do half a dozen sprints and probably a walk around the pitch and if there was a five-a-side going on – which probably the remainder of the first team had – and the ball rolled to him, he probably wouldn't touch it. He'd just walk by it, but give him a ball on a Saturday and he wanted it all the time.

Dave Mackay: It all depends where you are. At Tottenham, we played every Friday in the gymnasium, every Friday with the ball. I couldn't say there: "Eh, I ain't going to kick a ball." The manager would've sacked me. That was in the gym.

Roy McFarland

Brian Clough: I got annoyed because people criticised him because he wasn't 6ft 4ins. Silly, silly. He was vicious. He'd snap a centre-forward in half as soon as look at him and headed a ball as good as anybody playing. He'd got an all-round talent, the ability to play a ball. Now, for centre-halves in our day – and I don't mean that to be rude – that was unheard of. Centre-halves didn't play a ball. Occasionally Billy Wright, maybe.

Roy McFarland: Yes, I had ambitions of signing for Liverpool, very much so in fact. Being a Liverpool lad and travelling across the Mersey to Birkenhead to play for Tranmere Rovers...there was a lot of talk in the local paper, the *Liverpool Echo*, that I would sign for Liverpool. And, of course, Liverpool was my football club. Shankly was, in a sense, my hero and he made my team great. That was the club I wanted to sign for, that was the club I always wanted to play for. It never happened and, without doubt, if I look back on my career, there's no regrets that I never played for Liverpool Football Club because signing for Derby County was the best thing that ever happened to me.

Kevin Hector: He was such a good footballer. He reminded me of Paul Madeley at Leeds, in that he could have played anywhere. I went to school with Madeley. Roy was like Madeley, but with a Mersey streak. The thing about Roy was that if you'd have put him anywhere on the field, centre-forward, whatever, he'd have done a good job.

Roy McFarland: Dad was a keen footballer himself, played local football and was a very talented player. He told me that he'd had an offer of a trial with Sunderland. He didn't take that up, funnily enough, and I was bit reluctant too in my early days. When I was first offered a trial at Tranmere Rovers, I turned it down. In fact, they wrote to me twice and I turned both letters down and didn't turn up and surprisingly to me, I got a third letter inviting me for a trial. I went to that trial and, eventually, signed for Tranmere Rovers, but my father was a very good footballer. Again, a left-footer like I was. Always talked football. His idol was Dixie Dean and he was an Everton supporter.

Ron Webster: I don't think you ever saw the best of Roy Mac. I mean, he was great, but when Cloughie was there he never used to train with us, he always had a groin injury and he just played the matches and I don't think we ever saw the best of Roy because of that. He was great player anyway, but...

Roy McFarland: Our rivalry was never great but it was touched, in a sense, by what Everton were in the past. They were the glamour club, Liverpool were in the Second Division. Liverpool was the club that I followed all the way through and when Shankly went there and got them promoted from the Second to the First Division and a few years later they won the First Division championship, of course I rubbed it in with my father, but there was never any real arguments. We just had differences of opinion. In a nice way, I supported Liverpool, he supported Everton.

Dave Mackay: McFarland was, for me, the best player. No question, overall. You had your Todds and Gemmills, Hennessey and O'Hare, Hector, the whole lot of 'em, but to me McFarland was the best player, no question.

John O'Hare: He was an all-round footballer, Roy was. Dave was an all-round footballer. Mackay and McFarland were, to me, the two best all-round footballers I've ever played with. Toddy was a great defender, with his pace and his tackling. People talk of his reading of games, but I tend to think it was more his pace than his actual reading of games. To me, though, McFarland was a better all-round player.

Roy McFarland: My father never pushed me, never demanded things from me. He used to watch me play occasionally, but he wasn't a parent who was obsessive and made me play football. I was a kid from the back streets of Liverpool and I learned my football in the streets. In those days a lot of kids came through into the game from the back streets. I think football has changed now. Obviously it's for the best that the worst back streets, the slums, have gone – but I wonder if we've missed one or two good footballers because of that.

Gordon Hughes: I remember the day he signed for Derby County, as a young lad. I think Cloughie slept outside his house and that sort of thing, like he used to do to get his man. Roy came in for training the next day. Within half an hour or so, the older pros were saying: "What a player this lad's going to be." You could tell straightaway. His aura, what he was trying to do, what he did do. He was only 19 years old you know, but you could tell, immediately, that this was going to be a player. Oh yes, he was special.

Steve Powell: For a centre-half he had a tremendous amount of skill. He was a good defender, he was strong in the air and it was very, very unfortunate he didn't play a lot more games for England and become a household name. Well, he is a household name, really, but become even more well known internationally.

Willie Carlin: Oh, he had everything, Roy McFarland. I used to say: "He's an inside-forward gone wrong." He could play anywhere, Roy McFarland. He had aggression. I remember I was playing for Notts County against Derby in the FA Cup and they beat us 6-0. At the end of the match Les Bradd – who was a big lad, about 6ft 2ins and 14st – was in the bath and said: "I thought this McFarland was a footballing centre-half?" I said: "He is, why?" He said: "Well he hit me twice and he nearly killed me!" I said: "That's what centre-halves are for."

Colin Todd

Gordon Hughes: I remember Brian Clough said to him: "You make me bloody sick." "Why's that then?" "When are you going to make a mistake?" Honestly, he did. Colin Todd – he was very unlucky on the international scene because of Bobby Moore, but what a sweeper he was. He was virtually unbeatable, he was so quick on the turn, you see.

Alan Hinton

Bill Brownson: He was a really great player, at passing the ball. I don't think there's anybody playing today who is as good as him on crossing.

Colin Gibson: Favourite player? Of that era, probably Roy McFarland in defence and Kevin Hector up front, although I fancied myself as a bit of an Alan Hinton because, being left-footed, I'd always play out on the left wing. And I'd always take penalties in the school team, so I suppose if I really had to pick out one player it would be Alan Hinton. Of course, again it's this great thing about memories isn't it? Alan Hinton was a great player and he could ping a ball in however, but he used to get some frightful stick from the Derby supporters. If ever things weren't going quite in Derby's favour, Alan Hinton or John McGovern, they were the first two players the crowd wanted taking off. I think it was a game against West Ham in the old First Division – I could be wrong on that – on a real Baseball Ground quagmire and Alan Hinton wasn't having the best of games and the crowd were shouting: "Get Gladys off." That was his nickname. "Get Gladys off, get him hitting somebody with his handbag." He came down the left wing, cut in from the right hand side and let fly with his right foot. Top corner. Soon changed the crowd.

Willie Carlin

Kevin Hector: Willie had been around a bit. He did the shouting for everyone in midfield. He was an organiser. He was a good competitor.

Dave Mackay: Super little guy. Talked a lot on the field. Great, for his height, great in the air, as well. And tough. Tough little guy and a marvellous wee footballer.

Leaders

Dave Mackay

Bill Wainwright: He was certainly a leader, but he was very easy to get on with, Dave.

Roy McFarland

Brian Clough: A bit quiet. Didn't shout a lot, didn't do anything. He led by performances. I'll be repetitive, he was vicious on the field. He'd cut anybody in half.

Alan Hinton: He was a good leader. No, not demonstrative. He didn't need to be. He'd let you know when he wanted you to put out more, but he used to get a goal, make a tackle with his big left foot sticking out all over the place. Best player. Good captain.

Wonderful Days
...Magical Nights

THE Seventies is arguably the most dramatic decade of all in Derby County's history – from the heights of two League championships in four years at the start, to a slide towards relegation at the end. Managers came and went almost as quickly as players. Supporters were bemused. At the cramped Baseball Ground in 1970, the average attendance was an amazing 35,924. By 1980, it was down by 17,000 – and falling.

Despite the fact that Arsenal, in 1971, had became the second team to do the 'double' in the 20th century, Liverpool and Leeds United were always the teams to beat in the Seventies. Liverpool won the championship four times, whilst the great Leeds United team began by finishing runners-up three seasons in a row, the third time, in 1972, to new champions – Derby County.

Rams ruled okay, but before glittering European nights against the likes of Benfica and Juventus had been properly savoured, suddenly, Brian Clough and Peter Taylor were gone.

Dave Mackay took up the manager's baton in amazing and difficult circumstances. He secured another championship in 1975, then he, too, fell foul of a divided and arrogant boardroom, the members of which were clearly out of their depth. Panic spread and Derby County began to sink, rapidly.

Despite the problems, the acrimony, the bitterness and the decline, the Seventies will be remembered primarily for being football days of wine and roses. The Midland Hotel became the players' second home and the bond between players and supporters was never greater. Magical moments to remember, when Derby County was the club to be feared and the Baseball Ground was a cacophony of noise and passion. Those were wonderful days and magical nights that those people, lucky enough to be there at the time, will never forget.

Colin Gibson: Derby got into the First Division and then I really started going on a regular basis. In saying that, I wasn't there the day of the record attendance against Tottenham, the 41,000, but in that season I saw them beat Everton 2-1 and I mean, Derby were playing some fantastic football at the time. Then they beat Manchester United 2-0 and I remember going down to the Baseball Ground, queuing to get tickets to see the Manchester United game and having to queue a long time, but boy was it worth it? Seeing Derby beat the great Manchester United and we're talking about Kidd, Law, Charlton, Best, Stepney in goals. It was terrific and seeing your Derby County team beat them. It was a wonderful time.

Wonderful Days ... Magical Nights

Brian Flint: Every night you tended to look in the paper, once they got to be successful. Well, they were connected with every big name, weren't they? There was always an interest. I remember Brian Clough once saying about the young Steve Powell. He wanted to go to university and I think Brian Clough said: "If he comes to Derby, he'll be able to buy the university." Or words to that effect. Whatever he did, he managed to stir things up, come up with something to stir up the interest, kept it going.

Gerald Mortimer: I came into journalism in 1970. There'd been a yen there. I'd worked in the *Telegraph* for two summers when I was at Oxford and had really rather enjoyed it. Then, when I was teaching in Richmond, North Yorkshire, I did a few bits here and there for *The Guardian*. The life appealed to me and having spent ten years in teaching, I had this uneasy feeling that I wasn't going to get any better at that. Just having observed schoolmasters in various places, you could see outstanding ones, who were still outstanding at the age of 60 and somehow maintained a rapport with the people they were dealing with, and others who were dying off after 50 and just had no contact with their raw material if you like. Plus the fact, I don't think teaching is getting any easier. I wouldn't fancy going back into it now. Like many important jobs, it's desperately undervalued. I quite fancied a change.

Dave Mackay: "No, no. I didn't miss many matches. I think for the first time in my career, I actually was ever-present in the last season. As I say: "It's easy at the back." [*Mackay missed four out of 126 possible League appearances in three seasons.*]

Willie Carlin: We played Chelsea and got beat – 2-1 I think it was – and Keith Weller scored both their goals. It was funny. I used to get *The People* and *The Sunday Express* delivered from the newsagents and she was a big Derby County fan. Anyway, she sent me the *News of the* World as well and on it she wrote: 'What's this all about?' The first thing you do, as you know, is to look at the report of the match and as I read it, the phone went. It was Peter Taylor. The wife's gone to church with the other two kids, I've got my six-month-old child in my hand. So I answered the phone and he said: "Do you fancy going to Leicester?" I says: "No, I don't." So he said: "Well, you're going. Frank O'Farrell's coming at midday." So I said: "I ain't coming down." He said: "You get down to the ground." I says: "I ain't going." I put the phone down, picked up the paper and there was the headlines 'Carlin for Leicester'. I hadn't seen them. Anyway, eventually I went down to the ground. O'Farrell came to see me and he said: "Well, why are they letting you go?" I said: "I don't know, I don't want to go." Anyway, we had a talk about contracts and everything and he says to me: "It might take a few weeks to sort this out." I said: "It could take a couple of months or a couple of years. I'm not bothered. I don't want to leave."

Steve Powell: Well I was fortunate to join the club at the start of a very successful period. We won the championship in 1971-72, so I was very lucky and the atmosphere in all those years, in the Seventies, was absolutely fantastic. Not just for big games, but the whole week, the whole build-up, certainly to a home game. The whole town buzzed and even though the club's playing in the Premiership now, I don't think there's that atmosphere leading up to the games. Not just big games, but any game. It was the main talking point in a lot of business places or works or wherever you used to go. It was a big topic.

Willie Carlin: I went into Cloughie and said to him: "Why me? Why?" So he said: "Well, you don't have to go." I said: "Hey. You've agreed to let me go. You've agreed. If anything goes wrong, I'll get the blame." Anyway, Frank O'Farrell came back that night and said: "Everything's agreed." So I went, but I'll tell you what, it broke my heart. I travelled for six weeks on that train to Leicester: "Why? Why me?" I couldn't believe it, for at the time I was playing some good football. They knew and I didn't know, even though you have full medicals, that I had arthritis. I didn't know I had it, I thought it was my groin. I was taking six distalgesic a day, getting cortisone and no one ever told me I had a problem with my hip. I always thought it was my groin.

Roger Davies: It was a successful year when I came in the 1971-72 season, when the first team won the League championship and I came into the Reserves and we won the Central League. I played my first game against West Brom Reserves at the Baseball Ground. We won 1-0. I scored actually, so I remember that game. The second game I played was in midweek. We played at Everton, and Alan Durban and Terry Hennessey were playing. In the dressing-room they introduced me: "This is Roger Davies." I was in awe, you know ...Terry Hennessey. We lost. We got stuffed, actually, but from that game on – I came in the September – I think it was something like March time before we lost again. We never lost a game and we won the Central League – quite comfortably in the end.

The Midland Hotel

Bill Wainwright: I went to the Midland in 1963. The team didn't stay there in the years immediately prior to Brian arriving, but it was because of the head porter, really, how I got involved. He said: "There's a new football manager arrived and his name is Clough. Why don't you give him a ring?" It shows how terribly naive I was because I said: "Why?" I didn't know anything about football. I hadn't been to a football match in my life. So he said: "Well, Derby County used to practically live here when Mr Jobey was manager." The head porter had been at the Midland man and boy and he said: "There might be some business again."

Willie Carlin: Staying at the Midland? We did. Yes, a lot. It was to get you away really, from your family, before a match. It was unusual at the time.

Bill Wainwright: So I phoned Derby County. It was a bit like it is now, when your calls are stacked. It was a case of: "Well, he's very busy. It might be a day or two before he gets back to you." Time went on and nothing happened. So I phoned again. "Terribly busy. Terribly busy." It was apparent I hadn't got to the top of the queue yet. Anyway, the Mayor of Derby was a lady and her chaplain, during her turn of office, was John Tudor, who was vicar of the Queen's Hall, just round the corner in Midland Road opposite the Derbyshire Royal Infirmary. I told him who I'd been trying to get in touch with and he said: "I'll tell you what. If I can get in touch with him, I'll ask him to read a lesson at the carol service at Christmas." I think it was then, late October. He said: "You can read a lesson as a local businessman. I will sit you next to him. He'll not know you, but you'll know him because his photograph will have been in the *Derby Evening Telegraph* every night since he arrived."

Roger Davies: We stayed there before every game. We stayed away every Friday night no matter where we were playing, home or away. Midweek games we would be there in the afternoon.

Bill Wainwright: So the day duly arrived. I went across. There's Mr Clough. "Good evening, Mr Clough." "Good evening." The service starts. He reads his lesson. I read my lesson and when it's all over, I say: "Hello Mr Clough, my name's Wainwright." "Are you that character who keeps phoning me?" I said: "Yes, actually. I've been trying to get in touch. It's nice to meet you." I said: "The Midland Hotel is just round the corner. Would you like to come for a drink?" "Yes, why not?" And we clicked. Just like that. I won't tell you his words, but we got up to the flat and he walked round and round the settee and I said: "For God's sake Brian, sit down.

You'll wear the carpet out." That's it. That's how we met. That's how I came to meet Brian Clough.

Bill Wainwright: We clicked, just like that. I think we had the same kind of humour, same style of many things, otherwise that wouldn't have happened. Yes, he liked to keep people on their toes – and he did as well. In fact, I would say we were great friends, but so far as looking after the team was concerned, you were no different to a player. He'd tell you just the same as he'd tell a player at half-time if he felt like he needed to, but somehow it didn't matter...because you deserved it. Fair? Oh, fair. I don't think you could meet a fairer person.

Steve Powell: That's right, we stayed a lot at the Midland Hotel. I think he was one of the first managers to do that. Also he was one of the first managers to take players away mid-season, abroad. He was very innovative in that respect. I mean, most teams would just report at the normal time, half-six for a half-seven kick-off, but we used to go to the Midland Hotel in the afternoons before a night match.

Bill Wainwright: He was early 30s. Libby had just been born. She was just a baby and Nigel was only a little boy. No, the children never stayed at the Midland. No. Brian kept the football very separate.

Willie Carlin: Can you remember when we played Leeds on Easter Monday? We won at Man City on the Friday. Then we went up to Sunderland on Easter Saturday and we drew. So he said to us: "Right, you're all back to the Midland." That was Easter Saturday night and we were playing Leeds on Easter Monday. He said: "I know what you fellows will be up to if I send you home. I know what you'll be..." Well, we had to go to the Midland over Easter and we were bored out of our bloody brains. There was no one there, no staff, it was terrible.

Bill Wainwright: The Midland Hotel at Derby is in two separate halves and we used to be able to use one half for visiting teams, the one next to the station, and Brian had the garden side, so they didn't really need to meet. I think there was the odd occasion when it was a big affair they might stay two or three nights. Maybe, two or three. I don't think they stayed for any undue length of time, though.

Willie Carlin: So anyway, it comes to Easter Monday and we're ready for our steak and Leeds came walking in and we didn't know hardly any of them. They'd sent their reserves down, hadn't they? Because the first team were playing Celtic in the European Cup. So we went out and beat them 4-0 and were booed off the park! I could have gone home and had a couple of nights on the ale and still beaten 'em, but that's how he was.

Bill Wainwright: On Friday they used to come, usually about five o'clock. They'd have tea, then they'd have dinner. Invariably, from what I can remember, dinner was Dover sole. Brian liked Dover sole, so they all had it. They had a proper menu, really, there was no restriction. They stayed the night. If they wanted breakfast they had breakfast and if they didn't, they didn't. At about elevenish, they went for a walk. They usually went down London Road. They didn't go to any parks or anything like that. Then they came back for lunch. I think lunch was always about midday. It was always fillet steak or again, Dover sole. They didn't have vegetables. Nothing to start with, but they always had baked rice pudding with skin on top. Nice, with a bit of nutmeg and butter. If they wished, they could have Wilkin's jam with it, strawberry or raspberry or whatever. That was always their lunch and they'd leave for the ground about one o'clock or a bit after.

Steve Powell: Before the Liverpool match I would have got a lift with one of the lads. I don't know who it was. Obviously I wasn't driving myself at the time, but I'd have got a lift down with one of the other lads. I think probably nowadays it's coach everywhere, but certainly at that time we used to park the cars at the back of the Midland and go down in cars. No, we didn't walk down, not while I was involved with the first team.

Roger Davies: A curfew on Friday nights? No, not really. He didn't have to implement a curfew because people knew what they had to do. They were responsible. I don't know what you'd call them, professionals or adults? We'd sit around the hotels and he'd let you have half of lager or whatever. Even in Dave's time we kept it through at the Midland. Later on, as they started having the financial troubles, they started to change, but in Dave's era, we were always there before games.

Bill Wainwright: A curfew? No. Brian was always there. They never went out after dinner – but they weren't allowed to go to bed until...I'd hazard a guess and say it was about 10.30pm. That was the earliest they were allowed to go to bed. They'd got to stay up, play cards, read a book or whatever. Play chess because some of them played chess. No, it wasn't a case of being in bed at eight o'clock and lights out at nine! I think the earliest was about 10.30pm. "Can I go to bed, boss?" "No, you can't."

Bill Wainwright: If they stayed the Friday night before an away match it was usually because it was close by, so they went by coach to Leicester or Nottingham. Always twin rooms. They always had the garden side because that is quieter. They also travelled by train for some games.

Bill Wainwright: Occasionally they came back and had 'a do'. They'd phone and say: "We'll call in on our way back." I wouldn't say it happened that many times in the eight and a half years I was connected with them, but on occasions and, of course, when they won the championship in 1972. Or was it 1969, the promotion year I'm thinking of? They had a cocktail reception with their wives before they went to the Council House.

Bill Wainwright: Occasionally, Brian came on social occasions. I don't know whether he signed any players there. British Transport Hotels managers were most intrigued about me because they said: "He knows nothing about football. He knows nothing about this, nothing about that and yet, look how involved he is." I mean, I wasn't really involved in football. I still don't know anything about football. I like to watch football. I certainly knew nothing about it in those early days. I don't know much about it now.

Roy McFarland: Yes, I lived in the Midland. Actually, when I first came to Derby, I lived in the Clarendon – in the Clarendon Hotel – and John O'Hare, who had signed the week before me, was living in the York Hotel with his family. We lived there for three months and, eventually, I got myself out because I was a single lad and I got myself in digs. I was in digs with Jim Walker. I was then in digs with John Robson and then they signed Dave Mackay twelve months later. Cloughie said: "Would you like to live in the hotel?" He said it would be good for me. There was food there, a bed there and all that kind of thing and really, I was Mackay's batman. I looked after Dave, as such. He had the big, plush room and I had the little tiny box room in the corner, but it was, I think, maybe the making of Roy McFarland.

Bill Wainwright: Dave Mackay? He lived in, all the time. I'm not sure whether Roy lived in for too long. Invariably, new players lived at the Midland until they'd built a house or bought a house. Archie Gemmill stayed for a long time. Stuart Webb stayed. I might be exaggerating, but I would say about six months.

Roy McFarland: It was typical of Clough and Taylor, typical of Cloughie to put me in there to look after him, maybe to learn. He knew what Dave was. He knew Dave was a great player and, I mean, I had many evenings sitting round a table having dinner with Dave. On the odd occasions, we had the odd drink too. He taught me about life and he taught me about football – and Dave Mackay talked a lot of sense. He'd been there, he'd done it. He'd been at the top and everywhere I went with him, people admired him. Asked him for his autograph and people pestered him and I couldn't understand it and I didn't like it. Not because it wasn't attention for me, but it annoyed me because people disturbed us. We sat in restaurants and people used to come up and say: "Mr Mackay, can I have your autograph?" Dave would sign them and then somebody else would come and I'd say: "What are you signing them for? Tell 'em to bugger off." Dave said: "You can't do those things. These are supporters who follow football and they love football." I learned a hell of a lot living with Dave in the Midland Hotel. Both sides, in a sense. How not to live maybe, at times, but really how to be a good professional. He was a very good professional.

Bill Wainwright: Brian leaving? I wasn't there. I left in March 1973 and Brian left about October time. I went to Sheffield and the night before I left, they played Leicester and after the match was over someone said: "Brian wants to see you in his office." So I said: "No, I must get back. It's nine o'clock, half past nine or whatever." They said: "He wants to see you in his office." So I went down to his office and he's shuffling a few papers or whatever he was doing and eventually he said: "Okay, we'll go down to the Midland."

Bill Wainwright: I would have thought he knew pretty well what was going on at the Midland, but when I left at – half past seven it would start, wouldn't it? – it didn't seem to be anything other than an ordinary night, but when we got back, all the team were there, all the directors, Sam. Brian took me down. Peter was already there and they gave me a wonderful reception on leaving. Yes and I was presented with – the names are nearly obliterated – the ball they played with in the match. You can hardly read the names now, they've nearly all faded off. The next day, I left and came to Sheffield and Brian brought me. At the Victoria Hotel they used to hold FA disciplinary meetings. Anyway, the player, whoever it was, had to be there, so I came with Brian and, of course, he'd got a Mercedes. In those days, the Vic, which is near the railway station, was always covered in grime. The inside was glorious, but the outside was awful. God, it looked a bleak place and as we turned up Station Road, Brian turned to me and said: "If this is where they've sent you, it's the sack next time!"

Administration

Michael Dunford: I was at Wilmorton College, which had opened a couple of years earlier. I was doing my 'A' levels and in the summer we had quite a long vacation. My father was a residential policeman and he met Brian Clough one morning outside the ground and Mr Clough always had a great deal of time for the police and the services. He got talking to my father and he asked – in his own way, of course – "What's young Michael doing nowadays?" My father said: "Well, he's at home at the moment." So he said: "Tell him to get off his backside and get down to the Baseball Ground here because we need extra hands in the ticket office." This was at the boom period. We'd just won promotion out of the old Second Division, so young Michael could not quite believe his luck because at that time I was wanting to train as a draughtsman, although I think at that period of your life, you don't really know exactly what you want to do.

So I went down and worked in the ticket office. Malcolm Bramley was the secretary. Malcolm was very young. He'd joined us from Sunderland, I think, the previous year and he found it quite hard going and he didn't last too long. He was replaced by Alan Collard, before Stuart Webb came along. Alec Miller and Cyril Annable had both gone. Both of them were characters.

Whether it's folklore now or whether it's true, the first game when Taylor and Clough were at the Baseball Ground, I think Peter Taylor came in and asked Alec Miller whether he'd got a referee and linesmen. Of course, being the old traditionalist, Alec told him where to get off in no uncertain terms.

Stuart Webb: I was assistant secretary at Preston and Jimmy Gordon used to come across from Blackburn Rovers and he got to know me. He then joined Peter and Brian at Derby. They needed a secretary. There had been administrative problems because they'd been banned from Europe. They'd suggested that Dave Mackay, as part of his contract, did a weekly column in the programme, for which they paid him about 2s 6d. The FA found out and so on. In fact, it wasn't a good time because the club had qualified for Europe – they'd finished fourth and they were brought down to the FA and I remember Sir Robertson King looking at the minutes after that. Anyway, to cut a long story short, they got rapped over the knuckles. They got fined a few bob, but they were banned from Europe. No one really accepted what a ban from Europe was at that time because nobody knew. Only afterwards you realise it could have been a couple of million quid down the line. So the administration was changed and they were looking for a new secretary and I was asked: "Would you like to join?"

Stuart Webb: It was a shambles, an absolute shambles. The administration had gone and Alan Collard, who was with the cricket club, had stepped into the breach to help out. To be honest, he was a nice chap and a great administrator at cricket, but football was different and he was glad to get away from it really. It was a mess because three or four people had been around over a three-year period and there'd been no continuity and it needed sorting out.

Michael Dunford: There was, in the early days – the early Seventies – conflict between Brian and Stuart Webb. Now Stuart, really, was in his own way very professional. He'd come in from being well respected at Preston and felt that all the administration and that side of the club was under his jurisdiction.

Stuart Webb: It was a difficult time because they had to get it right and Brian was sort of dictatorial and tended to get involved in administrative things because he felt as manager, he had to be 'the man'. The board were of the opinion that, yes he had to be 'the man' and he was the manager, but on corporate and legal matters and secretarial matters there had to be somebody responsible to the board of directors and I was put in that position. Not a good position because I was only a young guy anyway. So there had to be a demarcation line between the playing side and the administration and legal side. So that had to be sorted out. It wasn't a pleasant time to do that.

Brian Clough: Jimmy Gordon said: "I know a secretary, an assistant secretary." He was assistant secretary at Preston. I said: "Well, I'll go and see him."

Ernie Hallam: When Stuart came he reorganised travel, the Supporters' Club, all that sort of thing. Through Stuart, who asked me, I organised a senior citizens' branch and we developed the foreign branch too. We got a lot of foreign branches, some of them still exist. London and Norway, up to when I departed from the set up last year, were probably our biggest members. Amazingly, the headquarters, Derby, aren't as big as them. Of course, the local people here in Derby don't have to belong to a branch. They feel they belong anyway, whereas the other places feel more remote. When Sam Longson was chairman, there was a tremendous following from up there. High Peak.

Stuart Webb: Preston played an FA Cup-tie against Derby at Deepdale and the replay was on a frosty night down here. At Deepdale, Peter Taylor got hold of me in the corridor and said:

"Oh, I think Brian would like a chat with you." Then Jimmy Gordon rang and it started there. I was asked to come down at Easter to see Brian. We came over – me, Josie and Beverley, who was probably about five then – and we stayed at the Midland with Bill Wainwright. I took a day off from Preston. They didn't know what was going on. Came down, found it, met Brian: "You must stay overnight." Comics in the bedroom for Beverley, all the usual stuff. "I want you to meet the directors."

Stuart Webb: There was a board meeting at Derby the next day, by chance! So at ten o'clock that morning I bounded down to the Baseball Ground with Brian and was thrown into the boardroom. A knock on the door. He said: "Gentlemen, this is the new secretary. Mr Bradley, sort him out will you, Mr Chairman?" And pushed me in. I was stood there with these five guys, who looked up and said: "Oh. Right." Everyone was so embarrassed, but that was how it was. I sat down with Sydney Bradley, who was chairman. Sam took over later. It was the time when the chairman changed regularly. Sydney sat down and I agreed a deal and that was it. Then I had to crawl back to Preston and go and tell them I was handing in my notice. The secretary at the time was George Howarth, who had been there a long time. I was 28, 29. The directors called me in and said they would like me to stay. So that was a dilemma in itself because I was born and bred up there, my family was there and I thought: "Blimey." So it took 24 hours before I could decide: "Should I move down to this great Derby County scene with these eccentric guys or should I stay where I was and get the top job in due course?" Anyway, I decided to come down and we moved that summer and I joined on 1 June 1970.

Stuart Webb: Michael Dunford came in. Michael was good, actually. One day a policeman knocked on the door and said: "Can I see you?" It was Mr Dunford, Michael's father. He was the bobby who patrolled the area. He said: "My son, Michael, has been working here in the ticket office during the school holidays and Mr Clough's just kicked him out and he's very upset. He's at home and I just wondered if you would look at the position." So that was the first job with Michael, to check round and find out what had happened. Why he'd been kicked out and then to take him back on. That was my first clash with Brian, in a way. This guy, myself – and Michael. It was all quite funny really. In fact Michael came in and did a good job and, obviously, has had a good career in football and has gone on to Everton

Michael Dunford: The Ley Stand was just about to be opened. I went to work there in the summer, continued my 'A' level studies for the following year, then started full-time. The first game at the Baseball Ground when I was working there, albeit on a part-time basis at that point, was the opening home game of that season when we played Burnley. We drew 0-0 and Frank Casper missed a penalty. About ten or 15 minutes from the end, as I remember. Strangely enough, that day, Neil Hallam, who was then working for Raymonds was phoning through an after-match report to the equivalent of Radio 5 Live. Bearing in mind the previous year, we'd had a problem with Burnley in the FA Cup with the 'Battle of Turf Moor', when Colin Blant had 'gone through' Roy McFarland and we'd lost 3-1 and John Richardson, I think it was, had got sent off. Anyway, Neil was phoning through his report after the match from the general office because the press facilities were pretty dismal in those days and he'd continued to say that the Burnley tactics were 'a continuation of the brutal tactics they had performed at Turf Moor the previous year'. Harry Potts, the Burnley manager, walked into the office at that very point and ripped the phone out of Neil's hand. There was a sharp exchange of words, which came over live on air. I thought: "If this is football, do I really want to be part of it?" We laugh about it nowadays, but that was one of the incidents which sticks in my memory.

Michael Dunford: I had no official title. I was just 'a worker'. Office boy. I would do anything

I was told to do, as most office juniors would. I used to watch the game after the first ten or 15 minutes. You didn't get the chance to watch too many away games in those days because the Reserves also played on Saturday afternoons. Saturday was the traditional football day then. I liked Derby County and what I was doing. They liked me and I stayed on. I was very fortunate because not many people get the chance to work at professional football club.

Stuart Webb: Yes, I had already been to the Baseball Ground. The impressions were that Derby was a vibrant and quite exciting place to be. Deepdale was a bit like the Baseball Ground. They're all the same, the football grounds, lots of corridors. So there was no difference to me being backstage at Deepdale or the Baseball Ground, but it was the feeling that the club had a sense of achievement and excitement surrounding it. No two days were the same, so there was that challenge for me, to come into this environment.

Stuart Webb: Those three, to me, were the basis of the team – Mackay, McFarland, Todd. Quite a lot was built around them. There were some great players, wonderful players: Bruce Rioch, when he was sticking them in from 30 yards; Francis Lee coming in. But from a Derby perspective, I think you've got to say those three people gave more to the club in the transitional period and that continuity of success. The other guys, Franny came in, Charlie George, they were there for two years, three years maybe, but I'm talking about a longer period in that era where they were the foundation.

Michael Dunford: One thing you learn in football, bearing in mind I was very young in those days – when I was appointed secretary I was only 26, which was very young by anybody's standards – one of the first things you realise, if you want to keep your job, is that you are an administrator, and football management and judgment of players is down to the manager. That's the way it should be at any football club. A pity some directors don't realise that.

Champions of England

'ON the evening of 8 May 1972, the streets of Derby were alive with people celebrating the fact that for the first time in history, Derby County Football Club were Champions of the Football League.' – Anton Rippon and Andrew Ward, *The Derby County Story* (1984).

Hereford United beat Newcastle United in the FA Cup that season. Ronnie Radford's rocket goal from out of the clinging mud at Edgar Street became immortalised on television replays and boosted the young John Motson's career as a football commentator. European Cup winners Ajax, with Johann Cruyff the conductor of 'total football', won the World Club Cup by beating Independiente of Argentina, but in England more people knew that Ted McDougall of Bournemouth topped the League scoring charts with 35 goals in the season.

'Very hard to beat,' was the critics' verdict of that first championship-winning team and there's no doubt that Brian Clough and Peter Taylor liked a clean sheet. Derby County kept 23 clean sheets that season, from a 42-match programme, but they were still an attractive side to watch. The skill of the defenders and the quality of the passing saw to that. Kevin Hector wasn't the club's leading goalscorer. That honour went to Alan Hinton, with 15 goals in his white boots, although penalties were part of his tally. Hector, though, and Colin Boulton were ever-presents and an average of 33,150 spectators crammed into the Baseball Ground to watch.

In the end, the players were sunning themselves on a beach in Majorca when news came through that Leeds United and Liverpool had failed to take enough points from their last games on the Monday evening, to deny the Derby County the title. Then came the dancing.

Colin Lawrence: I remember watching, in 1960 and 1961, Spurs. I thought they played some of the best football I've seen. I also remember watching Spurs in the late Forties when Alf Ramsey was playing right-back and they had Sonny Walter, Bill Nicholson Len Duquemin, George Robb, Eddie Baily, and I thought that was a good 'push and run' side. Then I saw the 1961 side, when they got the 'double'. When we were in the Second Division, I thought when we played with Brian – when we came up and won the championship – I thought that season we played some tremendous football. I would take the next season following on from there, when they beat Tottenham and Arsenal, then I thought: "Well, I've seen some football on here that can never be taken away from us." Absolutely superb, to be along there, with the atmosphere.

Graham Sellors: I know that watching football on television isn't the same, but to illustrate the difference between eras, a good example is the Tottenham match when Derby won 5-0. Recently I watched the highlights of that on Vision Rams and then went up and watched that afternoon's game live. There was no comparison in the quality of football been played then and the quality of football being played in 1969. And that was against a team that had Greaves, England, Gilzean and all sorts of people. In any department, but particularly midfield, there just wasn't a comparison.

Todd and McFarland

Gordon Hughes: I would say the perfect partnership was McFarland, winning and using the ball and Colin Todd sweeping up. They were an incredible back two. They were different types of players. I would say Colin Todd was the best defender because he read the game and he snuffed out things. Roy would play the ball more. In fact I'd fault Colin Todd when he used to try, at times, to come forward and lay the ball off. He couldn't do that. He used to win the ball and lay it off immediately, like Batty does in midfield. He was quicker and brilliant at sweeping up behind the centre-half and the full-backs. He was brilliant at that. McFarland was more the classy player. He could come forward, play the one-twos and go right into the other box. Scored goals, too. Colin Todd couldn't do that. He was more the defender, snuffing out the attacks. That was his forte.

Gordon Guthrie: I can't ever remember them two panicking. Even some great players do, but I can't recollect them panicking. I mean, you used to think: "Toddy's done it now, he'll never get out of there." But he did and he'd just roll it and Roy, with that left foot, it was like a snake. I used to call it the 'snake' because he could do things with that, well. And for a defender...

Steve Powell's home debut (aged 16)

Stuart Webb: Brilliant days. Fantastic. Again, that was a great match, wasn't it? Liverpool. He was a man, playing in short pants really, and he was brilliant. He stood up to everything Liverpool threw at him and he came through it. He grew up that day and played a great part in us winning that championship.

Steve Powell: It was a very big game for the club. They needed to win it to stand any chance of winning the League. The game went very quick. At the time, I didn't feel any nerves about playing. I suppose if it had been later on in my career, it would have probably been worse, but with me being young, I just wanted to go out there and play and I enjoyed it immensely.

Tommy Powell: I was at work at the *Telegraph* and it was a night match. Somebody came up and said: "You're wanted down the front office." That was the old offices. It was Brian. He said: "I'm playing the bairn tonight." I said: "You're joking, aren't you?" 'No," he said, "he'll be all right. I've just left them and he's gone to bed." That was it.

Steve Powell: The general format on a match day was to train in the morning and then have a bit of lunch at the Midland Hotel, go to bed in the afternoon and then get up at about half-three, four o'clock for some tea and toast and then carry on to the game. So I just carried on with the normal routine.

Tommy Powell: It didn't worry him at all, it didn't bother Steve. Yes, I was nervous, a little bit. I knew he could play, but whether the occasion or what would affect things. He was playing against Keegan, Toshack, Emlyn Hughes, Steve Heighway and players like that. I knew he wouldn't flinch from anything.

Colin Gibson: I remember that, yes I do. Yes, that Monday night. I mean, what a time to play football, on a Monday night, at the Baseball Ground. I don't know how early I got there for that game, but I knew I'd got to get in early because I hadn't got a season ticket and there was no way I was going to miss that game. It wasn't his actual debut was it? But it was one of his early games and what a game. Derby had to win it to have any chance of winning the championship and everyone remembers John McGovern falling on to his back and hitting the ball with his right foot as he did so. Top corner, Derby win 1-0, but this other thing was that this ball came down, a long ball came down and Steve Powell takes it with one foot – I can't remember the name of the Liverpool player – over his head and plays the ball away. Terrific.

Ernie Hallam: I don't think we knew he was playing until we got to the ground. I don't know whether Steve knew, but I don't think it was generally known by the public until we got there. By gad, what a game. Of course, everyone remembers him putting Tommy Smith on his back – and his flick over Heighway.

Steve Powell: I knew the morning of the match, actually. Ron Webster had a bit of an injury and the manager at the time, Mr Clough, he came and told me I was playing. I had an idea I might be because I'd been called into the squad and Ron was injured and in those days, you didn't carry too big a squad, so there was only 12 or 13 anyway. So there was a good chance I was going to be involved somewhere.

Colin Gibson: The other thing I remember about that night is that there were thousands and thousands of Liverpool supporters outside the ground and 15 minutes before the end of the game, they opened the exit gates and all the Liverpool supporters who were outside the ground, came in. There was a real crush in the Baseball Ground that night. I clearly remember that and, suddenly, the volume of noise and the atmosphere and the feeling really reached a cauldron and Derby won. Then they had to kick their heels to let Liverpool and Leeds finish their fixtures and they were the two that could rob Derby of the title. That was decided on the Monday night, after the Cup Final I think. Leeds only had to draw, Liverpool had to win. Liverpool could only draw and I can remember sitting round the radio listening to the Leeds versus Wolves match at Molineux and Wolves got a 2-0 lead and then Leeds pulled one back and did everything but equalise. They only needed to equalise and they would have taken the championship away from Derby, but the gods were smiling on our team that night.

Preparation and match days

Kevin Hector: I was fairly laid back. I didn't really get nervous or anything until I started getting my gear on. We didn't go out and warm-up like they do now. We didn't want to get our boots dirty for a start. We always stayed overnight on a Friday before a home match, at the Midland. Cloughie wanted a tightly knit group before the match. The wives didn't like it much. We hardly ever stopped for a meal after an away match. Straight back, sandwiches or fish and chips. Brian was a big family man. Eric Kitchen, the bus driver, was a brilliant driver.

Gordon Guthrie: Alan Hinton would come in at 20 to three, put his gear on and be ready, but some of them would be here an hour or an hour and a half before the game and putting a little sock on here and a sock on there and then they'd sit a bit longer. A few players put their left boot on before the right and things like that. Some want to go out last, some want to go out in the middle and others want to be right up at the front.

Roger Davies: I think I was always quite relaxed. Early days, I was a bit nervous going out there, but once you get into it... We had a good atmosphere in our dressing-room. I probably had procedures where I put things on last, whatever. You follow superstitions and things.

Steve Powell: We used to arrive at the ground an hour, hour and a quarter before the game. Have a cup of tea. Then I used to get warmed up and go on the pitch for a while, knock a few balls around and then we'd be back in for ten minutes or so before the start. As far as I can remember I've always done it from day one, which is what, early Seventies, but when it came in I'm not sure. I thought I'd always done it, but you're probably right, perhaps we didn't at the start. At that stage it was getting changed at half past two, doing a couple of stretches in the changing room and straight out to perform, which is obviously not the best way to do things, but I'm not too sure when players got into the habit of going out on to the pitch early.

Roy McFarland: Going out early? It started, without doubt, from the Europeans. I can remember going to Anfield and watching Inter Milan. I saw Ajax, I saw Cruyff play – we didn't call them 'Ay-ax' then. In Liverpool we called them 'Aj-ax' – and all of a sudden this team called 'Aj-ax' came to Liverpool and won 1-0. They absolutely mesmerised Liverpool, the great Liverpool team, but the point about it is that they came out and did a warm-up and we thought: "By the time the game starts, they'll be shattered." I think it started with the Europeans. We copied them.

Gordon Guthrie: I think it's something that's come over from the continent. A lot of these continental teams, it seems a part of their programme and they seem to have brought it over here.

Brian Clough: I remember Tom Finney once got beans and bacon off my flannels before an international match. I was scoffing into beans and bacon and the plate went 'bump' right on the flannels. I'd only got one pair. It's all I could afford. He said: "Don't bother. We'll get those cleaned." We scraped the beans and the bacon off. Tom took them away. Cleaned. Back. Put them on. I had to. I hadn't got another pair.

Clough and Taylor – the Departure

THE departure of Brian Clough and Peter Taylor from Derby County must rank as one of the most bizarre episodes in the history of football. Apart from the sheer ineptitude of losing a manager of Clough's capabilities so soon after winning the League championship for the first time, the sequence of events which finally saw the duo disappear from the Baseball Ground had more in common with a John Le Carre novel – and sometimes even a dash of 'Carry On' farce – than reality. Strong personalities were involved, of that there was no doubt, and perhaps, with the benefit of that most precise of sciences, hindsight, a collision was inevitable. The irresistible force meeting the immovable object? Almost, but not quite.

Brian Clough: I left Derby over a row with the chairman. What he said eventually, was that we were pushed.

Michael Dunford: It was a strange period because make no mistake about it, Brian was to everybody, really, 'the Boss' – and he liked to be seen as being 'the Boss'.

Bill Brownson: It was through the Supporters' Associations that I got to know Sam. He was very much the chairman and very much 'the Boss'. That's the way he wanted to operate. You can only have one boss and Sam was 'the Boss'.

Gerald Mortimer: It was an utter absurdity that they didn't stay. Utter absurdity. You just got two stubborn people going at each other and neither would back down.

Sam Longson

Brian Clough: He lived in Chapel-en-le-Frith and he used to have a board meeting on a Sunday morning with his mates. One of his mates, who was there, said: "Who runs Derby County, you or Brian Clough?" He said: "I do." Then it was a case of something or whatever. Having encouraged me to go on television, go on the radio, go on this that and everything, he then said: "I think you're doing too much." He was having board meetings on a Sunday with his mates – I'm being repetitive here for emphasis – and his mates were saying to him: "Who's running Derby County? Are you, the chairman or is Cloughie running it?" All he had to say was: "Cloughie's running it!" because I was. That's all he had to say. He didn't have to say nothing else.

Bill Brownson: I'd got a lot of time for Sam and I think that Sam did an awful lot for Derby County. He had a finance side of his business in addition to the transport side. He sold out on that and he put all that money into Derby County. That money bought Toddy and Nish.

Gerald Mortimer: He was a very uncouth man. He also never really put two bob in, Sam. He was a bullshit artist. He was desperate to be on the Management Committee, which he never was, but Brian got too close to him, that was one of the problems. Brian got too close to him. Sam liked to treat him as a son. After Len Shackleton recommended Brian, Sam took him on...he wanted to treat Brian as his son and Peter used to say: "I keep telling Brian, don't get too close. It'll end in tears." Of course, it did. It was absurd.

Stuart Webb: He was a successful man, a very good chairman for Derby. He had the club at heart, there's no doubt. He saw the big picture. I mean, Sam was quite interesting. He had a big camel coat and he portrayed the director as people see them, the stereotype exactly. Big cigar, loved it. Loved his sport cars and liked Brian. Got on with Brian. Brought Brian down from Hartlepool and drove that forward and backed him very much. People used to say to me, when we were at Derby and top of the League, against Man United, the Liverpools, the Evertons of this world, the big giants: "How are you succeeding?" Sam used to have this myth that he'd put millions into the club. It was great. I mean, it was all showbusiness. I remember the chairman of the League, Len Shipman from Leicester, in those days. I mean, Leicester were more powerful than we were. We came from nowhere and took over and he said: "Will Sam ever get his two million out?" I thought: "Two million what?" I couldn't give away the secret, obviously, but Sam portrayed this, that he'd invested vast amounts. That was it and it was great and they all went along with it and the board too. There was no power base because nobody actually owned it, so they all had small shareholdings themselves. Sam had to be a strong character to hold the board together. There was no control as such, like now because Lionel's got control. He owns it and that's it.

Gerald Mortimer: It was like many of these sporting disputes, like the one at Derbyshire Cricket Club recently, it should be sorted out behind closed doors in about ten minutes, but Brian was a stubborn bugger as well.

Bill Wainwright: I wouldn't say the directors came to the Midland much, but Sam Longson did. Sam and I got on like a house on fire. I would think probably because of the connection with Brian, but I found Sam a very nice chap. A very nice chap. I mean, I knew the directors more through travelling, than anything else, but I knew Sam better because he did used to come down to the Midland.

Ernie Hallam: He liked his football. Sam would put in his time. It's a fair way from Chapel-en-le-Frith a few times a week. I think people said about Sam: "He didn't put any money in." Well, he didn't buy the club and he didn't sell it, like they do now, but it's a different game now. He owned shares when they didn't give him any benefit, but I liked Sam. I think he got a lot of stick over Cloughie, but he thought the world of Cloughie really.

Bill Brownson: He started by driving an ambulance. He got sacked from the ambulance service when he took an ambulance to Derby one Saturday! I don't like saying this, but he wasn't very articulate, but he was a damned good businessman. You don't get to be a millionaire, as Sam did in those days back in the Sixties, without something.

Stuart Webb: Brian got into a situation where he was in great demand from the media and he was going down to London for interviews and he'd miss board meetings because of his charisma and so on, so there was no continuity of what Brian did. What Brian wanted he got because he was running the club and the board allowed him to do that. Then there was a lot of feedback from the authorities, the FA, from the League, particularly from Alan Hardaker, who was secretary of the League then. He was writing to the chairman saying: "We don't want your manager coming out with this and that in the press. Please control your manager." So that problem was starting. We were being told by the authorities to try to knock Brian into shape and stop his explosive press comments and he wouldn't do it. That was the problem. The authorities were telling the board: "Control your manager or we'll fine you or we'll fine him." There was always an inquiry going on, something going on. Then there was the situation where Coventry were trying to take them, Barcelona were trying too. It was like an never-ending press circus, that something was happening at Derby. All that was going on, so it was an exciting time and the team were winning matches at the same time. We were signing players and there was always something going on and the club was going forward at a rapid pace.

Bill Brownson: Sam Longson was a Cloughie man, until the League brought about the break-up. The League summoned Sam to a meeting and said: "Look, you've got to control your manager, otherwise you're going to be in trouble." I know that was the truth and that's why he did it. People didn't like Sam after that because he accepted Cloughie's resignation. Cloughie thought that Sam was behind it, that Sam was in cahoots with the League, but he wasn't. It was the other way round. He did think a lot of Cloughie. Sam Longson made Cloughie, and Cloughie made Sam Longson. He took him – he was only at Hartlepools – and he hadn't done anything at all, but Sam put his faith in him and he repaid that faith. I think Cloughie should have stopped with Sam a little bit longer and really got to know what was going on, but at that time, he'd got so big-headed as a manager. He was a good manager – and he knew it. It wasn't the first time he'd resigned you know.

Stuart Webb: All the directors had small shareholdings. They were voted on by shareholders really and by a caucus of friends. No, Sam was a good operator and it just went sour with him and Brian. Sam always liked to be a football man. He liked to be at the top table at Wembley and a power broker within the League and he was getting earache from all these other chairmen and particularly from the League and the FA saying: "Will you sort this manager out?" That's where it all went wrong.

Brian Clough: The Football League were thinking that I was having a go at them and so they were having to have a go at me. They're still having a go at me now. It didn't bother me. It never bothered me then – and it doesn't bother me now!

Stuart Webb: It was frightening. If there could have been some understanding. I mean, Brian needed a strong chairman. He needed somebody who said, you know: "Look here!" I mean, there was suggestions he was going to work for Coventry with Derrick Robbins and all that. I think he needed a strong guy who probably owned the club, to say: "Look, this is what I want you to do. Now go and do it and don't do this and that." You know, whatever. He hadn't got that control, nobody to control him, and we just went further and further and when it went too far one way, it had to swing back the other way and it was wrong. It should have been controlled on a day-to-day basis because the chemistry was there. Everything was there. He was just allowed to go and do his own thing to such a degree that at the end of the day, something had to happen. It was a great pity.

Bill Brownson: The thing was that it was mainly a clash of personalities, Mr Kirkland and Mr Longson. You see, Kirkland wasn't on the board, Sam brought him on. Sam's idea was that if he was going to stir things up, he would be better on the board, which was a sensible thing to do.

Colin Lawrence: We went down to the Baseball Ground, went up to the Sportsman's Bar and we were playing darts and a couple of directors came in and Brian said to one of them: "Good evening." He then said to me: "I shouldn't be speaking to them. If you'd seen the letter that came through on to my desk this morning saying: 'On no account must you speak to any member of the board. Everything has got to go in writing, through the secretary'." He was absolutely livid. That was leading up to the climax of everything. He said: "When I think they used to say to me: 'Get on television.' We'll drive you to the studios at Aston, to get on." Midlands TV hadn't opened here then. He said: "Every time I'm on, it's Derby County that's going on."

Bill Brownson: It had got to the stage where Sam and the board were fed up, although I can't speak for the other members . I think it was the fact that the League had been at Sam for a long time, which they had. I think this was the problem that Cloughie had been at him so much that he decided: "Right. He's resigned and that's it." Everybody was shocked and thought Sam Longson was in the wrong. They don't know about these things and it's like anything, a little bit of information is very dangerous. If you know it all, it's not so bad and you can then judge, but you can't on something like that. It was just one of those things. It was sad. It was sad for Derby County. It was sad for Sam and I think it was sad for Cloughie because he always wanted to come back.

Stuart Webb: No, I never felt threatened. The board used me as their instrument. When communications broke down with Brian, I was the guy that had to go with news... It wasn't pleasant, I can tell you. I could see it brewing up and up.

Brian Clough: Stuart Webb? He's not worth bothering about.

Stuart Webb: Being the general manager-secretary and an executive and not a director of the club, I therefore, had no vote within the boardroom on this issue. Or in fact, on any other. Once the directors had made a decision, then it was my responsibility as company secretary to carry out the board's instructions and implement the various legal requirements that would effect Brian and Peter's departure. That, in itself, wasn't a pleasant task and I did at the time feel quite exposed, but it was a duty I had to carry out under the responsibilities of company secretary, responsible to the directors and shareholders of the company. Whilst having been brought to the club by Brian and Peter, my duties and responsibilities were to the board of directors and shareholders, whilst at the same time working successfully with Brian and Peter during what was a highly successful period.

Colin Lawrence: We went in the Standard at Newton Solney. We were having a game of darts with the publican. It was about seven o'clock at night, I think it was – it may have been nearer eight – and a 'bobby' came in. He looked across the bar at Brian and he said: "Oh God. They've got Derbyshire Police looking for you." "Well they ain't looked very far," said Brian, like he does. "Well, I'm telling you," he said, "that there's a call come through on our radios that if we see you, we've got to take you in hand and arrest you. We've got to point out the fact that you have stolen company property. That is, you've taken a car without permission and you're running around not covered on insurance etc., etc."

Stuart Webb: This situation was when he'd gone that Jack Kirkland and I handled it. Brian had left and we had another classic with Sam. There are photographs about this. We played Leicester on the first Saturday and there were protests – 'Come back Brian' and all that – and Sam Longson arrived at the ground and, I mean Bill Rudd, one of the directors, just didn't want to go in the stand. He was visibly shaken he was so upset. There was all this hype going on and Sam walked out to the directors' box two minutes before kick-off. The players were kicking in and all that. He waved at the crowd and the crowd stood up and roared at Sam. He didn't realise that Brian had come out on 'C' stand, on the next gangway! So they both waved to the crowd and, I mean obviously, the fans were saluting Brian, but Sam thought they were saluting him! It was farcical. Brian went down for the *Parkinson Show* that night.

Dave Mackay: Nottingham Forest Reserves were playing at Northampton and a fellow called Mr Longson came to that game. I didn't think he was interested in the game, but was interested in the manager. It happened from there. Sam said he'd like me to come back, so everybody's saying: "Don't come back." Things like that.

Stuart Webb: Then there were the players' meetings. Players would come in and say: "There's another protest meeting." So we had to get the PFA down. Terry Hennessey was sensible. He was the players' representative on the PFA at that time and he said: "Look, lads." You know, to Roy McFarland, to Alan Hinton, to Kevin, he spelt it out: "You're breaking your contract if you do this." All of that was going on and I was the guy between the board and all this. It wasn't an easy time. Then the board decided to look for somebody else, and the chairman and Sydney Bradley. We drew a short list up. Bobby Robson was it. So I rang Bobby Robson and he said: "No thank you." He was happy at Ipswich. Then Dave's name was thrown in. Dave, who was at Forest, as you know, was approached and he said: "Yes I would like to come." He wanted about a week, I think. He had a couple of games to play before he'd actually do it. So that again was turmoil: "Will he come? Will he, won't he?" People trying to put pressure on him. I know a couple of players rang him saying: "Don't come." You know... "There's a lot of trouble here, better if you stayed away at Forest." Dave soon put that right because he'd made his mind up.

Gordon Guthrie: It was a hairy time, wasn't it? The town was in upheaval. No one could believe it. When you think back, Dave Mackay really did a tremendous job because talk about walking into a hornet's nest that day he came here, he did do. There was a bit of a rebellion on with the players. They didn't want to play for Derby County any more, they wanted Brian back. There were petitions in the streets, there were meetings all over. Of course, they got advice from the PFA about their contracts. Anyway, Dave steamed in that first day as manager and that was it. He was like Brian in a lot of ways. He could handle it. When I think back, had it been a lesser manager, I think they'd have just said: "No thank you." And just gone out again.

Stuart Webb: So the players were on strike and Dave was coming, the next day. This was the Wednesday night and players were demanding to see the board, to see what was going on. The board didn't want to meet the players because they couldn't tell them Dave was coming. It was a difficult situation. Everybody was playing for time. Everybody was keeping their head down because a statement was going out in the morning that Dave Mackay was coming and Dave said he wouldn't do it until he'd played his last game at Forest, which was that Wednesday night. He said: "If anything leaks, I won't be coming." So we had to honour our agreement with Dave, so that's why nobody would face the players or the press or anybody. That's the reason why Jack Kirkland and I locked ourselves in the boardroom. The directors had met and left. They were leaving, and I was going too, then all of a sudden...the players arrived. That was it. It was the Wednesday night. It was the night that Forest were playing, so after 9.30pm, we were all right. At 9.30pm, we walked out and we answered the questions because Dave had released it from the other side as well.

Dave Mackay: No doubts at all. Fearless. I always have been if I make my mind up. Roy McFarland, Henry Newton, two of my pals, they said: "Please don't come back." Because they knew there was going to be trouble, but did I listen to them? No. So I came back. I more or less said: "Hey, if I don't take the job, somebody else is going to have it. Brian's not going to be back there as long as Mr Longson's there. He ain't going to get it back, right? Somebody's going to get it, so hey, it's going to be me."

Alan Hinton: Absolutely brilliant, Dave. Brilliant. Never ever got the credit he deserved for what he did at Derby County Football Club. We were all disappointed when Clough and Taylor resigned, but they did resign. They weren't fired and what happened was that Dave came in. He had some problems with some players when he came in. He had no problems with me because he made a speech that was sensational when he took the job. He said: "Look guys. I didn't look for this job. Clough did resign. You may not want me to take this job, but if I don't take this job, somebody else will and I'll be angry with myself for not taking it. I want this job and I want it to work." He made a monumental speech that certainly for me, as an older player who was pretty mature, meant everything because Dave Mackay was so honest and genuine.

Stuart Webb: Yes it would have been awkward had Dave Mackay not come, but there's always something comes out when people sit down to make a decision. You look at it and see who's available and whatever. Had it been Bobby Robson? Well they all come in and do their own job, just as when Jim Smith came into Derby. Robson was the first choice because the board thought Derby were a big club, in Europe, so they wanted to go for a proven manager. Dave's managerial career had just started and he probably had a lot to prove as a manager. But Robson turned it down and Dave was then the obvious choice and, of course, went on to do a brilliant job.

Gerald Mortimer: It's possible that no one could have done it as well. It's something we'll never know. Bobby Robson was offered it. Even Brian in later years, would say quite categorically, that Dave didn't get the credit he deserved. I don't know. He was respected. He was loved at Derby really, as a player. Yes, I think I'd accept that. I don't think anyone else could have done it better.

Dave Mackay: Most of it was rubbish anyway. The players ain't going to turn up, they ain't going to do this or that. They ain't going to train, they ain't going to play. I said: "Okay, we'll play the Reserves." I would have done anything anyway, but it was hard work, first of all. We didn't win in nine matches and we had the AGM. It was there they had the League table, Brian's supporters. Who was bottom of the League after those nine matches? Derby County. When I went there they were third in the League and we finished the season third in the League, which was great.

Stuart Webb: I think Brian thought that I was part of it. I think he felt, you know: "There's always him down the corridor." It was always me who was close to the board and the administration. Disagreements? Correct. Very clear. The board had given me instructions what the demarcation lines were, having been brought in following a League enquiry and an FA Enquiry and the club being banned from Europe for a year. So they made it very clear that I had to be responsible. I was prepared to take the opposite stance to him. I think he resented that. The fact that he'd encouraged me to come meant he felt I was his man, but I soon found out from the board that I couldn't be his man. I had to take the legal position and the shareholders' position. The board's position was that there was a legal entity there and if anything else had gone wrong administratively, the club could have been in severe trouble with the authorities. There was a high degree of respect on both sides, but I had a position to play within the club and hold, so whether he held me as part of that team that which had to restrict him...I'm sure I was. There's no doubt about it, but I was very sad to see him go and was always part of the team trying to get him back, but it wasn't my decision. The board were powerful men, all successful business people in their own right and they made the decisions. There's no doubt. I was just merely the servant of the club and the shareholders.

Regrets?

Brian Clough: Yes. Despite all the friends and success I had at Nottingham, I felt at Derby, with the very young side we had – we'd signed David Mackay who was the guiding light, we'd got Colin Todd, Ronnie Webster, Pete Daniel, John Robson, you name it you can go right through them – I felt we had the nucleus, if that's the right word, of a side that could have gone on and on and on... So, that is my one regret. Then I went to Nottingham and fulfilled what I wanted to do.

Champions Again

IN the FA Cup Final of 1975, West Ham United beat Fulham 2-0. The Football Writers' Association chose Alan Mullery of Fulham as their Footballer of the Year, but the players really knew. They chose Colin Todd as the Professional Footballers' Association's Player of the Year.

Roy McFarland ruptured an Achilles tendon whilst playing for England at Wembley, which meant he played in only four matches of the 1974-75 season. Peter Daniel deputised and was a hero, as Derby County won the title for the second time in three years, this time under Dave Mackay. Daniel won the Derby County supporters' Player of the Year award, but the players really knew. Todd was magnificent.

Colin Boulton was ever-present for a second championship season and Bruce Rioch also played in every game. He was leading goalscorer with 15 League goals from midfield and some hit the net with frightening power. As in the first championship success, Derby County used only 16 players in total, with McFarland returning to the side for the final four matches. Up front, Francis Lee made a great impact with 12 League goals, whilst Roger Davies took over from John O'Hare as Kevin Hector's strike partner. Lee, of course, had won a championship medal with Manchester City in 1968 and his experience was vital. The following season at the Baseball Ground, he fell out with Norman Hunter, violently.

'More flair' they said about the second Derby County championship side, although, paradoxically, the team scored two goals less than their predecessors in 1972. Equally strange, the average attendance at the Baseball Ground fell by 6,431 to 26,719, but there can be no denying that Dave Mackay and his assistant, Des Anderson, did a magnificent job in restoring Derby County's fortunes after the turbulence of the Clough and Taylor departure. It did seem, though, that some people were becoming a bit blase about success.

Alan Hinton: Dave didn't always play me in the team and at the same time, I was getting older, but he treated me nicely and treated me particularly nicely when my son was sick with cancer. My son eventually died, but Dave Mackay and Des Anderson, for me, were giants and they won the championship and I was a part of that in 1975. Dave never got the credit he should have got, but I'm very pleased to say that Derby treat Dave Mackay like a film star today and he goes to most of the games.

Gordon Guthrie: I was with the Reserves mostly, when Brian won his championship, but I used to travel with them, of course. Then Brian went and Jimmy went and Dave took over and I was moved up then. That was it, I stayed there ever since.

Michael Dunford: Dave, in fairness, brought in some quality players like Bruce Rioch, Francis Lee, to supplement Brian Clough's team. Went on to win the championship. Afterwards he bought Charlie George.

Dave Mackay: Best buys? Francis Lee, Charlie George, Bruce Rioch. Bruce was probably the best...middle of the park...his first full season he scored 15 goals from midfield. He'd be worth about £25 million now.

Roger Davies: They were magnificent players. I mean, they always say: "The better the players you play with, the better it is." To play in the Derby side I played in was quite easy, actually, because of the calibre of players around us. Like McFarland, then we had the skills of Nishie at left-back. Rod Thomas came in and the others. It must have taken me – I don't know whether I really ever got used to it – I mean, it was years later, when I was a regular in the first team, I'd still sit there and look in awe. I'd sit there, getting changed and I'd look round the dressing-room and think: "What am I doing here?" I mean, I was in awe still, of some of these players, even though I was at the same level and still playing. I used to look round and think back to where I was a few years before and think: "God. I'm playing with these guys."

Charlie George: They had some great players, McFarland, Nish, Gemmill, Todd, Francis Lee, my old mate Rod Thomas. The thing that struck me immediately was the way they played it out from the back. That's what I noticed straight away. It was different to what I'd been used to. It's a pity they didn't win anything because I think with the players they had there – I mean, Kevin Hector as well – they should have gone on and won things. I was a little disappointed I didn't win anything at Derby because I thought they were a real quality side. I was fortunate enough to play with them and scored some important goals. I rented a house in Derby for a while before moving up, that wasn't a problem.

Roger Davies: We had ability because Roy McFarland could have played anywhere. He wasn't frightened of receiving the ball. You could give Roy the ball at his feet and he'd knock it anywhere you wanted. I mean, you had people at the back, really, with as much skill – and maybe more – than some teams had in midfield and up front. Roy could've played anywhere, Toddy was great on the ball, Nishie had silky skills and Thomo and Ronnie Webster could play a bit too. So we did play good football. That was the main thing about Derby.

Dave Mackay: When we won the championship I brought Roy McFarland in for the last four games. If you'd have asked another manager, they'd probably have left him out, saying: "Hey, leave Peter Daniel in there for the last four." I think if you look – I really haven't checked – with nine matches to go we got beat 2-1 by Stoke at the Baseball Ground. That was like the death knell. Not everybody, but most people said: "Oh, you've had it. They've had it." From then on, to the end of the season, we talk about attractive football and scoring goals and all that, but we hardly let a goal in. I remember drawing 1-1 at Middlesbrough, but we certainly didn't let in more than a couple of goals or so in the last eight or nine matches.

Roger Davies: Playing up front, when you're playing like that with players who have got a good touch on the ball and know when to give it and where to give, well. I mean, with David Nish and all of them, when you made your runs, the ball was always in the right area. It wasn't up here, like six feet above your head. It was right side, chest, left side. It made you favourite. I mean, the balls to you were so good, it made it a lot easier for you. You weren't always turning, facing balls because they could play it to feet or play it to your chest, whatever. Made you favourite for it. It made it a lot easier for a front player.

Dave Mackay: Was I tempted to buy when McFarland was injured? No. Peter Daniel had always done well. Yes, Peter Daniel and Colin Todd did well. Colin Todd was the PFA Player of the Year because he was doing what McFarland was doing previously, as a leader. He was a bigger man, not size, but in status than Pete Daniel, but he was a super guy, Pete Daniel. Archie Gemmill did well. Everybody did. If you win the League, everybody's got to do well, haven't they?

'Champion Years' speaks for itself. Derby County supporters lived off the fat of the land in those glorious times. Celebrities abounded. Everybody who was anybody strolled along Osmaston Road and down Shaftesbury Crescent, for the Baseball Ground was the place to be, especially when the floodlights lit up European nights or when Arsenal, Tottenham Hotspur and Manchester United were being beaten. Charlie George became the 600th player ever to appear for Derby County, when manager Dave Mackay signed him after the championship triumph of 1975. His injury before the FA Cup semi-final against Manchester United in 1976 proved to be costly indeed.

Leeds United were runners-up in 1972, Liverpool in 1975. Matches against those two fierce rivals were matches to remember.

Roy McFarland: The hardest and the best team – League team – I played against was Leeds United. There was that rift, in a sense, that argument and rivalry between Clough and Revie, but Revie's teams were tremendous teams. They were very efficient, very professional. If the word 'professionalism' came into the game, they took it to the extreme. It was too much and it was poor, but it picked up a lot of points for Leeds United, in terms of how to slow the game down. Liverpool picked a lot of things like that up, I think, from Leeds United. Things like how to slow the game down without annoying the opposition, without annoying the supporters, without annoying the referee, but Leeds took it to the extreme and upset too many supporters, upset too many referees and, in a sense, upset too many opposing teams. That maybe backfired on them, but without doubt they were the best League team I played against. They were a tremendous team. When they had the ball, you had to work hard to get the bloody thing back and when you got it back – and gave it away – it took ages to get the bugger back again– and that's the sign of a good side.

Gordon Guthrie: I think there was always that tension, that we wanted to beat them, which was natural against any team, but more so against Leeds. Remember at that time, a lot of the papers quoted them as being arrogant and all this and that, but for me, I always say they were a great side, when they had Bremner, Giles and all the others, Jack Charlton and everybody. They should have won more things than they did.

Stuart Webb: Well, the Leeds games were always interesting weren't they? Franny Lee and the punch up. They were fantastic, weren't they? Leeds always had an angle, always had aggravation. I think the Leeds matches were better than Manchester United or Arsenal. Leeds had always got that little edge, hadn't it? You'd get that tingle at the back of the spine before you ever walked down to the Baseball Ground, there was so much going on. They were a powerful side and for us to get up there to challenge them then was tremendous. There was always a lot of aggravation, which came out, of course, with the Norman Hunter, Franny bit. No, they were great days.

Lee v Hunter

Gordon Guthrie: That was some incident, that. As you know, we'd been awarded a penalty and Franny was quite famed for getting penalties. Anyway, that had upset Norman and something else had gone off a bit before. Next minute, there's a little incident just outside the 18-yard box and then there's blows going in. I mean, really, they could have hit each other with a handbag, as we thought from here. The next thing, the referee's amongst them and pointing to the tunnel. They're off, pair of them. So I've got out the box and I'm walking towards Francis and, as he's coming towards me, I could see him and he's touching this lip of his. Of course, it's bleeding isn't it? All of a sudden, he's put his tongue up to his lip and his tongue's come through the lip. It's cut right through. Yes, right through the lip. Then he realises what Hunter's done and, of course, they're at it again and I'm on and you know the rest. The rest's history.

Charlie George: I think there'd been a bit niggle about a penalty incident earlier. Anyway, they certainly had a go. It's hard to imagine what would have happened these days. It was a good contest.

Gordon Guthrie: We'll it took three of us, really, to get Franny Lee into the medical room. Down the tunnel, into the medical room, and we're holding him down there, two of us, on the bed. Slammed the door to and the doctor's come in and, of course, the doctor's trying to have a look at Franny to see what he can do for his lip as regards sewing it. Franny, he's trying to get off the bed: "I'll murder him," he says, "I'll murder him." Of course, the blood's all over the place, I'm trying to wipe Franny and get it cleaned up and everything. It was a while before he cooled down and, actually, even after the game he hadn't cooled down much.

Dream challenge match: 1972 Championship side v 1975 Championship side

Kevin Hector: That's a good question, a very good question. Hard to say, of course, but perhaps the 1972 side was a little better defensively. If I had to say which side I'd choose to play in, I would choose the 1972 side.

Michael Dunford: 1972. I think so. I'm not so certain that the 1969-70 team wouldn't have beaten the 1972 side. I think when you look at all the teams, I think the team that the supporters of the club, who'd had very little success to shout about for years, they grew up with that team. I think the team that came up out of the old Second Division – Les Green, Jimmy Walker, John McGovern, O'Hare, Kevin Hector, McFarland – were a very, very strong team. All right, maybe lacked a little bit of individual flair of the 1972 and 1975 teams, but I think as a team unit, their record stands comparison with many. The first year we came out of the Second Division, Tottenham 5-0, Arsenal 3-2, Liverpool 2-0 and 4-0. You know, the best in the country were coming and getting beaten. We went the first 12 games of the new campaign after we got promotion before we lost a game, at Sheffield Wednesday 1-0. Very strong team. I have to say, that was the strongest team I've seen play, as a unit.

Voices of The Rams

Brian Flint: I would probably say the 1972 side. I think the 1975 side was more attack-minded, but sometimes, you can trip over yourself like that. If it doesn't come off, you can get rolled over. The 1972 side was more of a unit. I think there were more individuals in Dave Mackay's side.

Alan Hinton: I think it would have been close. The 1975 side had unbelievable dynamism from Bruce Rioch. I mean, Bruce Rioch playing right-side midfield scored 15 League goals that year. I don't think any player ever played more powerful or stronger than he did. Francis Lee. Later of course, we had Charlie George. I filled in on occasions, but don't forget, the 1975 team still had McFarland and Todd and Gemmill, who was a 'horse'. I mean, Gemmill was like an athlete you'd never seen before. He was up and down that field like a horse. I mean, he was fantastic. At the same time, in 1972, we had John O'Hare, who was one of the most undersung heroes of all time at Derby County. A lovely man, wonderful player, good soldier for the club. Colin Boulton played in goal again, didn't he, in 1975? He did a great, great job. Safe hands.

Steve Sutton: I think possible the 1975 side. I think it had a little more finesse about it. The 1972 side was a very gritty side, a very hard to beat side. It would have been a magnificent game wouldn't it because there were hard men at both ends? Of course, some played in both sides. You'd have had to give them yellow bibs, to play for both.

Lionel Pickering: The 1975 side, obviously. You can look at it both ways because you could say: "Yes. Dave Mackay improved on Cloughie's 1972 side." It was a more attractive side. I mean, he signed Bruce Rioch, Francis Lee – Charlie George afterwards – and they were entertaining, but okay, Cloughie did it first and it was a good team that he produced, but I do believe that the 1975 side was more entertaining.

Graham Richards: I think the heart of every true Derby fan would say the 1972 side. It's a bit hard to rationalise because I think the 1975 side had more talented individuals. There wasn't a Charlie George, though – he came later – and there certainly wasn't a Francis Lee in the earlier Clough team, but I just think the 1972 side was a great side that never quite came to the culmination it should have done because Clough left. It contained Todd and McFarland playing at their best. They'd be hard to get past. Kevin would be three years younger, although he world, of course, be one of several who would play on both teams, but I would feel that, perhaps, the 1972 side would out-think the 1975 side. It'd be a game I'd like to see.

Mick Hopkinson: You mention the 1972 side and the 1975 side, but the team I enjoyed most came out of the Second Division. Maybe not such big names, but obviously you'd got Carlin, Dave in his heyday, Mac as a young lad coming through, Ronnie Webster. Young Robbo. Up front, could you get a better forward line than O'Hare, Hector, Hinton? McGovern, Durban, Toddy. Useful.

Roy Christian: I think Mackay's 1975 side possibly had the edge, but it was an older side. I mean, I thought Mackay, as a manager, didn't look to the future. I think he only saw as far as the following week's game. I always thought that was the weakness with Mackay. He was more a chequebook man.

Michael Gretton: Ah, well. There were some great players in both sides, but I think BC's team would have done it.

Roy McFarland: The 1972 team were quite hard to break down. They could grind out a 1-0. The 1975 team couldn't. They were more open, more attacking. If the words would be 'more modern', yes they were more modern. That was Dave's philosophy: "If we win 6-5, so be it." With Cloughie and Taylor, it was: "Let's get a clean sheet. Let's make it hard for the opposition.

Let's hit teams on the break." So we did that quite successfully. If the 1972 team played the 1975 team, it would be difficult to say who would win. I obviously – and I don't meant that disrespectfully in any sense – enjoyed the team in 1972. It was the first time we'd won the championship and that will always stand out. It was a little bit special because of that. I think the teams we beat that year, the Arsenals, the Liverpools and Leeds Uniteds, in their day, were great teams. The fact that we beat them on goal-difference or one point or whatever it was at the time, didn't matter. We still beat them and finished top.

Stuart Webb: That's an interesting one. I've never looked at it that way. If you were going to play Manchester United tomorrow, in the Champions League, which side would you put out against them? I mean, it's horses for courses. I personally feel that Dave's side was a better side. More flair, more attractive, but Brian and Peter's side was solid, didn't give much away. So they were two different sides. It's like a European Cup-tie. You'd have one for a home match and you'd have one for the away match. If it was a European Cup-tie, the home team would be Dave's team, Brian's team would be when you went away to, say, Juventus. One was based on defence and counter-attacking in many ways. The other was based on flair and attacking ability. I don't know. Difficult. I'd have to think about who the opposition was.

Colin Gibson: There's a question now. I don't know. People say to me that the 1975 team had got more style than the team that won it in 1972 and, again, if I pick out games, I would probably pick games from the 1974-75 season which would stand out more than games from the 1971-72 season. I think it probably took us so much by surprise in 1972, that Derby County were champions, but I wouldn't really like to say. I mean, you think about the players that were playing in the Derby team then and, of course, there were some players that were championship winners with both sides, but the addition of somebody like Bruce Rioch in the 1974-75 season...you're talking about inspired signings. Derby go out and sign Francis Lee, who has done it all, seen it all with Man City, and comes to Derby and wins another championship medal. That football that the 1974-75 team played was terrific, but I can't answer your question. I don't think so.

Roy McFarland: We were a hard team to break down in 1972 and the one thing that's never ever talked about and mentioned, except probably by our supporters, was that we had a goalscorer who could score a goal from nothing and, maybe, he didn't get the credit he deserved. I'm talking about Kevin Hector. I know our fans loved him and called him 'the King', but maybe overall, Kevin never got the recognition he deserved. We hit teams on the counter attack, maybe more than the 1975 team did, and Kevin was the key to that. O'Hare was the one who could hold it up, but Kevin was the one who could take it through and, if you look at the videos, you'll see the angles and the positions that he scored goals from and his movement on his left foot, his right foot. He was the key.

Alan Hinton: I remember Peter Daniel filling in very strongly for a long time and it was very special when the crowd started singing: 'Daniel for England'. That was wonderful, wasn't it? I remember being on the bench one day and Peter Daniel came out from the back against Liverpool and passed the ball through to Francis Lee, who went through and scored the winning goal. Des Anderson said to me: "Did Peter mean that?" And I said: "Eh, Des – if that had been Toddy, you'd have said it was world class." Toddy was very supportive of Peter, who was voted Player of the Year that year. It was a great, great story and I think if that type of thing had happened today, there would have been, maybe, a hundred times more publicity about it because it was what the real stuff is all about. Plus, when we were at Derby, the pitch wasn't very good and you think back to the times when somebody had scored a goal and somebody else would put their hand on the dirt and get a pile of mud in their hands and rub it down your face and say: "Great goal." 1972 and 1975 were special times and the crowd played a big part in it too. The fans were so proud of that team, and so they should have been.

Steve Powell: I think it's very difficult to compare different times in football. You can only be as good as you can, at that particular time. I mean, there were a lot of talented players in both teams and it would be very, very difficult to predict a result. So I'll sit on the fence with that one. Call it a draw.

How champion were the champions?

Charlie George: Leeds were a great side, although they didn't win as much as they should have done. Liverpool won things in Europe, didn't they? I think it was a pity that the Derby side didn't win more. I think they could have done, but the best sides do win things, don't they? Derby on a scale of 1-10? If you put Liverpool and Leeds at nine, seven and three quarters, perhaps.

Steve Powell: I would say in relation to Liverpool and Leeds, I would say they'd be around the eight mark, certainly. I mean, to win a championship is a really difficult thing to do. You had to play consistently well over 42 games; you couldn't afford to lose too many. People said in 1971-72 that the club was sort of lucky the way the results went, but it wasn't luck at all. They accumulated enough points over the season to win it and they won it fair and square. It wasn't luck at all, it was just through sheer talent.

Colin Gibson: If you're looking at the Seventies then, yes, Liverpool were the team of the Seventies and that was because they went on to have the European success, which Derby, I suppose you might say, were slightly cheated out of it. They reached the semi-finals in 1973, with all the bribery scandal that didn't really go in Derby's favour, despite the investigations. But Derby were a top team along the way. Again, they always say that if Brian Clough had stayed at Derby, Derby County would have been the team of the Seventies and not Liverpool, not Leeds United. Liverpool and Leeds, nine out of ten? Again, Leeds didn't have the European success that Liverpool did. They reached the European Cup Final in 1975 and lost to Bayern Munich. Derby only got the one real stab at it. They lost to Real Madrid, the second time around. Again, another great game at the Baseball Ground. 4-1, Charlie George's hat-trick. You're thinking: "Okay. That's some lead." And they lost 5-1 in the second leg! So I suppose, if Liverpool are on nine and Leeds are on eight, I'd put Derby on eight as well because you can't have Leeds going ahead of Derby. They were a loathsome team. They were a very talented team, but oh, they were a loathsome team.

Roger Davies: The Derby County sides in that era always had a chance of winning the championship. So to put us up at seven and a half was probably about right.

Graham Richards: We reached the semi-final of the European Cup. We were swindled out of it. Maybe Juventus were the better side anyway and our success was over a very short period. Their's - Liverpool's - was infinitely longer, so I wouldn't argue about with that assessment of seven and a half for us. In those championship seasons, we were as good as Liverpool and Leeds and finished above them and if that had continued for another three or four years, at the expense of Liverpool and Leeds, then you'd say yes, but Derby County came in two very short bursts, with two different teams and I certainly think the 1972 team - which I prefer - would have to be judged a little below those two eminently successful sides.

Today

Roger Davies: I don't think this Derby County side has a chance of winning the championship. It's not their fault; a lot's down to business now. The big sides are pulling away now and the Premiership is probably three divisions in itself. You've got the money guys pulling away; the middle ones; and those battling to stay in the Premier League. So I would probably, if I say middle of the table, say five for the present Derby County side.

Colin Gibson: Five. Some of the football we saw in the first season at Pride Park was reminiscent of the football Derby played in that championship time, but then again, I don't whether you can compare like with like. You don't feel now that Derby or Leicester or any of the other surrounding teams in the Premiership now, can really make the challenge needed. There's always the chance you can beat them, as Derby have done. They've beaten all the big teams in the Premiership, with the exception of Leeds so far, but you just don't feel that the title is there for winning any more, whereas back in the Seventies, although there were great teams like Liverpool and Leeds, you knew that you'd got a chance. There was a chance to come through and that your team could go on. I suppose Blackburn have been the last team to do it, but you just don't feel that it is a prize that's attainable any more, which is a shame. Yes, the current Derby team, maybe five in comparison to those teams.

Steve Powell: As I say, it's very difficult to compare era to era because the game's changed, certainly. I mean, the pace of the game's certainly changed. I've watched the current team several times in the last couple of seasons and there's been some good games down there, but the fact that they haven't really won anything, I would say would mean they'd probably be around the six mark, six and a half, at the moment, perhaps.

Graham Richards: You can't really equate them with the championship sides at all. The only way you can compare eras – and football is totally different in formation and pitches and scheduling in every way – is to pick out players of the present team you'd think would get in the championship sides and that's difficult, almost straightaway. Mart Poom would have a shout as the goalkeeper, but he probably wouldn't make it against Colin Boulton. Igor Stimac, in my view, fully fit as he was in his early days at Derby,was as good a player as many that were in that side, but after that...hmm.

European Nights

Gerald Mortimer: The first away one I think, that was exciting. The whole thing of going to the airport, representing England, off to Yugoslavia, Sarejevo it was. Bill Wainwright probably did go. He went on quite a lot of trips and pre-season tours and that kind thing. He came along to look after the catering and generally, to be Bill Wainwright, really.

Bill Wainwright: Juventus. We went to Juventus. Oh yes. I didn't go to many away matches in this country, but all the abroad ones. I didn't miss one. Exciting? Oh. It was wonderful. Don't ask me about the match. If I remember rightly, it poured with rain, that's about as much as I can remember. We all got presented with a radio clock. It's still up in the bathroom.

Stuart Webb: The Real Madrids, the Benficas. They were fantastic. They were absolute classics, weren't they? Big nights at the Baseball Ground. I remember Matt Busby coming on one occasion and sitting in the stand. Derby were playing Real Madrid, it was THE big match of that year. People like that. People came to see the big teams and we were hosting them, which was great. We were the club of the moment and it was good, we were carrying the flag. People wanted to be there, in that ground, sampling the atmosphere and the big occasion and the world class stars.

Bill Wainwright: Another one I remember was going to was Sarejevo. When you think of war in Sarejevo and it was a lovely old city. I don't know what it's like now. Bashed to pieces I would think. That was exciting. It was in BEA days – British European Airways – and the club hired a plane for that, with the journalists.

Stuart Webb: Juventus? Brian Glanville did a piece on that, didn't he? It's still a hobby horse, what he felt the referee was doing. Lobo wasn't it, Senor Lobo? I felt the Haller penalty – when he came on, when Alan Durban just brushed him – it was a joke, but you do get those things in a lot of other matches. In hindsight, you push it all together and it locks in. Yes, the referee was obviously biased towards the home side, there's no doubt.

Gerald Mortimer: I wasn't too happy with the bookings because you knew who needed to be booked, to be suspended – and he saw to that. Suspicious at the time? No. I don't know, probably not. We very quickly knew afterwards because Pete had a row about Haller – Helmut Haller – going into the ref's dressing-room and that kind of thing and he was saying: "Fix, fix." They'd taken his passport away from him. They'd a pretty murky reputation, at the time, Italians. Even if something wasn't obvious immediately, nothing surprised you. They could so easily have gone all the way that year, they really could.

Roger Davies: I'd torn my groin when we went over to Juventus and I failed a fitness test there, so I didn't play. I was sitting there watching some of the antics going on. It was terrible. Before the home game, I had an injection on the Saturday – the Saturday game, before the Wednesday game – and I was clear to play and it was just the combination of things right the way through that resulted in me losing my head at the end. I'd never played against teams that every time you went to make a run they'd either give your shirt a little tug or just step across on front of you. More so if somebody was just hitting you from behind as the tackle was coming in. Part of the game, but I'd never played against teams that every time you went they gave your shirt a pull or blocked you. I just got fed up. I'd whacked him once and I think it was just after we'd missed the penalty as well, which probably added to it and I just gave the guy a whack and deservedly got red carded. Had we scored the penalty, I don't know, it's problematical. I might not have got sent off.

Stuart Webb: Yes, in hindsight you feel that something has gone on. Then Lobo was contacted by an agent acting, reportedly, for Juventus and offered a Fiat car, which was never proved. FIFA looked at it, UEFA as well, and decided that as he'd reported it, he should be given the match at Derby, and I think he did very well. He sent Roger Davies off in the end, but no, I think he did all right. In those days there was a lot of suspicion, a lot of people were talking about what might happen in Europe.

Gerald Mortimer: Benfica, at home, was a great night. That was a great night because they were a big name and everyone had said: "Oh, they're out of their depth now." Brian and Peter had been off to see Benfica, and Brian told me later: "Eh, when we came back, we daren't tell them how bad they were." So they did all the old counter- publicity thing, pinning up all the reports saying 'Derby are out of their depth' and so on and, of course, they paralysed Benfica by half-time.

Bill Brownson: Benfica. They all played so great that night and particularly Alan Hinton. I would think it was probably one of the best matches he ever played. The perfection of his passes, his crossing, was out of this world.

Gordon Guthrie: Benfica, oh yes. That was one of the most exciting games that I've ever been privileged to be part of and if you was here that night, the crowd was terrific. They had some great players: Eusebio, Torres, the big centre-forward, Coluna. But our fellows were magnificent. The crowd that night. Anybody who was here, I don't think will ever forget that night. Then when we went over there, of course, it was 0-0. Over 75,000 in the Stadium of Light. I'll always remember it because for the first 15 minutes or so, I don't think we got out of our penalty box. They was hitting us with everything. Colin Boulton was magnificent that night, magnificent.

Graham Richards: Real Madrid and Benfica, when we're talking about particular matches. Both of them at the Baseball Ground, both tremendous wins. 3-0 over Benfica, when the Portuguese side, I think, were three down at half-time and they were flattered to be only three down. They'd been destroyed and Derby played brilliantly in Lisbon, too, with Colin Boulton at the very top of his form, and Benfica gave up. After half an hour and they hadn't scored in Lisbon, they gave up. That was wonderful to watch, the two games against Benfica.

Roy McFarland: I think of the European nights and, obviously, our first real experiences were when we qualified. We won the League championship and that year we got to the semi-final of the European Cup, at our first attempt. You know, I can still remember the Benfica game and Eusebio playing. What stands out more than anything else is, maybe, the game away from home in the Stadium of Light in Lisbon and we drew 0-0. We had our backs against the wall, it was tough. We beat them quite easily at the Baseball Ground and that was a memorable night, too. I scored a goal and it was lovely to score in the European Cup, playing against Eusebio, playing against Benfica who were world-renowned, but the interesting thing was going to the Stadium of Light and playing there and drawing 0-0. That night Terry Hennessey was outstanding in midfield. He played in front of Colin and myself and he was really outstanding. Virtually nothing got through to us. We were like the backbone. When they did get through, Colin Boulton was tremendous in goal. We were told before the game: "You'll know when you've won the game because they light the bonfires. They just put piles of rubbish down and set them alight." About ten minutes, quarter of an hour before the end of the game, around the stadium we could smell the smoke and see the fires being burnt and we knew we'd beaten them. That was a great night.

Gerald Mortimer: It was still an interesting night in Lisbon because that was one of the best games Colin Boulton ever played. He had Eusebio coming down on him about three times and he clutched the lot. And it was also one of Terry Hennessey's best games. That bald head kept coming up and heading it away. Then, of course, after Dave's championship, the Real Madrid night, although that turned into a nightmare in the second leg.

Graham Richards: Real Madrid, here. I think Real Madrid were unlucky here. They might well have got an equalising goal that was ruled offside by the same linesman that gave England the goal in the World Cup Final! Those were the great European nights, but I also remember Zeljeznicar coming here from Sarajevo and a tremendous sense of: "Now we're in the very top flight of football."

Charlie George: One of the best goals I scored was in Madrid, but people forget that 'cos we lost 5-1, after extra-time. I scored some good goals for Derby. I always fancied scoring and I was able to hit the ball well. The goal in the Madrid game was a good move. It went from left to right and then back again. When it came back to me, I just hit and it went in. Sometimes they do and sometimes they finish in the crowd, but I think the best goal I scored for Derby was against Burnley when I chipped the 'keeper.

Dave Mackay: I always say 4-1 at home and 4-1 away because they scored the fifth in extra-time. We were disappointed with the penalty – Rod Thomas it was – because it was doubtful. You didn't see as much of it on the television as you do now. I was very disappointed that we weren't able to sustain it in Europe. You are talking about Real Madrid, though, who were an excellent team.

Roy McFarland: We play Real Madrid, we beat Real Madrid; we lose in the Bernabeu. We go to Turin and we play against Juventus. Those European nights were, without doubt, a bit special and more than anything else, when the Baseball Ground was full, it had a tremendous atmosphere. It was lovely to play in front of your own supporters when the house was full.

Changing Times

IN NOVEMBER 1976, Dave Mackay and his assistant, Des Anderson, left Derby County. Mackay had asked for a vote of confidence from the board of directors, which was not forthcoming. It was three years earlier that Mackay opted to take over at the Baseball Ground after the turbulent departure of Brian Clough. Few managers would have been capable of handling such a situation, but Mackay did. Another League title, a Charity Shield victory, an FA Cup semi-final and twice a place in the UEFA Cup were tremendous achievements, whilst signings like Rod Thomas, Bruce Rioch, Francis Lee and Charlie George reflected the way Mackay liked his football to be played.

Third, first and fourth respectively were the positions which the Rams finished seasons 1973-74, 1974-75 and 1975-76 in Division One under Mackay and, although they were in 19th position when he departed, the team recovered to 15th by the end of the 1976-77 season. Colin Murphy took over, but there was always the feeling around Derby that Brian Clough would return. He didn't and eight years later, Derby County were in Division Three.

FA Cup semi-final 1976: Derby County 0 Manchester Utd 2

Dave Mackay: We deserved to lose on the day. We didn't play as well as we could. David Nish? Ah, well. Jack Taylor, who was the referee, he said for sure, afterwards, that if he had been able to realise what was happening, he would have never have given offside, but that's dead and gone. We can forget that.

Charlie George: We beat Newcastle in the Cup, 4-2 at the Baseball Ground, and I think we played Stoke a week later or maybe the following week, and I dislocated my shoulder and fractured my elbow. I honestly believe that if I had been playing, we'd have gone on and won the Cup and the League. I really believe that. Not that I'm giving myself a gee-up, but I was on top of my game and I think the players were responding to how I played and we had mutual respect for one another. I'm very, very, very, very sure that we'd have definitely won the Cup. We'd have beaten Manchester United because we took three points off them that year. I scored both goals at the Baseball Ground and we lost at Hillsborough to Jack Taylor, the referee, who doesn't feature too highly in my mind. A lot of funny things went on in that game.

Michael Gretton: The most disappointing match was, obviously, going to Hillsborough and seeing Manchester United beat us in the FA Cup. I'm still convinced that we would not have lost if a certain gentleman had been playing, Charlie George. He was a great character. A very nice gentleman. I've since been privileged to meet him two or three times. Very nice gentleman.

Dave Mackay: I was very disappointed to lose because we had played them previously in the League and done exceptionally well. I think we drew 1-1 at Old Trafford and we played much better than them, so we were really confident of doing something. Franny Lee, he didn't play on that day, which was a bit of a disappointment, but we didn't deserve to get there. Previous to that, we'd beaten Newcastle, I think 4-0, Everton, we'd paralysed them all and it looked as though we were on a roll, but we never managed it.

Clough and Mackay

Dave Mackay: Nobody's got the style of Brian Clough. As I say, I'm a great admirer of Brian. I know when I was manager, he was trying to get back with Peter Taylor. I'd never say Brian Clough without Peter Taylor because the two of them together were magic. Don't ask me how. How does he work? Nobody knows. Everybody's trying to copy him, all the ex-players. None of them's done any good. Nothing like Brian or Peter Taylor. My style was my own style. What I wanted was good players out there on the park and let them play.

Roger Davies: The biggest difference, I think, was with Cloughie, the way he spoke to people. Dave believed everybody was like Dave, who gave 150 per cent. He couldn't understand how things were going wrong. Why you hadn't got your sleeves rolled up and bawling because that's how Dave was. I still think – and they were two great managers to play for – it was good fun playing for Dave Mackay. As long as things went okay, he'd be part of it. He loved the five-a-sides and you had a laugh and, I suppose, it was quite easy at the time. You know, I wondered how it would have been if things were going the other way. Because I'd just left when they were having the bad run. Things always went well with the managers I played under then, so I didn't know what the other side would have been like.

Mackay departs

Stuart Webb: That was something that was a total shock. Dave was highly successful. Into Europe, played the right sort of football, attracted a different team to what Brian had and a lot will argue that it was a better team because it played more attacking football and I tend to agree with that.

Dave Mackay: Dave Mackay sacked himself. It was probably the paper boys saying I got the sack, but that's not the same. Most of the directors wanted Brian back and Brian still wanted to come back, don't forget that. Him and Peter Taylor, me and them, okay, no problem. No fighting each other. Peter Taylor was a great mate of mine and the same with Brian, but they were trying to get back to this club. They wanted to knock me out because I'm the manager, but they wanted to jog back to knock other people out, too, and I'm talking about the boardroom. When I took over, even as the manager, everybody – except Sam Longson and probably the vice-chairman, Sydney Bradley, who'd go along with Sam Longson – all the rest of them would've liked Brian back. So I had this situation – I mean, you would know being in Derby – of meetings on a Saturday night, when they're down at Brighton. Coming up for meetings. There were also the car stickers: 'BBC – Bring Back Clough' – all the stickers in the cars – and I used to drive up beside them and these people were really embarrassed because I'd been a good player for Derby and I was doing a reasonably good job for Derby as manager and when they saw me, they would blush.

Stuart Webb: It was incredible because from my perspective – secretary-general manager – you know a bit about what's going on. It came as a total shock. It came from the board, basically, I think. Dave's lifestyle, his management style, people in the boardroom, golf club Sunday afternoon people this that, the other. It wasn't a footballing decision.

Dave Mackay: They had the stickers in the cars – 'SOS – Save Our Soccer'. The best thing of my life is that every team I've been with, we've played fantastic football. I'm a football nut and I want us to play good football. I wanted us to win trophies, but first of all, I wanted to entertain and play football. They had 'Save Our Soccer'. That really annoyed me.

Roger Davies: Charlie George came the year after we won the championship with Franny. He played in the Charity Shield. I did my cartilage in a pre-season game at Celtic and so missed a chance to play at Wembley. I didn't play in the first game of the season either – and we lost 5-1 to QPR, at home. Reigning champions and we lost 5-1, at home! We didn't play that badly, actually, but every time they went up, they scored. Charlie came in and, as I say, I had the cartilage injury, but I got back in the side. It was probably the year that the 'super sub' thing started coming in and I was on the bench quite a bit and I didn't actually play much with Charlie, but I was still enjoying it. I was part of the squad.

Roger Davies: I didn't want to leave really, but Bruges came in for me and I thought: "Well, why not? Go and have a change" So I did that and ended up winning the 'double' in Belgium in my first year there.

A rapid slide

Stuart Webb: Innuendo was a problem. They had an exciting, extrovert, dressing-room. There were stories coming out all the time because they were big guys and big players. That didn't help and the fact that Colin Murphy was thrust into the hot seat, that was a total surprise. Colin had been reserve-team trainer- manager. He used to go away with the directors – there was always a director went on the coach with the Reserves – and Colin was putting himself out as being the man who was doing this that and the other. The choice of replacement for Dave was done more or less, just like that. Not like: "Who shall we look at?" Not like the Bobby Robson situation before. There was only one man for the job this time, it was Colin. Then it was free-for-all after that.

Stuart Webb: There was talk of Brian coming back. It wasn't easy. It wasn't a good time. It never is when things aren't going well on the pitch. There's too many distractions.

Michael Dunford: We had the situation where Colin Murphy took over for a short time and we signed Derek Hales. Then we had the Tommy Docherty era, where players were coming and going and, in fairness, most of the quality players we had were allowed to drift away.

Gerald Mortimer: Like most rapid slides, it's always lack of leadership at the top. You have two different managers who have won championships, for a club that's never won championships before. Each of them lasts 18 months afterwards. Now tell me, what's the sense of that? There was then, of course, the shadow of Brian Clough at Forest, so instead of saying: "We need such and such a manager to run this club properly," it was always: "Well? Can we get somebody to outshine Brian Clough?" I mean, some of the directors and some of the boardroom decisions, in those years, were utterly incompetent. They just made a complete shambles of it, really.

Stuart Webb: Totally too much change. The successful clubs, in any era, are created by a stable board of directors, a charismatic manager, who's allowed to manage and drive the club forward under the control of the board. Under the guidance of the board, but without interference. You look at the great clubs, Liverpool, Man United now with Fergie all of that is controlled, sensible. These guys, like Jim now at Derby, they know what they're doing. They respect the board, but they are given guidelines and within those guidelines they get on and manage it and they're allowed to be their own man and that's it. So the stability was never there. There were changes at board level, there were changes at management level, there were changes throughout. In any industry, whether it's ICI or Manchester United or Derby County, it has got to have that stability and control from above. If it's controlled in the boardroom, then it filters right down to the pitch and everybody is pulling together. But during that period there was total change. There was change every six months. There was always something happening.

Brian Flint: Well it came so quick. Nobody stays at the top forever. Manchester United went down, Spurs went down, but this came so quick and I think it was the way it was done, as well. I mean, you've got to be careful you don't start calling players. Well, you're not calling them if they've less ability because it's not personal, but I don't see how you can replace the likes of Charlie George with Roy Greenwood. You'd got Alan Hinton, but you ended up with Gerry Ryan. Now Gerry Ryan got a Cup medal, but I'm talking in general. Your Billy Caskeys, Morelands. I mean, it was so short a time. There was such a gap in ability that we didn't go down gradually. There was such a drop and it was a shambles. I suppose it's bad management, but bad management is allowed to happen from higher up, from the directors.

Gordon Guthrie: Tommy Docherty was quite good. I mean, for some unknown reason as you're aware, Tommy's not got too good a reputation in Derby, but I think he was a brilliant manager to work for and, honestly, he knew football inside out. When you go back over the history of the teams he had, he's brought a lot of exciting young players through, especially his Manchester team that did us in the semi-final in 1976. You don't just do that on luck. He was fun to work with, yes, but he was also serious. He was great. I enjoyed the time I worked with Tommy tremendously and I learned quite a bit off him. I know why he got the stick at Derby. He started to get rid of some of the good players, but the good players, really, were on the other side of the age barrier. I think what Tommy was trying to do what he did at Manchester United, but of course, he could never do it at Derby because Manchester United had more money and glamour. I admired Tommy Docherty, though.

Michael Dunford: One of the biggest problems I did find was that one side of me was the supporter and the other side of me was the paid professional and it's very difficult to bring the two together. When you're losing players like Charlie George and Colin Todd and replacing them with what I would call – with due respect to them, Vic Moreland and Billy Caskey – moderate players. When you see quality players going out of the club, it's a great shame.

Brian Flint: I think at the same time, Nottingham Forest were on the way up under Cloughie. They got promoted, won the championship the year after and the European Cup the year after that, which didn't help. I know we're old enough to know that it could be anybody, but that success was so close to what had happened at Derby and that didn't help either.

The Turbulent Eighties

DERBY County nearly went out of business in the Eighties. Relegation from Division One in 1980 was followed by relegation from Division Two in 1984. In March of that year, Derby County had a vital fixture in the High Court, with debts owing to VAT and the Inland Revenue. Thanks largely to the efforts of director Stuart Webb, bankruptcy was avoided, but it was a close run thing. The average attendance the following season, in 1984-85, was 10,381, the lowest since 1914-15.

In May 1984, Arthur Cox was appointed manager and Derby County began the climb back to safety, solvency, respectability and the top flight. In 1985, John Gregory became the 700th player to play for Derby County and by 1987, the club was back in the top flight of English football. It was a marvellous achievement. In contrast, between 1984-86, Wolverhampton Wanderers dropped from Division One to Division Four in successive seasons, whilst Lincoln City became the first club to be automatically relegated from the Football League in 1987. They were replaced by Scarborough.

Stuart Webb: I left in 1979, 1980 time. I'd decided that my life was going other ways. The club moved on. Then there came all sorts of changes and we got the bankruptcy situation. It was a time when – again – there were part-time directors as such, trying to run a company without strong administration and so, eventually, Derby County couldn't pay its bills.

Michael Dunford: The early Eighties was when football started moving into big business. Nowadays, most Premiership clubs' wages bills exceeds gate receipts. In the middle to late Seventies, when lotteries were first introduced, that was a boom period for football and a lot of people made an awful lot of money out of the game.

Stuart Webb: I came back. I was asked by Mike Watterson, who was on the board. That was in 1982 and within a month, he'd left. I came back as a director and Michael was secretary. Freddie Fern was a director. John Kirkland was chairman, actually. He took the chair after Mike Watterson, for a time. I went to one meeting in his offices and he said: "Look it's not working. We're verging on, well there's the fear of bankruptcy." So we took advice from a leading practitioner in bankruptcy, who said to that meeting: "You, gentlemen, are trading illegally because you are trading beyond your means. You could all be held responsible for this." There were some very white faces around the table, I'll tell you. Geoff Glossop, who I'd introduced to the club, was going to join the board at that time and invest some money. To his credit, he stayed on. I mean, he could have walked away and said: "Look, gentlemen, this is not for me." But he stood in and I asked the board, would they stay in place for six months while I went out to try to create a rescue package. Everyone to a man said: "Yes." John

Kirkland stayed on as chairman, Freddie Fern stayed on, Geoff Glossop joined and I went about trying to get some funding, which was very difficult. We went to the County Council, we went to the City Council, all obvious places, but no one was in a position to help football in those days. Then I hit on the big city and approached Robert Maxwell. He was understanding, he wanted to listen. While those negotiations were going on, the club received a writ from the Inland Revenue and the Customs and Excise. It was a joint writ, £130,000. With that, Bob Maxwell just pulled away. He said: "Look, I can't get involved with this. You sort your own mess out. If you sort it out, come back. I'm quite interested in investing in a football club, but sort yourselves out first."

Bobby Davison: The team weren't doing so well. I think they had a mixture of old players and some young players who weren't as professional as they should be. I mean, Archie Gemmill – I've a lot to thank Archie for, he looked after me when I was there, he was a great professional – and I think if more players had looked up to Archie, to see how professional he was, the team wouldn't have been relegated and those players would have gone on to play a lot of games. I think for some lads, everything was a joke. They thought they just had to turn up and they didn't have to work hard in training. You don't mind having a night out and having a laugh, but you've got to work hard. A percentage of that squad didn't do that.

Stuart Webb: So we were left high and dry and that was the day when we had the Plymouth Cup replay, when we lost at home. That was a terrible. It was a very low time for us. Maxwell had said: "No." The writs had arrived. We'd lost a chance of the semi-final. So the whole thing was terrible. I then went round about six to eight people and got, well we put the cash in, the board themselves. We put in £10-15,000 each and we got the £130,000 and luckily, just managed to pay off the Inland Revenue. We went four times to the High Court. The judge, on four occasions, said: "This is the last time I want to see you Mr Webb." It was touch and go.

Stuart Webb: The board had put the money in and I was to draw the cheque from the bank down there. I was waiting and the bank manager was talking to someone else, having a cup of coffee. I was looking at the time, it was 10.20am, we were on at half past and if we hadn't got it then, well...! So I sort of banged the door down and said: "Look, there's a cheque coming through, there's a draft." Got it, ran along The Strand up to the High Court steps and Arthur Willis, who was our solicitor at the time, did a wonderful job for us. He got the solicitors for the Revenue and the VAT and we all went in the gents' toilets and exchanged the cheque and came out and all went smiling into court. The judge said: "Right. Derby County. Next case." And we were clear, but he did say, on a few occasions: "I don't want to see you again."

Stuart Webb: We were treading on very thin ice. There were conditions every time we visited the High Court. We couldn't hire a bus to take the Reserves to away matches; the kit couldn't be sent to a dry cleaners, we had to wash it by hand. All those things that people don't know about, but the judge said: "Yes, you can go. I'll give you another fortnight," – I kept asking for another fortnight – "but you can't spend another penny because it's not your money. It's the shareholders' money." We knew what was coming in, so we had to promise and sign statements that we wouldn't do this, we wouldn't do that, but he did keep giving us extra-time because he thought we might see some light at the end of the tunnel, which we did, eventually.

Peter Taylor – manager

Bobby Davison: I got on fine because it was all new to me. Peter was a sort of larger-than-life character and he did all his work in the office. He wasn't a training ground man, he was a suit man, so it was all new to me. His team talks were on a Friday. We'd meet in the boardroom and we'd all sit round and he'd come in and he was very lighthearted. He'd come in and always have a go at me about my tattoo. I had a tattoo on my arm and every team talk he'd come in and point to me and say: "Get rid of that tattoo." Micky Brolly came from Grimsby and he'd say to him: "Where's my fish? Have you brought me any fish." He was lighthearted and joked about things.

Players and a changing business

Bobby Davison: When I first joined there was Archie, Dave Watson, David Swindlehurst – he was a fantastic player. Then, obviously, Arthur came and moved them on and we got some younger players in and some others who were a bit more experienced, like Kenny Burns.

Eric Steele: I looked forward to the challenge. Once I'd made the call to Arthur Cox and I came up and I spoke to Roy McFarland as well, there wasn't much indecision. I spoke to Bruce Rioch, funnily enough, at Middlesbrough, at the same time and contemplated that. Possibly a good move for me, but no, in the end I chose Derby.

Bobby Davison: Then he brought Rob Hindmarch, who was an outstanding captain who led by example. If the ball was there to be won, he'd go and win it. He was a leader. Rob will tell you himself, he wasn't blessed with pace, but what he didn't have in pace, he had in knowledge. He read the game well and he'd give 100 per cent.

Eric Steele: There weren't too many players about when I got here. I remember the day I came, there was Rob Hindmarch and Charlie Palmer, who came from Watford as well, on the same day. We were all free transfers. I asked for a couple of days to think about it and Rob Hindmarch did the same. I already knew Rob. He was at Sunderland, but I'd known him from Wallsend Boys' Club days in the North-East and he was one of the reasons I came. When I saw Arthur was signing people like Rob, that was one of the reasons, not just for the club. I thought: "Well, that's the calibre of player and you're getting him on a free transfer:..." How he managed that I don't know. It was a good opportunity.

Eric Steele: First year I was fine. It was the second year I broke my wrist, then I broke my fingers. Unbelievable. I'd not had any breaks for eight or nine years and my mother was convinced it was semi-skimmed milk and I'd got ricketts because I'd gone eight years without breaking a bone. It was the wrong time to do it because to be fair, the financial situation at the club was changing. In the first year, Arthur obviously wanted to run with one experienced goalkeeper and another young one. The change started when we began to sign the likes of Micklewhite and Geraint Williams. Then the second year, we'd finished seventh, eighth, we had to have another goalkeeper and Mark Wallington was brought in and it was a competition between him. Obviously, if we were to go anywhere, we had to have two goalkeepers.

Steve Sutton: Yes, 1985 I came on loan. I had a bit of a back problem at Forest and had been out the side. Arthur Cox was manager, he took me on then and I came across, really, to get some fitness playing in the Reserves because I think the reserve-team 'keeper, Ian McKeller I think it was, had got injured. Within me playing two reserve-team games, Eric Steele was injured down at Bristol City, so I had to play the next 14 games, until Eric was fit again and came back for the last four games of the season. I stayed three months and thoroughly enjoyed it.

Eric Steele: I think in the first year, three different 'keepers were brought in to cover for me There was Mark Grew. And Steve Sutton had to play a lot of games when I broke the fingers, but it's just too vital a position not to have two experienced goalkeepers, so when the financial situation was eased, that was one of the priorities for Arthur to say: "I've got to get another goalkeeper."

Michael Dunford: People investing personal money into football changed it. Most football clubs would see their way through in the normal course of business up to maybe the late Seventies, early Eighties, but really when the transfer market started to boom and you had £1 million transfers for the first time, you then saw, gradually, an influx of people like the Maxwells and people like that, who wanted to invest personal money into football clubs and gain control of them. Okay, you're probably looking at O. J. Jackson at Derby and there was talk maybe at one point of Sammy Ramsden coming in and buying the club in the late Sixties, but really the Eighties was a period where supporters or people from the world of commerce or industry, started to put personal money into it. Then, I think, there was a change of philosophy.

Eric Steele: Paul Hooks was here, Bobby Davison, Kevin Wilson, people who have gone on and done various things in the game and improved themselves as players and gone on to the managerial side too. Steve Cherry was still here at the time, but it was decided he was moving and he ended up going off to Walsall. That really was most of them at the time because that was all we had.

Graham Sellors: George Williams played then, didn't he? I moaned about him as much as everyone else. About the fact he couldn't pass it ten yards and get it to his own man, but I think when he went, you realised how effective he'd been. How he'd shuttled back and how he'd closed down spaces and how, quite often, he'd be the last man tidying up and nipping in and playing it back to the goalkeeper and all things like that.

Eric Steele: I always remember Arthur Cox and Roy changing the way we played, halfway through. We tried to get out of that League playing what you would probably call 'proper football', but we realised that we weren't going to get out of that division like that. So when Trevor Christie arrived, we became a little bit more direct. Before that we'd had Bobby Davison and Kevin Wilson, who were very good at accepting the ball, good pace, but we were being outmuscled a few times, especially away from home, so that was the side evolved then.

Bobby Davison: My favourite partnership was with Trevor Christie. He was an unsung hero. I enjoyed playing with Trevor Christie immensely. He was a big target man, took a lot of weight off me. He was left-footed and it balanced us and seemed to work.

Eric Steele: Jeff Chandler was an underrated player, very much so. I think the biggest compliment you could pay Jeff Chandler was that we replaced him with Nigel Callaghan, who'd played for the England Youth team and England Under-21s. It was a big, big signing, getting Callaghan, because Arthur, as you know, liked to play with these two wingers, who tucked in when we lost the ball and he favoured having a right-footer in the left wing position and so, when he felt Chandler's 'sell by date' had arrived, the greatest compliment to Chandler was that he bought Callaghan. Jeff Chandler chipped in with some very valuable goals for us. He wasn't just creative, he shared the goals with the front men.

Bobby Davison: Arthur played with two wide men. It was great because you'd got Gary Micklewhite and Jeff Chandler. Them two, well they used to work hard. I mean, Jeff Chandler scored 15 goals one season, playing as a wing man, and he used to cross balls as well. Chandler was at Bolton, he was at Leeds too. He'd lot of ability, and Gary Micklewhite had too.

Promotion: 1985–86 and 1986–87

Bobby Davison: Great years. Football is about winning. Everybody who plays football wants to win football matches and when you're successful, it's great and we had some good times.

One year, we just couldn't get promotion, but I always remember Gary Micklewhite – I think we drew our last home game, with Swansea – and Gary said: "You know, it's like a habit you get into, winning. Let's win our last game to carry us on to next season." We won that last game, at Newport, and carried on the next season. We won the opening game and went to get promotion. I always remember that.

Eric Steele: Highlights of the Third Division promotion? Well, the main highlight was it was a scrap, a fight, a battle. We only just got up and the night we'll always go back to was the night against Rotherham. I can remember games at home where we drew – like with Bury 1-1 – and we should have won. We had a good home run-in but we didn't win enough of those, which caused some of the problems. As ever, as you get near the finishing line, you're thinking: "Just two wins." But we just couldn't get them, we just couldn't put two wins together and, in the end, it really came down to the wire. Fortunately, the year after was completely different.

Bobby Davison: I think Gary Micklewhite came from a good school at Queen's Park Rangers. He used to work hard, he could cross a ball and he had that bit of steel. I still talk to my players now about Gary Micklewhite and John Gregory. They came from Queen's Park Rangers and could be nasty. They could mix it with the best of players. Players now think: "Gary Micklewhite? John Gregory? No. They wouldn't be hard men." I'll tell you, they used to get stuck in.

Arthur Cox in the Eighties

Eric Steele: I know he might have had some criticism in the later years, but those first three years, the signings he made, his knowledge of the lower divisions, his knowledge of what players could come and do well was frightening really. You look at the free transfers he brought in. The value he got from myself, Charlie Palmer, Rob Hindmarch, then it wasn't big money for Trevor Christie, then Geraint Williams arrived, Gary Micklewhite arrived and then your bigger people started to come in. John Gregory arrived and that was when you started to see a change in the fact that we became a buying club again. Before, it was a survival club. He got John Gregory and then Ross MacLaren and you could see there was the nucleus of a very, very good side and in the final year Nigel Callaghan arrived, for good money as well, from Watford. He could have gone elsewhere, but there were some very, very good buys by the manager, at the time.

Ted McMinn: A great manager as far as I'm concerned. Jock Wallace was a great manager and Arthur Cox was just as good. Disciplinarian. He got hold of me at times, he had me in his office more than once, but rightly so. I stepped out of line and Arthur was putting me back in line, as soon as possible, with as heavy a fine as he could.

Eric Steele: He had this image of a sergeant major. I thought he was very fair. I respected him greatly the three years I played here because he would tell you straight. He would tell you on a Tuesday, if you weren't playing. He wouldn't hang about. Some managers wait. At least you knew where you stood and I think the players respected that. He'd have the gravelly voice, that would happen, but he was very good at sitting back and assessing players, early season. "What do we need? Are we going the right way?" Didn't go in a great deal for team talks, no. Not a great deal. He was always very respectful that we were doing it for the public. The public were very important. I think the base he had at Newcastle probably taught him a lot of that; that we worked for the public. If ever we did have a dip he would constantly remind us that: "You might let yourself down, you can let me and Roy down, but..." I can remember sitting in the Baseball Ground in the away dressing-room. We knew if we were going to get a rollicking, it was into the away dressing-room and I can always remember him pointing to the stand a few times. It was a respect, but it was something at the time people didn't realise. The players he brought in contributed to the spirit.

Eric Steele: There was a great spirit. We used to go out and it was sensible. We'd go out on a Wednesday night every fortnight and we'd meet in a local hostelry and everybody would turn up. We didn't all drink and at the end of it, some would go for a meal, some would go home and it was brilliant and you'd be scared not to go. Now Arthur Cox didn't do that. What Arthur Cox did was bring the players in and we generated our own spirit amongst us and we had some characters. Jeff Chandler arrived, Gary Micklewhite with a bit of southern humour, Mark Lillis arrived.

Bobby Davison

Eric Steele: Tremendous. He'd be worth a fortune nowadays, absolute fortune. He would fit into the modern game. He was fit, he was sharp, he was a strong runner, a good leader of the line. I mean, we had talkers right through the team. At the back we had Hindmarch, we had John Gregory in midfield and you'd have Bobby, who really did talk. He brought Phil Gee on. I thought Bobby was underestimated, in terms of his skill as a finisher. He was a worker and I don't think people ever gave him the credit he deserved. Some of the finishes... I remember at Swansea, we won 5-1 away and he took a ball and bent it. If a Brazilian had done it they'd have been showing it on TV every week. What struck you about him was that when you really needed it, he'd pop up with that goal.

Bobby Davison: It was a fantastic time, at a big club like Derby, because you had to be at your best every week. You're up there and opposition players and fans, they all want to beat you, a big club. Our lads had to stand up and be counted every week and that was a credit to the players and to Arthur and Roy McFarland. I've got some photographs, a diving header against Ipswich. I was just happy to score, whether it was from outside the box or from a yard out. They all counted and I enjoyed every one of them.

Eric Steele: Last game of the season against Plymouth, who are trying to get into the play-offs. We're struggling to win the championship. We've had a torrid first 45 minutes and we've gone in 1-0 down, and then all of a sudden Bobby crashes a volley past Steve Cherry and I'll always remember, sunshine at the Baseball Ground. We never looked back. We went back to that flowing football. Three goals in the last ten minutes and we were champions. I thought Bobby was one of the best strikers I've ever played with. I've often said that the best defender I've ever played with was Mark Lawrenson, when I was at Brighton. John Barnes would have to be the best creative player, but surely the best striker I ever played with was Bobby Davison.

John Gregory

Bobby Davison: John was a fantastic player. He's one of the best I've ever played with. I don't think people at Derby appreciated what John did. He could pass, but he had that mean streak in him on the field. I think that came from being with Terry Venables. His knowledge was fantastic. When he played golf, he played percentage golf. He played football that way too. To be fair, John was a great athlete as well. He could get about a football field and he could pass the ball.

Graham Sellors: I think I might be wrong about Gregory because he had a big reputation and everybody was impressed by him. I was impressed by him to a certain extent, but I thought he didn't always help some of the younger players, who weren't as good as him. I thought, quite often, he off-loaded the ball when it was tricky, to somebody else, who was perhaps in an even more tricky situation than him. He did a lot of little kind of, push it on to Harbey and land Harbey in a mess, but he had got the nous to direct things, hadn't he? I remember being in a drama group once and there was a chap called Frank – I've forgotten his second name. If he forgot his lines, he looked at you. So everyone thought you'd forgotten your lines! You know, you can sometimes off-load to somebody else which makes it look as though you're all right. I'm probably being unjust to him, but I did think he was a little bit like that.

Eric Steele: Played with him twice. Played with him at Brighton. He came to Brighton from Northampton. We'd gone up the First, as it was. I did Third Division to First with Brighton and John Gregory was a major part. Again, Alan Mullery sensed that we needed more quality and 'Gregs' came and played as a right-back at Brighton, but he always had too much about him for that. I think he led by the way he played, not as much by what he said. He was a deep thinker. He was a good captain on the field because I think Arthur knew as well, we could put things right on the field ourselves, which is something we say that's lacking in the modern game now. You look at the successful three or four, sides. They've got people on the field if, when they cross the white line, if it isn't going right, they can put it right. I can remember 'Gregs', in certain games if we were overrun, we wouldn't look to Arthur or Roy, Greg's would sort it out midfield: "You stay with him for five minutes, you stay with him, and I'm holding in here." We'd just kill the game off for ten minutes. That was the sort of player he was. Well, he had a brain, as you well know. Again, ten or 12 goals from midfield. Free-kick specialist.

Bobby Davison: Phil Gee was a raw talent we took from non-League. I think if somebody had gotten hold of Phil and coached him a bit better, he would probably have gone on and played at a high level. I know for a fact what happened. John Gregory and one or two other players, including myself, we spoke up and John went in to see Arthur Cox and mentioned we needed to coach Phil Gee more and Arthur's reply was: "He's raw talent, just leave him alone." We used to see Phil do very good things in a game or create goals, but then he'd seem to try something totally stupid, where he's out wide and instead of trying to cross a ball or keep the ball, he'd shoot. Goalscorers win you football matches, but we just felt Phil needed to be coached a little bit more, but it worked quite well anyway. We scored plenty.

Goddard and Saunders

Graham Sellors: I think they played well together didn't they? Also Micklewhite on the right wing. They played very good little triangles and things like that. I never believed in selling Goddard, I thought Goddard was great. I never thought that was good business. It can't be good business can it? It's only good business if you then sign a player better than him or at least as good as him – and they signed nobody. Events proved it wasn't good business, it was bad business. It was nice to have a player with so much knowhow and skill and experience who was able to bring other players into the game.

Ted McMinn

Ted McMinn: I'd played in Scotland and then Spain and then to come to England, especially at the Baseball Ground, everything was 100 miles an hour, which at first, I did struggle with. The rest of that season, from February to May, I picked up an injury and then I came back the following season, had a good pre-season and then missed the first game and then played the rest of that season, which was, probably, a very good season for me. That was the season we ended up fifth in the League, which would have been the Premier League now. It was a great achievement, really.

Graham Sellors: I enjoyed Ted McMinn. Everyone enjoyed Ted McMinn, didn't they? I just wonder. He seemed to get less exciting as time went on. I wonder whether there were instructions for what they should do?

Ted McMinn: To play over there, against Real and Barcelona, Athletico, Zaragoza, you were playing against world-class players every week. Lineker was there, Archibald was there, Mark Hughes was there, but there was only about six Brits, I think. You were safer with the ball. When you had the ball, you wouldn't get spat on, elbowed or whatever, but as soon as you released the ball, making a run, there'd be an elbow coming across your face. They didn't like British players, that was my feeling, and the referees were always very, very strong with British players. Even the way they spoke to you. They swore at you because they just didn't like British players there.

Graham Sellors: When McMinn first came he was uninhibited. You never knew what he would do, shoot with the left foot, shoot with his right foot. He gradually became more inhibited as time went on and I wonder if it was the discipline imposed from the side.

Ted McMinn: I preferred the left wing. Not because my left is strong – it is the weakest of my two feet – but because I could always come inside and hit it with my right foot. I could cross it with my left, but it always gave me an option to come back and cross with my right or to go down the outside and cross with my left. You can come inside at pace because you're on your strongest foot.

Robert Maxwell

Robert Maxwell's involvement with Derby County was a strange affair. Some would claim that without Maxwell there would be no Derby County and they would have a case.

It all began so promisingly in 1984, but it ended in acrimony. Promises, promises, but in the end, disillusionment. Maxwell was not a football man, football was not his business. He saw it as a tool to further other ambitions.

The exact nature of his real business has been the topic of much discussion since he mysteriously disappeared from his yacht, the *Lady Ghislaine*, whilst cruising off the Canary Islands. Suffice to say that hindsight is a wonderful thing and many people who have since spoken out and claimed to be fully aware of Maxwell's business activities, were conspicuously silent at the time.

Graham Richards: First impressions of Maxwell? Oh, enormously positive. A brilliant brain and a proven, successful, great businessman. A linguist and a character that must be equal to anybody I've ever met, really, and remember, in my lifetime I've met one or two quite experienced kings and few cabbages too. I've met people at the very top of the legal profession as well as in politics, but Maxwell I would rate with any of them.

Stuart Webb: I first met Maxwell down at his office, during that worrying period. I'd rung for appointments and got the usual stuff. Nothing. So I went to see Jack Dunnett, who was then the president of the Football League and I said to Jack: "Come on, I think I've got a chance with Robert Maxwell." As president of the League he had to look at the clubs. He didn't want clubs dropping out, going bankrupt. So he helped to get a meeting one evening, for dinner at nine o'clock, in Worship Street, where his office was. So I went down with Josie and Beverley and went to a show. I said, at half-time in the show, I would go out. We'd arranged to meet at this restaurant, Joe Allen's in London, afterwards because I didn't know how long I was going to be, what was going to happen, and I said: "I'll see you there, as long as I know you're there, 10.30, eleven o'clock. I'll come and join you." So at half-time in the show, a West End musical, I cleared off for my appointment.

Graham Richards: Great charm. I think all great men have great charm when it comes down to it and he could ladle it on and turn it off like it was powered by an electric battery, but he would always remember, whenever I talked to him and whatever the circumstances, that I was in the legal profession and he knew lots of the famous people in the legal profession. Not the people I knew, but the really famous people. They were all confidantes of his and I believed what he said was true. My initial impressions of him were tremendously favourable.

Stuart Webb: I had a quick gin and tonic and off I went. Rang the bell at Worship Street at ten to nine and was met by the night watchman, ushered into his private lift, up to the tenth floor. I walked out and there was this Filipino houseman there, all dressed up: "Oh do come in." At the far end of the corridor, coming towards me, was this great bulk striding down the corridor: "Oh Mr Webb, how are you? Good evening." You know, as though I was a long lost friend. Shook hands, went into this boardroom on the right. A massive room, massive table, probably could seat 20. At the far end, there was one place set and then one next to it. So we went down there. I can remember it vividly, we had prawns and avocado. We had chicken, glass of wine usual stuff. He had a coffee cup with 'the Boss' printed, big thick letters. So we talked. I wasn't rushed. It was a good meeting. He asked me all the questions. What the future of the club was, as I saw it. He said: "Yes, I'll have to pass this by my advisors." Could he have my contact numbers? "I'll come back to you." All the rest of it. We finished off, took the numbers, exchanged pleasantries, went to the lift, said: "Cheerio." Down the lift, on to the street, looking for a taxi. I looked at my watch and it was five to ten! I'd been and done all that in under an hour, had a meal, everything was set up, no time wasting. So I then went to the restaurant, got there and was sitting on the bar stool as Josie and Beverley came in. Josie said: "Wasn't it all right? Was it a bad meeting?" I said: "No. It was good." Everything had happened and it was wonderful. That's how it started.

Graham Richards: I was involved with Stuart Webb in the very first discussions about Maxwell coming to Derby County and I remember one very cold, snowy, January day in 1983, when Stuart phoned me and asked me to go to Derby and we'd go on to his home at Headington, in Oxford, to begin the negotiations. I remember going into Headington Hall – which, it was later revealed, was rented from the Oxford City Council for £20 – and being terribly impressed by the battery of secretaries all on duty on a Sunday afternoon and the fact that we were squeezed into the schedule and that we began to talk about Derby County. Overall, he came over as one of the largest people I think I have ever met.

Michael Dunford: Well, he was a big man. My first meeting with him ever was when Ian Maxwell was at Derby. I was summoned down to Headington Hall, on a Sunday. We were going to produce a brochure. Now the previous week, there'd been an article in one of the Sunday supplements regarding Fillipino servants being at Headington Hall. I got down there on a Sunday and apart from three cups of coffee, I'd worked from 9.15 in the morning until seven o'clock on Sunday night. No sight of the Fillipino servants, but the 'old man' was coming back from China that day and both sons were fighting among themselves as to who had to fetch their father from the airport. Neither of them wanted to and as soon as the 'old man' walked into the room – bright red polo necked sweater – he filled the room and the atmosphere changed completely. It was a reign of terror. I've seen Derby directors squirm in his presence because he was so... well, he could pick up the phone and speak on first name terms to Gorbachov, Margaret Thatcher, Reagan, anybody like that. Incredible man, but when you read his life story and the formative years – when you realise the problems his family experienced – he had a hard side to him.

Jim Smith: When I got the sack at Birmingham, one night before that I went out with Ron Atkinson. He had a friend called Paul Reeves, who was a director at Oxford and we went out to dinner in Stratford upon Avon. We'd drawn at West Ham funnily enough and unbeknown to me, I'd got the sack. I didn't know that, but that decision had been made before the game and Monday I knew that. Paul Reeves rang me and said: "Sorry, blah, blah, blah. Would you fancy the Oxford job?" I said: "Well, I need to get a job quickly." So I went down to see Maxwell – I don't know, about two o'clock, half past two – but we were leaving about 11 that night from Manchester airport to go to Majorca. You know, when you get the sack you always try to get away, and Doug Ellis had lent us his villa. I got there and he keeps you waiting an hour. Then he meets me. At that time, the chauffeur lad was called Charles, I think. I said: "How long have you been working for Mr Maxwell?" This lad said: "Twenty years, no, 18." Then Jean Badderley came in, his personal secretary: "How long have you been working?" She said: "Twenty years." So if they'd been working 18 and 20 years, it can't be all bad, can it?

Stuart Webb: He wasn't so bothered about being chairman of Derby when we were in the Third Division because that's when it all happened. So when we did come through the High Court, then going back to the High Court, coming back to Derby, the club was saved. Clean bill of health. We had our first board meeting because I was chairman at that time. I'd taken the chairmanship up. I'd decided I'd run with it and take a gamble, which I did.

Jim Smith: Mind, I think a lot of people got him mixed up with Murdoch in the early days because he only had the Pergammon Press, which was a very successful business. Anyway, eventually, he said: "Right. I've got a dinner party over the road, I've just got to go and meet people. I'll be back." So I said: "I'm going to Majorca at eleven o'clock tonight from Manchester and time's getting on." "You go tomorrow," he said. "What's your wife's name?" I said: "Yvonne." So he rings Yvonne up on the loudspeaker phone, to let you know everything that's happening. "Yvonne, would you like to go on your own to...?" So she said: "Well, whatever Jimmy..." What I'm getting at is, we cancelled that flight and he arranged us flights from London the next day. That's how strong he was.

Jim Smith: I'd got the job when I left, but he said: "You can't go for a fortnight, you've got to get back." I understood that, to be fair. So I came back a week early. I never had many problems with him because he hadn't got *The Mirror* at that time and he was grafting away at this BPCC. He never interfered very much. I only saw him occasionally – I didn't go to board meetings. He used to arrive at the game, at home, at five past three and leave at half past four and then ring me up at ten to five, to see how we'd gone on. I asked him to buy Aldridge and he bought Aldridge. It was only when we got promoted or when we looked as though we'd get promoted and he'd got *The Mirror* then, that he wanted to force the council into getting us a new ground. He said: "We will not play there." I said we would play there because we can't play anywhere else.

Stuart Webb: From then on, once I got my foot in the door, I didn't let go. At the same time, he was courting Manchester United and there was one occasion when I went down and halfway through the negotiations I was ushered in another door by the secretary because Martin Edwards was going in the other side. All of that was going on. Would he come to Derby, would he go to Manchester United? All that was nailbiting. Every day was a crisis.

Michael Dunford: I think prior to him getting involved at Derby, he had an involvement with Oxford and prior to that he tried to gain Manchester United and he also tried to gain control of Birmingham City. He'd been refused or had those overtures rejected on both occasions. He had a big printing works in Derby, so there was, obviously, that aspect to be considered and, in fairness, by his own personal wealth standards, the investment in Derby County was quite minimal really.

Lionel Pickering: I think if he'd had been half as brilliant as I used to think he was, well...! He phoned me up and he said: "I understand you're a bit disillusioned at the print works, with the unions." I said: "Yes, that's right." He said: "Well, what do you want for the Trader Group?" As if I would be interested, maybe in off-loading the print works. He said: "What do you want for the Trader Group?" I said: "You've taken the wind out of my sails. I haven't even thought of that, Mr Maxwell." He said: "By the way, do you pay corporation tax?" I said: "Yes. Yes I do." He said: "You've got a lot to learn about business, haven't you?" So I went hurtling to my accountant and said: "Are we doing anything wrong?" You know, he didn't pay. He just bought more businesses. Always made sure, officially, that he made a loss, whereas we used to make profits and pay our tax and it was quite lot then, wasn't it? 40 per cent, maybe 45 per cent of your profits went in corporation tax. I could see his point, after it was explained to me.

Michael Dunford: When Maxwell became involved, he insisted on gaining 76 per cent of the shares, which meant, from a tax point of view, any losses incurred by Derby County Football Club could be offset against profits from his other companies. Therefore, it didn't cost him that sort of money.

Lionel Pickering: I do think this, getting back to where he missed the boat. I mean, he was talking about getting Manchester United for £10million. I mean, had he bought it for £20 million, wouldn't he be laughing now? I mean, look what it's worth now. So he didn't really understand what was going to happen in the Premier League and didn't understand the magnitude of it. I mean, the business of ringing me up about the print works was about at that time. He said: "Look, I'm coming up to Derby in about two weeks time. I haven't seen the Derby print works yet." I think PSG it was called, Product Support Graphics. He said: "I'm coming up there to see them, so I may as well see you and we'll have lunch together. It'll be probably in about ten days' time." The secretary confirmed: "Yes, ten days' time." On the day he was supposed to come up, she said: "I suppose you've seen the papers?" I said: "No, why, what's happened?" She said: "Oh, he's up at Manchester. He wants to buy Manchester United. He can't make it today." So he never did actually come and, of course, he was all for Manchester United and I think he was arguing over twopence-halfpenny, wasn't he, really? It was £10 million or £12 million. There was Knighton there and he was going for £12 million. If only they had been half as brilliant as I thought they were, they would obviously have been laughing away today.

Jim Smith: He said to me: "Jim, I'm going to Manchester United, but you're not going to be the manager, big Ron's staying there." You know what I mean? Typical Maxwell.

Stuart Webb: We said, as directors, what should we do? We were in the Third Division then and we were skint. We'd put all our money in – dead money – to pay the debts off, so there was no money for new players or transfers. It was: "That's all gentlemen." So my first decision was to say to the board: "Look. Do we go back to Maxwell or somebody else who we might want to bring in? Or do we try to do it ourselves?" We decided to go to Maxwell, which we did.

Brian Flint: At the time, early on, you thought: "Wonderful." Then it didn't take long to realise he'd do anything to get his name in the headlines and sell his newspapers. It was a publicity stunt, wasn't it, Maxwell? I mean, we hadn't got any money and didn't he lend money to Spurs, money for Gary Lineker, because it was news?

Stuart Webb: He took a look at it. It was a better proposition then. There were no debts. It was a clean company. He came in and he appointed Ian as the chairman and asked me would I stay on. That was a condition of him coming in. So I stayed on as managing director and I worked, sort of, part-time for Derby County and part-time for Lonsdale. That was the deal and first year we did all right in Division Three. The next season we got promotion and came through Division Two into Division One. The point is that about that time there's a quite interesting story in view of what has happened to Derby since. I got Arthur Cox as manager. Went to Newcastle, got him signed. "Very good," I thought, "we're on the way here." Just during that period – it was when the board was deciding whether we should go to Maxwell or should we do things ourselves – so having then got Arthur in place, contract signed, Arthur's moving down and everything else, Maxwell joins. Within a week of this happening, I get a call. I can remember it vividly. I'm in my bedroom in South Avenue, looking at my garden. Maxwell's on the phone. Picked the phone up. He said: "Everything's going well, I'm delighted to be on the board. I've got ourselves a manager. I've got the manager for us, Mr Webb." I said: "Oh yes." He said: "Yes. The Bald Eagle, Smith. He's my manager at Oxford. Smith will be appointed on Monday morning, as the manager of Derby County." I said: "Well, I'm sorry. We've just signed Arthur Cox on a three-year contract." "Cox?" he said, "Sack him." That was my first crisis with Robert Maxwell, to persuade him. The only manager he probably knew was Jim, from his Oxford days, and he trusted Jim and knew he was successful. So that was my first problem: "Hang on mate. This isn't how it works." It's quite ironic how Jim's come back into it.

And football?

Michael Dunford: What he was very good at – and my dealings with him were somewhat limited – was that whenever you had a meeting with him, he'd had very thorough preparation. He had been briefed prior to the meeting with you. I've heard Arthur Cox and people like that say they've been summoned down to Headington Hall or Maxwell House, for an half an hour meeting and by the time they got into the meeting, he would have been briefed by his staff on the particular issue he was going to discuss and, if you thought you could pull the wool over his eyes, you were in for a rude awakening. He was no fool at all, but certainly not a football person.

Graham Richards: Kudos, pure and simple. He'd been an enormous success in business. He'd never got any headlines. He was known for Pergammon Press, he could be big news on the financial pages, but never make it to front or back pages. He was an MP. He achieved a lot in life, none of which had got him the publicity he got immediately he became involved in football. He'd previously tried to buy Manchester United, believing that was the proper foundation for his own ego. He hadn't succeeded, therefore, Derby County were interesting to him because they were a club with history, a point which was very much sold by Stuart Webb and then, in the middle Eighties, of vast potential. Far more potential than Oxford United, that he'd chaired for a number of years. Eminently successful, but it was all done so that you could see Robert Maxwell having breakfast, Robert Maxwell wearing a funny hat, and Robert Maxwell's view on great players.

Gerald Mortimer: Maxwell had discovered, at Oxford, that although he might be a major publisher and might have been a Labour MP and he might be this, that and the other, no one knew who the hell he was until he linked himself to football and started galloping round the pitch at the Manor Ground.

Jim Smith: Well, the story at Oxford – and I don't know how true it is – is that he wasn't going to bale them out. He was hoping – because it was a fantastic site – to close it down because the site is, apparently, now worth about £8 million -£10 million. It was quite near to where his business was and he could see the potential, but what he didn't realise was that the publicity that the football club gave him, free, was a big bonus to him because he was an egotistical guy. If things had have gone wrong, he'd have walloped it or whatever. I don't know what leases are on that ground or whether he could have done that. They all said he baled them out, but he tied all the ground and the supporters' club up to him. They all said that it had gone wrong – maybe even, he was hoping it would go wrong – it would be: "Thank you very much, sorry" Then the club's gone.

Stuart Webb: I think he'd had a taste of it at Oxford and he was a politician and he liked the big stage. He'd come out of politics and he saw football as a way to get into the newspapers and give him the media coverage. It was a stage, like politics had been a stage. Local hero, building a ground at Oxford. He saw Derby as the next stage and even at Derby, he was looking at Leeds and he wanted to get into that scene. Of course, we're jumping on a bit. After Ian and I had run the club for those three years and had come up, as we hit the First Division, he decided then that he would like to be chairman. He wanted the big stage.

Gerald Mortimer: Actually, I thought it was pretty well run in the first two years of Maxwell, when he kept fairly clear and Ian ran it and, I thought, ran it pretty well. Difficulties arose when Maxwell wanted more of a major part and suddenly discovered the people of Derby didn't necessarily love him and actually did want somebody as chairman with whom they could identify, someone who was present.

Michael Dunford: I suppose it sums up supporters, generally. They just want to see a winning team and if Maxwell comes in and owns the club and invests the money so that they can see quality players, like Mark Wright and Peter Shilton arrive, they're not bothered.

Brian Flint: We got to fifth, didn't we? Fifth. You're fifth on merit because everybody's played everybody, but I don't think there is a lot between fifth and 15th, at any time. Over 42 or 38 matches, it's worked your way that season, but you can't stand still. People work you out and you've got to come up with different things, haven't you? People knew the threats, knew the dangers – and snuffed them out.

Did Robert Maxwell save Derby from extinction?

Michael Dunford: No. I don't think that is true. When we were going through the High Court, it took a group of people. People like Stuart Webb and the other directors, John Kirkland and Arthur Willis, a local solicitor, who did an awful lot work and the unsecured creditors, at that time, mustn't be forgotten because they accepted 50p in the pound settlement, which to some of the smaller companies was quite a considerable loss. The National Westminster Bank wrote a considerable amount of money off, so all those factors coming together allowed the club to be saved, but I still believe that, had Robert Maxwell not come in, somebody else would have come in to save the club. Whether it be an involvement of the City Council, the County Council, I do not believe for one minute that, given the tradition and history of the club, they would have allowed Derby County to have disappeared into obscurity. Somebody would have saved them. Accrington Stanley never had the tradition of Derby County, did it?

Graham Richards: I don't think it is too much to say at all. Someone else may have come along and saved Derby County from going down the financial pan. The club might not have actually died. Might not have not gone bankrupt, but it's unlikely. The debts were pretty big in those days and Maxwell came in with, today, what seems a pathetically small sum of money – well under a million pounds. Well under and probably under half a million, and he got the whole club. No one else would put in the half million at that time, for, to be sure, they didn't come forward and offer anything. Maxwell was the only person willing to negotiate and take the club on.

Gerald Mortimer: No, because although it might not be as big a club as it thinks it is, it is a big enough club and somebody would have come in I feel sure, somehow. We weren't talking about huge sums. They were significant. I know nobody had come in, and people kept saying: "Oh, Frank Cholerton's going to put some money in." And so on. Nobody had come in. The trouble is, of course, when you're in that position, you're ripe for exploitation.

On the board, with Maxwell

Peter Gadsby: The first time – because I was a director twice – was when we'd conceded seven goals at home to Liverpool. By then I wasn't playing football, I was going to watch Derby quite regularly and had established myself with a profile in business, quite a substantial business. In 1987, which was when I actually started the business, three or four quite successful business people came and said: "Look, this has got to end." Maxwell had actually said the club was up for sale and all sorts of situations were being suggested. I said that I would be prepared to have a look at it and wrote a letter to Maxwell, via Brian Coxon, I think it was, who still owned business in BDC, the communications network. I had a letter back from Mr Maxwell saying: "You are indeed a fit and proper person with whom I am prepared to do business with." I think he'd had a few altercations with a few people in his time. So a meeting was arranged a week later and I went down with a fellow finance director, who helped prepare some of the figures, alongside other people who were prepared to put some money in. By this time Mr Maxwell was hitting the headlines every day for reasons that he was taking over companies and suing people and issuing writs. Afterwards people said: "Why didn't you spot it?" Well, many of the leading institutional houses hadn't spotted it. They'd actually allowed him to carry on trading, when he didn't even have the shares! When they asked him for the shares, he just told them who he was. So you had to put it into that sort of perspective.

Lionel Pickering: I agree with everything that's been written about him. I mean, I suppose in one respect he was a brilliant businessman, but on the other hand, if you're playing with other people's money and fiddling the books, you're not so brilliant at all. He had great charisma and great presence. I don't think he was very interested in football. I think he was interested in Robert Maxwell. He'd got himself the *The Mirror* and he was publicising himself all the time.

Peter Gadsby: I recall going down there and we'd almost assumed that we'd be dismissed. We'd spend all day there because that was the way we understood things were done down there. This was at Maxwell's place in Holborn, the communications headquarters. We arrived at quarter past ten. The appointment was at eleven o'clock. At three minutes to the hour we were taken up to his room. We were introduced straightaway to a large man, round a large table, with a booming voice: "Peter Gadsby, you are indeed somebody I wanted to meet." I was always impressed by that, but I was reminded afterwards by the agent, that he was standing behind me with a blackboard and he was writing on it 'Peter Gadsby'. Apparently, Maxwell kept calling me Peter Litting. He had a way that his mind worked, so it was almost as though he was saying: "Who are you?" We sat down and he told me: "This is how we are going to do the deal." I said: "That's going to be too much money." So he said: "I thought it would be. Now go and have something to eat upstairs." So we went upstairs and, let's say, we were very careful what we said – for entirely different reasons. Kevin Litting was with me. When we came down we were expecting to be dismissed as time wasters, but he then said: "Right. I would like to have your money and I'd like you to be involved, along with Brian Fern." He was in the next room, actually. Brian Fern had got 60 per cent of the old company. That came out at 51 per cent and we formed the new board. The new board was a, sort of, creation by Maxwell, which was never going to be a very happy situation. The board then was Fern, who was the chairman, Colin McKerrow, the vice-chairman. There was Billy Hart, there was Stuart Webb, David Cox, myself and Arthur Cox and John Kirkland. We had very little money. Maxwell's first stroke was to withdraw his £300,000 shirt sponsorship, which he had promised because that was part of the deal. He immediately reduced that to £50,000. We were clearly under-financed and I think we even had difficulty becoming soluble because finances were not balancing.

Michael Dunford: I think Bob Maxwell misunderstood what the potential was at the time. I think I'm right in saying that for a long time the club had never averaged more than a 19,000, home League gate. All right, the Baseball Ground was a potential problem and was always going to be. Sooner or later, that had to be addressed, but even when we got into the First Division, with the Shiltons, the Saunders and the Wrights, the average attendance was never much above 19,000. Now he'd invested a reasonable amount of money and he questioned the commitment of the Derby public to support a team.

Lionel Pickering: Then I heard nothing and it was Radio Derby, of course, that caused all the kerfuffle. I think we lost in the Cup didn't we, in January, and this was about September time. This was the season before the Premier League started and had Derby stayed up they would have been in the Premier League.

Graham Richards: Banned me? Yes he did. Me and Lionel Pickering. Just the two of us. Ironic isn't it? He banned Lionel on the basis that he actually tried to buy the club. Yes, well, perhaps you should explain that to me. Lionel offered him £3 million and he wanted £4.5 million and, consequently, he banned him from the ground. The fact that Lionel never went to matches anyway made no difference, so Lionel didn't lose out at all, beyond the fact that he got the clear impression that Maxwell was ungrateful to him. Me, he banned for a different reason.

Graham Richards: I actually had the temerity to criticise him. I did say, after a very disappointing FA Cup defeat at Newcastle, where the side had not played well, we're clearly short of players and the whole thing was drifting under a quiescent manager called Cox. I openly criticised him in my match report, which was re-broadcast on the Monday night talk-in show and the listenership to that programme, which was extended to two hours, was such that the whole mood of the programme was virulently anti-Maxwell. Not that Colin Gibson or I, said very much or anything really, but I was simply saying to the audience: "Well, don't complain to me, I largely agree with you. Phone Robert Maxwell. His number is in the telephone book, in London,...his premises on Fleet Street. It's this." And everybody phoned him!

Lionel Pickering: Yes, he banned me. It was thanks to Radio Derby really. I was nothing to do with it at all. It was just that Graham Richards was telling everybody: "This is Maxwell's private number, this is his fax number. Get on the phone." It was all supposed to be confidential, obviously, when someone's asking you what you're offering. I think I offered him £3 million for Derby County and, as Derby County was bankrupt, that was a very good offer. I mean, well, you'd think the Baseball Ground's got to be worth something wouldn't you? Now they tell me it's only worth about half a million. So it was way over the odds.

Graham Richards: The phone apparatus in London blew up. Anyway, he was in New York on his boat and he couldn't get through because his fax machine was on fire and he made some enquiries and it appeared he'd had 3,000 telephone calls during the night, from Derby. I was telling everyone to phone at nine o'clock in the morning. So in the morning, there must have been an even greater pressure and he made investigations, found out that it was Radio Derby, and me, he thought, was at the bottom of it. So he banned me and he called me the worst epithet that you could ever call anybody – a Nottingham Forest supporter, along the way! On that he showed what excellent judgment he had, even if his grip of the facts wasn't clear.

Lionel Pickering: It all went quiet. So as I say, Derby County lost and I don't know why Radio Derby phoned me up on that very Monday and somebody said: "You've actually made an offer for Derby County?" I said: "Oh yes, that's quite some time ago." They said: "What did you actually offer?" I said: "Well, £3 million." "What! £3 million? What happened?" I said: "Well, I've heard nothing." Graham went spare then, telling everybody that I hadn't had the courtesy of a reply from Maxwell and because of that and because of the hoo-hah that was caused on that Monday night talk-in programme, Maxwell banned me. I saw an article on the back page of *The Mirror* saying I wasn't 'a fit and proper person' to deal with. I mean, that more or less sums him up doesn't it? He was really not the 'fit and proper person'. I was, therefore, banned.

Michael Dunford: I think we were going to Manchester United for an evening game. We heard it on the radio that he'd put Mark Wright and Dean Saunders on the transfer list. That came as a complete shock. That's the way he was. He just decided to make a decision and you were lucky if you were told about it. Normally it was an exclusive in *The Mirror*. I think he was probably misled as to what the potential was and when he'd had enough, decided to sell up.

Jim Smith: Of course he'd no idea of which way the game was going, television and that, but having said that and it must have been at Oxford, not at Derby, he went to the chairmen's meeting, the League AGM – and actually, he used to get on the top stage because Dunnett was his man – and said: "Gentlemen, the deal you've done on television is a joke. I can get you £111,000 million," or whatever and people said: "Don't be so daft." He was right, though. All I'm saying is, whatever happened with him elsewhere, I actually haven't got too many bad memories of him. I've got to say, he was an unbelievable bloke to be in his company, to see him perform. He was ignorant, he kept you waiting, but he was fascinating also.

Graham Richards: I hate to say it, but Maxwell was right about everything in football and has proved to be right since. One of the first things he said was that the BBC was paying by no means enough for the right to televise games. He was very pro live football, but it being paid for properly. He sat on the Football League Management Committee with television and I think he resigned from it on the basis they settled far too low for his approval. A lot of his ideas were big, with him in the middle of it. He was, in one sense, a Jack Walker before Jack Walker came along. The difference is, as we know now, Jack Walker had the money, Robert Maxwell just thought he'd got the money.

Some Great Centre-Halves

IT'S strange how some clubs are noted for having outstanding players in one particular position. For example, Everton are famous for centre-forwards like Dixie Dean, Tommy Lawton, Alex Young, Joe Royle, Bob Latchford, Andy Gray, Graham Sharpe, Gary Lineker and Duncan Ferguson. Newcastle United, too, with Hughie Gallacher, Jackie Milburn, Len White, Malcolm Macdonald, Kevin Keegan and Alan Shearer. Derby County have had some great centre-halves, like Jack Barker, Leon Leuty, Roy McFarland, Mark Wright and in the modern era, Igor Stimac.

Roy Christian: We always had a very good centre-half. Funny, I never remember a Derby team, really, that hadn't got a good centre-half. A bit like Derbyshire cricket and the wicketkeepers. Seam bowlers, too.

Jack Barker

Tommy Powell: Well you're talking about different eras, but I think Jack Barker was, probably, the best centre-half I've ever seen. He could mix it and he could bring it down on his chest and send it this way or that way, no problem, right or left foot, sweet as a nut. I wouldn't say he was blessed with terrific speed or anything like that, but he wasn't slow. He was masterly.

Tom Stubley: The best centre-half I ever saw, in my opinion, was Jack Barker, by a long, long, chalk. He'd got a charisma all about him. He didn't have to do any stupid things. The very fact that he was there meant you'd got a solid base. All the time he was there you knew perfectly well that nobody would get past Jack no matter who they were. In the old days when Jack was playing we'd got two very fine wingers remember – Dally Duncan and Sam Crooks – and Jack used to bring the ball down off his chest and give it to the wingers so they could take it in their stride no trouble at all because the ball would come to them within a foot of them travelling towards the opposite goal. As a matter of fact, that was one of the best features of his play.

Ernie Hallam: Jack was supposed to be the last of the old type centre-halves, after the third-back centre-half came in. Jack was still the old-type centre-half, who wasn't afraid to go forward. His outstanding quality as the game was in those days, was his ability to swing the ball out to either wing. It would probably never get there now, it would be cut out. But in those days, before the marking got as it is, he was able to find Sammy on one wing or Dally on the other. That was his great quality. He was a strong chap and a very hard, opinionated man, I think. He wouldn't do anything if he didn't think it right himself.

Roy Christian: He was a good defender as well, but what I remember were those lovely passes out to the wings that he gave. Like Carbonari, who is good at that too. He had good ball control. Centre-halves weren't always good footballers, but he was, and he was a very tough defender. I wouldn't say was dirty, but he was very hard. He was big chap, he'd probably be 13 or 14st.

Alf Jeffries: I always rate Jack Barker as one of the best centre-halves in the country. Of course, you can only talk about the era he played in – the ball was different, the rules were different, pitches were different – but I reckon Jack Barker was really, one of the best centre-halves I've ever seen. When Jack was playing, they played the attacking centre-half, but for some reason or other, Arsenal's centre-half suddenly decided to revert to the defence. So Jack had to revert to defence. But he was the one who used to fling the balls out to Dally and Sammy, either feet. Jack's trouble was his mouth, you see. That was Jack Barker's trouble, otherwise he'd have got more England caps. He couldn't hold his tongue with the powers-that-be. He was a lad, but he was a good player. A tough sod he was. He came out of pits, did Jack Barker.

George Beard: Jack was a tough centre-half. Burly bloke he was. Jack Barker was a hero of mine, but Mac...! Jack Barker was a solid bloke. With his left foot, he could hit that heavy ball and drop it straight at Sammy Crooks' feet. If the ball was on the right, he could swing it with that right foot and drop it straight for Duncan.

Tom Stubley: During the war, Jack was stationed at Barton-under-Needwood. He was a PTI. Now Jack Barker's wife, Annie, lived with us at the time and Jack used to come and visit every weekend. In those days, I think he was even bigger than when he was playing football – and he was a hell of a size playing football. I always used to meet him in Babington Lane and we'd go to the first house at the Grand Theatre, no matter what was on. Even though it was wartime, there was still some damned good programmes on at the theatre. On this particular Saturday night, it was raining like hell and the bus was late. Jack got off the bus and he was in one of those greatcoats, which came to about three or four inches from the floor and it made him look even bigger. I always had the two seats right in front of the stalls, in the middle. We had those week after week after week. This time we got in rather late and the star of the show, on this particular occasion, was Tommy Trinder, who went on to be chairman of Fulham. Now Tommy Trinder, if anyone was late, tried to take the mickey out of them – and so on and so on. Now Jack was easily upset and it got right under Jack's skin, what Tommy Trinder was saying. Well, it took at least three of us to stop Jack going on stage and clocking Trinder one. He'd have clocked him, sure as houses. Jack, though, was a great lad.

Leon Leuty

George Beard: Leon Leuty was damn good. Precise. A wonderful header, heading out of the goalmouth. It always went in the right direction. It wasn't slid out for a corner, it was headed to somebody, but Mac...! He was brilliant, wasn't he?

Tommy Powell: He was a good player. Yes, a very good player Lee Leuty was. Brilliant in the air. He'd got that little knack of brushing up the back of a centre-forward and then backing off. In 1948-49, in that side, there was myself, Reggie Harrison, Bert Mozley, Jackie Parr, Leon Leuty, Chick Musson. Six local lads, all in the First Division. Georgie Poppitt also played.

Bill Brownson: Jack Barker was great, but the best centre-half in my time was Leon Leuty, without a doubt. Very stylish. Leuty was very unfortunate because he came up when Neil Franklin of Stoke was at his best. That was unfortunate because it kept him out of the England team. I think if Leuty had got into the England team he'd have stayed there. I would have to think about either Leuty or McFarland. Maybe Leuty, much as I thought of McFarland.

Ernie Hallam: Ah, great player. He wasn't a great big fellow, but amazingly good in the air. Unfortunately, died early, didn't he? Had a bit of class. He played well in the Cup Final. The centre-forward who played for Charlton never had a kick.

Tom Stubley: Lee Leuty was a very fine player and there was no doubt about that. In those days, he had two wing-halves, Tim Ward on one side and Chick Musson on the other, although the lad who played in the Cup Final was Jimmy Bullions. For the most part when Lee was playing, he'd got those two wing-halves and he used to bring the ball down, pass it to them and he was finished. He'd nothing like the charisma of Jack Barker or even Roy McFarland for that matter, but he was excellent.

Ray Young: No, I didn't see Jack Barker play. I saw Leon play. Leon was still there when I signed for Derby. I – sort of – tried to model my style of play I suppose, on Leon Leuty. When I wasn't playing I would watch both number-fives. I'd watch the full 90 minutes and I'd be watching the number-fives. Stylish, but hard as well. Oh yes, he was hard. Only about my height, about 5ft 10ins. Oh yes, a good player. I think he was the best centre-half I've seen at Derby.

John O'Hare: I was talking to some people the other night and there was an oldish guy from Ilkeston and he was talking about Leon Leuty being a fantastic player. He must have been useful. I never saw him, of course.

Don Hazledine: Leon Leuty I would pick out as the best, but I did like McFarland's play. I think he was a tremendous player as well. Lovely style, Leuty. Cultured.

Roy Christian: He was very good. Now he was a different type altogether to Jack Barker. He was very much the 'gentleman' centre-half. He was very cool and calm and collected. I don't think it was a pose, I think it was his natural style, but sometimes he seemed so calm. Actually, a bit like Stimac. Stimac made his one mistake every week and Leuty was a bit like that. So was Toddy in a way. I mean, Toddy was a great footballer, but he made some, at times, astonishing blunders, as Stimac did. I can't remember McFarland ever doing that.

Gordon Hughes: I saw Leon Leuty and he was a stylish, good, centre-half, but Roy McFarland had the power – and he had the style.

Graham Sellors: I can remember Leon Leuty, yes, and I can remember him being a favourite of my aunt's. I've actually got a rosette – that someone gave me that they said came from off the Cup – that Leon Leuty gave to their sister. It certainly is a Cup Final rosette. In our house the conversation was all about the fact that Leuty should have been playing for England, rather than Neil Franklin. That he was a much, much better player, than Neil Franklin.

Johnny Morris: I thought Neil Franklin was the best at the time. Then there was Leon Leuty and Allenby Chilton of Manchester United. Leon Leuty was a little bit better footballer, but put the other way round, Allen Chilton was a strong man and he made his players play around him. He was the making of Johnny Carey and Johnny Aston, his full-backs.

Gerald Mortimer: I saw him play a bit. Not enough to form a judgement. Leuty was obviously very good, I wish I'd seen more of him, but I'd have to have been older. He must have been on the decline at Notts County because of the leukemia. He died at 35.

Phil Waller: I saw Leon Leuty at Notts County. Good footballer. I think there might have been players who didn't mind playing against Leon, whereas they bloody hated playing against Roy.

Roy McFarland

Tommy Powell: Good player. It must have been nice to attack balls, knowing you'd got a bloke like Toddy speeding about behind you. That makes a difference. They were a good back four then.

Roger Davies: I would say, in my era, he was the best centre-half I've ever seen, bar none. I mean, there were some good centre-halves around, but he was the best. He had alongside him, Colin Todd. You know what Toddy was like, his pace, his passing, his tackling. I mean, the two of them together must have been awesome. I wouldn't have liked to be a front player playing against those two.

Geoff Hazledine: I'd put McFarland first, without any question. Then Leon Leuty and Mark Wright. I never saw Jack Barker. I think without question McFarland, as far as brain power, judgment, and all the attributes to play centre-half, he had all of them. I don't know how many times he was capped for England, but in my book, he should have had more than 70 caps. I think it was a travesty of his football career that he couldn't account for 70 caps. I thought he was totally brilliant.

John O'Hare: Roy had everything really. Attitude, apart from just ability. Head it, play it, pass it, Roy could do everything and he had that aggression, too. I'm not too sure about this business that he could have played any position on the field. They tried him in midfield, once. He wasn't as good there as he was at centre-half!

George Beard: He used to come out almost to the touchline, tackle somebody, get it and then deliver it. The best of all the lot? Different styles, of course, and my favourite was Jack Barker, but McFarland, I think, as a general all-rounder and bringing the ball forward and wiggling his way though, Mac had to come up as the best.

Ray Young: I thought Roy was a good player. Wouldn't say he was completely commanding in the air. I think there were players who gave him trouble and one was Peter Withe. Always struggled against Peter Withe, in the air. And I suppose Roy only had one foot; left foot. I remember asking Roy why he didn't kick the ball with his right foot . What he said to me was: "Were you sitting in the stand? Because if I'd have hit it with my right foot, you'd have been in danger of being hit!" That was Roy. At that time then, there were quite a few players in the Derby side who were good one-foot players. Archie Gemmill only had a left foot. He just stood on the other one. Nish also, with his right. Roy was the same, all left foot.

Michael Dunford: People talk about whether he was the best centre-half ever to play for Derby. Jack Barker, Leon Leuty – different generations will give you different versions – but I think as an all-round player, Roy McFarland was the best I've seen pull on a Derby County shirt.

Roy Christian: I think my best centre-half would be Roy McFarland. Jack Barker would be a close second. I was going to say that Barker was a different type, but that wouldn't be true because McFarland was a sort of throw-back in some ways. I mean, McFarland didn't hesitate to go upfield – and he scored nearly 50 goals for Derby – but Barker was one of the last of the attacking centre-halves.

Tom Stubley: I would say, of the three, I'd put Jack Barker at the top of the tree, I'd put Roy McFarland second and Lee Leuty third. That's the way I would view it.

Mark Wright

Bill Brownson: Not compared with Leuty, I'd put Leuty first.

George Beard: Yes. Mark Wright was another splendid centre-half, but not like McFarland.

Gerald Mortimer: Yes, he was a good player...I'm sounding slightly defensive on that one. He always struck me as being a slightly unfulfilled player. I think he was as happy with anyone, playing with Rob Hindmarch.

Phil Waller: I think he had a couple of good years. One good year at Derby, certainly. I think he was a volatile character, wasn't he? Off the pitch as well as on it? Roy was just hard. Didn't often lose his head. I mean, not totally, like Wrighty. He's always been the same. He had strong opinions, Mark Wright.

Tom Stubley: I never saw much of Mark Wright because at the time he was playing for Derby, I was working away from Derby and I didn't see an awful lot of him. I saw him on the television a time or two. I thought him a very fine centre-half, but I can't pass a lot of opinion on him.

Ray Young: I think he improved while he was at Derby. Whether Coxie had anything to do with it I don't know. He didn't do too well to start with. He improved. Toddy was like that, too.

Michael Dunford: I don't think he was in the same class as McFarland. In fairness, remember, he broke his leg in the FA Cup semi-final at White Hart Lane before he came to Derby – he was playing for Southampton. I forget which leg it was, but he very rarely tackled with that leg afterwards. Probably slightly better in the air than Roy. Very cool, comfortable with the ball, but not the temperament of Roy McFarland. Wrighty was very hot-headed, although he improved as he matured, but I'd certainly have to go with Roy McFarland.

Rob Hindmarch

Gerald Mortimer: He wasn't in the class of the others, but equally, you knew what he was going to do. I thought he played a huge part in the first half of Arthur Cox's management and those two promotions. I just thought he was a sort of man's man, which was what you wanted then. I remember seeing him once, playing for Portsmouth – when he was on loan from Sunderland – and I thought: "What a camel." Then when you had him, although you knew he was slow, you also knew he'd put his lot in. It's a bit like Spencer Prior. I don't think he's ever going to play for England, but if he did, you know what you'd get. I thought that was marvellous that you buy a guy for £700,000, to replace one you've sold for £5.3 million. And you're not sure – well, I think I am sure – who's the better defender of the two.

Igor Stimac

Bill Brownson: Stimac's good, but he got a bit over confident and did some silly things sometimes.

George Beard Yes he's good, isn't he? McFarland was better.

John O'Hare: I think he's a very good player. I think he's got quite a bit of arrogance as well. Winds people up, uses his arms, things like that. Whatever he does, needling people, he's certainly a top-class player.

Ernie Hallam: You wouldn't like to leave him out from that group, from that quality. No, Stimac is in that group.

Tom Stubley: Stimac? He's a very fine player, a fancy player, but I don't think he is an out-and-out centre-half. He plays wonderful football, but he doesn't seem to have his heart in it as far as people like Roy McFarland or Jack Barker, did. Now, I might be totally wrong in that respect, but that's the way I feel about things.

Ray Young: Never really rated him. I don't think he commands enough.

Gerald Mortimer: Igor's coming was like Kevin Hector or Dave Mackay coming. He doesn't owe Derby County anything. He brought a swagger and a confidence and a skill and a personality to the whole thing.

Steve Powell: Again, a very good player, but I would worry a lot about his appearances, really. When he plays he's an influential player, of course he is, but he doesn't play often enough.

Keith Loring: I thought it was very significant to buy Igor Stimac, at that particular time.

Igor Stimac: I just tried to do my job because I know that I am a good player. I know that I can play very well, so I just tried to stay inside the team. I didn't want to go out of it or to make players in the Derby County team jealous. I just wanted to stay inside the team. I am very ambitious and I wanted to be one part of Derby County team that did well in the Premier League. I always want to go up.

Horacio Carbonari

Roger Davies: He looks so laid back doesn't he? Nothing seems to flummox him. He's flicking balls up at the back, flicks them over people's heads.

Graham Richards: A good player, who will get better and I hope he stays at Derby County. He had a difficult start and then an injury and we were all a bit dubious about him coming from so far and for so much money and not, incidentally, from a town where you find talented Argentinean footballers. The best players are very quickly into Buenos Aires, almost as teenagers, if they're not born there already, which nine-tenths of the country is. Rosario is quite a small town. I think he's an outstanding player, whose reading of the game is excellent and whose contribution going forward will be one of the aspects of his game that will improve. He scored more goals in his last year in Argentina than some acknowledged out-and-out strikers did. That shows two things, one of which is that Carbonari is a good footballer.

Geoff Hazledine: He's a mystery to me. Sometimes he looks a class act and then, he looks really leaden footed. He looks like when all the lads are out training and the trainer shows up – and he's only got wellies. So he's played in his wellies. He looks very leaden-footed to me, at times, but he does some wonderful things. He's got great composure. He strikes a ball well, as we all know, and then, at other times, the contrast is so great that you cannot believe it's the same person in the same shirt. He seems to get lost in the game sometimes.

Graham Richards: If Derby County have got a reputation in one position, it would have to be centre-half, wouldn't it? I think Carbonari's off the pace yet. You've got to have a lot of good seasons before you're in the same breath as those mentioned previously. Carbonari's good in the air, very strong, but we live in a different world now.

Phil Waller: He looks a good yard short of pace, but it might be deceptive. I think players come off him and he doesn't track them too well. I see him too often turning round and chasing players down the channels. I mean, one or two people say he's improved and I think as a constructive player he might be getting in Roy's class, but as a defender, well. He's got good feet for a big lad, hasn't he? It's a big step when they come from the continent or even further. It was a big enough step for us when we moved ten miles down the road!

Graham Richards: He doesn't come from a mining town, he comes from a town that grows beef the other end of the world and you feel, necessarily, as he gets better and more prominent and everybody sees him on television, the greater the likelihood is that he won't have a career at Derby County at all – and that's the shame.

Steve Powell: He's an excellent player. I think he's got the potential to be in the top bracket, but it's difficult to say. He may need to move on to a bigger club to do that. I don't know whether he can achieve that at Derby.

Other centre-halves

Roger Davies: Some were difficult for different reasons. Some were harder than others. When I say hard, I don't necessarily mean hard physically, although when you used to play against people like Chris Nicholl and Stuart Boam...! You know, they were the big raw-boned ones. When you went up, you knew they were going to clatter the back of your head. You would be shaking your head and they would just walk away. You'd go back to mark them at corners when one's hanging there. You knew what's going to happen when you were going up to head it. You're going to get this belt on the back of your head. From the point of view of other centre-halves, there were quite few. I mean, Paul Madeley, when he played at the back for Leeds, was a very, very good centre-half. Very quick, good reader of the game. I always found him difficult to play against.

Ray Young: I suppose Billy Wright overall. He was smaller than me. I think he was a superb centre-half. Adams is not my sort of player. Jack Charlton. He was a useful player. Yes, Jack Charlton of the more modern ones.

Roger Davies: As opposition, there were some you didn't like to play against when things weren't going well. No one really bothered me, as such, but there were some. As I've said, I'd have hated to play against Roy McFarland and Colin Todd because I think they were the best at the time. Best centre-backs in the country.

Don Hazledine: Ray Young tried to play like Leon Leuty. He wasn't as good, but he did try. He was quite a useful player, Ray was. He was a bit unfortunate he didn't play in a higher division all the time. He played most of his games in the Second or Third, didn't he?

Roger Davies: When you look at other people, like your Norman Hunters and Tommy Smiths even though they had this reputation as being hard players, they were fair with it. They'd take it as well as give it. They weren't always wanting to give it and then moan. You knew what was going to come, so if you wanted to compete, you'd got to do something about it. You couldn't just roll over and die. You'd be gone.

The Nineties

THE last decade of the 20th century opened with Derby County struggling to stay in Division One. In season 1990-91, the year before the Premier League was formed, they were relegated and so began a struggle to get back into the top flight which wasn't achieved until Jim Smith led the club into the Premiership in 1996. That first season in the Premiership was the last at the Baseball Ground. Pride Park Stadium is now the club's home, rising majestically in the middle of an industrial estate, a symbol of the new football age.

In 1992, Marco Gabbiadini became Derby County's second £1 million pound player and Peter Shilton qualified as the oldest man to play for the club when he made his last appearance for Derby County against Watford in February 1992. The following year, John Harkes became the 750th player ever to play for Derby County.

Off the pitch, there were political and power struggles for control of the club, until order was restored when a local man took up the challenge. Lionel Pickering began his career as a junior reporter, covering matches at Chesterfield in the Fifties, before emigrating to Australia, to become sports editor of a Sydney newspaper. He returned home and eventually made his fortune by selling his interest in *The Trader* group of free newspapers.

Trust is something that is becoming increasingly absent in football, but supporters seem to trust Lionel Pickering. He is known to be a lifetime follower of the club and has a fan's feel for the game. Supporters appreciate that Lionel Pickering is in their corner. Most admire the gamble he took when he put his money into Derby County. It was at a time when returns on such an investment were not likely, but neither was the move to Pride Park. For that decision alone, Lionel Pickering and the board of directors deserve every credit.

Ted McMinn: As a winger, you rely on crossing it and we were lucky enough to have two great wee players like Paul Goddard and Dean Saunders, who could finish for fun. Then Mick Harford came, which suited me because he was a big target man.

Lionel Pickering: I'd been out. I'd not seen much football for quite some time. I became interested again, I think it was 1990, it was the World Cup and I noticed we'd got Shilton in the England goal and Mark Wright was centre-half and then, of course, we'd got Saunders and it occurred to me that Derby had got the makings of a team and right out of the blue I was contacted by Derby County saying: "Would you be interested? Maxwell wants to buy Spurs or something like that and he can't have two teams." I did get interested. Stuart Webb it was, who rang.

Ted McMinn: Well, we had the best goalkeeper in Britain at the time. Shilts was number one. We'd big Mark Wright and Deano and Paul Goddard and a lot of young lads breaking in, Mel

Sage, Micky Forsyth, they were there. This wasn't a team full of big names and that's why we were a great team together. All the lads were close and we always had a laugh at the right times and we took it seriously at the right times. All the lads that were there got on absolutely great.

Peter Gadsby: I was off the board because I think really we hadn't seen eye to eye with Brian Fern, who was running the club. He promised, as I understand it, to put finance in. We were all asked to put more finance in and there was an imbalance and he was basically looking for us to put more money in and he called at one stage saying: "You're a very successful person, you've got a big business, put more money in." And I was saying: "Well, sure, I'll do it for equity." And he said: "I'm not losing control." At that point it was really better that we went.

Lionel Pickering: Of course, they got relegated and I went off to Australia thinking: "Well, that's dead now." Then the following December 1991, I was contacted again and I thought: "Why not?" They'd been relegated, were going downhill fast and Maxwell had sold all the bloody family jewels, hadn't he? To Liverpool. They really looked in a bloody mess, so I said: "Yes, I'll get involved."

Michael Dunford: If you remember at that time, Lionel Pickering had been banned from the Baseball Ground by Maxwell because there was a story in the paper about Maxwell had rejected an offer from Lionel. Maxwell had said that he didn't think Lionel Pickering was a suitable person to be involved with Derby County Football Club and so Lionel was banned from the ground. We then get a phone call one day at the Baseball Ground to Brian Fern, from Lionel, who was sitting in his house at Ednaston. He said to Brian: "Can I have a chat with you?" Now Brian had just left a board meeting – he was on his way back down to his house in Hertfordshire – and he turned back and went back to Ednaston, saw Lionel – at that point they seemed to get on quite well together. They hit a basis of agreement, those negotiations went on for a few weeks involving solicitors and accountants, and Lionel then got the controlling interest in the club.

Peter Gadsby: The board wasn't a happy board. From day one that was quite clear and the club was going through a difficult time. I suppose you could say that Arthur Cox was not a happy man, and discontent was going all the way through. So what I think therefore happened was that the board decided they wanted to find somebody who could finance it and Lionel Pickering was introduced. Basically, Lionel Pickering would only come in if he had control. We were asked to pass over shares. I'd done business with Lionel and knew him for many years, being an Ashburnian person, and was fairly happy that he would be taking over my shares.

Peter Gadsby: Lionel had had a go earlier, yes, and Maxwell had banned him. I think it was simply that he was a bully, you know: "If you upset me in any way, I don't want to see you." I mean, Lionel, well we know his qualities, is very simplistic. He says what he thinks and he'll make his own mind up and he made his own mind up and I think he was ahead of the game. I think he actually spotted it. Certainly he spotted Maxwell as a bully.

Lionel Pickering: As I wasn't going to Derby County I'd got a bit disenchanted with football. I thought it had gone very negative in the Eighties and, as I say, it was was only because of the 1990 World Cup on television, that I thought: "Mmm. It's picking up a bit and England's picking up a bit. We've got a couple of Derby players in the England side." So it rekindled my interest, but I wasn't watching Derby County because on the very few times I'd been, in Brian Coxon's box or something like that, I thought it so sterile and uninteresting and unadventurous, negative and, apparently, in the old First Division we played this negative stuff and we finished sixth or fifth. I thought that if that's the standard, I don't want to know – but Cloughie banned me twice, as well!

Michael Dunford: Politically at that time, it got very nasty. There was a lot of infighting and such. I don't know what figure Lionel sold out to Thomson, when he sold the Trader Group, but he invested an awful lot of money into Derby County...Arthur Cox was pushed to spend. No manager is going to refuse that type of money because he's judged on results and, make no mistake, the better quality players you have, the more successful you're going to be.

Steve Sutton: I came at the back end of the season and during that summer, that's when Arthur Cox went out and bought Pembridge, Kitson and those sorts of people. Gabbiadini was here. Kitson was also here while I was here. He came just after me, I think.

Michael Dunford: The problem was that everybody assumed that investment would continue... but all of a sudden Lionel, for whatever reason – and he knew what he was doing – said: "Enough's, enough." Now, at that point, the club had invested heavily in players and associated with that were the overheads incurred with servicing those players – wages etc. The club couldn't sustain it and, therefore, the better players had to go.

Lionel Pickering: I did not like what I saw at Derby. I was asking questions: "What about the training? What about this, what about that?" I was told: "Leave it to the professionals, Lionel." I thought: "Well, I'm probably out of date anyway because I can remember when they had two wingers, five forwards, half-backs etc." I thought: "Maybe yes, I'm probably out of date." Therefore, I sat back.

Michael Dunford: I think it proved that football is still a team game and you can bring the best 11 individuals into a club and it doesn't guarantee success. I think if Arthur was to look back now and have his time again, maybe where he didn't quite grasp the nettle was bringing a couple of old heads in. Like another Gordon Cowans or somebody at that time, to supplement the Kitsons, the Johnsons, Pembridges, all great players.

Steve Sutton: They were kids. They were all potential, weren't they?

Michael Dunford: Lionel wanted to get Derby into the First Division, now the Premiership. Once he saw, after a couple of years, it wasn't going to happen, I think he became a little bit disenchanted. He probably thought: "Enough's enough." The problem was that not everybody realised there was a limit to how much money was available. Had they done, then they might have acted differently.

Steve Sutton: The quality, for the amount of money spent, wasn't instantaneous. If they'd still been together three years on, possibly it could have worked out, but not at the time. Not the amount of time it was given.

Lionel Pickering: Then I thought: "It's boring, this is." To be honest – and now we can say it – I always defended Arthur, but...! I don't think he bought the wrong players at all because they've been recycled. It's like when people say to me: "Well, you never gave McFarland money." Well, the money was on the field wasn't it? McFarland had exactly the same money as Jim Smith. Jim Smith, of course, just sold them and got the players he wanted.

Michael Dunford: There was certainly a big clash of personalities in the boardroom. John Kirkland, to a certain degree, was somewhat removed from it. Wherever the shares are, there you have the power, but for a while Lionel didn't want to take the chair. I've been there when Brian Fern said: "Any time you want to take the chair, you take it."

Peter Gadsby: I think things combined then in getting to a point where the Extraordinary General Meeting came in because Lionel had said at that point, he wanted to take the chair. I think he owned then, at that point, 79 or 80 per cent. He had an agreement that at any point he wanted the chair, he could have it, and Lionel actually went to the board meeting and asked to have the chair and the board said: "No."

Michael Dunford: There were a lot of things said at that particular time which, as secretary of the club, unfortunately you become embroiled in. But the only thing that mattered as far as Derby County Football Club and their supporters were concerned was that the team continued to struggle for another 12 months, in as much as they could only finish ninth. Jim Smith was then appointed and they soon got back into the Premiership. Since then, it's all been rosy – and that's the only thing that matters.

Peter Gadsby: Well they misread the situation. They thought the voting system was okay. They didn't want to leave really. They were enjoying it, weren't they? The money was there, they had no responsibility – well, they had got responsibility, but they hadn't got any real cash in there – and they probably misread Lionel to some extent.

Steve Sutton: It was good to be there. You could see that if it all just clicked. I think that was the thought. You could see, on the day, we murdered some sides, but we just didn't get the results to help us.

Ted McMinn: We got through to the Anglo-Italian Final, which was a good achievement for us because we played a lot of hard games away and at home.

Lionel Pickering: Don't forget we did get to Wembley. We nearly got up straightaway, when Blackburn beat us, if you remember, in the Play-offs. Then, of course, two years later, with Roy McFarland, we got to Wembley and it was the best thing that happened that we didn't win there because we'd have come straight down again. We would have had about six players there who were Premiership players. We'd have had to have bought another six. I mean, some of them, like Pembridge, just didn't play did they? Really, it needed tougher management. If they didn't play – either sell them or drop them. I thought in some ways, we weren't tough enough with them. Yet they played really well in that semi-final against Millwall. The two Millwall games, we were brilliant. It's a fine line, isn't it, between success and failure?

Michael Dunford: I think it would have been very difficult to have changed a successful formula, in as much as had the club been successful under Arthur Cox's management and under Brian Fern's chairmanship, I don't think Lionel would have wanted to have rocked the boat. He would have taken certain kudos, quite rightly, from being the owner, and making a lot of money available for players. That would have gone with that, but I don't think you'd have found too many changes had it been successful. We'll never know that, will we?

Arthur Cox in the Nineties

Steve Sutton: I thought he was very, very good. Yes, a disciplinarian, very much so. I think if he made a mistake, it was bringing too many kids too soon into the side. I think the core of experience went and with that went a little bit of discipline because the kids didn't respect him. They didn't respect him as I respected him, and as the players who had been here respected him. I think that caused him a few problems and it didn't work out with the kids, as we all know to our cost.

The EGM

Peter Gadsby: The Extraordinary General Meeting was a very high profile and unwanted thing for the club and still, to this day, I will never understand how when people are put to a position on a vote, that says that one person has got in excess of 85 per cent of the shares and is going to an Extraordinary General Meeting, why would you want to go through that? It was a demonstration. People standing up making speeches. People put up to make speeches. It was like: "Hail to Caesar, to the board." I think that the board, particularly the chairman, assumed that Lionel wouldn't go through with it. Once it had been done, that was it. Roy was then the manager and Roy was given the opportunity to take the club forward, but I think he still carried on the same way as in the Cox era, so it wasn't a new era, I would say. Really, that went on for so long and it wasn't going to work and that, of course, is when Roy went.

Going forward

Keith Loring: My first day here was a Monday in mid-July 1995. We'd arrived back from America on the Sunday, on a flight through the night, so you know how you feel. I came up on my own at first and Jim Smith arrived the same day. I was in San Francisco when Jimmy got the job. I got the job at the end of April, early May. I got a phone call from Stuart Webb back in February time. Over the years I'd had about six offers to go to other clubs. I was at Brentford and we'd done a good job. Yes, I was chief executive. I went there as a commercial consultant on a six-month deal. It was on the shake of hands and I was there ten years, without a contract. I never had a piece of paper all the time I was there. Got on very well with the chairman. He owned it, rather like Lionel, and he left me to get on with it. It was fine, but obviously, there was a limit to what we could achieve because we were never going to be a rich club.

Lionel Pickering: I think it was certainly Jim getting hold of Igor that was a turning point. I remember we were up at Sheffield United and Jim was saying: "We need some cover at centre-half." He'd heard about this guy called Igor Stimac, but you know, unfortunately, it was over a £1 million. I said: "What's he like?" Jim said: "Different class." I think they were telling us he was the captain of Croatia, at the time. I think he captained them once! Even so, we said: "Well, can we organise it?"

Igor Stimac: Tranmere was a big shock for me. I was so frustrated after the game. I was thinking about the next game because the next game was my first game before the Derby crowd. It was the most important game for me. The Tranmere game was a really big shock. We lost 5-1. It was my debut and I scored a goal and I didn't play so badly, really.

Lionel Pickering: He was different class, as Jim said. He showed that you just didn't have to belt the ball up the field. You could just, slowly, roll it to somebody five yards away and it's still a good pass and it takes the heat out of the situation.

Keith Loring: At Brentford we had to be the best community club in the country. It was the only way we could take the gates up and we were were fairly unique. We went in with two councils and ourselves. Two other partners as well. The PFA were in the north then and weren't doing the south. We had to do it ourselves. We got grants here and grants there. It was a completely independent system and we did it really, really well. We won the national award, twice. The best club in London, in the middle of that, and you know, in fairness, I was very proud of it because it was original. I can show you a book with all sorts of things in it, but it was just something we were very proud of at Brentford.

Igor Stimac: Why Derby? It just happened. It seemed a good idea at the time. I was playing in Croatia and I wanted to go abroad to play football. My agents were in contact with a couple of clubs, Derby was one of the clubs which was in a hurry to sign a new player. It just happened.

Lionel Pickering: The one nice thing about dealing with Croatia, as opposed to an English club, is you can pay them over three years. Say you buy a player for £1 million in England, you put 50 per cent down – that's half a million – and then you pay the rest in a year's time or in dribs and drabs – quarterly after three months, six months, nine months and then the final payment. They get the full £1 million after one year. I think Igor was something like two years. We put down something like £500,000 and then another £300,000, another £250,000. It was easy payments, which enabled us to go for Igor. We were hoping to get him for less than we were quoted and we finished up paying a little bit more, but I think it was definitely a turning point.

Bringing in the money

Keith Loring: At Brentford, we also got a reputation for being commercially aware. A reputation for innovative ideas, on gates and things like that. We'd already filled the ground for an Under-21 international, but it didn't get the headlines because filling the ground at Brentford meant less than 12,000. So that wasn't such a big story, but we still filled it. We filled it for an Under-18 international, as well. It was Brazil, though! Of course, at Derby we got a record gate for an Under-21 international.

Keith Loring: Stuart Webb phoned. Met him. Met Lionel, at the Yew Tree. Spent the evening with Lionel. Nothing then happened. Met Mr Gadsby the next day. Nothing really happened then for about six weeks and then I turned it down. What I was concerned about was that I hadn't told my chairman. I'd never ever done anything like this before and we had a great relationship. I didn't want it to leak out. I thought it had gone on long enough. I phoned Stuart and I said: "I am writing to you, but I will just take my name of the list." I must admit, when I was invited, I didn't realise there was a list because I don't do interviews you know. That sounds really arrogant, but I don't. Stuart said: "Keith, there's a lot going on here at the moment, which I can't explain to you over the phone. It needs a little bit of sorting out. Once it's sorted out, I may well be down the motorway with a contract." I said: "In which case, we'll talk again, but at the moment I don't want a sort of drawn-out situation." I said: "Of course I'd love to come to Derby, but I can't be in a situation where I come second or third in an interview situation. Nor do I want my chairman to find out before I've told him." So I told my chairman and told him I'd been interested. It's a funny thing. All my friends were pleased. Lesley, my wife, was pleased at the time. When I told my chairman, he didn't handle it very well. "Well Keith, you've never had a contract and I'd never stand in your way." I think he was trying to do the right thing and he was a bit shocked, to be fair. I always remember David Webb saying to me: "Martin Andrews was very upset, the way he handled it." He said: "But don't worry, I told him you'd never leave Brentford." I walked out of that office and I'm thinking: "Hang on. I'm not even 50 years of age yet and people have actually got me sorted out. That's no good" Stuart rang me again. I came up and met Lionel at The Manor. Shook hands.

Keith Loring: David Webb said the people here at Derby treated him magnificently. He loved the people of Derby... Jimmy and I stayed at the same hotel, at the Breadsall Priory. We only stayed there a week, though. We didn't know who was paying the expenses at the time, so we got out quick and we went to the Mackworth.

Keith Loring: We agreed the deal but I wouldn't tell a soul until the last ball of the season was kicked at Brentford. I think that by the time I got the job, we were already in the Play-offs. It was the only year that two clubs didn't go up. It was a nightmare. We finished second. We played Huddersfield in the Play-offs and drew 1-1 away. We came home and were 1-0 up, finished 1-1, lost on penalties. I'd a golf tournament the next day, which we did every year. Big day and everyone was there, feeling flat. I still hadn't told the chairman. I didn't tell him until the Friday afternoon and that's when it was announced. I came up here the following week.

Keith Loring: I came up and interviewed all the staff. One bloke walked in and I asked him some question. He said: "Well, we won't get on." I thought: "This is interesting, I normally decide that." "Why's that?" He said: "Well, everybody out there has to save money, but I'm the one who spends it." I said: "No. You did spend it." I have to say, he was on my list of six people that I didn't think would survive with me. The other five didn't, but he turned out to be such an important person. It's David Holland, operations manager. David was such an important person in the move to Pride Park. He had been in senior management in the police force, so there was going to be a clash of wills for a time. Once I knew what David did, I had such respect for him, I didn't argue with him. I didn't need to because he knew his subject better than me. Being at a smaller club, I'd done all the jobs. I may not have been as expert as these guys, but at Baseball Ground level, I wasn't far away from them. Obviously now we've moved, it's a whole different situation now.

Keith Loring: I always knew Derby was a football town and I always fancied working at a place where the ideas I had in my head and the ideas we tried at Brentford could work. We had limited success at Brentford because – well, we had no daily paper for a start. We had three local weekly papers so, if you had an idea, it would take you three weeks to get it going. Here, you go like that, snap – and everyone's got it. It happens. Radio Derby's got it, the other radio stations and the evening paper. You can make a decision on a Monday, which is how we got the Crystal Palace game organised. That was a Monday morning decision. We needed to do something to wake everybody up – because everyone was a bit depressed over the Birmingham result – and turn that into a positive. Make the crowd feel they could achieve something and be part of it – and we did that.

Lionel Pickering

Keith Loring: Lionel is unique. I describe him as the shrewdest man I've ever met. I was a croupier for a number of years and I learned a lot about people and their habits while sitting there waiting for the bet. Sometimes Lionel will say something to you and you'll think: "Behave yourself." Then you're driving home – or it might be two days later – and it hits you and you think: "Hang on a minute." He's done that to me ten or 20 times, when he's had an idea or he's made an off-the-cuff remark, where he's said: "Why don't you...?" or, "Well have you thought of...?"

Keith Loring: Lionel plays it ever so clever because he's the local man done good. Legend is not the same as what happens is it? Legend is that you paint the story anyway you want it, but I do love the idea of making money, then buying my local pub and local taxi company because you've got everything sussed then! Obviously there's a lot more to it than that, I realise that. Lionel is always very accessible and very 'there'. Some people may want to try to take advantage of that, but I think they'd be very foolish. He doesn't suffer fools. I think a lot of people may have tried, but he doesn't suffer fools.

Alan Hinton: Don't forget 1972 was when Rolls-Royce went belly-up in the eyes of the bankruptcy courts. I think Derby County Football Club kept the town alive then. Today, when you talk about soccer in America, like I often do, they say: "Well how does it work in England?" And I say: "Well, it works in Derby because the whole town supports the team. Everybody supports Derby County Football Club. There's a prince of a guy at the top, Lionel Pickering, and everybody supports the team. Whether they go to the matches or not, they support the team. They get big crowds and as a result they're able to attract some of the best players in the world. They've a terrific manager, who's a personality on his own, Jim Smith." For me, it's always a pleasure to be back here in Derby.

Keith Loring: Name me another club that does a three-year season ticket? By the way, here's an example of Lionel. I did the three-year ticket because I thought there'd be a market for it because people would like priority for the new stadium. That's fair and you can wrap it around with a few bits and pieces, but really it was knowing they'd be at the front of the queue for the new stadium. You can only do that once. You don't build stadiums very often. Also, it would raise necessary income at a time when we didn't have loads of money. Some people moaned about the three-year ticket: "Oh, you've created an elitist group." I say: "No." Those people helped because that was the down payment on Dailly – because it was down payments at the time – Asanovic and Laursen. End of story. It justifies it. Also, I know people who did overtime for eight or nine weeks to raise money to get that three-year ticket. Lionel said to me: "Are you going to do it again?" I said: "Chairman, I don't actually think there'll be a market for it." So he said: "Well, a few people have mentioned it to me." And I said: "Funnily enough, one or two people have mentioned it to me." So I sent out a letter to people and we got quite a good response...it's again an example of Lionel thinking ahead.

Jim Smith

"Jim Who?" they said, when in June 1995 Derby County appointed Jim Smith as manager of the club in succession to Roy McFarland. "Too old," said others. Smith was approaching 55 years of age at the time. Few say it now, of course. Jim Smith has stayed longer as manager at Derby County than at any of his former clubs and is immensely popular in the city and around Derbyshire. His achievements speak for themselves and he doesn't really look much older.

The fact is that Jim Smith was well respected in the game. A hardened football man, he knew his business from the groundfloor upwards. At various times, he had been manager of Boston United, Colchester United – both as player-manager – Blackburn Rovers, Birmingham City, Oxford United, Queen's Park Rangers, Newcastle United and Portsmouth. By the time he got to Derby, Smith had learned a thing or two about football, about players, about directors, about chairmen, about survival – and, probably, a lot about life. As a schoolboy, he was runner-up for the Yorkshire Boys' county boxing championship title. He lost that decision, narrowly on points, but over the years, Jim Smith proved he could ride a few punches.

More importantly, from Derby County's point of view, Smith's teams were always worth watching. Supporters, who had become frustrated with the lack of success of Arthur Cox's spending spree, were equally disappointed with the dull spectacle being provided on the pitch. In the event – and well beyond anyone's wildest dreams – Jim didn't disappoint, although even he would be hard pressed, despite a glass of red wine and a cigar, to claim: "It was all planned folks"

Brian Flint: He was certainly somebody we'd never thought of. I think we'd heard about Neil Warnock and Brian Horton, Barry Fry. All those names were bandied about and whatever the date was, I was sat there in the kitchen and it came on the radio: "They've appointed Jim Smith," I said to my wife, Di: "Well, I don't care it they don't win anything. That'll do for me because what I watch will be entertaining." So I was really chuffed to bits at that.

Gerald Mortimer: It's always a decision of magnitude, appointing a manager. There were one or two who appeared to be in the frame about whom I was less than enthusiastic, I must say. I don't think the appointment of Jim, let's be fair about this, took the town by storm. There were people who were thinking: "He's past it...." We thought: "He's experienced, he knows what he's doing, etc." I think it's turned. Perhaps they were lucky. Perhaps they deserved to be lucky, but I guess Jim is happier now, in management, than he's ever been.

Ray Young: I think he's done superb, brilliant. I think he's a likable person anyway. I don't know him much, really.

Peter Gadsby: Tremendous character, very strong. Very respected and respectful, too. Someone who will listen to a discussion, may not agree in many ways, but will not discourage you. Will talk it through. There's a tremendous trust and that's the thing that matters. The relationship with Lionel has got better. It's just been one of those things that has worked.

Mick Hopkinson: At Boston, brilliant. A bit like Cloughie. That type of character.

The player

Gordon Hughes: Jim was there as a player, at Lincoln. Ron Gray was manager. Wing-half. A bit one-paced, but used the ball very well. He was a good footballer. A 'Blanchflower type' player, pulled the ball down well and used it. He was a footballing player. Read the game well. Very competitive. I remember when he was released by Lincoln, he was 28 years old. He was really upset, as you can well imagine. Within a month of being released, at 28 years old, he was manager of Boston United. That's where Jim's career started.

Mike Hopkinson: At Boston, I played full-back and Jim played midfield. Right-half. Good player. Not the quickest of players, but a good passer of the ball. Very intelligent player, I used to think. He could mix it a bit, as well. He'd come through a hard school down in the lower divisions, Halifax, Aldershot. Howard Wilkinson signed at the same time as me. He was on the left-wing, I was the full-back.

The manager

Gordon Hughes: At that time, at Lincoln, there was Jim Smith, Graham Taylor, Ray Harford, Mick Brown, who was on the England staff, Billy Taylor, who was also in the England set-up. Poor lad, he died at an early age. There were five in the Lincoln side who did tremendously well in coaching and managing. Graham Taylor was a Scunthorpe lad. He was left full-back.

Mick Hopkinson: Oh, aye. Jim used to throw the tray, never mind the cups. He used to throw trays at you, sometimes.

Gordon Hughes: He always had a lot to say on the pitch. Into team talks, too. Yes, he would always give his input. I can remember him saying to me: "I always felt I could be a manager." That was in those days, when he was 20 years old or so.

Mick Hopkinson: Jim used to put on some great training sessions. So much better than we had at Port Vale. You could see that Jim was going to be a top manager. I can see him in his red track suit now, Jim, shouting and bawling.

Gordon Hughes: Howard Wilkinson came to Boston and he was starting on the coaching ladder. They're both Sheffield lads, Howard Wilkinson and Jim. Howard used to take a training session or two. Jim used to supervise it, but he used to give Howard experience, as friends. I remember Howard starting like that. He was going to Lilleshall at that time, as well.

At Boston United

Mick Hopkinson: They were always a leading club in the Northern Premier. Terrific ground. Always near the top of the League at that time. Paid good money. I reckon I got about £30. I wanted to get away from Port Vale. No money. Boston were far more professional than Port Vale, but the manager was good, Gordon Lee. Yeah, a down-to earth-character. I got on well with him. Reading offered me more money, but Pete Taylor rang me up and said: "There's a young manager at Nuneaton wants a word with you." That was David Pleat. I'd already decided on Boston, but I did meet Pleat at Pat Wright's house, but I preferred Boston.

Gordon Hughes: I was at Lincoln when Jim went there. I was wanting to wind down. I'd joined Rolls-Royce and I was part-time. I was starting on the career I wanted to pursue. I'd served my time and I wanted to get back in. I wanted a more stable situation. My wife wasn't too pleased about moving around all the time. It's very precarious. Even so, when I was at Lincoln, I thought I'd like to have a go at managing. I applied for the Exeter City player-manager's job. I went down for the interview and going down on the train I picked a newspaper up and it said the longest-serving manager in the Fourth Division was Ron Gray. He'd been there a year and a half! I thought: "I'm going to be out of a job in six months." That was no way to go. The reason for me was I had something to fall back on. Engineering. Now Jim hadn't, you see. People like Jim had to have a go. If they didn't, they didn't have much else and, of course, Jim made a great success of it, didn't he?

Mick Hopkinson: We had a good team at Boston. All ex-pros, some from Notts County, Sheffield Wednesday. There was a little inside-forward, I've forgotten his name now, it'll come back to me. Jim used to give him a rollicking regular, but they were a good midfield. Aye, a good mix.

Gordon Hughes: Part-time? Yes, working at Rolls-Royce. I used to travel from Derby to Louth. We used to train at Louth, which was between Lincoln and Boston.

And at Derby County

Gordon Hughes: It's funny how that happened. At that time Jim was living in Portsmouth and he'd just been released from Pompey. I went down with my wife and we spent three or four days with him. He had this Managers' Association job. I was talking to him and he says: "Yes, the job's all right." Then, next minute, he was saying: "I think I've got a chance for the Derby job." I says: "Well, are you going to leave this?" He said: "Aye. I miss the involvement. I miss the everyday involvement."

Jim Smith: Well, the phone call wasn't quite in the middle of the night. I was, at that time, the chief executive of the Football League Manager's Association, living in Portsmouth, although we were on the point of moving back to Oxford. I had a phone call from a Graham Smith, who I know very well. Graham used to play for West Brom and Notts County, I think it was. I know I tried to get him to sign when I was at Boston. He'd been in Adidas and he's an agent, really, and he asked me if I'd be interested in a chance to join Derby County. I think it was a contact through Stuart Webb, to be honest, via the board. At that time I was about three months into my job. I wasn't particularly happy in the job and there were lots of jobs, football manager's jobs, available that summer, funnily enough. It was one of those summers. There were about six or seven jobs available, but Derby was one I was very, very keen on. Any time you came to the Baseball Ground – I'd been with Birmingham, Blackburn, I'd been with Portsmouth, Oxford – it always had, well, a good feel. A football feel, really.

Peter Gadsby: There was a number of people interviewed. Jim Smith was not necessarily top of the list when you looked at it, but he hit it off straightaway with Lionel. ... Jim had had a difficult time at Portsmouth. He'd done a good job, but he'd obviously fallen out with somebody and the club had lost its way. He took the job with the Managers' Association and, in his words, it wasn't a job he enjoyed, shuffling paper, dealing with people's pensions, patting their backsides etc. He was very clear that if and when he came back into football he would do it in a different way. He would go for a young coach and tackle it in a different way. The rest is history, isn't it?

Gordon Hughes: It was funny. We travelled up to Wembley from Portsmouth. England were playing Japan that day and whether it was coincidence or not, who was sitting next to Jim, but Stuart Webb. Whether it was coincidence, but they were having a natter. I'm not saying he was being interviewed for the job, but they were having a natter and, probably, he was being sounded out then. So I had an inkling and I knew Jim would take the Derby job if it was offered – no doubt about it. And what a wonderful job he's done.

Stuart Webb: When Jim came, we were looking round and wanting to make sure we got the right guy. It was a difficult time because managers were tied up on contracts, but I knew Jim was available because he wasn't a manager of a club. So you hadn't got the compensation and the League and the allegations of 'tapping up'. That was a big plus and he had a good, a great track record. One or two people said to me, a bit like the press when we signed him: "Jim who?" But you look at the guy. He's a football man and he's done remarkably well and I thought he'd a lot left in his engine room, at that stage, but it was whether he wanted to come back in or not, that was the thing. He'd been in, he'd gone out and that was what he wanted to do. I think that was his decision that he didn't fancy the administration of the Managers' Association and he wanted to get back in. Soon as that was agreed, he was our manager.

Jim Smith: No, I'd never played at the Baseball Ground but I always had a tremendous feeling for what we would call the 'old fashioned' football club and that's what it was. I said I was interested. I came up and had an interview with Mr Pickering and Mr Webb, a preliminary interview. No letter came. Stuart Webb rang me.

Peter Gadsby: I've never heard a bad word about Jim. All the managers and all the directors that come to Derby, I can't recall anybody saying: "We wouldn't want him." Or anything uncomplimentary about him. Actually, to have gone through football for those many years and to have that respect, well. We noticed, in the early days, when it came to dealing, that respect was so important. When he spoke to people, there wasn't any messing around. That still exists today. I think that is one of Jim's strengths, the respect and, of course, the enthusiasm hasn't diminished. I think we've travelled on a very interesting course these last few years, haven't we?

Jim Smith: When you're talking in terms of management jobs, I've had a few and I've only ever applied for one job. That was at Colchester. The other ones have been an approach from someone or other. I've had an approach and turned the job down, but I've never had an approach and lost the job. When I joined Oxford and met Mr Maxwell and I was going with my wife and family for a fortnight's holiday, he told me to only go for a week, which I did. But I was still a little bit concerned that when I came back I'd still have the job, but I did. To be fair, Derby was a little bit like that, in so much that I was in the frame, obviously. Then there were stories about Barry Fry, I think. Stories about Steve Bruce, other people, and obviously, it was a nervous time. It was on-off, on-off. Then the chairman, Mr Pickering, more or less stepped in with the final decision and said: "You know, we're faffing about. I want Jim Smith. Let's go and get Jim Smith." Fortunately for me, that's what happened.

Gerald Mortimer: He's always, as he's said, had the knack of being at the right clubs at the wrong time. He'd been at Newcastle about three weeks when John Hall was starting his campaigns and saying: "The first thing I'll do is get rid of Jim Smith." Well. Thanks very much. He was at Blackburn when they couldn't afford to buy Steve Kindon for £60,000 or something, to make the difference. Here at Derby, he obviously gets on extremely well with the chairman. There's a rapport there and I don't think a football club can exist without that. That's what

Alan Durban used to talk about, the triangle'. Chairman, manager, secretary, whatever you liked to call them, working on the same wavelength, going in the same direction. Then you've got a chance. It's still difficult, but you've got a chance. Yes, it's suited him down to the ground and he's been around long enough not to be surprised about anything. If players act up, they act up, and off they go, quite soon. Can't be bothered with that.

Lionel Pickering: He's a first-class person as well – and that's saying a lot for managers because they always want the best team. They always want an extra player, they'll do anything they can to get him, to convince the board that you should buy this extra player or that. Nevertheless, I saw Jim at his very best when he sold Christian Dailly. He definitely did not want to sell Christian but it got up to about £4 million – I think they came in at about £3.5 million, which meant they were serious. They wanted Christian Dailly – although look what's happened to them now – and they were due to play in Europe the following week. They wanted Christian in their European team. So when it was £3.5 million, Jim said: "Oh no. No way." "Four million? No, no." When it got to about £4.5 million, he said: "Well okay. Give me two weeks and I'll get another player and he can go in two weeks." They said: "No, we want him now." When they got to £5 million, he said: "Well, he's got to go now. I'll put somebody from the youth team in." Managers want to win matches. They're not really bothered about all the directors' problems of paying for stadiums and things like that. They like a nice stadium, they like a nice ground, but the fact that we owed so much money and borrowed so much to do all this, it's nice for the fans, it's good for everybody, but we've still got to pay the money back, so when it got to £5 million – and it finished up at £5.35m – he said: "Oh we're never going to get that again. We'll never get that, even on a good day in the close season and on a day we *want* to sell him. We won't get more than about three and a half to four, on a good day." So he put the club first, second and third there. Even though he knew he'd have to put someone else in. Then, of course, without telling us, within about half an hour, he'd bought Prior from Leicester. He'd already got somebody at the back of his mind, which we didn't know about.

Jim Smith: First impressions were of meeting the board again and getting a good feel about it. Because, as I say, people ask you advice about how to do it. What you do as a manager. What you do and that. You can't really give them too much technical advice because you have to do it your own way I think. I felt very comfortable walking into the Baseball Ground, albeit small offices and small corridors, but it was just a nice feeling. The staff there were very, very good. As always, they're all waiting to see who the boss is going to be and they want to try to please. The only people who didn't want to please me were two or three players who came straight firing in to say they were not stopping at Derby. By being out of the game three months or so, which was the longest period I'd ever been out the game as a manager, I quite enjoyed the challenge. It was quite easy to go in trying to persuade the players to stay. It was also quite easy for me to say to the players: "Well, off you go then. We'll do our best to get you away." Obviously, that helped in my rebuilding plans.

Keith Loring: I've always had a thing in management myself, that you can shout at people and scream at people: "Do this, do that," but people have got to want to work for you. Not work for Derby County. That's important, but if they don't want to work for you, they'll not respond to you. I was taught that by one of my old bosses. I only knew Jim, briefly, before I came here, but Jim has this incredible knack of having people wanting to please him.

Jim Smith: It was 1 July and I had about a week solid up here. Organising pre-season, organising staff. I'd got Steve McClaren in and he was on holiday. Then I was on holiday, but the individual players, like Pembridge, Williams and Short, who were desperate to get away, they came to see me and knocked on my door. I obviously knew the story because I'd had the background and there's no point keeping unhappy players. In Short's and Pembridge's cases it was in their contracts that if the club didn't get pomoted, then they could go. So it was a quick welcome back into the hurly burly of the football business.

Lionel Pickering: I think by Premier League standards, we're like a lot of clubs. We're not just on our own in this way, but we have got limited resources really. I mean, we'll never get more than 33,000 people in this stadium as it is and there is a limit as to what you can expect the fans to pay. I think we've gone a far as we can go in that respect. I mean, the fans want the best, but where's the money coming from? We've really got to do something about the wages or the agents. That's all got to be sorted out again. That's the club's problem, it's not necessarily Jim Smith's, so when you consider his limited resources, I think he's as good a manager as any in the Premier League. I really mean that. I used to joke with him: "Well Jim, if you get the England job, I've got somebody in mind to take your place." Things like that, but to be honest, it would be very difficult to find a replacement for Jim Smith because he is very good.

Keith Loring: I have two or three very simple theories. The first theory is that you hire a manager, you back a manager and you fire a manager. There's nothing in between. The minute you stop backing him, you're in trouble. The other thing, too, is that I run the business and our number-one job is to support the manager...For while we make his job easy – easier rather, we can't make it easy – we can take the pressure off. Anything we can do to take the pressure off him, to allow him to be clear minded in what he's doing. We all know how easier the job is when we're successful. Now, we can't make it successful, but we can bloody well make sure we support him. The next job is to bring as much money in as we can and to stop as much going out as we can. Now that's a very simple way of saying it, but it's not much more complicated is it, really? All we're ever trying to do here is to try to find some more money.

Jim Smith: I knew the players, but I didn't know them particularly well. I knew the Gabbiadinis, I knew the Simpsons and others, but I'd never had any of the players with me at a previous club. An advantage? I think in the summer it's an advantage. Possibly if you're walking in during winter, it might be handy to have some people you know enough about to get some information and rely on them a little bit. I think the good thing for me was, by virtue of the fact that a lot players were disillusioned, it was a chance to clear the decks and start afresh. The chairman said: "This is going to be a hard task. You're going to have to reduce the wages and stop in the First Division." So, yes, we got promotion. I suppose that helped, if it was people's expectations. They weren't my expectations. No, no. The chairman, credit to him, wouldn't want to put you under any pressures too much, would he? He said: "You've got to get us up – in the first year!"

Keith Loring: Jim gives you every emotion and he brings out every emotion in you. He'll bring out anger, I'm sure, but he'll bring out pleasure. He'll bring out laughter. He'll make you cry. He'll make you cry tears of laughter because he is some funny man when he's in form. He'll hurt you because he's blunt. He'll say two words when other people will say ten. One of them might be 'off', I don't know. He's very impatient, very, very impatient. He demands support, if that's the right word. He knows what he wants and what you want to do is to get it done and you don't want the phone call when he rings you and you haven't done it. There's no fear there because you can go nose-to-nose with him. We've only had, probably, two cross words since I've been here. One of those was about a tent on the pitch, in which he was absolutely spot on because I was trying to please too many people in too short a time. It was only on the pitch that much – inches – but you'd have thought it was in the centre-circle. So I learned that one pretty quickly and I'm pitch mad anyway. I never use the pitch. It was something I was seduced into doing by someone who shall remain nameless. The tent pegs were just on the pitch – inches. Jim rang me the next morning!

Jim Smith: We made a lot of changes. It was funny really because some of the football we played in our pre-season was as good as I've seen and, as soon as the season started, we had injuries, suspensions and we set off very ordinary. Drew the first game, lost the second game, lost out, drew, lost. Took us about seven games, I think, to win our first game. 'When Saturday comes...' it's a good saying. I mean, it's better when they're bad in training and good in playing and, as you know, we got a few results together, but we'd got ourselves together a bit but were still short. At that stage, when we went to Sheffield United, I'm guessing now late October, early November, we were in the outside frame if you like. I'd got this information and seeing Igor Stimac, I thought he'd be the man for us. By virtue of the fact we had pulled ourselves together in results, it had whetted the chairman's appetite on spending. Gambling and spending some money.

Paul McGrath: He didn't have to say a lot. Obviously, I'd met him before, through Ron Atkinson. I've the utmost respect for him. We sat down for a quarter of an hour or so, but I always wanted to sign. He's got that type of magnetism, really, that a few managers have. It makes players want to play for him

Lionel Pickering: Tactically he's very good. He might be criticised, but I can't understand when people criticise him for playing three forwards up front away from home. It shakes people. It frightened Arsenal. It frightened Man United. It's positive play, but you've always got to understand, it's possible for the other side to get four or five against you. If they catch you on the break they can, and some of these teams are good on the break. Then you are going to concede the goals.

Eric Steele: I've found a change. When I was self-employed and doing other clubs, when I came here for two or three days a week, I'd see him, although on some days not see much of him. He hates goalkeepers, so why he employed a full-time goalkeeping coach I'll never know. It's the one position on the field: "Oh look at him. What's he doing? Why doesn't he come and catch that from 16 yards?" I've found the change since I've come in full-time great because he's always receptive and I do a lot of stuff on video analysis and we discuss things. He leaves me to run the goalkeeping department. He's brilliant in that respect. He draws on his staff. He still makes the ultimate decisions, but anything we've done on the goalkeeping side, he's always sought my opinion. He will make the right decision. I might not always agree, but that's why he's the manager.

Jim Smith: When Igor came in and didn't know the players, we went with a straight back four and got hammered at Tranmere, in a funny kind of a game. I decided to go with three and Igor knew the three system. Ronnie Willems, funnily enough, behind the front two, was as big an influence on the next 20 games as anybody and, obviously, we went those 20 games unbeaten and that turned everything around.

Success a surprise?

Gordon Hughes: I'm surprised because I thought he had a tremendous amount of work to do when he came here and he did it in quick time. I knew he'd get it right, but I thought it would take him longer.

Style of management

Jim Smith: Changed? Well not really. Adapted. You look at how you treated your own children and how they treat their children. I remember how the bobby used to treat me when I was playing football on the street. Get a clip round the earhole. Then you go and tell your mum and she'd give you a clip round the earhole as well. Well, those days have changed because everything changes. So you can't steam into the players like you could yesteryear because they won't have it. So my ideals haven't changed, but the method of trying to achieve them has.

Is it Lucky Jim?

Gordon Hughes: I think he works tremendously hard at his job. And he picks the lads to work alongside him well. He's shrewd. He got Steve McClaren, who's a very enthusiastic, a young chap. Of course, they got everything worked out, what they were going to do every day, and Steve implemented it, after discussing it with Jim. Jim brings in the people he knows he can work with. He's never really had a lot of money to work with, wherever he's been, Jim. At Newcastle he had that problem. He hasn't really a lot at Derby either, compared with many clubs.

Lionel Pickering: He's come up through the ranks, yes, but don't let's forget that he was the first person to sell a player for a million quid when he sold Trevor Francis from Birmingham to Cloughie. Every year he was at Portsmouth, he had to sell. I mean he's found Les Ferdinand, Anderton, all sorts of players. He's got a very good track record of finding centre-forwards, for instance, then having to sell them. What we've tried to do at Derby is get the players and let him hang on to them. Obviously the Bosman ruling changed things. Paulo Wanchope hadn't signed his new contract. If he hadn't signed by the end of January, he'd have been able to start negotiating his own terms with another club, just as McManaman did. Therefore, a player that you may think is worth £3 million or £5 million can go for nothing if you leave it too long. Paulo would have been worth nothing to us. There is an art in this game now, of selling players on. Selling them off and not having a McManaman situation at Derby County. Okay, reluctantly, let some of them go, but knowing Jim's track record, he seems to be able to pluck them from anywhere, all over the world in fact. I'd like to see him probably get one or two more English players, but there's no doubt about it, these continentals have improved the standard of our team. Our players now realise what standards good football is all about. They've got heroes for people to look up to.

The survival secret?

Gordon Hughes: I think he believes in himself. From an early age he fancied being a manager and he's always believed in himself. Also, everybody likes Jim Smith. I'm talking about the Fergusons at Man United, I'm talking the Pleats, the top people. Everyone likes to be in Jim's company. So if he relates that to his players, you know? I mean, we know of Jim's tantrums and things like that, but I think it's for a reason. He wants to show them that he's cross – "We want a bit better effort from you lads" – by getting a little bit over the top and irate.

Gordon Hughes: I've known Jim since 1969, 1970. He's a very shrewd lad. He never misses anything. He's very aware of what's going on. He's looking at players, he's knowing their moods, he chats to them if he thinks there's something wrong. Jim doesn't miss anything. All right, we've all got to have a little luck in life, but I think he makes it. He's no fool, Jim Smith.

Influential players

Jim Smith: My very first top job was Birmingham City. They were bottom of the table when I went and I've forgotten exactly how many games – I think there were 16 games to go – of which we lost only one and drew about three. Trevor Francis was playing then and he scored nine goals in those 16 games. And they came in nine games. They weren't three here and two there – and most of them were winning goals. A mark of how influential he was, was that in the next year, my first full year when we got relegated, to be honest, he only scored nine goals all season. He was injured most of the season. So the influence of someone like Trevor Francis on a team was immense because he could score goals from making his own chances and he'd win you games. Some people score goals and they don't necessarily win you games. He could win you games. He would be one of the best two or three players I've had.

Jim Smith: Colin Todd was an outstanding player, and Archie Gemmill, for me, also at Birmingham. When we got relegated, he and Colin came into the old Second Division and Archie was tremendously influential in getting us promotion because he was a leader. I wouldn't say he was a captain as we usually reckon, but on the pitch, he was a captain. He led by example and his endeavours in training and on the park to win games, he was very instrumental in us getting promotion. John Aldridge was as good a goalscorer as I've been involved with, but Trevor Hebberd, funnily enough another ex-Derby player, was probably the most influential player at Oxford. Just by his running and his work rate. He was an unbelievable athlete, really, who could play. I never thought Trevor achieved what he should have because he could have played anywhere.

Jim's office

Gordon Hughes: You could write a book on Jim's office. You could interview the Allisons, the Fergusons, whoever you want to say, the top managers in the game, and they're all roaring and laughing with Jim. He's a great personality. You could write a book on Jim's office, the people there. When he was at Newcastle, I've gone in to Jim's office, say half past five, and I've been there at ten o'clock, talking about the game. And the wives? We've arranged to meet the wives at a restaurant in Newcastle and we've never got there, you know! It was just total, total football, with managers. At times, the staff of say, Arsenal or Manchester United, have come in: "Come on boss, we've got to move." And they just can't leave Jim's office, you see. The tales that I've heard and they've all let their hair down when the adrenaline is just coming down after a game. Wonderful. Wonderful conversation, if you're a sportsman, football. Tremendous. Of course, there's things you'd never dream of repeating. Honestly, Jim Smith has enlightened my life over the last 20 years and yes, privileged is about the word. He's a tremendous lad, tremendous human being, which is the most important thing, isn't it? He's just a nice lad. He never misses a trick. If your wife's there or if your friend's there he's making sure everything's all right – and he's got a match on! He's unique, Jim Smith, as regards those things.

How long?

Gordon Hughes: You never know with Jim. I think, a couple of years, that's my view. Because Jim puts a lot into it, he really does. He'll be a big loss to the game. Every manager likes half an hour in Jim's office.

Training

TRAINING has to be done. Some like it more than others. Often it depends on what form training takes, but fundamentally, football is a running game. As times have changed, conditions of play have changed also. Today's players are athletes playing football, the players of the past and distant past were more ball players, who ran. 'Make the ball do the work' and 'there's no substitute for skill' used to be the maxims. 'Make the body do the work' could be a slogan for today's all action, fast moving, running sort of game.

Football requires someone to play, a ball and a pitch. Simple really, but those requirements do condition the game. Remember the brown lace-up, leather ball? Remember the Baseball Ground, after a week of rain, on wet Saturdays in February?

Now, it's different. Think of the shiny white, high-bouncing, swerving ball. Think of the pitch at Pride Park, in February. Marvel at the state of pitches throughout the country though the season. Conditions have a big influence on the sort of football we see and the types of matches played. Training programmes, too, have changed.

Alf Jeffries: Jobey left it to the trainers. Alex James' father-in-law, Dave Willis, was the first-team trainer. Old Bill Grummett was the reserve-team trainer. Nice fellow was Bill, but I didn't like Willis. No, he was a nasty piece of work, he was.

Reg Harrison: Dave Willis was trainer. He must have been about 65 years old. He'd been trainer for a long time. He was a rough sort of chap, not a good mixer I didn't think. He'd played for Newcastle. Jack Bowers was his assistant.

Johnny Morris: Jack Bowers was the trainer, with Jack Poole.

Alf Jeffries: Jobey used to be there at practice matches. Talk about practice matches! He used to come out with some funny things. Reg Stockill was finished when they got him from Arsenal, I think. He was like a rocking horse when he was playing and he was quite lazy. In this practice match the ball came to Reg and he kicked it over his head and old Jobey shouted: "You can't kick it straight to them when you're looking at them. Never mind kicking it over your head, you'll lose the bloody thing." He was right. He had all his buttons on did Jobey.

Johnny Morris: We did some training running round the roads. Great fun, but it didn't do the football much good. Stuart McMillan said to me one day: "I'm bringing in a well-known Derbyshire long-distance runner called Jack Winfield." I says: "I don't believe you." I was captain then and I said: "I don't think that's a good idea. It's bad enough going round the ground. Monotonous." He said: "Well, we'll give it a try." Well, I'm not kidding, we used to do it a couple of times a week. He used to send us seven miles out, then make us run back and he used to time us getting back. I can tell you this, we were the fittest team that has ever been – up to half-time. Then second half, we'd got legs like lead, especially with the grounds we had to play on. Anyway, we started dropping down the League because we'd always been second or third or so. It went on for a couple of months or something like that, then he was sacked.

Reg Harrison: It started to change. First season I went back, you reported back about five weeks before the season started, and in the mornings you walked. They'd got Sinfin then, but most of the running was done at the Baseball Ground. Lapping then sprinting and building up like that. What I didn't like was, after that, you went in the gym and were left to your own devices, really. It wasn't organised until Ralph Hann came. He came at the end of the Forties.

Tommy Powell: Ralph Hann used to do the training. Ralph was a good trainer. He was a good player. He'd got two good feet, Ralph. He sort of took over later, when he went to right-half and Jack 'Nick' went to right-back. A good player, Ralph was. He was a lovely bloke. He took it all to heart Ralph did. On match days he used to eat the same as the players. Boiled chicken or fish, in case he had to play. He was a nice bloke and a good trainer. From Sinfin, we used to run right up through Stenson Bubble and up to Twyford and come back the other way.

Alan Durban: Ralph had fairly high standards and I enjoyed that. He expected people to be as squeaky clean as he was. Tim liked the lighthearted side of it, whereas Ralph was fairly dour and serious.

Ray Young: Easy. It wasn't difficult really, training. Mostly stamina training, more than anything. It did change later. When I first went, say pre-season, it was mainly on the road. They didn't do much at all in the early days.

Frank Upton: I enjoyed it. Jack was purely running, running, running. Ralph was a lot of running, too. There was a lot of running in those days. That's what we used to do, but I enjoyed every minute really. You learn from it. It was a bit monotonous, but coming from where I did, everything was brilliant. I was being a professional footballer and I thought that's what everybody did. Of course, when I look back, it was very boring. Very, very boring at times, but it was one of these things you have to do. You have to run when you play football, so to get the stamina you wanted, you had to run.

Alan Durban: We were a bit more creative at Cardiff. We had a good trainer, but also at Cardiff, we had top players. We did have seven or eight Welsh internationals, so when I trained with the first team, training was more imaginative and also, we were able to get on the pitch quite a bit at Cardiff. Ninian Park wasn't enclosed, there was a lot of air in there and it was fairly dry, whereas we hardly ever got to train on the pitch at the Baseball Ground. We got round that track a few times, though.

Reg Harrison: People say: "What do you know about it? It wasn't like this in your day, Reg." I say: "Well I've never been out of it." I mean, if it wasn't like this in our day, who started changing it? It was the people before me, the Ralphs, who changed it. I say gradually it's changed, but the people who've changed it have been each successive generation. I bet, basically, training's not much different, really. Running's the same, isn't it?

Ron Webster: I thought it was great. I used to enjoy training. I found it easy. I wasn't a bad runner, I found it quite easy really. Even when Cloughie came and altered it a bit, training never bothered me or affected me at all. He changed it from all physical work. We used to do a lot of physical work.

Phil Waller: Well, of course Cloughie had Ralph out, didn't he? He started with Jack Burkitt. Of course, he wanted Jim. He couldn't get Jimmy Gordon in, so he got Jack Burkitt in. He knew what he wanted in terms of shape of the team and that sort of thing.

Training

Willie Carlin: Jimmy Gordon was the old type trainer. Football was changing even then and training was changing. Brian used to train us some of the time and I remember one morning, we got changed at the Baseball Ground and we went off down to the Municipal. We'd only been training ten minutes and he sent us home. He knew we were fit enough and we didn't need it anymore. That was the beauty of him. Plus, all his training was for mental alertness, not physical, mental. That was what his training was all about.

Ron Webster: He always worked on you mind. Once pre-season was over – pre-season was hard, very hard – he said: "Once you're playing two games a week," – which we was at that time – "all you've got to sharpen up is you mind. You're fit enough." We often used to come in on Wednesday or something like that, after a match on Saturday. He never bothered. We never did any hard training in the season, really. I think he used to work on your mind, to get you that yard quicker, rather than your physical stamina. You used to do a bit of work, of course, but I'm sure it was his thing, that he got your mind working and you seemed a yard quicker...

Kevin Hector: Training at Sinfin was good. It was different to Bradford. They didn't have their own training ground, but Sinfin was good. Jimmy Gordon used to do the training to start with. Cloughie would arrive after a bit, in his kit. Then we'd play five-a-sides. He liked five-a-sides. Jimmy Gordon organised free-kicks and things, but we didn't practise them much. We did score a few goals, though, from corners and free-kicks.

Dave Mackay: Coming from Tottenham, it was like chalk and cheese. Like when I came into Tottenham every morning, everything was pressed and laid out, everything. At Derby – especially when you went pre-season – you had the same clothes on in the afternoon as you had in the morning. All stiff and that. At Tottenham, every day, you had nice new kit, all pressed and that and after lunch at the training ground, you'd have another set of a new kit. Of course, I had to go with the boys. I never ever complained. I never would because I thought if I complained, it would show up the system.

Willie Carlin: Oh, pre-season was fantastic. We used to go to Colwick Woods and it was absolutely murder. We used to run up a hill, we called it Pork Chop Hill. Oh God! All day, pre-season and I lost seven pounds. Me! Now can you believe it? Seven pounds. Me! That's how hard our pre-season was. As Shanks said – and Cloughie – "If you're going to play Wednesday, Saturday, Wednesday, Saturday, the game's are going to keep you fit. You don't need training much."

Ian Buxton: Once pre-season started, if there were gaps in the cricket when there was no match, I would go to training, although I can't remember doing it very much, except when Cloughie came. I went to Colwick Woods for two or three days then – and wished I hadn't.

Dave Mackay: The training itself wasn't that much different, no. Training was quite good. Jack Burkitt, he used to take the training, mainly.

Colin Lawrence: Peter used to wander down sometimes. Not a lot. Towards the end, he didn't go anywhere much.

Kevin Hector: No. Peter Taylor didn't go to the training ground, not to mean anything.

Willie Carlin: Who? Pete Taylor? Well, he used to give us tips. The only training he knew was racehorses.

Gordon Hughes: What struck me about Brian Clough – and I played under quite a few managers – you could have a bad game on a Saturday and he used to say: "I don't want to see you, you little ... until Thursday." With previous managers, you'd be in on Sunday and by the time the next Saturday came on, you had so much in you mind you were a little bit stale.

Mick Hopkinson: We trained hard. Now in his later years, Cloughie used to give them time off, if it was a Saturday to Saturday match. It changed in that he took the training sessions. In the Tim Ward days, Ralph used to take the sessions. Ralph was a good trainer, but I used to think that Cloughie worked you harder for a shorter period. We used to spend a good hour playing like, 'piggy in the middle'. Two players in the middle and the others on the outside passing the ball and you'd got to win it. I used to get with Ronnie Webster. Ron could run and I was pretty fit and I could run and we used to win it back ever so quick, but then you'd get one like Durban and people like him, who weren't so quick. You could keep him going for ages, Durb. In fact, he used to finish up trying to tackle, diving at the ball, trying to tackle. Brilliant on the ball, but he was the slowest player ever. Feet wise, though, he was brilliant.

Brian Clough: I'll give you one secret. Now it's not a secret because you're going to share it! We were playing in the European Cup. We were a close knit group. We got in the dressing-room and I said: "Right. We're off to Spain." So we went to Spain, simple as that. Jimmy Gordon was a sergeant major with a stick. He used to hit me with it. I said: 'We're off to Spain. We're going to get some sun on our backs." So, we got on a plane at East Midlands and off to Spain. I ordered the breakfast, which I used to like and they liked it. If they had a beer, I didn't mind. We went to Spain for three or four days, I've got a lot of friends where we went. Some of the lads had a few beers and messed around and what have you. Every morning, Jimmy Gordon, every morning: "When we're going to train? When are we going to train?" I said: "We're not training. We've come on holiday." He said: "We've got a European Cup match on Wednesday." I said: "Well, we're not training. We've come for a break." Now I used to treat Europe as a holiday because it was away from the environment that we were in, away from the normal routine. The bairns were left behind, so no problem there. The wives could get on with what they had to do. We were off, on a plane. Eating what we wanted to eat, drinking what we wanted to drink. It worked, no problem. We went to relax. By the time you play European Cup Finals you're tired, mentally. That's the real problem.

Gordon Hughes: You need a certain level of fitness to be a professional footballer. Sometimes you go down and sometimes you go up. If you go up you need to be eased off, but you don't really know which one you want. You don't know whether you need more training or less training. Cloughie seemed to have it: "I don't want to see you lot until Thursday." He thought we'd had too much. We'd ease down. Hard day on Thursday, a light day on Friday and you were back fresh for it. He seemed to have the gift to get the best out of the players. Every 90 minutes, on a Saturday, when it matters.

Mick Hopkinson: I used to enjoy Cloughie's training. We used to do more ball work, whereas with Ralph, he'd kill you in the first hour, running. Then all of a sudden, he'd throw a ball on and you'd have five minutes each way and then it was back to running again. I couldn't play perhaps, but I could run, I know that.

Roger Davies: Training was different. Part-timers and local players don't realise the difference. I remember, Friday afternoon, I had to report. I signed on the Wednesday and I didn't finish my work until Friday. I came on Friday afternoon, for a training session. It was just like a limber-up thing round the Municipal really and we were doing this little thing and I thought: "What!" I was tired with just this bit of running we were doing and I thought: "Whew, what a session." And we were only doing a Friday afternoon warm-up. Then I got into full-time training and it was hard work for me, I must admit, to catch up with these other guys who'd been doing it regularly and had done pre-seasons, with the hard work. I would think non-

League players now are probably fitter than non-League players used to be in my era, but I used to enjoy training, actually.

Charlie George: Training was pretty much the same at Derby as at Arsenal. We used to play plenty of five-a-sides. We did when I played for Cloughie at Forest. When you've got good players like Derby had then, you don't want to be messing them about a lot.

Willie Carlin: The year we won the Second Division we played at Chelsea in the League Cup and so off we go to Bolton and we're 2-0 up at half-time. Anyway, we finished 2-1 up, but in the second half we struggled. We really did struggle. Even so we win 2-1, away from home, and we go in and we're all full of it and he came in, Cloughie, and he went berserk. "You shower," he said. "Ten thousand from Derby come to watch you and you play like that second half. You're in tomorrow." So we were in on Sunday. Then we play Coventry, first year in the First Division, and we get beat 3-1 at home on a Wednesday night. So him and Taylor are in the corner, talking. Next minute he says: "Have you got your wives and girlfriends with you?" We all said: "Yes, why?" And he said: "Right. Down to the Midland, we're having a party." So off we went down to the Midland Hotel and didn't finish until eight in the morning. So you lose at home and have a party, you win away and you're in on Sunday!

Ray Young: If you're fit by doing the pre-season right – your month's pre-season – you're fit, but I always used to say that it took me probably five or six games before I really felt match fit. I don't care how many friendly games you played, to me they didn't count, but once I'd played five or six League games, then I didn't need so much training. You needed your energy for playing. It has changed. Stampie and them hardly did anything on Friday mornings. When I first went to Pride Park and saw them warming up, I thought that I'd be knackered doing all that before a game. When we played, there was more emphasis on stamina and strength because of the grounds.

Peter Newbery: Monotonous? I didn't feel so at the time, but there was a great emphasis on running and the physical side of the game and not sufficient on the use of the ball. We didn't train a great deal with the ball. If you wanted to do that, I remember, you had to go back in the afternoon and we used to try to improve our skills then.

Eric Steele: We used to catch people out because when the ball went out of play we got it back so quickly and we used to practise that. We used to go on, on a Thursday, if the groundsman would allow us – John Dodsley used to go crackers – and again, it was John Gregory: "If the ball goes out, first 20 minutes get it back quickly." We used to do it. Ball came back off a board, pick it up, in. Normally on a ground, you've chance to turn away and get your breath, but we used to catch people. Special, special times.

Steve Sutton: Differences? No not really at that stage, before all the technical stuff they're getting now. I wouldn't say it was basic, but it was fun. A lot of five-a-sides. Obviously, Roy mixed in with the five-a-sides and he was head and shoulders above everyone, even if he couldn't move with arthritis. He was still head and shoulders above most of the players in the five-a-sides. He was top quality. It was enjoyable, although there were one or two undercurrents with the young players there at the time. I was enjoying myself, anyway.

Jim Smith: We actually used Lippi's Juventus pre-season training plan ourselves because it was unbelievable. In fact, we toned it down because, in all honesty, it was really intensive and they do work very hard, but there are two things. Firstly, the game has changed over there. It does tend to be a slower game, but Juventus and Milan in the modern era – and getting the success they got – became more 'English'. They've become more English and they marry the two, but their fitness training abroad is very intensive, but they can do because secondly, they don't play midweek games.

Peter Newbery: Certainly in training itself, it was very physical. We were very fit. Strength rather than athleticism, very much so. A different type of fitness to what they have today. We needed it for the Baseball Ground pitch. Not only that, but other pitches were very heavily used and not particularly well drained and, of course, you had to play Christmas Day and Boxing Day, so you had to be fit to do that, two consecutive days at Easter, as well. It was a very physical game.

Jim Smith: When I first brought a foreign player over, Tarantini at Birmingham, he couldn't believe how hard we worked our young apprentices. They were educated to sleep in the afternoon, abroad. He said the senior players worked harder than the junior players. They were educated to sleep and the foreign players have educated us to sleep and rest in the afternoons and, to be fair, I think more and more of our players are doing that now. They're not going off. Not many go golfing now like we used to do, or to snooker halls or whatever. They tend to look at the method of conserving energy for Saturday. That's one of our problems... the foreign players have come in, and playing Wednesdays regularly and three times over Christmas is unheard of for them. So they find it hard and I think we do sometimes cram too many games in.

Steve Powell: It was certainly not as scientific as today. Well, during the championship year, the main thing was just keeping ticking over in the week. We used to play a lot of five-a-side football. Very little purely physical work. A lot of short, sharp work, but nothing too strenuous or long. A lot of it consisted of five-a-side football.

Gordon Hughes: I question all these modern training methods. They've got a psychologist now, although I do think that's important. In any game, your mind's got to be right. You've got to be positive. I don't think there are less injuries now than there was when we played. Lads are off quite a lot now with injuries, as much as what we were, so I don't know whether that means anything. All right, the game is quicker.

Steve McClaren: What coaches are trying to get and develop are more intelligent players because there are some people you can give information to and it's never there – and will never be there. They don't learn. A famous manager once said: "You can tell them once, you can tell them twice. After that, get rid." We want to develop a more intelligent player. We have the information, but the ability to take in that information is up to the individual player and his intelligence. It's only like in school. Some are top of the class, some are bottom of the class – and that's like it is in football.

Jim Smith: There's not the same loyalty to a club that there used to be. Yes, they want to play, and they want to play as well as they possibly can, but you can easily see what they feel: "Well, I'm too tired. I can't play. We're playing too many games." I think that if there was anything in yesteryear that was a problem, they did play too many games. The games yesteryear, technically, were probably better with some individual skills, certainly no worse, but it wasn't as quick. It's got quick to a fault, to be honest. Now they've got to be athletes to play and so, consequently, it's far more difficult to keep that fitness level up and you do need to swap them a little bit – but they do want to play. You see it now, your top players at Chelsea. When they had the rotation thing, they all wanted to leave because they wanted to play. But the fitness thing means that sometimes they do need to come out and then go back in. But if you drop them, they'll soon let you know they want to play!

Training

Gordon Guthrie: Looking back, in Brian's time and Dave's, when he was manager, they all must have trained hard for the number of years they stayed in the game. I think as their ages increased, it must have paid them dividends. Look at Dave, coming back from three broken legs. He must have trained hard. Look at Roy. He was another example. I've always said about Roy: "He should have had 100 caps." For me, he was the best centre-half I've ever worked with. Unfortunate, of course, injury told, but he kept coming back because he was that sort and he had that spirit. There was no way he was going to say: "Well, that's it."

Roger Davies: You never knew what he was going to do. Brian would come when it was just the first team, but a lot of the time first team and reserves used to train together. Not like they do now. They probably split them up. When we were going well, sometimes we'd play on Saturday and he wouldn't see us until Thursday, but a lot of players used to come in anyway, even though he'd given us the time off. We couldn't keep away and we used to go and do skill things. When he used to turn up at training, he used to take us when we were going round the Municipal and doing all the games and stuff and over the fences and that and he, obviously, loved to play in the games, Brian. Play until he scored. He'd always join in, until he'd won the game. He was still sharp. Still sharp round the box. I never saw him play. Not in his heyday. Obviously, when he scored, everybody knew about it. He was a bit like Dave was in the latter days. You played until he won. Yes, until he won.

Ted McMinn: Seville is one of the warmest areas in the world. We trained at eight o'clock in the morning for two hours because it was so hot after ten. Then we trained again at eight o'clock at night, for two hours because it was nice and cool. We always trained in the north. We used to play Osasuna in Pampalona and we trained up there because we did altitude training, but training was mostly with a ball. Everything was with a ball in Spain. We trained on the pitch all the time, which was an absolutely tremendous stadium. We used to have 4,000-5,000 people watching us at training at night because that's what the people did at night. Everything was always changed when a coach was sacked and after Artur Jorge came in, the Uruguayan, he changed everything. Everything was with a ball again.

Steve McClaren: You win football matches with team players, not individuals. If you can have a plan and prepare and get the individual player into your way of thinking, it makes the rewards bigger than if they were just an individual. An example in basketball is Magic Johnson. He won individual awards galore, but the Chicago Bulls never won anything. This new coach, Phil Jackson, sat him down: "You'll never be identified as a great player, until you win things with a great team," he said. They won the championship four years on the trot. Magic Johnson's reputation went up.

Jim Smith: They pay a lot more attention to detail in training now. Timewise there's not much difference. In the old days training would be a practice match, reserves versus first team or whatever, just to get a game on a Tuesday morning. I always remember going to Sheffield United and if you were young you didn't get in because Joe Mercer wanted to play – and his son used to play, too! Set plays and things like that, they weren't worked on in the early days like they are now. And probably to a false degree, you've more awareness of your opponents now. They weren't too concerned with opponents then. They were concerned with themselves. Another thing, which people forget, is that you talk about squads, but you used to have 40 or 50 professionals at a club. I never made the first team at Sheffield United, but I remember the Reserves and there used to be three, four, five internationals or ex-internationals in the Reserves. Reserve-team football in my day would be comparable with Second and Third Division football now. Today, it's like a youth league.

Steve Powell: Pre-season was probably more difficult than it is now because we had more chance to get out of condition. We had two or three months close season, so there was a lot of time when we didn't do anything. So we got out of condition and it was a hard slog when we got back. Nowadays the close season's so short, players don't have chance to get unfit.

Gordon Hughes: Can you imagine pros now? I served my time in the coal mines as a mining engineer. I can remember coming out of the pit at four o'clock on a Friday night, getting in the bath and catching a train down to London and going to play Arsenal, Spurs. It was a way of life and you didn't think anything of it. You had a good night's sleep and you turned in a good performance. I think there's a lot of baloney talked about tiredness and staleness and: "I brought him off after 60 minutes because...!"

Paul McGrath: I think training has probably changed quite a lot. Not for me, of course because I don't do too much training nowadays. I got a shock when I came up from Dublin, what with the training regime even then, but now I think it's a lot better, especially for the younger players. I think the game's quicker, there's more athletes now. More speed merchants.

Jim Smith: Changes? Yes, just in terms of your staff. You have a full-time masseur, a full-time fitness coach, a part-time sports psychologist – just those three added to the normal coaching staff is a major difference. It's all changed in the last five years, although maybe seven years ago, fitness coaches were coming into it. Masseurs have been brought in by the foreign players. They can't believe the situation in England because they normally have three or four at the clubs they've been at. Funnily enough, the Stan Cullises of this world were major believers in massage. Then it disappeared and now it's come back again. To be fair, the old trainer used to do that side. Poor beggar, he was there all Friday morning, wasn't he? Now they're there every morning and after every training session.

Steve Powell: Brian Clough believed in the relaxation thing. I think most people in sport, at a high level, need to have a certain amount of lack of tension to be able to perform. If you're up-tight, then that's only detrimental to performance and I think his whole attitude was to try to get players relaxed in order that they could perform to the best of their ability.

Alan Hinton: First of all, Clough and Taylor didn't want the players to leave all their energies on the practice field. It was just fun. It was a pleasure to go to training. We didn't want to leave. He used to make us very angry when he cancelled the five-a-side halfway through on a Friday, when we were playing great and having a good time. He'd say: "Stop. I want you to keep this energy for tomorrow." You know, it was phenomenal leadership from Clough and Taylor, through the whole club.

Eric Steele: It's changed for goalkeepers because of the rules. Goalkeepers are becoming outfield players who are good with their hands. Once they changed the rules, when the ball came as a back pass and you couldn't pick it up, couldn't bounce it four times, have a look, throw you're cap in the back of the net and then kick it, then the pressure came. They wanted the game speeded up, but I don't think it's particularly helped at times. Then they had the time when you could roll it out and get it back. Then it changed again. It means that goalkeepers are even more important to the team. I can say when I started in 1992, 70 per cent of my job with the goalkeepers was concerned with the catching, the dealing with crosses. 30 per cent was distribution. The last two years, you've got to split that differently. 60 per cent is to do with the hands, 40 per cent is to do with the feet.

Weight training

Bert Mozley: I was the first one to do it. Jack Barker was manager. It would be about 1953. I won an award in London for bodybuilding and I went in training one day and Ralph Hann – he was the trainer – said: "The boss wants to see you in his office." Jack had got this magazine and he threw it on the desk. "What's all this garbage?" he said. I said: "What do you mean?" He said: "You, weightlifting. You'll get yourself musclebound." I said: "That's stupid. Can you explain to me what musclebound is, Jack?" And he couldn't. I said: "I'm not weightlifting, I'm weight training and there's a big difference. I'm keeping my body toned-up to keep fit." So he said: "We can't have that." So I said: "That's fine then, Jack. Just transfer me because you'll never stop me. Just transfer me and I'll go." He said: "Hold on a minute, hold on a minute." Well, I'd been picked to play for England and I was classed as one of the quickest recovery full-backs. "It's never stopped me, has it?" I said. "Oh, all right then," he said. So then Norman Nielson and Cec Law came to my house and did a few weights with me and we found out that Tottenham Hotspur had heard about us and they'd got some weights.

Ray Young: Bert was doing that when I got there. If we ever had photographs taken, he always wore short sleeves. What he did was to roll his shirts sleeves up and always have his fists behind his arms and, if you look at Bert, he always used to push his muscles out.

Bert Mozley: I think I was the first to start weight training in English soccer, but there's a big difference between weight training and weightlifting. After I left England and went to Canada, I got into weightlifting and became Alberta champion for four years, Olympic lifting. Then champion power lifting for four years. I won the Mr Western States, Mr Physical Fitness and became Mr Calgary. I've always enjoyed being fit. I used to go back in the afternoons.

Special training

Bert Mozley: I think it was a waste of time. Eggs and sherry. It used to be cheap sherry, so as it wouldn't kill the egg! Nowadays, if a fellow can't keep fit with the equipment there is, well. The nutrition there is on the market, they should be the fittest guys in the world and when you're fit, injuries come less.

Coaching and tactics

Roy Christian: Managers weren't built up celebrity figures as they are now, like George Graham and people like that. Raich Carter always told the story about their manager at Sunderland, Johnny Cochrane, who was a useful player in his time for Middlesbrough, I think. Well, all they saw of him was at quarter to three on a Saturday. He would walk into the dressing-room after a very good liquid lunch and say: "Who're we playing today?" They'd tell him and he'd say: "Are they much of a side this season?' They'd tell him again and he'd say: "Well, do your best lads." They saw him again at quarter to three, the following Saturday. Of course, often the directors picked the team then and there were lots of rows about this.

Reg Harrison: For years Bill Bromage was the assistant trainer, but he had the sort of attitude that, to me, was absolutely great. He'd get you arguing about football. Not rowing, arguing. When you'd all finished arguing, he'd say: "I'll tell you what I think." Arguing about who takes penalties, for instance, who takes them, this fellow, this fellow, what have you. Bill would then say: "Well, if it was me, a left-footed player should take penalties and drive them because they always swing them that way, left-footers with the swing. Usually then, it's to the goalie's weakest hand."

Johnny Morris: I was a tactician. That's why I was an inside-forward. Don't forget I was one of the first coaches in this country. 1948, three of us went from United. They asked us to coach the England amateur side. We did it at Old Trafford. Three other lads went on the first FA coaching course, at Loughborough – Johnny Carey, Charlie Mitten and Jack Crompton. Johnny Carey had just captained Great Britain against the Rest of Europe, but he didn't get his coaching badge. When they came back, failed. All three failed. Waste of time. There was Stan Pearson and I and Johnny – his name was Jack – Warner, the Welsh international. We stayed back to coach these England amateur lads. When they got back from Loughborough and told us the tale we thought: "There's no chance, then." Anyway, we didn't go on the next year's course, but they did – and failed again! Third time they went, they decided to teach the book way, not the playing way. Got the badge!

Alan Hinton: I think Clough and Taylor were smarter than people thought. A lot of it was down to the fact that they didn't care too much about licensing or coaching awards. I remember being in Egypt with Derby County, about 1974,1975, and Alan Wade was sent on the trip from the FA to see what we were all about. We were around the swimming pool most days and it was a relaxation time. Their theory was to get the players away from the phones and the press. Alan Wade was there, around the pool, reading the coaching book every day and in the end, one of the players said: "Allen, why don't you throw that coaching book in the swimming pool and come to Derby for a few weeks and we'll teach you how to win games." That was a very important statement and I think that's what's been wrong with English soccer for years. The development programme has been screwed up big time, mainly because those that have licences and those who don't have licences don't like each other. I think it's hurt the game and it's why we've got so many foreign players in the game right now. I've got no problems with a couple of hundred foreign players being here, but 500? Too many. Bringing players in from little-known countries that don't have the soccer we have is particularly sad, but I think it's all down to the licensing – the coaching programme – and the development programme, which was very poor years and years ago.

Ray Young: I remember playing on the Baseball Ground mud when Storer was in charge and he wanted us all man-for-man marking. Hopeless. I went in at half-time and said: "This is bloody stupid. I'm playing like a centre-forward." My fellow was going back, almost to their penalty area and I'm thinking: "It's hard work in this mud." I said to Harry: "There's no way he can run from their penalty area to our penalty area in this mud." I said: "He'll be knackered by the time he gets to me, he's got to pass the ball. If I stay, it's not drawing anybody out." I mean, we had a spell where the full-backs were going different ways and nobody knew where they were.

Ian Buxton: I played very little under Harry Storer. I was signed by Storer, but played very little in the first team under him. I played mostly with Tim Ward. I do remember Storer telling the full-backs that if they'd got a winger with any trickery at all: "Put him in the crowd in the first minute." And if they didn't, Storer wanted to know why. That's how football was. Every club was the same.

Johnny Morris: We all think we're good players, don't we? Anybody that goes on a football field thinks they're a good player. Winterbottom thought he was a good player, but he wanted the game played as though he was centre-half and with him not being the tops, he wanted everyone to stand behind him, didn't he? I've been in team talks with him, and Stanley Matthews has come out afterwards - the best I've ever seen, winger - and he's said: "What does he mean?" Tom Finney's the same you know. Nice lad. Brilliant player, but I'll tell you this – it's no use telling him how to play the game. That's what the coaching school does. It tells you how to play.

Reg Harrison: When we had team talks, the people who took over were the Raichs, Peter and that. They didn't say: "We're going to do this, that and the other." They talked. They went right through the opposing team. They'd start with the goalkeeper: "Anyone seen him play?" They'd start with him: "Does he come out for crosses? Should we get some high ones in early on?" Then they'd go to the right-back, the left-back: "Anyone seen this lad?" Right through the team. That's how the team talks went. They didn't say: "We're going to do this or that."

Ray Young: I suppose in the early days most centre-forwards, played upfield. It hadn't come in, centre-forwards dropping off. That came in with Revie really, didn't it? Lying deep.

Roger Davies: I often tell people, very rarely did Brian Clough talk about the opposition. He always said to us: "Go out and play. Do your thing." Very rarely did he talk about the opposition. He used to do his little spiel down at the Midland Hotel before the game, when we'd had lunch. He'd do about 20 minutes about the game. What he wanted from us and probably on the day, at game time, he'd not come into the dressing-room until ten to three. You know, we'd be getting changed, doing last stretches, as you would anyway, then he'd pop in.

Willie Carlin: No. Cloughie didn't go in for team talks. The only time he'd talk to you was on Monday. He'd analyse the game and then he'd give his version and that was it. No, not before the game. On a Friday? No, not at all. He got a team together that he could send out on the park and he knew they could do it.

Steve Powell: He tended more to pick out individual things, certainly at half-time, than general team things. Obviously we'd have a general sort of team talk sometime before the game, but most things at half-time were about individual incidents, which maybe, might have cost us the game or won us the game.

Roger Davies: Half-time he'd probably be more verbal, depending how the game was going, but before games, no. One thing, in particular, Brian Clough was good at, he used to speak to individuals. He didn't tend to talk to 15 players. He'd come over and talk to individuals: "You're the best at this." Things like that. He knew how to gee people up. Sometimes he'd really have a go at them because he'd know that they'd react to that, like: "I'll show you." In anything you're doing, everyone can't react to the same statement and Brian Clough was very good at that. He used to give me stick because if someone has a go at me, I'll react. Do that to other people and they'd go into a shell and you wouldn't see them again.

Reg Harrison: We never did much on free-kicks, just played what was there. I remember Jack Stamps said to me very early on: "Get these balls across Reg. It's our job to make something of them." So I never had to bother about picking men out, really. They made the crosses, those in the middle. If I was out on the wing, I got them up, but if I was coming into the box, they were driven because they'd be cut out if you tried to get them up from there. Too close.

Eric Steele: Arthur didn't do anything on free-kicks. No, John Gregory did. We used to do it all in training and Arthur would make sure it was practised, rehearsed, but John had something he'd got with Terry Venables at QPR. When we had Gregory, Ross MacLaren, Callaghan, we got some goals. Free-kicks won't lose you games and we won a few games on those.

Ted McMinn: Arthur never told me what to do. I don't think any manager, any manager I've worked under, has told me what to do because I think they might have lost the best of me, because nobody in my life has told me how to play. If I didn't know what I was going to do, I don't think they'd much chance of telling me what to do.

In the dressing-room

Roy McFarland: When Cloughie came in the dressing-room at the Baseball Ground, the sign was already up there: 'The biggest crime in football is to give the ball to the opposition.' Who was the manager who put that up there? It wasn't Cloughie, it was Harry Storer. Harry Storer put that up and when I signed for Derby County and to the people who came after me, Cloughie said: "Keep reading that. That's the most important rule you'll ever want to know in football." It stayed there and I had it put up at Cambridge United and it's true.

Gordon Guthrie: Yes, I've had 11 managers. Some came in straightaway after the match – and some didn't. It varied. Some went to the office first, just to get their mind clear. There's an old adage in football that if you steam straight in, then you might slaughter the wrong player or describe the move or whatever, wrongly. Then after a few minutes, someone says: "It was me, boss, it wasn't him." Then, of course, you've caused yourself more aggravation. Mostly, they pop into their own office, just to have a few minutes to get themselves sorted out. Compared with Brian, Tim Ward was pretty quiet. Dave was quite composed, then he talked football.

Roy McFarland: When David Webb signed for us, he would get ready in the last quarter of an hour and he virtually wouldn't come in the dressing-room. That was his preparation. The majority of players are all different and they all have a different approach. I liked to be there maybe an hour before. I had a certain preparation, I had a routine. I even put my kit on in the same way. On the odd occasion, I'd put my socks on before I put my shorts on and I'd say: "Oops." Take the socks off and put the shorts on. So there was always a particular preparation.

Gordon Guthrie: Brian would sometimes come in and just say a few words and go. Then, of course, Peter Taylor would take over. He would probably go round one or two. If Brian had slaughtered one or two, he'd pull them back up. He'd tell the whole team what he thought, briefly. Then he'd probably walk over to an individual, who was having a cup of tea or whatever, and have a few words with him.

Roy McFarland: I remember Willie Carlin. I used to go out fourth and all of a sudden in this game, fourth's gone out and I'm fifth and I'm panicking. Carlin says to me: "What are you bloody on about? Get out. Get on with it." So Cloughie, very quickly, turned round to him and said: "Willie, why do you always go out last?" For the first time ever, Willie Carlin didn't have anything to say. He couldn't turn round and say anything. So we all have a preparation and we all like to do what we want to do. The only thing is, like most footballers, you don't like to show it.

Gordon Guthrie: Colin Murphy, he was quite excitable, as you know. If you could understand his London accent and slang, you were halfway there, but I think he wasn't the best at giving pre-match talks. Largely because no one could understand him. He spoke in this London slang.

Are players – different? Have they changed?

Eric Steele: I don't think they want to play all the time, the foreign players. Straightaway they've got another agenda. They're not going to make a total career in this country. There's not one foreigner going to come here at 19 or 20 years of age and stay here for 15 years. So nine times out of ten, they've got another agenda. They've got to go home three or four times a year. It's a case of: "Yes, we want to play in the Premier League but..." It was the Italian League and the German Bundesliga ten years ago.

Colin Gibson: I don't necessarily think they have changed. On an individual basis, they very much want to look after themselves and when they are in the team environment, it's very much 'us' and 'them'. Yes, I get close to them because I go along to interview them, but I think there are areas you don't overstep. If the players are together at the training ground or at the ground, in the dressing-rooms, I don't think that's any place for the media to be. That's their environment and you don't step into it.

Gordon Guthrie: No I don't think so. About the money? Well, it's something that's gone along with the game, hasn't it? I always say good luck to any player, whatever he gets he earns because it's a very short life. I think if they get ten good years now, they've got a lot of their lives afterwards, still to live. I think it's down to individuals really, how it affects them.

Jim Smith: In their inner selves, they're just like footballers always were, but everything else is different. I remember, when I first joined Sheffield United, leaving Bramall Lane after training and going to catch the bus. Alan Hodgkinson, their England goalkeeper, was walking behind me and I was embarrassed when he caught me up. What I'm getting at is, he didn't drive home, he walked into Sheffield city centre to get the bus himself – and he was playing for England. Now they come in Ferraris or whatever, but when you get them all together and the camaraderie and playing tricks and that, they're no different. The dressing-room is just the same. It's got to be, hopefully. I think some clubs have the problem that the dressing-room has changed. There's always been a bit of jealousy or a clique somewhere or other, even in the old days. There's got to be, it's human nature.

Eric Steele: The Scandinavians are very much of the English way of thinking, but when you start involving the Latin temperaments, that is when you start to notice a change in the players because they tend to have different cultures and different attitudes. When you think what we've been used to, coaches and managers have had to adapt as well.

Colin Gibson: They have far more power than they ever used to do because of the money and the way that football is run and the way their contracts run. Derby sold Paulo Wanchope because if they hadn't, they'd have got absolutely nothing for him. He could string them along. So in that respect, yes they are millionaires very, very quickly. Very easily, if they've got the talent, if they've got the good fortune, but in terms of their attitude, no. I think when it comes to getting out on the pitch, they want to be out there, want to be winners and want to do their thing.

That Baseball Ground Magic

IF YOU never went to the Baseball Ground, you missed a little bit of football magic. Not all the time, of course. Magic only appears fleetingly, but when it does, you remember it, especially at night, with the floodlights glinting off that notorious wet playing surface, sometimes known as that @$!?--- pitch'. Tight, compact, cramped, a cockpit of noise and passion, supporters and players were always involved together, sometimes literally, notably when a visiting prima donna found himself upside down in the Popular Side, after the attentions of someone like Chick Musson, Frank Upton or Dave Mackay. Thrusting hands aided him back to reality, shaken and probably stirred. Some of those hands are represented in this chapter, as well as the feet.

Gordon Guthrie: When you walked in that top gate at the Baseball Ground, straight away you felt you were in a proper football ground. Now, you don't always get that at some grounds, but you always got it here and people who came, referees and everybody, said it's an atmosphere that you can't describe. Visiting players, internationals, everybody, they all loved to come to Derby County.

'Ned' Mee: I thought it was a dump. Well it was, to what it is now. There were stands, aye. There were not many, but there was a lot of rails to lean against, on the 'bobs'.

Ernie Hallam: At that time, there was just a sort of curved roof over both ends. There was no stand on the Leys side and at both ends there was just a sort of shelter, with the curved roof. In the Thirties – 1932, 1933 – both those ends were made double-decker stands, and basically, they're still there.

'Ned' Mee: I remember them building the Osmaston and Normanton Stands. It didn't take them long.

Tommy Powell: I played on there about 1934-35. They used to play the schoolboy finals on there. I'd seen Reggie Harrison and Lee Leuty play the year before because they'd played – Reggie for Notts Road and Leon played for St James' Church, you see – so I'd seen them play the year before. I always say to Reggie, "You old so and so..."

Peter Gadsby: You always have your team, there's no other team. I've always said: "I can't understand how anyone wants to be a director at any other club." When the decision to move from the Baseball Ground was being taken, it was taken with trepidation. I remember how I could smell the place, smell the game. It was always a decision taken with trepidation. You thought: "Gosh. Is this the right decision?" There's been so many memories there.

Bill Brownson: I always used to stand on the little terrace, in front of the Main Stand. If you got down there, you didn't notice the crown on the pitch, until you'd sat upstairs. Then, after you'd been up, and then you came down, you noticed it. You noticed it more, anyway.

Bill Wainwright: I sat in the directors' box unless it was full, then I sat on the steps. Graham Clarke, who did the hospital broadcasts, used to have a special box and sometimes I'd sit in there. But usually I'd sit on the steps if the directors' box was full.

Tommy Powell: I saw the last game before the war. I can remember Derby beating Villa 1-0, when Jack 'Nick' scored from a penalty. That was on the Saturday and war was declared on the Sunday. I was in the boys' pen in the corner.

Brian Clough: I certainly played there. Once we won there 7-1 – and I didn't score! It was just another match really. It was ironic that I finished up managing Derby.

Dave Mackay: No. I'd never played there before. Not being big-headed, but when you were in the old First Division, anyone below that, you didn't even know the names of the grounds, really. Even when I went from Hearts to Tottenham: "Who's Tottenham?"

Ray Young: Wragg's, the bookies, on the corner and a fruit and sweet shop on the other corner. In fact, many people used to park their bikes there. One shilling to look after your bike. The players' entrance has never changed, it's still the same, exactly the same. I suppose the only thing that eventually improved was the playing surface. Prior to that, I mean, it was just a brown diamond with four corners where the grass was.

Bobby Davison: The Baseball Ground and Highbury are the two favourite grounds that I played at. The Baseball Ground was tremendous. The atmosphere, the supporters, so close to the pitch. Night matches were great.

Eric Steele: I'd played there before. I remember Roger Davies scored a hat-trick past me when I'd played for Newcastle Reserves. We lost 4-1. I was only 17 and Roger scored a hat-trick. He still doesn't remember it. Yes, I knew all about the atmosphere and what that was. Everybody knew of the place. Still even now, even with what we've got now, people still talk about the Baseball Ground and what it was and what it meant. I saw the changing faces of it. Fences up, fences down, seats, standing up, mix of both. Everything...

Ted McMinn: No. I'd seen it on television in the early Seventies, on *Match of the Day* in Scotland. It was the only time I'd ever seen it. It looked like a building site every time I'd seen it on the television. This was the days when Derby were winning the League and things like that, but the pitch. Phew! It looked like it rained every single Saturday.

That ******g pitch

Roy Christian: Dreadful. Ankle deep in mud really. It must have been a dreadful ground to play on, especially when the ball got heavy. Mid-season it was terrible. On the other hand, in April, when there was no grass left or virtually no grass, the ball was uncontrollable, virtually. It would be bouncing very high and there were all sorts of bobbles. A player would miss an open goal, but if you were looking very intently, you'd see the ball bobble at the last minute and the poor chap would be lucky if he got his foot on it at all.

Jimmy Bullions: I loved playing at the Baseball Ground. It slowed all the others down to my speed! It's not surprising players get the ball stuck under their feet in such conditions and with someone like me ploughing into them, they often packed it in. There was a fellow called Ray Bowden, played for Leicester – I think he was an Arsenal player really, but this was in 1944-45 time – and it was one of the matches when we played Leicester a lot – and Notts County and Nottingham Forest – in that little Midland League, before the big League started again. Anyway, this Bowden said to me: "'Have you just come out of the Reserves, eh?" I never said anything. I just ploughed into him.

Johnny Morris: They used to have to put these coke burners on it to dry it out. They used to have about six of them in each penalty area. It was a real muddy field. We trained on it, aye, when it was fit to go on it.

Roy Christian: It was all right at the beginning of the season, but there were players... Jackie Stamps was one, he was a marvellous player in the mud, but in April, he might as well have taken his summer holidays. He just couldn't control that ball. It was terrible to watch him. Embarrassing.

Frank Upton: It wasn't so much hard work because I thoroughly enjoyed myself, so to me, it was just a job and I looked forward to it. The pitch must have been one of the worst in the League, I would have thought. We used to have to plough through mud. I'd say it was four to six inches deep at times, which you know yourself is hard, especially in the middle of the park. Yes the pitch was terrible. It must be beautiful to play on the pitches they play on today. It must be a treat to go out there on those pitches.

Ian Buxton: Ah, the pitch. Well, we signed Frank Upton back one season because he was big and strong and could kick it out of the mud. The pitches in those days were sometimes unbelievable. No, that's not right, they were normal then, it's today's pitches that are unbelievable. It's fantastic how they keep the grass on them all year now. We just played in thick mud all winter.

Steve Powell: Well, obviously going back to the mid-Seventies there was a lot of talk about it. If you look back at some of the games, I can't believe how we used to play such good football on it because it was an absolute mud heap. Compared to the pitches nowadays, it's incredible the difference. Maybe it would be nice to see some of the so-called international stars play on that sort of surface. It would be very interesting, anyway, to see how they would perform on those sort of surfaces.

Charlie George: I liked playing there, it didn't bother me about the conditions. It wasn't a problem really, for me.

Gordon Guthrie: I can see Bob Smith in his wellingtons, the referee's halted the game and we thought: "What the hell's Bob doing?" Bob's out there with his whitewash bucket, stepping it out and measuring it out and putting the thing down and the referee's said: "Now we can take the penalty." That's after Bob's cleared off with his bucket. I don't think that's happened before.

Keith Loring: When I first came to Derby they asked me to do a press conference and I was on the side of the pitch. They wanted me to go back on to the pitch and I wasn't being clever, but I said: "No, no. This is where my job finishes." It wasn't being that clever, but it was quite a significant remark. As I was doing that, I was looking around me and it was 29 March and much as we were a small club at Brentford, we were bloody organised and the pitch was good. I thought: "This pitch is a disgrace." Little did I know, as much as you guys know about the pitch, but even then I thought: "This pitch should be better." So I phoned the chairman and I said: "Chairman, I think we've got a problem here." Anyway, I looked into it very quickly and, don't forget, I hadn't really started yet.

Crowds and atmosphere

Roy Christian: Not long after I started going, they put up that old shed that used to advertise Ind Coope's, then Offilers' Ales. There was some cover, but it was fairly well back and where we stood, we were in the open. We went there because although I was about as tall as I am now – I seemed to stop growing at about 14 years old – I couldn't really see much over the people ahead, so we usually made for right up to the front. There were these iron, sort of leaning posts, almost like a zimmer, that you could lean against. They were fixed. The crowds did used to sway in those days because nobody could see very well and everybody was peering over somebody's shoulder and you'd get a near miss at one end from a corner or something like that and everybody would sway up and down. It was really quite dangerous. I was a bit scared at times. As I got taller we moved back a bit to get against one of these barrier things.

Bill Brownson: On the Popular side, they did get a sway on. Of course, in those days there was no Ley Stand, either. It was more noticeable. There's always been a noise at the Baseball Ground. I've never known it when it hasn't been. The lowest crowd I can remember was about 8,000. I think we played Luton.

Alf Jeffries: The crowds were quite big. As you know at the Derby ground, they're right on top of you aren't they? My mother used to say to me sometimes: "Was there many there?" And I used to say: "I don't know." There was a lot of shouting, a lot of noise, but I never really noticed them. You kept you mind on the job.

Ian Buxton: You remember it as a small ground, but in those days it was quite a sizeable ground with 30,000 odd, I suppose. It was really the closeness of the spectators to the pitch that made the atmosphere at home always so good. You were expected to win at home. Unlike England at Wembley now, going out frightened of the opposition, Derby County always went out expecting to beat whoever came to the Baseball Ground, whatever division you were in. I think a bit of that was the atmosphere from the closeness of the spectators.

Tommy Powell: When you were at the Baseball Ground – the crowd and the players – they all seemed to be as one. They all seemed to be part of the atmosphere. You could hear whether they were slating you or what. My mates used to be where the little wall was and they used to be shouting and things like that. You could almost have a natter with the crowd. The crowd being so close was intimidating to other teams, I think. The crowd noise has won many a match at Derby. I know it has.

Kevin Hector: The second half of the Chelsea match was the best ever. The noise was incredible. There were some good nights in the European matches, but that second half against Chelsea was noisiest I ever heard the Baseball Ground.

Brian Flint: It was closed in, wasn't it? You'd got the streets right opposite, so I suppose the people walking about were crammed into a smaller space, which was bound to help the atmosphere.

John O'Hare: All those night games there. I think night games have got something.

Ray Young: You used to get some good crowds. In the Reserves even. Whenever you played at Burnley, for instance, you were talking of 15,000 to 17,000 at reserve-team games. Then again, they had good crowds at Derby in the Third Division North days. They averaged over 18,000 – and 25,000 wasn't uncommon. Superb atmosphere. Always got a good atmosphere at Derby. To stand in the crowd was superb.

Willie Carlin: We had some wonderful times, but the biggest thing was that the players belonged to the crowd and the crowd belonged to the players. I'll give an instance. My missus was in town and I remember her telling me: "I was in town and these women saw some lads coming home from the match and they said: 'How's our lads got on?'" 'Our' lads. That's wonderful. It was an affinity with the people.

Roger Davies: Ah, it was tremendous wasn't it? I mean, this place at Pride Park is good, but it was so close wasn't it, at the Baseball Ground? The terraces, so close to the pitch. It must have been awesome for the opposition to come in.

Steve Sutton: Tremendous atmosphere. I remember trying to get out after a night game. My Dad wanted to leave ten minutes early because he had to be at work on a night shift at ten o'clock in Buxton. So we had to leave ten minutes before and the number of times we had to try to find a steward to open the gates at the bottom of the Pop side there, behind the old Ossie End.

Roger Davies: There was a great atmosphere in our dressing-room. It wasn't 'whether we're going to win today?' It was 'by how many?' We actually believed that. It was a case of 'how many?' You could feel that when you went out, with our crowd, they really could lift us. I think they were louder than they are now. I don't know why they are subdued now, but the noise we used to have... Maybe some of the football they were watching might have helped.

Ted McMinn: You see the pace of the game now. It seems slower. Sometimes you come here to Pride Park and you watch it and it's slow, there's no atmosphere. At the Baseball Ground, whatever the score was, you always had an atmosphere and I love grounds like that. It's the only ground I've played on where everything was so close. This is a great stadium, Pride Park, take nothing away from it, but I'd always have the Baseball Ground.

Eric Steele: Oh, the crowd were a big part of it. I can remember, we weren't even in contention the first year and we played Newport County. We're losing 3-1 with 25 minutes to go and it was one of those days. It was throwing it down, but it was a typical Baseball Ground afternoon and I'm sure that crowd sucked two goals in for us! We were playing with the wind and, I'll tell you what, they were unbelievable. I was talking to their players afterwards and Peter Sayer, who I'd played with at Brighton and who had gone back to Wales, couldn't believe it. We drew 3-3. The crowd got us the draw on the night and there was only 11,000 there. The Taylor Report had to come for safety reasons, but there was something about seeing people standing and leaping and jumping and singing all at the same time. You don't just hear it, you see the atmosphere. People in waves, jumping up and down and it was just great to be there.

Ted McMinn: I think at the end of the day, the gaffer used to sum me up because every time I played on the side of the Pop side, I would play right wing one side and then go left wing, so that I was at the Pop side both halves. Then the gaffer, kind of clicked on. So I was always down that side because I always got a big buzz of playing on that one side, but he clocked on and told me we needed to keep our shape. Then the odd time I'd see him screaming at me and pulling his hat off, telling me we'd lost our shape and it was me that had lost it.

Jim Smith: It's been a big help retaining the Baseball Ground. They've put in a lot of work on the ground at Raynesway to try to maintain a decent pitch for most of the season, but with the water levels being what it is across over the hedge, it's always going to be heavy. You do need good surfaces now. Most pitches have good surfaces and the Baseball Ground, number one, for training with the first team, has been excellent. More than anything, it's protected Pride Park because we put our Reserves and youth team games on there. It's a marvellous facility, but obviously, we're hoping in the near future we'll have a state of the art training ground and all that goes with it.

On the way to the Baseball Ground

Bill Brownson: For a young lad in those days, it was quite something to go to the Baseball Ground because it was so closed in with all the tuck shops.

That Baseball Ground Magic

Brian Flint: Everybody had their routine. You either went on a bus from town or you walked up. You knew what time you had to go, how long it would take. You knew where to get your programme. Very few went in cars. Those who did had to park some way from the ground, so you were walking further, with people. You chatted to people more then.

Michael Dunford: Occasionally I went in the boys' pen – slightly cheaper than in the paddock – and I stood on the Popular Side, one game. I remember that vividly because I hadn't got enough money to go in the paddock. I must have lost it on the way to the ground. We played Southampton. That was the time when Terry Paine and Ken Wimshurst, people like that, played. Sydenham, the winger. I think it was quite a high- scoring game. I think we were beaten 5-3 or something like that at the time. Generally, though, I was in the paddock. You got to know the people. They were quite friendly. Then as we progressed to the late Sixties and the club became more successful, you ended up having to queue from about 12.30pm onwards to get into the paddock because it only held just over 1,000, as I remember.

Roger Davies: When you think we used to leave the Midland at around quarter to two to get there, the road would be packed. We used to drive up. From the Midland, to the ground. We nearly always went in our cars.

Bill Wainwright: When they'd had lunch and everybody had left, I used to go down to the White Horse in the Morledge. There was an elderly lady there. She was the licensee. It was a very good pub in those days. It had a very good buffet and I used to go down and have my lunch there. Then, I'd walk up to the Baseball Ground for the match.

Brian Flint: You used to be able to see the players. You can still see the players walking into the ground now, if you're lucky enough to get past the stewards, but then, they used to seem more like human beings, the players did. They seemed more on a level with the supporters and I think that made the supporters feel that it was all part of a thing, whereas now, you're nothing, really. You get an impression you don't belong, in general, these days. I think it's probably money, really. It's taken them away from the working man, but at the Baseball Ground, it was different. It really was. Different...

Peter Gadsby: There were elements of the Baseball Ground at Swansea when we played them in the Cup two seasons ago. To see the crowd and the way they were coming to the ground. What you'll never replace is parking your car about half a mile from the Baseball Ground and walking to the ground and talking about the game you're going to see, in anticipation. And talking about it afterwards. I noticed at Swansea, there was so much vocal support and some of that was because so many were standing, which makes a hell of a difference too.

Peter Gadsby: The issue of the stadium was quite interesting because there was a company called Stadivarios that had arrived on the football scene, with a quite interesting concept which involved approaching six clubs in the UK. Some of those clubs were already putting new stadiums up. One, in particular, was Middlesbrough, also Sunderland. They were saying basically: "If you put a new stadium up, we'll finance it, we'll own it and we'll rent it back to you, so that you don't have to put any money in at all. You have your gate and we have all the royalties and we'll have pop concerts and etc, etc." Well, you can make any figures work and it looked attractive. It was an English firm, but had come by an American system. It required quite an ambitious planning project. It projected about £45 million and I think it was like saying: "Would you like to have a new car for £1 or would you like your old one for £150 and you can drive it free of petrol."

Keith Loring: I realised the pitch was crap. Rang the chairman. The guy who'd been here before, not to criticise him in anyway at all, but he'd decided to franchise everything out, which I don't necessarily believe in because then you're just on a list of: "Oh, we'll just go and do the Baseball Ground pitch." Well, the Baseball Ground pitch, whatever we say of it, has to be loved and I'm quite proud to say that in the last two years we were there, it was a lot better than it had been in previous years. That's because we bloody well grafted on it – and it had to be grafted on, to give it a chance.

Peter Gadsby: If you go to look at the Nou Camp in Barcelona, it's basically just concrete. It's a very old stadium and it's got very little commercial things installed. Leasing back systems really require community money or ratepayers' money and that therefore, and rightly so, means access for the community. Immediately there is a conflict, in commercial terms.

Peter Gadsby: The club was again going through a difficult period where results weren't happening and the relationship with Lionel and Arthur Cox had deteriorated and also with the board. He'd been quite patient, but things were getting to a point of: "Well, what's happening?" The ground thing, I was trying to advise on and, as you know, my business does lead me into regeneration and I suppose I'd nailed my colours to the mast in saying that I didn't think the Stadivarios thing was going to happen. I didn't believe the six things were going to happen in time. £45 million in Derby was a fortune and maybe it was too simplistic a scheme. In any case, it was on record that I was not willing to move.

Keith Loring: The Baseball Ground was magnificent but in the Seventies commercialism in football was a necessary evil. "We've got to have it because they've got one; we'll have a shop because they've got one." I'm not criticising Derby because Manchester United and all these people didn't realise what was happening either. Clubs that had been in the top flight for years were still running their shops out of Portacabins. Anyway, I felt the ground looked tired. But the builders were in, so I knew that the Toyota Stand was going to look very nice with what they were doing over there because I'd seen the drawings.

Peter Gadsby: I was not willing to move? That is absolutely correct. That was about four years before we did move. It was because of £45 million and where the project was positioned on Pride Park, on the old tip. It needed developing at a cost of £8 million before you could even start. It didn't seem to me to be any good. Also, there was the amount of planning required. I think I was probably right in thinking they weren't going to get all the retail, all the things they – Stadivarios – were looking for. So I did a report through a firm of local solicitors who were involved and that report, when it was tabled, didn't please Mr Fern at all. I was almost asked to leave there and then, but I stuck to my guns and Lionel looked at that report and basically, that was the end of Stadivarios.

Keith Loring: I saw that Lionel had put his money in and it had all been spent on the team but very little had been spent on anything around us, to invest in us, to make us better. Now I knew that the ground situation was all over the place, the decisions. The thing that struck me most of all, though, was that we didn't have a word processor in the place, never mind a computer. Marion, who's still here, was using a typewriter and I'm doing a deal for £2.6 million for Craig Short!

Sunday, 11 May 1997

Jim Fearn: For the last League game at the Baseball Ground, against Arsenal, we'd come up with various razzamataz ideas for the crowd, which had worked to a certain extent. Charlie George took a bow and various other people were there for the day and it was nice. We did a minute's silence, which in retrospect was probably a bit over the top, but it was something we felt would work at the time. We also made the mistake of trying to put in an enhanced sound system and as always, I was the idiot on the microphone trying to make this work and the feedback all around the ground made it absolutely impossible. Again, I was just pleased when we kicked-off. I'm sure everyone was because it had been such a big build-up and I felt I had to get away and we'd promised we'd try to get a player down to the Assembly Rooms. We were doing a 'beam-out' because so many people wanted to be there. Martin Taylor was around the tunnel area as well, so I said: "Martin, let's go down to the Assembly Rooms. I've had enough of this now." It had been such a massive build-up. So we did. I drove him down to the Assembly Rooms and Martin came on to the stage at half-time, which was nice because we really looked after the fans down there. Then I came back and watched a bit of the second half. That's just another example of how the build-up to a game can actually take away everything, leave you absolutely exhausted.

Gordon Guthrie: The Arsenal game was the end of an era. A most exciting era, which I'd have never swapped for anything. It's mostly due to the players I've been fortunate to work with because over the years we had the best at the Baseball Ground. The best.

Can you remember when...?

"Time is but the stream I go fishing in," said Henry Thoreau. Derby County were one of the 12 clubs that founded the Football League in 1888. The great deeds of today are but the memories of tomorrow. "Can you remember when...?"

Ernie Hallam: The finest game I ever saw at the Baseball Ground was the 4-4 draw with Sunderland in 1933. Dally scored with almost the last kick of the game, to equalise. I was almost level with the goal and it swerved in. It was a tremendous game. We were winning 2-0 and then losing 3-2, 3-3, 3-4 eventually 4-4. We won the replay at Sunderland 1-0. Raich Carter was playing for Sunderland at the time. Chelsea in the League Cup in 1968 was a great game, as was the Everton League Cup game a few weeks later, but the one I'd pick out as the best ever was the 4-4 draw with Sunderland. Tremendous.

Gerald Mortimer: You could go quite a long time without too many memorable matches. One I do remember is in, I would guess, about April 1955, when they were just about to be relegated from the Second Division. They played Swansea Town, as they then were, at the Baseball Ground, when we'd had a long spell of dry weather and it was a dust bowl. It was the most appalling game you could imagine. We lost 4-1. That stuck in the memory.

John Bowers: I can remember one very nasty incident. Derby played Southampton at the Baseball Ground on a Wednesday night and it was quite a ferocious game. I think it was Huxford went in high on Glyn Davies and just split his thigh muscle open, just above the knee, just like a steak. It was parted like that and I walked over to it and looked at it and I thought I was just going to faint because it looked a real bad one. They strapped Glyn up and off he went and then the funny part after that was that Frank Upton spent the rest of the game chasing Huxford all over the pitch and eventually he did him, badly. His knee I think, in front of the directors' box. I think that's all the crowd wanted to see, retribution.

Frank Upton: Southampton. I wouldn't say it was a kicking match, but it was a hard game. When we played, there were a lot of hard men about, wasn't there, really? Well, so called hard men. People say to me: "Oh, you were a hard man." I can honestly say, I went for the ball. I tried to win the ball. I can honestly say that I never went 'over the top', to anyone, but I remember the Southampton game, I remember that. Oh yes. The lad Huxford, came over the top of the ball to Glyn Davies and ripped his thigh wide open just above the knee and the first tackle after, I lost my head I suppose. I'd seen the state of Glyn's thigh. The ref spoke to me and I said: "Fair enough, sorry ref." You know, like we used to, apologise to the referees. I settled down then. The last ten minutes, he happened to come for a ball, 50-50 just outside our box. He was going to do me. So I just went for the ball, strong like. I went straight through him and I won the ball, no problem, but they carried him off didn't they? I'd done the ligaments in his knee, but I just went for the ball, I just went for the ball. He was saying what he was going to do when we went down there, to Southampton, but he never came anywhere near. When we went down there, we never saw him. He was quiet as a lamb.

Ray Young: I remember seeing Glyn Davies getting done, when Huxford did him. Went over the top and Glyn's leg was split. Then Frank did him, sorted him out. One of the hardest I played against was Alex Dawson.

Ian Buxton: Huxford, that's him. Huxford did Glyn and Frank did Huxford, and Huxford and Glyn ended up in hospital beds next to one another. Both with about 15 stitches up the thigh and Glyn had stitches in the inner muscle as well! I think it was called a draw!

George Beard: 1946. We played Villa, at Villa Park. 76,000. Packed to capacity. You couldn't get your programme out of your pocket. Couldn't get your fags. Anything. So tight. The game, though, was terrific. We won 4-3. Then we drew 1-1 at the Baseball Ground, in the second leg.

Roger Davies: Probably all games are memorable. When you talk to a footballer and say: "Do you remember that game?" The detail they come up with. Somebody mentions the game to you and it's like the computer triggers it and you're away: "Yes, I remember it. I remember that move and he was doing this and he was doing that." It's amazing what memories you can come up with that's attached to a game that happened 20 years ago. If somebody just says something to you: "Do you remember that game?" And you'll be able to tell everybody what the team was, the opposition was, the score was. You'll remember things that went on in that game and it's amazing how you can pick it up.

Frank Upton: A Manchester United cup match. We lost 5-2 and I scored one of the goals. I remember a Birmingham game when my son, Gary, was just born and I scored a couple of goals that day, one from the halfway line! Anyway, it seems like it now.

Ian Buxton: Well, Man United in the Cup was the biggest match I played in. We were Second Division and they had Law, Best, Charlton and the whole lot. Foulkes, Gregg in goal. The whole town built up to that match. We lost 5-2, but that was, obviously, for me a memorable match and to play against people like that, a Second Division player. I played very early on, under Storer, at Liverpool, the year Liverpool got out of the Second Division. There was a full house there. I played at Newcastle in the Second Division and Sunderland, which I remember, again, for the crowd. They're the matches you remember.

Ray Young: A full house against Manchester United. 33,000 or something and I don't think the crowd had stopped cheering when we'd kicked off and I'm passing the ball back to the goalkeeper. I think it was Albert Scanlon, who nipped in and we're a goal down. What do you do? If there's a hole in the ground you bury yourself, don't you?

Charlie George: Arsenal v Derby County, FA Cup 1972. It took three games to get a result. First game was at the Baseball Ground. I remember scoring there and the fans were giving me some stick and I think I gave them the V-sign. Yeah, in front of the Main Stand. It's funny, a few years later I was playing there and I got on tremendously well with them. The first replay at Highbury was when the electricity strike was on. 63,000 people were there – and on a Wednesday afternoon. We ended up playing at Leicester. Why Leicester I don't know. I think they had a private generator for the floodlights. Only 35 miles from Derby and Ray Kennedy scored the winner, I think from a John McGovern back pass.

Roger Davies: Obviously the Tottenham game. For me anyway, the Tottenham 5-3, with us 3-1 down with 12 minutes to go and I got a hat-trick. That game I remember.

Bobby Davison: I always enjoyed matches playing against the clubs from the North-East. Before Arthur Cox took over we beat Newcastle 3-2, at home. Keegan, McDermott and everybody was playing and we won 3-2. I scored two. That was enjoyable. Leeds United. We beat Leeds United to go up and I scored against them. I think Phil Gee scored too. Mervyn Day was in goal for Leeds.

Michael Dunford: I can remember in the very early Sixties when Coventry were riding high, coming from the Fourth, to the Third, to the Second, when Jimmy Hill was manager. I think Derby went to Coventry twice in successive years when they were on a high and beat them. John Bowers was playing, Eddie Thomas and Alan Durban. Talking of Kevin Hector, when Kevin made his home debut against Huddersfield, although he scored then, Alan Durban got three on that day. I think we won 4-3.

Dave Mackay: Chelsea. Yes, we beat them 3-1. Do I remember the first goal? Only from 30 yards, that's all. A wee back-heel from Willie Carlin and I drove it past Peter Bonetti. Yes, they were great matches. Fantastic atmosphere. When you talk about 30,000, once nearly 42,000 at the Baseball Ground! I just can't believe how 42,000 got in. Fantastic atmosphere.

Brian Flint: League Cup, against Chelsea. Replay. Everyone says that one, don't they? I mean, that one stood out. I think it was the first time I'd seen a Division One side. We got a replay and I think the night that they played the first leg, the Reserves played and they kept giving the score over the tannoy, how the first team was going on. There was that much interest in it. Then the replay came. I mean, it was a full house, a night match. That all adds to the atmosphere, doesn't it, a night match, smoke coming over from the foundry and what have you, but they thoroughly deserved to win, didn't they?

Steve Powell: I certainly remember going when I was 13 or 14, when they played in the League Cup game against Chelsea and beat them 3-1. That was a fantastic night. Also, I think in the same competition, they played Everton and beat them 1-0 and I think we actually got in on old age pensioners' tickets. There were no tickets available and we somehow managed to get through with these old age pensioners' tickets. For about two shillings a time I think it was.

Michael Gretton: Oh, probably one of the most famous was Derby County versus Chelsea. The day after, when I went to work with some of the gentlemen who used to live in Shaftesbury Crescent, one of them said his front door actually moved with the sound of the Derby supporters. Great, great atmosphere.

Colin Gibson: The Chelsea game in the League Cup, when Chelsea were a good First Division team, Derby were coming out of the Second Division. That was terrific because Derby had drawn at Stamford Bridge – didn't go to that game – and got the big Chelsea team, Bobby Tambling, Peter Osgood, at the Baseball Ground. Of course, Derby had all the dominance and Chelsea go and score and could have made it 2-0. I don't remember the full details of it, but the ball was going in and I think it was Dave Mackay – I could be wrong there – cleared it off the line. That seemed to tip the balance in Derby's favour and Dave Mackay scored one of his famous free-kicks. Edge of the penalty area and he just hit it low and hard, right in the corner and Derby were back into the game. That was a terrific night. Again, under the floodlights. As was Benfica in the European Cup. The 'Eagles of Lisbon' in town, at this ramshackle little Baseball Ground, against Derby County, the Football League champions. That was amazing.

Willie Carlin: Oh, I loved Derby. The crowd was fantastic. The Chelsea match was unbelievable, but the best football we ever played, I think, was the Tottenham game. When we won 5-0. I thought that was fantastic. They did me proud because we beat Liverpool 6-0 in the season, which was great. 4-0 and 2-0. Not a lot of teams ever do 6-0 over Liverpool in a season. It's some going.

Dave Mackay: I loved the Tottenham match, obviously. Like when I was a player, we beat Tottenham 5-0, right? Bill 'Nick', he didn't want me to come to Derby. He wanted me to go to Hearts. Get me out the road! Then, when we came to Tottenham. First game, when I was playing, 5-0. Then, when I'm manager, we beat them 8-2. It could have been 12! Pat Jennings made three or four, fantastic saves in the last ten minutes. Liverpool came, 4-0. Chelsea. Everybody. Arsenal. The whole lot. We used to beat them all. Great days.

Roger Davies: I remember the Luton game when I got five plus two disallowed. I remember the Carlisle game and we paraded the Championship trophy, before the game. It wasn't the best game. I think we finished 0-0 and we were lucky to get that, actually. Carlisle got relegated. I remember that game because of the atmosphere. You know, when you go there before the game and you're running round with the League Championship trophy. That was one magic moment.

Stuart Webb: The Leeds matches. I think they've got to be the matches, for League matches. All right, we beat Tottenham five and eight and that. They're one offs, but I think the key matches – when you're looking for those big matches – are when there are crunches going on. They were the days.

Eric Steele: ...We played Huddersfield at home and won 2-0. Arthur Cox ran on and kissed me! That's a one-off, aye. I've got it on video. What a shame we're not doing a video, rather than a book! Yes, Arthur Cox ran on.

Colin Gibson: In the second championship season, Derby and West Ham were vying for position and Derby won a really close game against West Ham by 1-0 and to see the likes of Trevor Brooking playing for West Ham... Terrific players. That was quite a memorable game and there must be lots more along the way.

Graham Richards: In terms of League games, an Easter Saturday game against Leeds United, heading for the first championship, a 2-0 victory. Leeds were the team we had to beat and they were our dreaded enemies and we did beat them that afternoon. Getting promotion, against Leeds United and Plymouth Argyle under Arthur Cox were great occasions. The away win at Millwall, when the car got turned over in the car park, in the Play-off games. Memorable occasions.

Colin Gibson: The FA Cup quarter-final game, when Derby brushed Newcastle aside 4-2. Derby were terrific that day. Going to Wembley to see them play in the Charity Shield, Charlie George's debut. I suppose the games I'm picking out are all from the Seventies because I was young. I was at an impressionable age and here you have your club winning the championship twice in four seasons, seeing off the likes of Liverpool, seeing off the likes of Arsenal, the likes of Man United. It was terrific.

That Baseball Ground Magic

Ted McMinn: The one that really hurt me was Blackburn. That really hurt me, when we were 2-0 up after five minutes in the Play-offs and still lost. It was the season Blackburn went up. I think Speedie dived for a penalty against Leicester, when they won the play-off Final. Biggest disappointment that was, certainly because I was captain in that run-in and being 2-0 up and then we came to the Baseball Ground and beat them 2-1 and Gabbi missed a sitter with a couple of minutes to go. Just had to lob the 'keeper, and he went too high.

Graham Richards: In terms of Cup-ties, some great ones with Manchester United. Some good Cup wins, especially against Norwich, when we were doing badly under Peter Taylor and we went on to play Plymouth – and not beat them in the sixth round. Perhaps the best, the most exciting, was more recently, drawing 3-3 with Leeds United on the first day back in the top flight, in the Premiership. A very exciting occasion.

Eric Steele: Other great games, the 11th away win, when we went to Sheffield United. It was a good game. They had Peter Withe, experienced. We had to weather the storm a little bit. We defended a corner and I'll always remember Phil Gee streaking away and he put it through Burridge's legs. Again, the sun was shining...and our fans that day, well I'll always remember it, unbelievable. We stopped at a local hotel on the way back and Stuart Webb had arranged champagne because it was the 11th win, equalling the record. Great days.

Keith Loring: Making Jim Smith the manager of this club was obviously the most significant thing in this current period in our history. And the decision to move to Pride Park. But I believe that the job that we did off the field in the week up to the Crystal Palace match also played a part in our history. We went 1-0 up in eight minutes. We took the nervousness out of the situation. Of course, the team won the game, nothing to do with the administration, but I'll tell you something. Marco Gabbiadini came up to me at midnight that night and said: "Keith, I know you had a lot to do with what happened today. I just want you to know that the players appreciate it." Now that's end of story as far as I'm concerned because if a player says it, you can't ask for more than that. I'll tell you this, there was a great atmosphere that day and if I was a Crystal Palace player that day I'd have thought: "Bloody hell, I'm not sure about this." What was obvious was that if we won that match, it didn't matter what happened against Birmingham. It didn't matter what happened against West Brom. The job's done. So that was very significant, too.

Jim Smith: The Crystal Palace game, obviously. The drama of it. Not the game as such. When we beat Forest for the first time in nine years, my daughter – she sat with the fans – came in the office afterwards: "What a great game." I said: "Great game? It was crap." I said: "I expected that, to some degree." "No," she said, "I mean the atmosphere. Everybody was up for it and enjoying it and having a laugh." You know, people see things differently, but the Crystal Palace game, because of what it meant to everybody and to ourselves, obviously that game was memorable.

Jim Fearn: I suppose it would have to be the Crystal Palace game, when we got promotion. Nothing was really looking particularly good at the start of that season, as you know. We started with ten points from ten games, I think. Then we went on this incredible run and, suddenly, we're almost promoted. Had a bit of a blip. It got to the Crystal Palace game. We did quite a lot of building up towards that game and the fans responded tremendously. People talk about the Baseball Ground atmosphere and they compare it now with Pride Park. I don't think they quite remember that in the latter days of the Baseball Ground, there was no real atmosphere. We were down to 18,500, all seated. They remember 42,000 against Tottenham in 1969. Of course they do, and they remember the Pop side, but it's not really a like-for-like comparison. That's the point I'm making, but when we got to the Palace game and Sturridge scored within the first few minutes, we were on the way. A guy called Brown, was it? He equalised for Palace.

Keith Loring: It has got to be Crystal Palace which was a very big game for us. There is nothing more important than what we did that day...It was like a script wasn't it? It was quite funny in that I was sitting in the ground on the Saturday and they were taking these corners and we never scored a goal from them. It was a lovely sunny day and they were taking the corners, using the Baseball Ground, the day before a game. It was all very relaxed. I knew, we had done our bit and I knew the town was 'up for the game'. It was the anticipation. How many times in football have you had the anticipation, without the bit that goes with it? That was a 'bit moment'. Crystal Palace.

Jim Fearn: I was in a weird position. I was down on the touchline because there was a lot of television there. It was a 'live' game and I needed to be there to watch what was going on. But just after the start of the second half, I couldn't watch any more. I went to my little hole, as it was at the Baseball Ground, my office. I watched the game on television there because I felt somehow detached and it wasn't quite such a pressurised situation. Because of that, I always visualise Robbie van der Laan's goal as being at the other end from the end he scored. For some reason, I've got it down at the Normanton End, but it was the Ossie End. When he scored, I was alone in my office, just jumping up and down and thinking: "Wonderful. I can now go and watch the last little bit." I had to get away.

Jim Smith: The two other games were both away. Birmingham City, for it told us we'd a chance to go all the way, and Sheffield Wednesday. 5-2 at Sheffield Wednesday. What threw us a bit at that game was that Cloughie was playing and Carbone and Di Canio. We thought Cloughie was going to play 'there' and them two 'there'; but he was 'there', and them two were 'there' – and they were running all over the place. I thought: "What are we to do here?" Anyway, we got Jacob Laursen sorted out quick – and once we started to play, that was it. We got a lucky goal. I say lucky, but Jacob whacked it and we went on to win...Some of the football we've played at Pride Park has been outstanding. Perhaps we didn't get enough credit for it because we didn't score enough goals. For instance, when we beat Sheffield Wednesday 3-0 here, that was outstanding. It could have been ten. I suppose away results always stand in you mind, but the Birmingham one, for the significance and I think the Sheffield Wednesday one. It gave us the belief that we could go away – and win.

Steve Powell: All matches, in a sense, are memorable because I was just happy to have been involved as a professional footballer. Obviously the game against Liverpool that finally decided the fate of the championship was memorable. The semi-final, when we lost to Man United, was memorable too, from a different point of view. The games in the European Cup. They were all special games, so they were all good memories, even when we lost. Just playing football is a good memory.

Difficult Opponents

EVERY footballer can nominate at least one opponent who always gave him trouble, whether it was a full-back with a biting tackle, a centre-half 'who never gave you a sniff' or a centre-forward who always proved a real handful. There are others who were just a joy to watch playing. Here are a few...

Ted McMinn: Stuart Pearce. Only because the first five minutes, he'd be booked for tackling anything above the knee, but he'd stand over you and always tell you that he was 'going to come back'. So when you did get the ball, you always thought he was right up your back – and he wasn't. Then, when you didn't think he was – he was!

Ron Webster: The most difficult was Tommy Hutchinson from Coventry City. His end product was nil, but he was the hardest player. He'd want to beat you five times, if he could. The end product was nothing, but he caused me as many problems as any winger throughout my career. He had long legs and he'd beat you and then want to beat you again and beat you again and in the end you'd get one in, eventually. You always thought you were going to get it, but you didn't. I always liked to play against wingers. I always felt awkward if I didn't have a winger. I felt I'd rather play against a winger than not.

Ted McMinn: Pearcey was probably the only one I ever feared. Not so much feared before a game, but the gaffer always used to tell me: "By the way, you're playing against him." I always tried to go on the left wing then, but when I went on the left wing, Arthur used to see me: "You're on the wrong wing, Ted. I told you, you're on the right wing." I used to say: "Pearce is left-back, gaffer, can I go on the left wing and then I'll switch and go on the right wing?"

Ray Young: The player, to me, who was probably the most outstanding was Johnny Haynes. As a passer of the ball, almost perfect. Centre-forwards? I played against John Charles, when he came back from Italy. Probably a little bit past his best, but he was still a useful player. They used to have one at Fulham, Bedford Jezzard, and I thought he was a great player. He was one I had a little bit of a problem with. I played with David Dunmore in the Forces. Yes, good player David Dunmore. Good close control. One of the best half-backs was Duncan Edwards. He was superb.

Ian Buxton: George Curtis at Coventry is the one I remember. He was a hard man, but we got on fine together. They got promotion, promotion, promotion, so we played against them in the Second Division, on their way up. They came up Fourth, to Third, to Second, I think. We were the first team to beat them in 1964-65. We beat them at Derby and went to Coventry the following Wednesday and beat them again. Twice. It was the first time they'd been beaten and lost two matches for a long time. I was playing against Curtis. He was a strong man. Another one with big thighs.

Dave Mackay: The best player? I could name about ten I suppose. No, I never played against Pelé. I was lucky in one way, I suppose. Eusebio was a brilliant player. Johnny Haynes. He played for Fulham. He's forgotten about a bit because he only played for one club. Me, I've got chances that people will remember me because I played in Edinburgh and in London and played in Derby. If I'd been Johnny Haynes, I'd have loved to have moved somewhere else because I'd be looking to win something – and at Fulham, he wasn't going to be winning anything. But he gave us a hard time in international games. At Fulham he didn't give me a hard time, but in internationals, oh yes. He was a brilliant player. Denis Law, Jimmy Greaves. I played with and against them. Great.

Bobby Davison: I always enjoyed playing against Kenny Burns. I really enjoyed it because you knew what you were going to get from him. You knew he was going to kick you, but Kenny wasn't the most mobile, so he was kicking and I was chasing and he had to catch me. Difficult opponents? When myself and Kevin Wilson played against Ipswich in the Cup, we played against Osman and Butcher. We both played well and on the back of that, Kevin got himself a move to Ipswich. The most difficult opponent I came across was Chris Nicholl. I think Chris played for Grimsby before he moved on. Very difficult. Strong, knew the game.

Steve Powell: At that level most opponents are difficult, but funnily enough we were talking not so long ago and one of the biggest problems, the one I had most problem with, was a guy called Wyn Davies – and not even when he was playing at the highest level. It was a pre-season friendly and he was playing for Bangor, I think it was, in Wales. We were just playing pre-season, but in 90 minutes I don't think I got one decent header. I was playing centre-half and he was centre-forward and I didn't get one ball cleanly in 90 minutes. Every time the ball came up, he shoved his head in your face or something, so you couldn't get a clean header and he was an absolute nightmare to play against. Yes, Wyn Davies wasn't the most skilful player on the ground, but in the air, he was an absolute nightmare to play against.

Ian Buxton: You can name people at cricket better, just from the facts and figures and the time in which they got them and the style, whatever. Football's more difficult. I played Second Division, Third and Fourth Division. Mainly Second Division, so I didn't play against the greats, except when we played Manchester United in the Cup. Bobby Charlton had a magnificent match that day. He was a wonderful player. Law scored a couple. Probably tapped them in from four yards, but that's what he did, didn't he? That's what good goalscorers do. Obviously that was a highlight. I played against Liverpool and they were a good team, as well. No, I think Bobby Charlton was the best. He had the best match – in any match I've played – of any player, which wouldn't be a surprise when you think about it. He was a cracking player.

Steve Powell: As regards the top level, when we were playing in the First Division, I remember playing against George Best a couple of times and he was tremendous. He was almost impossible to stop. Most players, as you know, need to get up close to go by you, but he could beat you from three or four yards away – and you couldn't do anything about it.

Roy McFarland: George Best. He was the best. Most talented, most gifted, most balanced, change of direction. The thing you think of, as a defender, is that, if somebody beats you, can you get back at them. With Bestie, you never got chance to get back at him. Sadly, in his latter years, I can remember playing at Old Trafford and Bestie went across me, around the halfway line, went forward but across me and, sadly, I was able to catch him. I missed the ball, but I caught him and gave him a good crack and he got up and was aggressive, but I thought: "George, two years ago I couldn't have caught you. You would have been away from me." I would have had to make a short cut, in a sense, back to the 18-yard box or back to the goal, whereas I just chased him. Chased him and I got near him and he wouldn't release the ball and, like I say, I caught him a good one and that let me know then that maybe George was slowing down and that the problems he was going to have off the field were starting to happen.

Eric Steele: Best 'keeper? Gordon Banks. And I worked with Peter Shilton. Admired Shilts greatly. Admired Ray Clemence, in his day. Jimmy Rimmer, in his day. I grew up watching Lev Yashin in the 1966 World Cup at Roker Park. I was absolutely in awe. My mum says my mouth was open for 90 minutes because he dressed all in black, but Banks, for me, was the all-time best. I remember meeting him in Tunisia, when I was with Peterborough and we played an Under-21 tournament out there. Just to meet him and see the frame he had. When you watch footage of him now, how did he make it look so easy? I tell the 'keepers: "Why did he make it look so easy? He got in line." For a big man he had a natural movement, but he also had great perception of where it would go. He had to work at it. Shilts had to work at it. Clemence was a natural catcher, Jennings was a natural catcher. Banks had to work very hard on the technical side, but what he had was this great temperament.

Paul McGrath: I think one of the most difficult opponents – and I've played with him as well – is Mark Hughes. He's so strong, lot of skill. Mark Hughes has got a hell of a lot going for him. Obviously, Alan Shearer has to be up there as well. If you give him a second, the game can be over. Ian Wright always gave me a difficult time. Each in their own way had their own style. Kerry Dixon was another who always gave me trouble. My strength was heading the ball and he used to annoy me. Used to glance it on. Many people are surprised when I nominate him.

Jim Smith: My favourite player was Albert Quixall. He wasn't much older than me but I used to watch Sheffield Wednesday and I just loved how he played. Blond hair, a tremendous passer. First time, like Alan Ball. Then there was Joe Shaw, at Sheffield United, who was, what – 5ft 8ins? He was an unbelievable centre-half. Billy Wright kept him out of the England team but you could argue whether Billy Wright was much better. The only guy I ever saw turn Joe Shaw was Brian Clough and he got a hat-trick for Middlesbrough. I always remember the goals. They were brilliantly struck. Two were volleys. I was about 16. I'd just joined Sheffield United because I didn't watch them usually, I watched Wednesday, and can see two of the goals now, volleys. It was like poetry in motion and they flew into the back of the net and I'd never seen anybody do Joe Shaw, not to the tune of three goals. When you think back, there's so many good players that you saw. Dave Mackay and the Tottenham team, when they had Johnny White, Blanchflower and people like that. Greavesie. To pick just one...well. Three then? Well, Albert Quixall would be one. Tommy Taylor would be another. I'm talking about people who appealed to me. You could argue there'd be better centre-forwards, but players who I'd 'want to be' would be: Duncan Edwards, Tommy Taylor – and Albert Quixall.

Best Derby County player?

Steve Powell: I would say Roy McFarland. Not just because he played for England. He could have played in any position and still played at the highest level.

Graham Richards: Roy McFarland would run very high and Colin Todd not far behind him. Charlie George wasn't at Derby very long, but I think McFarland and Todd were the best players at Derby in my time. Dave Mackay was the man for the moment. Certainly he came in and made a huge difference, and Kevin Hector, although probably not quite as good as the other two. Brilliant player in his own way and such a pity he didn't get more games for England. If I was asked to pick players outside the usual bent, I would probably go for Colin

Boulton, in goal. Much underrated, brilliant 'keeper, undistinguished career apart from the championship years, but a fine 'keeper.

Mick Hopkinson: The best player? The best player or the most influential player? For me, this is a very hard question but I wouldn't go much further than Dave Mackay. Now remember, I saw Dave at the back end of his career. What would he have been like when he was 25? When he came to Derby he was 34, but for everything – I'm talking about, leadership, drive, personality, skill – there were not many better players than Dave Mackay. Now he sticks out in my mind. We all know about Roy McFarland. He was going to be a terrific player as soon as he came to Derby.

Michael Dunford: The best player or my favourite player? The best player? I'd have to say McFarland, closely followed by Charlie George. I thought Charlie George was an underrated player. Super person as well. Overall, though, I'd have to say Roy McFarland. My favourite player was, of course, Kevin Hector, but I'd have to say, as a complete footballer, Roy. He could have played in most positions. He wasn't the fastest player and I think today, more than ever, you need to be fast. You need to have speed, but the way he played the ball. He was comfortable on the ball, he was aggressive, he'd kick his grandma and when you speak to other players – and they're the best judges – very few vote against Roy McFarland.

Gerald Mortimer: Favourite Derby player? That's awfully hard isn't it? I can't really consider Raich Carter and Peter Doherty on the grounds that I only saw them as a schoolboy, although I was rather pleased once, when I tested out my schoolboy impressions of them on Tim Ward and he thought that they were about right. Raich continued to impress me later. I met him coming to a launch of a book that Anton Rippon did. I think it was probably Breedon's first publication. They had a launch at the Baseball Ground and old George Thornewell was still alive and he came. You went into that room there, which was entirely dominated by Raich – and he didn't move. Everybody went to talk to Raich, and Raich didn't go to talk to anyone else, and I thought: "Yes. I guess that fits in with everything."

Willie Carlin: The best player I ever played with was Roy McFarland. He was fantastic.

Gerald Mortimer: I think the best single season I've ever seen from a Derby player was Colin Todd in 1974-75, when Roy McFarland was injured for most of the season and Peter Daniel played next to him and did a splendid job, but Toddy was as near to flawless that year as ever I'm likely to see. He just made the game so simple in that he took the ball off opposing players and gave it to one of his own players and that was it. I think also, for a season when he first came, Charlie George was a bit special. In fact he was very special. I think if he hadn't have cracked his collar bone against Stoke, they might have won one thing – League or Cup – or even two things, I don't know. Perhaps that's pitching it a bit high.

Alan Hinton: Oh, I think McFarland was the best player. I mean, he had everything. He had time on the ball, he had elegance, he could score a goal, he could defend a goal. His preparation for the games was like he was going to war. The tragedy was he had so many serious injuries towards the end of his days, but he was fantastic. He did his Achilles tendon playing for England. He didn't do it for Derby, he did it for England and then many times he played with a serious groin injury. Many times, he told me, he would start to walk down to the boss's office to say: "I can't play tomorrow." But he'd turn back – and play. He played in pain, but he was a great winner.

Stuart Webb: Best player? Phew! That's a tough one. There's so many. Obviously, the Mackay era. McFarland, the Colin Todds. They were really class acts. Midfield you can go through, so many talented players, but I think you've got to go to that team of Brian's or Dave's. To me, that's the era. The strikers? No, I think the defenders. I think the three I've mentioned, Dave Mackay, Roy McFarland and Colin Todd, they were the class acts, for me. All had different talents. I liked Toddy, to be honest, the way he had that extra gear.

Gerald Mortimer: I remember when Dave was on the way to sign Charlie George and I thought: "Hmm. Interesting signing that." And then the immediate, selfish thought: "I don't think I'll get on with Charlie George." In fact, I never had a cross word with him, in either of his two spells at Derby. I thought he was absolutely wonderful. He was very funny and I find it significant now that if he ever comes back to present anything and be introduced, he brings the roof off every time. People love Charlie, at Derby.

Phil Waller: Roy McFarland. Best all-round player. I mean, Kevin was a very good forward player, but all-round player and commitment, that sort of thing, McFarland. He wasn't as one sided as people thought he was. He could play on his right side, he just didn't. He was different class to Toddy, I think. Toddy had such pace he could get away with things, but over a period of time, no. Look at Roy's goalscoring record. That's another thing. He got as many as some forward players, didn't he?

Gerald Mortimer: I've got to mention Roy in all this because I thought over a long spell of time, particularly before his Achilles injury, he was a magnificent player. You've got to mention Kevin Hector. Again, consistency over a very long period and I'm still waiting to see Kevin off balance or find a picture of Kevin off balance. I think those early Seventies sides, I got to know them probably better than any others and some of them have been, well I would regard them as friends for a long time. Very fond of John O'Hare. I think he did a wonderful job for Derby County, absolutely wonderful. One player whose style appealed to me hugely was David Nish because I just think he treated the ball like a valuable china cup. He had a beautiful silky touch and yet I remember when he first signed from Leicester City he could hardly get a kick for about two months. He had an absolute nightmare to start with, but he came through to be, I thought, a major, major player.

Graham Richards: John Gregory was a very useful player at Derby County. And I liked Bobby Davison and David Swindlehurst. Bobby needs no more testament from me. He's a proven goalscorer and a very reliable player, but Swindlehurst hit some marvellous goals at Derby and I think he was a player who could have reached the very top of the game. Intelligent, articulate, and despite his clear strength, he was also very unorthodox and if you watched him week by week, as I did for years, I think you'd have a very high opinion of David Swindlehurst. Not one of the great players, but certainly a Derby County player of significance.

Gerald Mortimer: Of the interim ones, I would put Bobby Davison very high. I think he brought a lot of excitement and colour to the place, as indeed did Dean Saunders in a comparatively brief spell.

Jim Smith: Coming along here, to Derby, Igor obviously, was tremendous, but Asanovic came in and I think, all right, we only got half a season out of him really or just over half a season, but it was a vital half a season because he lifted our profile and our expectations of play to the level that it had to be. Baiano and Eranio, again, took that on. What is quite amazing is what we did in a short time here – Igor, Asanovic and the two other lads. I could put Robbie van der Laan in there also, as a skipper in the First Division days. He was very instrumental in what we've achieved.

Jim Fearn: Now, I love to just listen to the older players talk about their favourites. John

O'Hare for instance. Alan Hinton was down here the other week at Pride Park and we interviewed him for the cable show. He said the fans didn't appreciate John O'Hare, but, as a player, you could play the ball into him any which way and he'd control it, make it look easy, keep the ball, retain possession and you were on your way. As a fan, you don't particularly appreciate players like that. Archie Gemmill will also talk about John McGovern, another player who the fans didn't appreciate while he was here.

Brian Flint: Well, we've often said: "Who's the best five players?" Generally, it's Mackay, McFarland, Kevin Hector, Colin Todd and Charlie George, too. Less of him because we didn't see him for so long. McFarland was something we'd not seen, as young ones. Of course, we were told he wasn't as good as what had been seen before, your Leon Leutys and Jack Barkers. Never as good as that, but that was not fair. He was the best we'd seen – and I've seen nothing as good since!

Dave Mackay: The best player? McFarland was, obviously.

Moving to Pride Park

IT'S always easier with hindsight, but very few people would say that the move to Pride Park Stadium hasn't been a resounding success. Of course, they say that now, but when the decision was taken to move from the beloved Baseball Ground, to what was simply a piece of waste ground, many people had mixed feelings.

Yes, a risk it certainly was – and on many levels. Financial, emotional and, not least, on a playing level. Few promoted clubs have survived in the Premiership and for Derby County, in that first season played at the Baseball Ground, it was a fairly close-run thing. A few hearts were pounding, especially of those who had taken the decision to build Pride Park Stadium when Derby County were positioned less than halfway up the First Division. Furthermore, wasn't the Baseball Ground unique? Would the move to a new stadium and new surroundings have a detrimental effect on winning home matches, the key to survival in the Premiership? Could it be paid for?

Roy Christian: I think on balance I was in favour of moving. I may say now, I'm very, very pleased we did. It was almost 50-50 with me for a long time, but I came to the conclusion that they couldn't develop the Baseball Ground very much. There wasn't enough parking for one thing, not that there's a great deal more at Pride Park, but it's a bit better, with a bit more sense of space. It's a very good ground, and they say it's the best ground in the country for the disabled.

Graham Sellors: Well, I was against it. I don't have an argument when the people who live near the Baseball Ground objected to it going up another tier or half a tier or something like that. If I'd have lived there, I might have not wanted it to be any higher, but I was against the move. I thought they should have tried to develop the Baseball Ground and kept it where it was because of history and tradition, and because all those years ago, when I was seven or eight, I'd walked down those streets with family, and I'd taken our John and we'd walked down those streets to the same ground. In a funny way there is a sort of appropriateness to it, in that the Baseball Ground was built in an area of terraced housing, next to heavy industry, and the money that football clubs had in those days would have come from people who came out of housing like that and who walked down streets like that, in their thousands, to football matches. Now, it is built in the middle of a business park, and the money that is keeping football afloat is coming from businesses, far more than it is coming from people who pay at the turnstiles.

Colin Gibson: Initially, no I wasn't in favour of moving. I thought that you couldn't leave somewhere like the Baseball Ground. It's steeped in tradition. Derby County and the Baseball

Ground – you couldn't mention one without the other. I thought their original plan to rebuild the Baseball Ground was a good idea, but then, when you thought it through – that you'd have been playing in the Premiership, initially, with a part-open ground, which could work against you, and that a rebuilt Baseball Ground wasn't going to be like the Baseball Ground as we remembered it – you think: "No, perhaps they've got to move to a new stadium." Then, you think: "Well, okay, we've seen Middlesbrough's stadium, which is what it's going to be based on. It's okay. It's nothing special. Let's hope that Derby do learn from the mistakes that Middlesbrough made and that they build a great stadium." Fortunately, they did.

Peter Gadsby: There's nothing like walking to the game and I still miss it. I enjoy the facilities of the directors' box and, recently, I was down at Swansea and remember saying to somebody: "I don't want to go back to this." With all due respect to Swansea, it was a culture shock, sitting in the front of the directors' box, getting wet, which shouldn't happen in the directors' box. The guest room was no bigger than a shoe box. You know, it made us realise how far we've come.

Michael Gretton: Did I want to move? Not really because the atmosphere was absolutely tremendous, and as a very famous manager said: "It is worth a goal start." Now, having seen Pride Park and after working there for three years, we realise why we had to move. It is mind-blowing when you consider what we used to work in and what we work in now. Everyone who comes from the press side or whatever side, say it's a vast improvement.

Graham Richards: Dubious? I wasn't dubious at all. I was against it. I didn't sit on the fence. I was against it – and I was wrong, no doubt about that. I never thought they'd get Pride Park so good. I thought it'd be a bit of a mix-up, that the money would run out. It was a brave decision because it was saved, in a sense, by promotion. Without promotion, it might not have turned out so well. But I do believe that fortune favours the brave, and if people make a bold decision and back it up, it is often the right one and palpably so later in life, and I think that was one of them. I think Peter Gadsby's got an enormous amount of credit due to him on that one, for his vision, and the entire board aren't far behind, and Lionel, whose money was very much involved. They made the right decision.

Steve Powell: At the time there was a lot of almost fear about it because there was a lot of nostalgia about the Baseball Ground and it was a very good place to go as regards atmosphere. But I think most people now would say that the move was a good one. Certainly from an access point of view – and it's a fabulous stadium. I don't think there's quite the atmosphere they used to get at the Baseball Ground, but apart from that, I have no qualms about things. I think it's a really good move.

Gerald Mortimer: I had mixed feelings. You're deserting an old home and that's always a traumatic thing. I think, possibly, the thing that said: "It is a good idea," was the fact that even had they stayed at the Baseball Ground, it wouldn't have been the same Baseball Ground. They would have to have altered three sides and then, probably, the fourth side would have looked very tatty. So, although the site would have been the same, it wouldn't have been the same ground. Now, that's worked very well for some people. If you look at Molineux now, for instance, I think they can still identify that as their home, although it's entirely different. Molineux in its pomp with Stan Cullis there, I thought was a wonderful ground to go to, and in their lean years, it became an absolutely appalling place.

Stuart Webb: Mixed emotions, yes, but I think we had to move, there's no doubt at all. It was a massive decision because we could only develop the Baseball Ground under restrictive conditions, so it was never going to be right. So you always felt you might be spending money just to be mid-table, as far as stadiums were concerned. Always looking to improve it. It was always a tight environment; houses back-to-back; a classic football stadium like the Evertons, the Liverpools. So you were spending money not on a greenfield site, but on just improving the stadium because you had to do under the Taylor Report.

Gerald Mortimer: Derby were in trouble, really, with the fire department, safety and so on. Although, I'd be interested to know how many millions of cigarettes had been trodden out on those wooden stands without a fire. Without wishing in any way to diminish the Valley Parade episode, we survived a long time without too many fires at football grounds. I can only think of about three in my lifetime and before Bradford City, only one of those, at Forest, was when there was a game in progress. Nobody was too sure – but then they got the right deal.

Graham Richards: They saw more than perhaps we did, that football was into a new era, and that which we love – terraces and male audiences and strong tradition and local loyalties – are on the back foot. That commercialism and family attendance and television and comfort, are on the front foot. Pride Park has been an enormous success. I think, perhaps, the most successful of all the new grounds. Not the biggest, not the most beautiful, but I think overall, and taking everything into account, the most successful of the new grounds.

Keith Loring: Brilliant decision, but I have to say, I followed it, I didn't make it. I think Peter Gadsby has to take a lot of credit for it. It was the end of a string of coincidences. The first coincidence was that Stuart Webb normally attended most of the Football League Management meetings and on this occasion – it was in December 1995 – Peter came because Stuart couldn't go. It was one of those meetings that dragged on, where we had to go out of the room while the committee discussed this, and there was all this talking and all this business, and unbeknown to me, Peter was talking, and he's come back, and the question in his head is – and I'm not being nasty to the clubs – "How are clubs like Reading and Oxford building new stadiums? Where are they getting the money from?" He got one or two people to investigate and found, as sometimes happens, that the tide in the city had changed and they were quite into lending money to build, whether it be for football clubs or not. And, of course, football was going through a better time, with the Premier League building a better image.

Gerald Mortimer: It was a brave decision. They were still in the First Division, as it's called now – it's the Second Division really – and they were handily-placed, but nobody was guaranteeing anything. You can't guarantee anything. It could have bounced back on them nastily. Yes, it was a very brave decision, and I think the current board, since Lionel became chairman, have got a lot of things right.

Jim Fearn: It had to happen didn't it? The fans, to be fair to them, recognised that. There was no big protest movement about leaving the Baseball Ground. We all feel very sentimental about it, no one more so than the chairman, but he realised. He's made the move now and you look on the Baseball Ground and you think: "It was nice, good memories." Good memories, but my goodness, when you actually go back for a reserve-team game it brings it home to the difference as to what we have here and what we had there.

Ray Young: When I went out on to Pride Park before the Sampdoria game and just put my hand on the turf and felt the pitch, I thought it was like Astroturf. There were no gaps in it. It was superb. I thought "Well, if you can't play football on this..." Also, from being a centre-half on there, if I hit a ball to left or right, there was plenty of space. At the Baseball Ground, if you weren't spot on it would be out-of-play. At Pride Park you can hit a ball and have plenty of room.

Peter Gadsby: When we'd gone through the scenario of Stadivarios and that wasn't on, Lionel had taken control. And there came a point where with the Taylor Report, we'd already had one or two years and we'd expended £360,000 in professional fees – which was when Lionel checked the books and found out – which was a huge amount of money gone out in this abortive scheme. The thing that broke it really was that. Stadivarios was telling everybody what it could do and what was going to happen. Anyway, there was a fee required – I can't recall what it was exactly, £8,000 or £18,000, but it wasn't a lot of money – to go further with the scheme and we suggested that Stadivarios should put up half of the money, but they wouldn't or couldn't. Talk about no cloth on the back. I think that really brought not only me, but a few people, to realise that here was a club that was in dreamland.

John O'Hare: I think it's a magnificent place. I think it's the best thing they've ever done, really. They had to move, and I know lots of people who used to go ten years, 12 years ago and now they've moved to Pride Park they've got season tickets and go again. Getting in and out isn't the best, though.

Peter Gadsby: We then got the Taylor Report and that was giving us trouble. I think we were due to go down to 12,000. We were on 16,000 or 18,000 and were due to go to 12,000. There was concern about the future; everybody was wondering. Jim was wanting to know what was going on, so based on what we had – I think we were about 14th then in the First Division – we decided to look at putting a new stand in. That was about £8-10 million. There was an awful problem with planning. We'd actually let the contract to Taylor Woodrow. We'd actually signed the contract, and I think they'd almost started to mark out and so on, but at least we thought we'd made a decision; we'd actually got something moving. We'd have gone up to 24,000 and, okay, there'd have been problems, but at least there was progress. Yes, it would have been like Leicester City's ground. We'd have had to bring the stand back and obviously car parking was a problem, but we had some contingency plans.

Ray Young: Oh yes. You've got to move with the times, haven't you? What could they have done with the pitch? It was four feet lower than the drainage outside at the Baseball Ground. You could see why they had the problems in draining it.

Peter Gadsby: It happened that with the Millennium bid for the Dome, Derby was one of three sites on the short list, and Derby had made a very spirited attempt to get it. They'd spent quite well, and local business people like myself had supported it, and they'd closed down any deal on Pride Park. Pride Park was not for sale at that point. It was thought: "We're getting on with the Millennium bid and that's it." The roads had been put in. I think I was then a board director with the Department of Trade and Industry and involved at that level, and I happened to get wind of the fact that it was going to go to London – to some extent that always was assumed, but we didn't know for sure until it was agreed – and I remember driving round the Baseball Ground and then I drove round Pride Park and then I, sort of, got a feeling of where some clubs were going, and there was some talk about what other clubs were looking at. And in development you get the magazines and feel for which way, after a time, things were going, and something told me it wasn't right. So I went to Pride Park, had a drive round, and I just thought: "It isn't right. We should be here."

Mick Hopkinson: Oh, brilliant. Well, there was nothing left at the Baseball Ground was there? Except it was a lovely tight ground, similar to Arsenal and places, and it always created a nice atmosphere. I think that's why people were a bit reluctant to leave the Baseball Ground because they didn't think you could create the same atmosphere at Pride Park, but you can.

Peter Gadsby: Arthur Burns was the project manager with me. Has been all the way. He's a retired engineer and he was supervising the contract with Taylor Woodrow. I think it was 6 January – we've always a slow start in this industry – and I sat him down at ten o'clock and I said: "Arthur, I think we should move. I think we should make the move." And he said: "Well, that's a big decision." I asked him what the contractual arrangements were, how we would stop it. Then I drove up to see Lionel, sat down, explained and his words were: "Well, you always knew I wanted to move." He backed me 100 per cent, and we rang the other directors and they said: "Well, if that is possible." John Kirkland knew a bit about what was going on because he's in the construction business.

Stuart Webb: We knew what we had to do, and then the opportunity of Pride Park came up. Peter Gadsby did an excellent job in that, put it to the board and it was a major decision. Not only were we in the First Division with no guarantee of promotion, but you were spending an awful lot of money in gambling the future of the club. Yes, they were difficult times and the board were, fortunately, as one, and were able to move it forward.

Peter Gadsby: Then we rang Ray Cowlishaw and the leader of the Council; then it was Bob Laxton, who is now the MP, and we went to see them. They were very, very guarded because they'd had a tortuous route before, where it was on and then off. They gave us five weeks. They said: "In principle, this bit is available." I think my view was: "Look, the Millennium thing's not coming." They said: "We know that now." So I said: "Why not have the next best thing – which will be the stadium?"

Keith Loring: The next thing we heard was that Pride Park was not going to get the Millennium site, and the combination of Peter Gadsby being in the building trade and having a couple of weeks off over Christmas, as they do, and so having another look at Pride Park, those three things came together, and then Peter spoke to the board and said: "I know you'll think I'm probably crazy, but..." I was very uneasy about the Baseball Ground because, although we had no other choice at the time, there were three things that bothered me: the residents had asked us to clip space off the stands, so we weren't building what I wanted; we were going to be knocking stands down for the next three or four years, so we were going to be playing with one end down; and we would only have finished up with 22,000-23,000 and therefore we'd have built something that was out-of-date before we started. That's hindsight. It's not being clever. We had no other choice at the time. At the end of the meeting, Peter said: "What are you doing?...Well, you're not. Clear your diary. We're off." Next minute I'm in the car to Middlesbrough.

Jim Smith: They didn't have to sell me Derby County, but one of the things that they showed me were drawings of the new stand, and the next new stand, and the next new stand, which actually, wouldn't have been built today on the plans. It was about a five-year thing. Then, suddenly, this opportunity came to come to Pride Park and, like you say, very bravely, the board seized on that opportunity, cancelled the rebuilding and that was also a very important decision. Not only an important decision, but we'd have been going for promotion on a building site with Portacabins because it was due to be knocked down that season. It's so difficult to play in those conditions and we'd also have lost spectators. We were only ever getting 17,000, and so the actual building of the new stadium, I think, helped us to gain promotion. The fact that we had one year at the Baseball Ground in the Premier League, I'm convinced also helped us to stay up in the first year, when many clubs who get promotion find it very difficult.

Stuart Webb: Having made that decision, then the thing was, were we going to get promotion? It's all right having this wonderful new stadium, but had we missed out with the Play-offs and missed out with promotion, it would have been disappointing for the fans, and that would have been a difficult time. But no, it all went well and according to plan. They were difficult times because key decisions had to be taken about the future of the club.

Ray Young: Let's face it, I'm lucky. I've got a car parking pass. The only thing that you can say is it's not like me going to the Baseball Ground. I would leave home at, say, twenty past two or probably later, half-past two. Park. Walk down and watch the game and I'd be back home for five o'clock. Now, I'm leaving home at twenty to two and I'm getting home at seven o'clock or something. That's the difference. I think it's superb, though, the view and everything.

Peter Gadsby: We went through some pretty detailed negotiations. The Council were very good; they were trying very hard. We had to use regeneration people, but fortunately, being in the business, I was able to use the people we employed to come in on a 'no way, no pay' basis – confidentially – to see what we could do. It's interesting, when people talk about which way the stadium is positioned. It's the only way it could be because of restraints caused by gas pipes and such things.

Roy Christian: I think it's got its own atmosphere. Not quite as intimate as the Baseball Ground, but it's a different atmosphere. I think it's developing its own. I feel quite comfortable there and I shudder at the thought of the Baseball Ground now, although I enjoyed it at the time, but I think it would have been a mistake to try to patch it up, rather than move to Pride Park.

Colin Gibson: No. The atmosphere will not be like the Baseball Ground, but then the atmosphere at the Baseball Ground, in the latter years, wasn't as good because people were sat down and there were only 17,000 people there. When you talk about the Baseball Ground atmosphere, you're talking about when there were 30,000 people there, perhaps 20,000-odd people there, but when there were people standing up, and when you stand up you tend to move about, and when you move about you tend to make noise. Whereas when you're sat down, you relax, and if the football is perhaps not quite right on the pitch, you relax even more. So I think, if it's going to be as good, you need to get a set of circumstances that can generate the atmosphere and get it going. It can be – the second half against Middlesbrough two years ago was fantastic, in adversity: "We're going to show this clown of a referee, who's sent Paulo Wanchope off, that's not going to stop us." And that was fairytale stuff, the way that Derby came back. They went behind, came back, won the game, and the stadium was absolutely electric that afternoon. Terrific stuff, but it won't be like the Baseball Ground.

Peter Gadsby: We entered into the agreement, and it's always interesting these things – the business plan and things we had to have. "Yes, we have a business plan." "Can we see it?" "Yes, here it is." "Does it work?" "Yes, it does." "Well, we want to see it again." And we said: "Are you backing us or not because, you know, the business plan can be anything?" I remember we pressed the button and we were still short. Sometimes I say to people, when they come to see me about business and things: "If you're waiting for everything to be right, you'll never do it. You'll never do it."

Charlie George: Yes, I'm always made most welcome. It's always nice. I was fortunate to play for two clubs where the supporters really took to me and they appreciated what I tried to do, and I built up a rapport with them. It's nice. Times have moved on up there and they've got a fantastic stadium.

Moving to Pride Park

Peter Newbery: I think it is a magnificent stadium. Absolutely superb and, of course, with the second team and possibly the youth team using the Baseball Ground, then they can preserve the quality of the Pride Park pitch. But it is a magnificent ground. The Baseball Ground was just outdated in every respect really. You can't rely on sentiment. You've got to move with the times. No, I think it's a great ground.

Peter Gadsby: So we set off and utilised the Middlesbrough stadium, their concept. We made 26 changes on it because we could see where we could improve it. We got a cracking price. I still say so now, that it's a wonder it didn't cost £6- £8 million more to build the stadium. We caught the market absolutely right. Again, luck was on our side. We were still in the First Division, remember – only 11th when we started. We hadn't got Premiership football in our minds. With regard to the situation, we'd probably get 20,000 – 24,000. People say now: "Why didn't you do both corners immediately? Why didn't you do this or that?" Lionel, of course, was always ready to do it, but in his own words he'll tell you he sometimes doesn't take on as much detail. But I'm a pretty cautious person, actually, and I felt that we'd have stretched ourselves and, who knows, had we tried to be too clever, it might not have happened. So we didn't do the corners to start with.

Gerald Mortimer: There's no argument at all, no argument at all. I think it's been done very well and I think they've been cute enough to learn from other new stadia and avoid some of the mistakes. It's obviously based around Middlesbrough; same sort of design, same contractors and so on, but it seems to me a lot nicer than the Middlesbrough one.

Keith Loring: I'd done my homework on new stands and I knew what I wanted commercially...One thing I'd been impressed with, having gone to other clubs, was the open-plan concept. That's what we've got...Open-plan gives you a multi-functional use, Monday to Friday, and it just struck me it would be such a shame to build anything that didn't have a multi-functional use. We'd have done it well at the Baseball Ground, but we wouldn't have done it as well as we have done it here, for all the obvious reasons. I mean, it's a bit different driving to Pride Park than it is driving to the old Baseball Ground, when you're talking about people who don't love Derby.

Don Hazledine: Oh wonderful, wonderful. No doubt about it, they did the right thing to move from the Baseball Ground, oh yes. There were a lot of reservations about it, weren't there? I think everyone realises now the advantages, but obviously they've got to get in that top five or six or somewhere. At least the top half because the signs are there – and I go every week – that if the fans get a bit disgruntled, the crowds can soon go down to 18,000. That's one of the dangers.

Frank Upton: I think we have to move on, and I thought with the Baseball Ground, although they did a lot of work to it and I thought it was a homely ground, the biggest problem was around it. I've got a lot of good memories of the Baseball Ground and I always will, but Pride Park's brilliant. I think what Lionel Pickering's done for Derby County is fantastic.

Peter Gadsby: What really made us realise it was going to happen was when we set up these computers with visuals of how the ground would look, and I think we had 86,000 people within a short time. The response, the excitement; it was there. It was something that, in their generation, was going to be built, and they were going to be part of it, and you noticed from the people coming in, it was a different type of person, as well as the ardent supporter. There was the 46-year-old lady, who used to go when Cloughie was there, and said: "I'm coming back now and bringing my son." This was tremendous, and once this got going, it was wonderful.

Keith Loring: The most significant thing, I felt, was the day we played Middlesbrough, when we had the little get-together to open the visitors' centre, and there was one piece of steel up. I know they could see holes going in the ground, but they'd seen that before. We were digging holes at the Baseball Ground. I felt the Derby supporters had heard so much, for so many years. I call it the 'gonna' syndrome – "we're gonna do this, we're gonna do that" – that suddenly there was this piece of steel and they thought: "This stadium's going to happen." I think that was very significant.

Geoff Hazledine: Absolutely wonderful. Breathtaking. It's like going on a trip to the moon, isn't it? Absolutely wonderful. The thing that amazes me about it is, it's showtime. That word sums it up, doesn't it? Like when you say: "A football match – and showtime." It's showtime. Its not like a football match that we knew. The pitch – it's nearly too good to play on! When you used to run out to play on the Baseball Ground...now you look at the lads going out there and you think: "You can't go out there on that wonderful surface with studs on." It's so perfect, isn't it? It must be absolutely wonderful to play on.

Steve Powell: The pitch is immaculate. One of the things that has improved at all clubs in the last few years is the playing surfaces. You never really see a bad pitch, every one's immaculate.

Keith Loring: I've got to tell you now, I asked for it to be put up, that bit of steel. It wasn't due to go up, but if we're going to open the visitors' centre, we'd just got earth there, so I said: "Could we not have something, just so you can actually see the sense of something about to happen?" And the fact that Lionel was saying it meant we'd gone past the doubt and suspicion period anyway. There was an incredible trust in Lionel. So if Lionel said we were building a new stadium, we were building a new stadium. We announced that at the Baseball Ground, but I think that day – the opening of the visitors' centre – was a big, big day, and then it was a roller coaster, wasn't it? You're talking about 250 days from then and I described it as 'the biggest non-moving, ride-in park, anywhere in the world'. We had 75,000 people through the visitors' centre – but that doesn't count the people who just came to look. I just loved driving past, just loved it. Wherever we'd been, Lesley and I – anywhere in the country – we just had to drive back through Pride Park.

Gerald Mortimer: There are a lot of people who are trying to make it a pleasant experience going to the game. On a purely selfish note, the treatment of the media at Pride Park is far better than almost any other Premiership ground, I think.

Bobby Davison: I was invited down for the first game, against Sampdoria. I'd have loved to play there. Yes, I think it's a smashing stadium. I've been down twice now and I think, maybe, they could have made it a little bit bigger. Once they get 40,000, it's up there with the best. Then you could hold semi-finals and that.

Geoff Hazledine: The thing that amazes me about it is the fact that at the Baseball Ground it was a compact little ground and it had a cosy atmosphere. Now you go to Pride Park, which is an entire world apart from the Baseball Ground, but somehow there's still that cosy atmosphere. It's to do with the people you know. All the people who work there, in the restaurants and that, are wonderful.

Peter Gadsby: There were some tricky times when I found it difficult. I recall one when we were sitting in the old Baseball Ground Sportsmen's Club, explaining the concept of how we were going to have a lease to a property company, who, in turn, were going to lease it back to the football club, and – rightly so – there was a lot of suspicion. What we couldn't tell people was that we had to create this lease to prove to our funders that a lease existed that we were the guarantees of, not the football club. The reason this was done was that Middlesbrough had got themselves into some difficulty because they had bought a player, whereas they should have made a payment and, as a result, they said to the contractors: "We can't pay." What our contractors were saying was: "We want you to be ring-fenced, so that you can't go and buy a player..." That's what we had to do, and we had to put some money in and be brave. Lionel was brave, and the directors were brave to do it, I think. We knew it was going to be tricky, but we couldn't say – and this was the crux – we couldn't say: "Here is a lease for 25 years – I think it was 25 years, it might have been longer – with massive rent to pay over, which is really a method of transferring funds, that will be torn up the moment we start the stadium or when we get there because it's a legal document." I could see people looking at us as we were trying to explain it and it was difficult times then, but that's the way we had to do it. That's gone now, the whole thing's gone.

Dave Mackay: This is progress and you've got to progress, simple as that.

Peter Gadsby: We've just reached a stage now when we need – to use a cliché – 'put a foot on the ball'. If we look at the ground, we've gone up to 33,000, haven't we? We've not had many full houses. There was the clamour we should have gone up to 40,000, that we should have put 35,000 on day one. That's all right for a cup match or when we play Manchester United, but if you take an average, we're still around 29,000 aren't we? Lionel's always been of the view that 30,000 is about it, but the reason we were able to build these other corners was, to some extent, more for the corporate side, although we've put more fans in the second one. We made an awful lot of friends at the England Under-21 match.

Roger Davies: You have to move on with the times. The Baseball Ground, you look at it, there's no comparison to this place is there? It's absolutely magnificent. The pitch is out of this world, even at the end of the season. If you can't play on there, you can't play anywhere. It's just a positive step.

Jim Smith: No I don't use the pitch much. Some managers, I know, certainly in the older days, used to go on the pitch regardless, and the poor groundsman used to get stick every Saturday because the pitch wasn't very good. I mean, if we need it we need it, but – and the chairman couldn't believe it at one time – I say: "I want the best playing pitch on a Saturday." You know, rather than doctoring it for other teams, but the biggest and best playing pitch. Obviously we'd have used it a little bit more if we hadn't got the Baseball Ground, that's for sure. I've been at clubs where we've had to train on the ground every day because of the weather, and you're absolutely right. When you walk in on a Saturday, it ain't got the buzz. It's just like going to work on a Friday, on a Thursday, especially late in the season, when you need to freshen everything up, yes very much so.

Alan Hinton: I think it's super. Before it was open, I went on a trip around and later saw Jim Smith, and I said: "Jim, don't go on a trip around the ground and see all the banqueting rooms and private boxes. Don't do it Jim." He said: "Why not?" I said: "It'll scare the hell out of you. It's so impressive. All of a sudden business people are going to be there, who are going to be drinking the best wine and having the best lunches before the game, and then, maybe, they'll become a bit more vocal than they would ordinarily." That increases the pressure.

Peter Gadsby: We've never, ever, touched the football money. The only time the transfer money ever does get touched is if it gets mixed up in wages. If the wage bill goes over, if something happens, then Jim, being the manager he is, will say: "Yes. Fine. That's down to me."

Alan Hinton: Every time I come to Pride Park it's just great. I'm not a part of any of it now, of course, but I'm a fan of Derby County Football Club – and I'm really grateful for that.

The Queen came too ...and the Duke

Lionel Pickering: The Duke was chatting to everybody. He surprised me because although he was two paces behind the Queen, we were having to wait for him because he was getting into conversations with the players and various people. For saying I wouldn't think he's the greatest football fan in the world, he showed a lot of interest. It was quite an interesting experience.

Lionel Pickering: I wasn't really nervous, no. I mean, I can say 'yes' and 'no' to that. One or two friends of mine have met the Queen and they say: "You don't have to worry about it." You say: "Well, what's it going to be like?" And they say: " Oh, she's so easy, she'll put you at your ease. She knows you're going to be nervous. You've got no problem." The other thing was, the Lord Lieutenant said: "Look, you know Lionel, when the Queen comes, you're in charge. She's never been here before. She's never been to the ground. She doesn't know the way through the corridors or the way to the pitch. You've got to actually take control. When you meet the Queen, call her 'Your Majesty' first of all, and then 'maam'." Rhymes with 'spam', apparently. Then say: "I'll show you the way through to the pitch."

Lionel Pickering: Was I nervous? I felt quite happy. I slept quite well the night before, and I was looking forward to it and then, about 15 minutes before the Queen arrived, I was just standing around, talking to people and all of a sudden, my throat went extremely dry, which has never happened to me ever before. I wasn't nervous at all, but something happened and I went so dry, that I nipped through the players' entrance – there's a little canteen there – and had not one, but two cups of tea. That's all. I had tea. Nothing else. It made all the difference and I was okay after that.

Lionel Pickering: It was quite true. The Queen was very pleasant and, obviously, she's done it many times before, and when I was supposed to show her how to pull the cord, to open the curtain for the plaque, I made some little joke: "I suppose you've done this a few times before in your life?" And I think I got the royal stare. I don't know whether she thought I was taking the mickey or not, but I was just meaning that because I had to tell her the cord was hidden behind the curtain...if she just gave it a pull it would open. It just occured to me that she'd done that a few thousand times in the past.

Lionel Pickering: I was extremely proud. It was a proud day for me. It was a proud day for Derby County, and a proud day for Derbyshire, I thought. I think any member of the Royal Family would have been a real bonus. We didn't dream of thinking as high up as that. We might have settled for some, I don't know, second division personality, but thanks to John Bather, the new Lord Lieutenant, he happened to know the Queen was coming to the Midlands and he phoned us up and said: "Well, you've got a new stadium. Will it be ready on 18 July?" We said: " It's not due to be finished until the end of July. Why?" So he said: "Well, would you like the Queen to open it?" We said: "It will be ready for 18 July, don't worry about that!"

Lionel Pickering: I was introduced to the Duke once before. I went down to one of those 'Water Rats' luncheons and somebody, quite out-of-the-blue, introduced me to the Duke of all people, who is the president. He'd obviously been tipped off because he said: "I believe you're building a new stadium. Will it be ready on time?" I said: "I can assure you that if you and your wife are going to be there, it will be ready on time." We had a little laugh at that.

Lionel Pickering: It was a very friendly, oh, emotional day. I do feel that. It was a great turnout. The fans thought so too. As we were walking through the corridors to the pitch, I said: "Derby County's noted for its roar. I think you are going to witness it for yourself, and it's for you. It's certainly for you." The Royal Family do get some stick at times, which I think is terribly unfair. They're in a goldfish-bowl, and it's nice to know that we are the silent majority of people that appreciate the monarchy, and I know Jim Bullions says the same. To me, this country wouldn't be the same without the monarchy. There was this tremendous roar, and I'm sure the fans just couldn't believe their eyes; we've a brand new stadium, a bright sunny day – and we've got the Queen. You can't beat it.

Lionel Pickering: It was a very proud day in my life and I'm not the sort of person to get proud of anything, to be honest. I get pleased about things, but I'm not particularly chuffed or proud, about Derby County or anything, but that day I was. I was very proud.

The Media and Football

WE live in an electronic age with television the new paymaster of football. The media has grown out of all proportion compared to what was the case a dozen years ago, and it has an insatiable appetite for information, information and more information – ad infinitum. Speculation abounds. Stories are trailed, credibility is stretched – and broken. The media uses football, and football uses the media. Television, newspapers, magazines, they all tap into the new rock and roll, the new fashion. Meanwhile, the public swims around in a sea of information. Information is the lifeblood of the media – and football is fashionable. Give us more; we crave more; we get more; football at every turn. Is there really so much to say? Is it really, after all, just more and more – about less and less? The media – and football.

Les Parkin: The first match? I don't really know, but I think the one that sticks in my mind was Boston United, when they came and gave us a good thrashing, 6-1. I did a lot more before that because I used to go to Chesterfield, Notts County, anywhere in the East Midlands basically. But Derby was the home side. We used to lie in the mud, with dirty old army sheeting underneath, and get kicked in the head sometimes – and sworn at sometimes.

Graham Richards: Yes, I remember my first match vividly, although I'd been broadcasting for three years with BBC Radio Nottingham. Barry Eccleston is the only other regular commentator that BBC Radio Derby have had in 30 years, beyond myself. Barry moved off to live in America after a dispute with the radio station about being the commentator and the news editor. The then manager said: "You can't do both." So Barry chose to do neither and departed to America.

Gerald Mortimer: I suspect that it was Chelsea, away, in 1970, when I did it as number two to George Edwards. I think it was a draw, I'd have to look that up. I think it was a draw, and I remember Hugh McIlvanney being wildly impressed and saying that Derby played football like a good jazz group – integrated and free-wheeling and so on. Just to be involved at the Clough time was exciting in itself, apart from the aspect of earning a living.

Les Parkin: I always thought that when you took photographs in those days, you could identify where they were taken. Nowadays, techniques are superb. I think they're absolutely magnificent, but they could be anywhere. They're really close-up, they're dramatic, you can see facial expressions. You know, the old black and whites are coming back again now, which I used to do, and they were big boxes and we used to take out what we used to call slides. Six slides and you had to press the button absolutely at the right time, but nowadays, they'll take 300-400 shots. We used to show-off a little bit you know, when we used to go and talk to the other press photographers. We were the boys then, but I do think you could identify. You had 'Offilers' at the top, over the stands and people in there, in the background.

Gerald Mortimer: Do on the day? Virtually nothing, for a bit. George did the running copy for the *Green 'Un* and, a bit later on, I did one or two to get the hang of it. There's a certain knack to it, really. There's a lot of words, and the worst thing you can do is give them too many words at the other end, when there's little time to chop things and change things about. So for the start, it was rather nice, really. I just watched the game. George did the main report and I did a, sort of, subsidiary report, picking out a particular aspect. Now, with the way things have changed, it would all have to be quotes and things, but in those days, I was just paid to give an opinion.

Graham Richards: John Bright, who was then manager of Radio Derby, and had been number two at Radio Nottingham and had known me at Nottingham – but knew that I was a Derby County supporter – asked me to come over. It took me perhaps three seconds, perhaps two, to decide that I would, and I dashed over to see him on a Wednesday at the end of October 1977 and said yes, I would come from Nottingham to do Derby County, although Derby seemed to be on the way down and Forest were definitely on their way up – heading for the European Cup, eventually. I'd no doubts about it and he said: "Well, tonight they're playing at Anfield. It's Liverpool in a League Cup game. Would you go and do it?" I don't know what arrangements he'd have made if I'd said no.

Michael Gretton: They call me the 'Press Steward'. I've done the job for something like ten or 11 years I think, on-and-off. I enjoy it very much because you meet some very, very famous people. I've met Sir Bobby Charlton, as he is now; Norman 'bite your legs' Hunter; and a fortnight before Billy Bremner passed away, he was in our press room. So we do meet some famous people.

Graham Richards: I drove straight from the offices, straight to Anfield, dashed into the stadium an hour early; I didn't arrive at the last minute at all because I drove up the M6 at about 110 mph, such was my enthusiasm to get to this team, this radio station, in this town. I thought it was an unrepeatable opportunity – and I didn't know half of it.

Jim Fearn: I joined Derby County shortly after Keith Loring and Jim Smith and, having worked with Lionel Pickering, he asked me to come and work here. I'm a journalist by profession and I was editing something called *Derbyshire Now, Nottinghamshire Now, Leicestershire Now,* which was something that Lionel was running and he asked me what I knew about football. I said: "Probably a little bit more than you're thinking." I'd played rugby at school.

Les Parkin: One of the interesting things, we used to take crowd pictures. I remember the *Derby Evening Telegraph* – I never worked for them because I was always agency – they used to say: "Would you send us some crowd pictures because we want to do 'a face in the crowd'?" Do you remember that? I used to get all these chaps with their flat caps on and their trilbies, and they all looked very respectable and nice and you look at them now and they're really interesting. I found them interesting anyway. I know I'm getting older, but they are interesting. I think now, they are the most attractive photographs.

Jim Fearn: I'm press and communications manager. I came as press officer. To be fair to Derby County, I wasn't the first press officer. There are still some Premiership clubs who don't have an established press officer now, but Derby had already seen the potential. A guy called Ian Guildford preceded me and he used to deal with the programme, principally. That's when I got rather stuck, at the start of my career with Derby County. The problem is that you just think: "Programme, programme, programme." It was just me. Very soon afterwards I had an assistant come in, but the PR side of the job was just something I did when I got time then.

Gerald Mortimer: I guess it was soon after five o'clock when the *Green 'Un* was on the streets, but then again, matches used to finish at twenty to five in those days. You're now, consistently, 20 minutes later. It's still, actually, out at a pretty good time, and if a few more people would pull their fingers out, they would be on sale around the ground more freely than they are. The time-scale has changed. Half-time is longer; no game is allowed to finish in 90 minutes. So really, they can't start slapping the final things together 'till about five o'clock. It's a miracle that it comes out as quickly as it does, really.

Michael Gretton: Personally, I think that the press room is far better behaved when there is a lady present because the swearing's cut down, and they have a presence about them. When I first started, there was only one, on Radio 5, as it is called. I can't remember her name, but she was a very pleasant lady. I can remember another lady sitting in the corner, and one of the local journalists asked me why she was in the corner and why she was in the press room at the Baseball Ground, and he said: "It can't be a very important paper that she writes for." It turned out that she was writing for *The Times*!

Jim Fearn: As time's gone on, the PR side has taken precedence, really. Now I've got people in the department to do the programme full-time. A full-time person, Amelia Clarke, does the programme. She's the editor, and Damon Parkin is the special publications editor and he covers things like the *Rampage* magazine and I've recognised – almost to be dragged screaming and shouting – that the PR side is where we're really at and have an overview of where the club's at.

Gerald Mortimer: Yes, in those days the Saturday night sports paper was big stuff. Obviously, the other arms of the media have come in to take over. If I go back to my earlier watching days, there was a time that I lived, sort of, at the bottom of Normanton Road and the top of Green Lane, and I reckoned I could just walk back from the Baseball Ground in time to catch the results on *Sports Report*. *Sports Report* was there and the results came, but there wasn't this kind of blanket coverage. Now you can get them on teletext, television, national radio, local radio. It's made things more difficult for the evening sports specials, plus the fact that newsagents are increasingly reluctant to stay open to sell it. You can take steps to combat it, but only to a certain extent, I think.

Les Parkin: Other than that – lying in the mud and getting kicked – I remember one super incident. I can't think who it was, but Glyn Davies was captain, and he was a lad – a bit of a rough lad – and I remember he got hold of this one fellow and he went about six foot in the air, came down on his back and screamed: "Oh Christ." All of a sudden, Glyn ran up to him, put his arms round him and said: "Well, we are playing for money." I always remember that.

Gerald Mortimer: The *Green 'Un* certainly was, and remains, a big part of the working week. I wouldn't quite say it was the focus. I think to me the match was always the focus, never mind what was going to come out of it. There's a lot of work goes into the green paper. As you can imagine, there are some very willing people, and very conscientious and reliable people indeed, who send in reports of local football, but they do need a bit of touching-up here and there. I think it's spread a bit now. Derby County used to be on page three. The Derby County 'notes' as it was, that old Mark Eaton wrote, in what I always call the longest longhand I've ever seen because he was from that old-fashioned school of journalists that wrote in pencil on bits of paper and joined up lots of words. It looked very long. Yes, it's now spread itself over about four pages, has Derby County, and there are times when you have an uneasy feeling that you might have said that last week, or the week before, because there are only so many approaches really, unless you've got a side like Manchester United or something, galloping away at the top.

The Media and Football

Graham Richards: Broadcasting has changed from the dark ages to the space ages, really. For many years, all we had was a telephone, on which the studio would ring you or you rang them when there was a goal. If you were lucky enough you had a phone with a dial, and the dial wasn't padlocked by the owner of the telephone because all the telephones were owned privately, not by the football clubs. You had to book them off local journalists, always from newspapers, who never understood the different disciplines of radio. You had to book your phone, go and do it and you'd do it week-in-week-out, like that. There was no commentary. You were restricted, I think, at worst, to two interventions each half, of less than 30 seconds, plus a half-time and full-time report.

Gerald Mortimer: I took over, I guess it was 1973, when George was promoted to assistant editor of the paper, and he's now, of course, editor of the paper in Swansea and, by all accounts, doing it very well. Then I was sports editor and football correspondent and cricket correspondent for, I guess, about 20 years, which I'm not totally sure was a good thing. In the end, a guy called Mike Lowe came as editor and he said he wanted a sports editor in the office – which was a pretty fair thing to ask really – and virtually said to me: "Pick whatever title you want and write on Derby County and Derbyshire." I was delighted. I'd made a list of, sort of, options and whether or not I'd accept them. I just really didn't want to work in the office. Some people enjoy working in offices. It's never greatly interested me, I'm afraid.

Colin Gibson: Beyond all recognition, it's changed. I've been following Derby now, with yourself and Graham, regularly since 1986. We're only talking 14 years ago but back then you were into shared commentaries with other stations because the broadcasting facilities at the ground were so basic. There was the one broadcast line coming out of the ground, which went to Radio-wherever and then the line was hooked on from Radio-wherever, back to BBC Radio Derby. So you had no choice, you had to share the commentary. Well, can you imagine sharing commentary with BBC Radio Leeds and doing Leeds against Derby commentaries? It's just unthinkable.

Les Parkin: Ten yards from the goal post. We used to draw an imaginary half-circle, and when the players came into that half-circle, that's when we shot because our lenses were short, you see. Nowadays, they've got the big bazookas and they don't get near the play. They sit on the sidelines and sometimes in the crowd. The can sit on the corner posts and they get really superb stuff.

Jim Fearn: To be fair to people like Keith Loring, he's given my role more than maybe it would have been in any other football club, certainly in the past, so I'm now regarded as one of the four key managers. There are four of us beneath Keith and so we do have an overview. It means that any of the managers sees what is going on at Derby County and we can say: "Right. There's a commercial decision to be made there." I suppose now the PR department is more an ideas unit, we're more pro-active than reactive. You can run the danger of sitting back and waiting for the phone to ring, talk to the *Derby Evening Telegraph*, talk to Radio Derby. Now we try not put a spin on things, but we do try to keep the PR of the club very, very high up on the agenda.

Colin Gibson: The two things that have revolutionised broadcasting, from our point of view, are the mobile telephone because that allows you to get into places that you never got into, and digital technology, which has brought in something called ISDN, and now every ground you go to, even the really small grounds – you think of some of the grounds we've been to in recent times, Exeter a few years ago in the League Cup, many trips to Southend United – you now have your individual broadcasting facilities, and instead of getting there and having

Voices of The Rams

to rig up boxes of tricks, telephone leads and crazy switching boxes, now you can arrive with your little black box, plug into the wall and nine times out of ten, it works. That has been the major change. It's changed beyond all belief in the last 14 years.

Jim Fearn: The change in emphasis reflected in the change in title? I suppose so. I mean, I didn't create it. One director wanted to call me the 'director of communications', but the chairman said: "He's not a director." And that was that! In America, as you know, they like that kind of title, 'director of communications'. I met a couple of them out there, but we all do the same job, basically. I don't suppose the title particularly matters and whenever I go on any other programmes or Radio Derby for example, I'm always regarded as the press officer and described as 'the press officer'. I'm not proud. That's fine by me.

Michael Gretton: Of course, some of the rules have changed. At the Baseball Ground, when Mr Cox ruled, ladies weren't allowed down the tunnel. It didn't matter who they were, whether they were directors' wives or what, no ladies were allowed down the tunnel. Then, we used to go and ask the players, plus the manager, to speak to the press. Of course now, I only look after the managers because the young lady looks after the press in a different area. The situation now is that the two managers, are escorted no matter where they are in the ground. After the end of the game, no matter what opposition it is, whether it be Sir Alex Ferguson, whoever – wherever he goes after he's given his interview, I have to be with him.

Les Parkin: Never, no. No, you don't get the ball going in the net now. You don't see goals now. I mean, later on when I used to do stuff, you'd have the *Sunday Times* or *Sunday Express*, *Daily Express*, they would phone you up and say: "Can you send us a three-column oblong?" Never mind what the photograph was, it had to fit the space. Now, they will go out – and I do really admire the photographs that are taken, they are very, very dramatic – but I think the pity of it is, you don't get what I call 'a feel'. You don't get 'a feel' because they could be in Italy, they could be in London, they could be in Derby or whatever. I'm trying to think of the guy who wrote in *The Guardian* and he wrote a piece on 'Days Gone By' or whatever it was. He wrote this superb piece on the photographs that I love, and he did a spread in one of the *Sunday Times* colour supplements, all in black and white. When I looked at it I thought: "Good God. I did lots of stuff like that." I only said to Lionel Pickering the other day: "Never get rid of your file because there's more golden opportunities in that." Someone's going to come along one day and say: "What were they like?"

Graham Richards: I don't know how it started. It carried on for a generation too long. The evidence was always the other way, that broadcasting would increase football's popularity, but the obdurate octogenarians who ran football in those days thought the opposite was true and didn't want any sort of change. Indeed, Jack Dunnett threw Radio Nottingham out of Notts County altogether when his gates went down. It was a bit disappointing for him when the gates went down even further, after Radio Nottingham were thrown out.

Gerald Mortimer: Treatment of the media? Yes, I guess it's altered, but then so has the media. You can relate this to football and cricket. One of the best examples of change is an England cricket tour, where once upon a time, everybody would travel happily together, and there was an 'on parade, off parade' understanding. Now, cricketers know that anything they do out-of-hours, they're liable to have news reporters snooping around or somebody flogging stories or something, and their lives aren't their own. The media has become very intrusive, and it intrudes in a lot of things that aren't necessarily anybody else's business. The great cry that goes up is 'public interest' and that is totally specious in most cases. The public is quite keen to know because it likes being titillated, but there's absolutely no reason why they should

The Media and Football

know a lot of things and, therefore, more barriers have come up. I think footballers are more distant, not only from the media, but probably from the public. I think there are fewer problems again, at Derby, than at most places, but I think, were they to win the championship again, I don't think access and availability and ease of communication would be the same in the new century, as it was in the Seventies. But I don't think in the Seventies we asked them for quite so much all the time.

Colin Gibson: The other thing that's changed as well, is that football clubs have finally got round to realising that radio commentaries don't stop people going to football matches. Up until six or seven years ago, the thought of doing the whole 90 minutes was just unheard of. The clubs would say: "Oh, you can't do the whole 90 minutes, people won't come along to the games." Well, that's nonsense. I mean, can you imagine those who were running football in the Sixties and Seventies being told there would be one, two, three, maybe four live television games on a week and the stadiums would be packed? Football, okay, is in its boom time at the moment, but that's the other big change; the attitude of the clubs has also changed, and now commentaries, radio commentaries, live TV games, are part of the norm. So there's the big changes, the technical facilities and the attitude of the football clubs, that actually, radio commentaries don't keep people away from the football match. If anything, I would say it encourages them to go along to see them.

Graham Richards: Today, of course, it's not for me to talk about the technical things. That's Colin Gibson's purview. But ISDN, and many lines and 90 minutes of commentary is excellent and is where we should have been since the Sixties. We've lost 25 years, through obdurate officialdom, from broadcasting the game properly. When they come to us at two o'clock now and go away at, let's say, ten-to-six, that's a none-stop broadcast of nearly four hours, yet football is more popular in terms of attendance than at any time since local radio has been available.

Michael Gretton: Managers didn't always do interviews. I can recall one gentleman who is very, very, very hard to get in a press room. I won't tell you who it is because I might upset him, but he was very hard to get in a press room. Not too many managers refuse to come into the press room. Obviously it's a matter of choice and we can't force them, but most of them are very good. Our present manager is very good, very, very good. Yes. I've only known him refuse to come in the press room once, and that was when he was taken ill.

Les Parkin: I hope I took more than just the best one, but I mean, I had a sports picture award from the *Daily Mirror* for the Midlands area. Funnily enough, it was a Notts County match and the manager of Wolves – who were playing Notts County, there was snow all over the ground – had one of his star players carried off on a stretcher. He ran out, had a look around, realised there was a big problem. The stretcher was being carried off by the ambulance people, and he was walking with a very, very glum look, with his hands in his pockets, and that was used very big in the *Daily Mirror* and a few other newspapers. I've even got it up at home, and I never normally put photographs up at home. I think one of the better pictures, I don't know about soccer, was a boys' boxing match. He'd fought his little heart out for three rounds, and he couldn't stand it when they said he'd lost, and he just burst into tears.

Colin Gibson: Chalk and cheese were the managers that I've had to deal with at Derby County. Let's go through them. Peter Taylor? I was wet behind the ears when Peter Taylor was here, but he was terrific. He was great entertainment. He'd always got a story, he'd always got a quote and by-and-large, he was very good to me. As I say, I was wet behind the ears when Peter Taylor was here. He didn't have any success and he was soon gone. Arthur Cox then came in and Arthur, by his own admission, was difficult to work with. You used to get this very short letter at the end of each season, from Arthur: 'Thank you very much for your help in the last season. I know I'm not the easiest of people to deal with.' Which I thought was nice. He was difficult to work with. He wouldn't tell you anything unless he really had to, and he kept everything very close to his chest. Didn't let his emotions show. He was enjoying himself with his players. He didn't let it show to you. Roy McFarland? Roy and I had a sort of strange relationship. I'd idolised Roy McFarland as a player. In terms of a working relationship, we never really hit it off. Jim Smith? You just couldn't have anybody better to work with. Again, he keeps things very much to himself. If he's got a transfer, if he's working on something, if he doesn't want you to know it, he won't tell you, but he's always got something to say, always got something interesting to say.

Colin Gibson: It's interesting. Someone said to me recently: "You don't interview the players anything like as much as you used to." Which is true, and there's quite a few reasons for that. If I go back to the days of interviewing Arthur Cox and the players Arthur Cox had in under his managership, Arthur wasn't necessarily the most interesting person to interview. If he had got something to say, he didn't really want to say it to the media. I mean, he had plenty of his own personal thoughts on football and he could be fascinating to listen to, but put a microphone in front of him and he gave a very straight up and down answer, but the players that he had signed were terrific to interview. Peter Shilton, Mark Wright, Bobby Davison who played for him, Ross MacLaren, Steve McClaren – loads of them – all really interesting characters and, of course, they could all speak English as well, which helps. So you tended to deal more with the players because the players were interested or interesting and, perhaps, Arthur didn't really want that side of it. It's gone, in a way, full circle, in that a lot of the players can't speak English or don't speak English that well, and when the manager has something to say, if you ask him about something fairly controversial, he'll give you a straight answer, whereas Arthur didn't really want anything to do with that. And Jim, you can phone him anytime and he might say: "I don't want to talk to you now," or "'Phone me back," or whatever, but he'll always talk to you and he'll always have something to say to you, and he's terrific to get on with. As I say, chalk and cheese with managers.

Media facilities

Graham Richards: Best positions? The big boys really. Liverpool and Manchester United, where the facilities are excellent. Everton is very slightly too high, so used to be the case at Newcastle, but they've all got excellent facilities – a bit of room. Somewhere to go at half-time, to get a drink and access to the players and management after games. I enjoy Arsenal, where we sit on the front row, often in the sunshine at the end of the season. Tottenham is too low, but then again, you get a real player's feel for the game, even though your angles are difficult on the far side to be accurate, and I've certainly announced an equalising goal for Spurs at White Hart Lane, that actually hit the advertising boards behind the net, some ten years ago, much to the annoyance of the listeners, who wrote to tell me so at the time...

Michael Gretton: Well, obviously it's more spacious, therefore you're not so cramped. It got very cramped in the old Baseball Ground and the facilities are so much better at Pride Park. The press are now fed – and they are fed. There's quite a selection of food in the press room now and they are allowed to drink as well. Obviously we have to keep an eye on certain people not to take drinks out of the press room into the viewing area itself, but, yes, it's improved. I prefer it because there's more room. It's very, very friendly, very friendly.

The Media and Football

Gerald Mortimer: Tools of the trade have altered. A lot of people now working at night for morning papers, or doing Saturday matches for Sunday papers, are permanently looking at a computer screen. I find it amazing that some of them produce such good match reports as they do under those conditions. Yes, the tools? There are a few plusses with those. You're cutting out two big areas of error, like the old copy takers and the old, stroppy printers, but the curious thing is, the better the means of production there are, the earlier papers seem to want to publish, instead of stretching it later. They seem to have got it the wrong way round, to me. Facilities? I think with a lot of them the press accommodation is a bit of an afterthought. I would particularly mention Tottenham Hotspur in that because it is a poor view down there and the sort of press room they offer is a palsied effort for another club that fancies itself as a 'big club' without huge evidence to support the idea.

Colin Gibson: Arsenal. I think it's a great stadium. Tottenham's is coming along very nicely as well, but Arsenal's has got tradition about it. It's got the streets surrounding it, the street vendors around it. Unfortunately, it's got the most unbelievable stewards running the place and commissionaires, but we needn't go into that right now. It is a great stadium. We are on the front row of the press box to watch the game. They've had a lot of success. They're playing in front of full houses, but it's just got the tradition mixed in with the new. It's a great stadium.

Michael Gretton: There's a lot more press around. Another thing I've noticed is that a lot of the clubs bring their own press officer with them, so on that occasion, he brings his own manager through. Arsenal have got one, Newcastle, Chelsea. In fact, the Arsenal one is a lady.

Graham Richards: Our own position at Derby County, at Pride Park, is very good. We'd lost a very good position at the Baseball Ground. You'll remember, we were just at the side of the directors' box. That was, maybe, the perfect position of all time, and I used that for two or three years at the start of my Radio Derby career. Then we were pushed to the back of the stand, which became a poor position, but now, at Pride Park, we are comfortable, very comfortable indeed and the hospitality at Pride Park is unparalleled, I would say, in my entire experience.

Gerald Mortimer: I was quite interested going to Maine Road for the first time for about eight years. The press box there used to be splendid. It was right behind the directors' box. It didn't surprise me that it was now right up at the back of the stand, given the relationship between Manchester City and the media or indeed, Manchester City and their fans. It was significant, but not surprising, and it was sad because it was a belting view and you felt right in touch with the game.

Colin Gibson: Unfortunately, the best broadcasting position is at Leicester City. It's absolutely brilliant. Paul Mace, who runs the press and communications department at Leicester City, really knows what it's about and he negotiated a great broadcasting position. The only trouble is that the broadcasting position and the press room are about three miles apart. It's not too high, it's not too far back, it's not too low down, it is in just the right position to commentate on the game and there's plenty of working area as well.

Gerald Mortimer: Favourite ones? I'm not too good on this. I think you like going to big grounds that have a history, irrespective of facilities and, indeed, present status. I honestly think that if there was one away from Derby, it would be Liverpool. It has a buzz about it, and I although I don't think they are as nice as they used to be, I always think they are nicer than Everton.

Graham Richards: The worst grounds are generally the small ones. It's ironic that Watford, who got back in the Premiership for a brief spell, is one of them. An appalling place, behind glass. I would now dread going to Oxford United. Awful place. Can't see the game at all at Oxford. Bournemouth is hopeless, but they're all lesser clubs because clubs have had to improve press facilities. Nottingham Forest is too far from the pitch, and is combined with the most unpleasant and offensive officials that the League has got.

Colin Gibson: Here we go. Selhurst Park. It's just an awful ground. A dreadful place. Dirty, filthy. It's quite a decent working area, but there's just nothing about the ground to recommend it at all. Coventry I'm not too enamoured with either. I had a bit of a run-in with the people running Coventry a couple of seasons ago and I've never quite got over that one. I don't like Coventry at all. I just think it's a bit of a soulless place. I'm sure they'll thank me for saying that, at Highfield Road. Other than that, there aren't too many that I really do dislike. We do have our fair share of fun and games, don't we? Stewards at Liverpool, vociferous supporters at Everton, sitting behind us, but I think it's all part of the fun of doing the job.

Michael Gretton: When you've worked as long as I have, you get used to the gentlemen. Most of them are kind and let me use their first name. There's one gentleman, though, who still insists on being called 'Mr', oh yes.

Les Parkin: I wouldn't say skill in photography has declined. I would say self-discipline. I couldn't afford to go out because I didn't use film. I used plates, in the back of the camera, to start with. So when you pressed the button, it had to be right. You talk about that picture of Reg Matthews. I remember taking a picture of Reg Matthews pushing a ball round the post and he wore a cap and it was six inches off his head, and it was a lovely shot. You're right. You don't see them today, and I think they would be interesting. I'd like to see a few of those coming back, but maybe they don't know how to do it today. They could do it. Technically they could do it, but they don't see it like that anymore.

Michael Gretton: No, they didn't used to have to sign in, but that was introduced at the Baseball Ground some years ago, after what happened at Bradford and Sheffield, so we knew how many reporters we had in the building. It got a bit lax towards the end, but now, on the insistence of the powers-that-be, you have to sign in basically for your safety as much as anyone else's because should there be a disaster, I'm responsible for getting everyone out.

Les Parkin: Precise is a good word. Less precise is exactly right. I remember going to a match at Wembley for the *Daily Mirror*. They said: "Look, we're going to send some messengers round and after the first 15 minutes, can you send some stuff back, and after 40 minutes, can you send another batch of stuff back?" I said: "Hang on a minute. I might send two or three or something." They said: "No, no. We want you to do this and it's all done on 35mm cameras." I said: "Okay." We did that. The messenger turned up and I did a roll of film. The message came back: "We want a lot more stuff than this." But in fact, they only used two pictures. I would have shot then 50 pictures, but it doesn't give you any pleasure because I think when you shoot that amount of photographs, a lot more are left in the camera that are never printed, never looked at because you highlighted the pictures which you thought, which were always goals, but today, goal pictures are not important. Maybe it's me getting a bit older and a bit old-fashioned and saying we were better, but no, we weren't better I don't think, but it was nice, the way we worked.

Jim Fearn: I tell a story about the Liverpool game, which was the day before Mother's Day. I got an e-mail from a guy in Australia, who said: "My mum actually sits just a couple of rows down from you. It's an aisle seat. Could you just tap her on the shoulder and say: "Happy Mother's Day". That brought it home. He described what she'd be wearing and what dad would be wearing, so it was easy to pick them out. So that was quite sweet, really. She didn't actually turn round and say: "Shut up, I'm watching the game!"

Michael Gretton: No, I've not had to throw anyone out, not really, no. Well yes, we've had people 'advised to leave', but usually it's very good. The only problems we usually have is when a certain gentleman, a very high profile manager, comes to Pride Park – he's a very good friend of Mr Smith – and we need a crowbar to to get them apart.

Jim Fearn: When we were in the States in 1999, I met a couple of guys who had actually worked in England. One is the director of communications for the Colorado Rapids... a very pro-active guy called Ben Grossman. He'd worked a couple of months in the Crystal Palace press office, so he knows what it's all about over here. The problem they have is the local media not knowing the sport. He'd got one guy in Denver who understands soccer, as they call it. But he feels they're banging their heads against a brick wall all the time. The Broncos play at the Mile High Stadium. They're high profile. Soccer, they just can't get any profile at all. By the same token, in Chicago, they've a guy there called Adam Lowe, who is a director of communications. They won 'the double' last season, a very new team. They won the Cup and the League and, as far as the Chicago media were concerned, there was no interest whatsoever. I suppose you feel: "What do I have to do? What do we have to do, as a soccer club?"

Michael Gretton: I was sitting in the corner having five minutes one day and there was a gentleman sitting in the other corner wearing an old mac and an old battered cap, and I thought: "I know you from somewhere." It suddenly dawned on me who it was and I rushed over and asked him for his autograph and he said: "You don't recognise me, dressed like this, do you?" I said: "Yes." It was Leighton James. He later told his wife he'd been recognised and she said: "Never in this wide world." Apparently he'd come straight from where he was working.

Jim Fearn: I suppose you can go too far with the PR. Forty per cent of the crowds in America are Hispanic. All the announcements are made in three languages. There are a lot of Poles there as well, so it's Polish, Spanish and English – but the PR guy said to me: "You know, if we signed a couple of Mexicans, the crowds would just go sky high." Then you've got the compromise of saying to your coach: "You might want that player, but would you please make sure he's Mexican." You'd feel then that something's a little bit wrong if you had to do that. I know Keith Loring has made the point – and it's quite true – that whereas grass roots is where we are at here, making sure our academy kids come through and maybe cutting out the need to go abroad and to bring in all the continental stars – there they really ought to concentrate at the head end because they're playing in massive stadiums – 75,000 seaters – and there's nobody there at all.

Michael Gretton: Yes, former players do come back. One of the nicest gentlemen is Mr Roy McFarland. Always got a handshake, always asks how you are. Always asks how the family is because he knows I've got a family and he has met the wife on various social occasions, both at the Baseball Ground and at Pride Park. Obviously the gentleman who normally comes every week is Stevie Cross. And Big 'Rog'. Very nice gentleman is big Roger Davies.

Jim Fearn: We get to play with all the toys now. We get to do a weekly cable TV show and, as a journalist, you quite fancy the idea of doing quite a few little things, doing a nice little feature, doing things for television, for radio. It's not much point if you're no good, but... There will always be people who are better than you, but the great thing about the department now is that we all get to play with these things and we're all getting quite good at it, without ever wanting to take the thing over completely. We have a guy called Ivan Gaskell, who comes in on a match day and pulls together *Vision Rams* because he's very good at what he does. There's only so much you can do and going back to where I used to escape from games, now my escape is to sit down and do the commentary. That is something I don't particularly prepare for and I enjoy it. That is the release now. To actually commentate on a game.

The future for the media?

Colin Gibson: Ever changing. From the radio point of view, I've mentioned how it's changed over the last ten to 14 years since I've been involved in it – that football has got this picture that, okay, you do radio commentaries and people don't stay away. The technical facilities for bringing the broadcasts have changed. We've seen that television has been the big player in football. Sky TV bankrolls the Premiership so that clubs can pay these fantastic wages. Yes, the stadiums are full, but without the TV money, a lot of the clubs you would feel, would be in trouble.

Jim Fearn: You feel that whatever happens, whichever way court judgments go, there will always be two or three clubs calling the tune. If you're talking about pay-per-view down the line, the big issue is that when Manchester United play at Pride Park Stadium, what is Derby County's cut going to be? At the negotiating table, what are Manchester United going to say about these sort of games because you can't get away from the fact that the people who will be interested in taking the pay-per-view will be, predominantly, Manchester United fans worldwide and the game at Pride Park will be going to attract millions of people because we're playing Manchester United. Well, it's what Derby County's cut in that game is going to be that is going to interest the likes of us. We have to accept that, although the support base is growing in America – we've attacked it through various ways, we've talked about the internet before and we've been very pro-active in that – you still have this Manchester United fairytale, where people who have never been to Manchester, never mind Old Trafford, still link to Manchester United.

Colin Gibson: I slightly worry about some of the developments in the future. The talk of pay-per-view television. Even the economy, getting radio broadcasting rights, the money for that. The money that BBC Radio Derby has to pay for commentary rights has gone up phenomenally since Derby were in the Premiership, and the only way that money is going to go, is to continue to go up. There's more and more competition. The national networks of the BBC face competition as we know. All we ever hear about these days is the BBC losing sporting contracts. The fact is, a lot of money is being bid to get sports broadcast rights because it tends to bring in an audience. It's a classic example with Radio Derby that the sports audience figures, which is effectively our coverage of Derby County, are phenomenal, but the costs associated with that are going up increasingly, and that's how I see it going. That there's going to be more and more competition, but that a lot of the terrestrial viewing, as it was, for television, is going to go more and more by the board. More and more is going to go on to satellite, but I suppose you've got to think that there has to come a point where it can't go any further. You just feel that football is on this high at the moment, and somewhere along the line, the bubble will burst. Goodness only knows what will happen then!

Jim Fearn: You could have Manchester United versus Arsenal week in week out and that might get a bit tedious. I think there's also the danger that the fans get forgotten and if you're looking in terms of, maybe, a European League and you look at the lack of interest in some of the Champions League matches last season, you really think: "Where are the fans? Is it worth it?" The atmosphere's nothing, That's the key. You do feel that, maybe, there's a bubble out there waiting to burst, if we're all not very careful about looking after the fans.

A Changing Game

IT IS probable that the Nineties saw a greater change in football than in any other ten-year period in the history of the game. Commercialism grabbed football by the throat in the Nineties, and those with a broad perspective, rather than narrow self-interest, fear that it might squeeze the life out of what was once 'the People's Game'. Finance now dictates the decisions that were once the sole preserve of football people. The culture of the game has undergone a transformation.

The Taylor Report of 1990 has had a sizable effect. Premiership stadia are money-making enterprises, far removed from the grounds that grew up in the shadow of the factories and amidst the back streets of Victorian England. In some cases, stretch limousines have replaced 'shanks's pony'. After the dark days of poor crowd behaviour in the Eighties, football has now become fashionable. A peg for anyone and everyone to hang a hat on.

The speed of change has been lightning-fast. Modern football reflects modern society and those who yearn for a slower, more leisurely pace and a return to the values of the past are whistling in the dark. Yet some things do stand the test of time. Good control, accurate passing and sound temperament are fundamentals of the game that have not altered and remain simple. It is why football is the most popular game in the world, and what happens on the field is still the thing that matters.

Roy Christian: Football was very much a working-class game in the Twenties, whereas now the working classes or what is left of them so to speak, they almost can't afford to go to every match now. There was always a sprinkling of women, but not so many as now. I think children or juniors, went as much. Maybe a bit of financial trouble there too, but I shouldn't think there is much difference between Under-16s then and now. I don't think there's a boys' enclosure anymore. Now, I suppose, it's the Family Enclosure.

Michael Dunford: I was box office manager, then I became assistant secretary. That was 1976-77. Then I became secretary on 1 September 1979, which was an away game at Crystal Palace. Box Office manager, assistant secretary, secretary, general manager, and – apart from three or four days in those 25 plus years – I wanted to go to work every morning, and there aren't many people who could honestly say that. I had a job that was my hobby. It still is my hobby. I was only a very average local player and I thought I had the next best job, working alongside professional players in a professional environment. Football has been very good to me.

John O'Hare: We used to say: "Can he play?" It's still the same now. All through my career, if you're talking about football, with people who have played football, the first thing you say to them is: "Can he play?" And they know what you mean by: "Can he play?"

Jeff Knight: The players have no excuses these days. Light ball, beautiful pitch. The pitch is marvellous, isn't it? When you think you used to be up to the knees in mud.

Mick Hopkinson: It's hard to compare eras. It's like saying that Matthews would never have played today because he'd have less space, but you learn to adapt to that, don't you? Skill is skill, isn't it? Fitness is fitness. Agents, of course, try to make out that a player is far better than he actually is, and the player, if he believes it, then you've got a problem, haven't you? Agents are a newish thing and they are important now.

Charlie George: The game's got so fast now, I don't know where it will all end. All the preparation is different. You can't compare eras. You can only be the best at the time. I enjoyed when I played. I think that was the best time of all to play. There were some great characters then: George Best, Rodney Marsh, Stan Bowles, Peter Osgood. We're a bit short of characters at the moment. Too many without a smile on their faces. My favourite player was Denis Law. He was a great player. Jimmy Greaves was fantastic. Dennis Bergkamp is a great player, too, and Kanu.

Bert Mozley: Reg Harrison said to me that if I was playing today, I'd have a birthday. Attacking, I'd have a birthday. I saw the shoes of a guy, about four ounces, and I felt the ball and the field – immaculate. The modern game is fast, but put today's players back then. It would be difficult for them. The leather ball, when the rain hammered down, felt like a ton of bricks when you tried to head it or move it.

Ray Young: You don't know the players now. I enjoy going, I've always enjoyed watching two sides, but you're never going to get a local derby again, are you? How can you get a local derby with no Derby lads in it? It's maybe versus Forest, but it's just a load of foreigners. People still get so miserable when Derby lose, though. It's amazing.

Bert Mozley: It has changed. I mean, it's faster, a lot faster, obviously. Lighter shoes, lighter ball and the grounds as they are now, but it seems as though the players nowadays don't want the ball. They get it, move it on and say: "That's my job done."

Jeff Knight: You don't see so many players today who are noted for one particular thing, like heading or shooting. Tommy Lawton or Dixie Dean, for example. Some of the way they play, the tactics and that, bores me at times.

Peter Gadsby: So much is down to television. In those days there was just about *Match of the Day* available to watch football on television. You didn't have action replays did you? You just missed it and you were perhaps better for it – and in black and white. If you take what has happened now, there's so much football on television.

Michael Dunford: I think, sometimes, the football club in Derby is too big for the city. You think of Derby, and you think of Rolls-Royce, you think of Royal Crown Derby and you think of Derby County Football Club. Maybe British Rail as well at one time, but the football club is such an integral part and its a county club. Forty-five per cent of the support for Everton comes from within the city boundaries, but at Derby, it's very much the 'county club'. I'm not certain it isn't too big, really, too important for people.

Ray Young: I think they're fitter. At least they seem to be fitter than I was.

Ian Buxton: I think the fitness levels are much higher than they were when we played, but

I'm not sure that's for the good of watching the game. You get a lot of boring first halves, and the more interesting football comes when people get a bit tired in the last half-hour, which is when the gaps open up. It's more interesting to watch then, I think. I'm of the opinion that players of our era would be good today, and good players of today would be good in our era, whatever the pitches. They would adapt to them. They'd have a different mental approach as well. They'd have the mental approach of 30 years ago, when they just got on with it.

Lionel Pickering: I think it's almost impossible to compare eras because it is a different game. It might have been, up to a point, more entertaining in those days, but there's no doubt about it, they are fitter and faster and it's a quicker game. In fact, it's sometimes too frantic. Back in good old Raich's days, he would get hold of the ball and just put his foot on it and look around him and people would stop. They didn't want to be made to look a fool. There's no doubt about it, the football was brilliant and entertaining.

Bobby Davison: I think the grounds were heavier, but I don't think you had the overall fitness in the team. Four or five would be exceptional athletes, but now, in this day and age, I think you'd probably find the whole squad are exceptional athletes.

Ian Buxton: They're might be better athletes than we were, yes, but we were probably stronger, generally. I mean, I never had a pulled muscle in my life, at least not until I was 61! That was playing tennis. Now I'm told: "It's a different game. It's more stressful, it's quicker and all that." I wouldn't argue about that. I don't know enough about the modern game, but there does seem to be a lot of injuries today which seems to indicate a lack of strength. They're more finely-tuned, perhaps, today. I'll tell you what, Storer wouldn't have entertained them being injured. They'd have had to play.

Stuart Webb: You cast your mind back to decisions. Decisions to go for Dave Mackay, decisions to go for Jim Smith, key decisions to move to Pride Park, all of these, yes, but as businessmen you make them. I make decisions here at Lonsdale every day, but they are not as important as those because they affect so many people. It's incredible how it affects the lives of thousands of people, being a football director. I always say, being a football director you are custodians of the club on behalf of the shareholders and the fans, for a period of time. You do your best in that time. You may get promotion, be relegated, whatever, but you do your best for the supporters.

The Premiership

Lionel Pickering: I think the Premiership is a damned sight tougher than the old First Division. It doesn't get easier, this Premier League. We've noticed it in the four years we've been in. It gets tougher and tougher. People are spending a lot of money now on these foreigners. The standard is so much higher. We're looking now for the guy who, with one touch, can control the ball like Igor could and like Eranio can.

Willie Carlin: I don't think the standard is as high as people make out. The game's changed, obviously, but I don't think it is more skilful. When we played most teams had very skilful players. Look at your Coventry teams, when you had your Willie Carrs, Ernie Hunts, even George Curtis at the back. QPR had good teams. They had Marshie, the Morgan brothers... Conditions have changed and training has changed. And God knows what they put in the ball these days. When we played the goalkeepers used to kick the ball to the halfway line, now goalkeepers are kicking the ball to each other.

Dave Mackay: The standard? I'm a little bit disappointed. Most of the teams are just trying to stay in the Premiership. Of course, money involves everything and when a good team in the bottom half goes to Man United, it's everybody behind the ball, that's what you're going to get. Then you get an occasional break and maybe win 1-0 and think: "What a lovely tactical move." It's fear. Of course, it's fear. In my time at Tottenham, teams used to come and try to beat us. Mind, they always got slaughtered, you know! They tried to come and beat us, but now everything's changed. Now, if you're an inferior team, then you get everybody behind the ball. You give me a team with everybody behind the ball, and I'll make it difficult for Brazil to beat us. They'll beat us perhaps, but not by many. That is becoming an art, everybody behind the ball, and if they win 1-0 with two shots at goal and one goes in, its a brilliant tactical move, which I don't agree with.

Roger Davies: The next step is probably the biggest of all, from where we've come, up to challenging. I think that is a difficult step and I don't know whether clubs like Derby can make that step anymore.

Gerald Mortimer: There was one FA Cup win in 1946. I think both looking back and looking ahead, you tend to think it was almost a blip in history, the two championships. It is increasingly difficult for a club of Derby's stature, or say Nottingham Forest's stature, Ipswich Town say, to win major trophies. Then again, if you look back in history, they haven't won major trophies very often. The pattern was set, initially, once the League had settled. I tend to think of Preston in 1888, rather like Derby County in 1946, they were just slightly ahead of the game. In Derby's case, they'd done a couple of shrewd things while wartime football was on, like signing Carter and Doherty. If you look at the list of champions, they're all big centres of population, aren't they?

Peter Gadsby: Success nowadays is measured. Whether you want to agree or not, success is measured on the ability to stay in the Premier League. It may not be right, but from our point of view – the finances – anyone outside of that Premier League, the way it's going, is in trouble.

Roger Davies: I think it's going to be a long, long while before a team like Derby County is going to win the championship again, unless a major benefactor comes in. Lionel has done a tremendous job here, but you're not talking £200-230 million, or Jack Walker megabucks.

Gerald Mortimer: Yes, the hope is certainly more slender now...you can hear supporters giving boards of directors stick because they're not as rich as Jack Walker, which is really pretty unreasonable when you think that most boards of directors are making more personal sacrifices than Jack Walker, who could subsidise Blackburn Rovers out of his interest. I'm not knocking him, in any way shape or form, because he was obviously a guy who wanted to put something back into his own home town and, although I felt Blackburn Rovers going down had quite a high chuckle factor, simply because they'd lashed out silly money so freely, you had to feel sympathy for the poor old lad, standing up in the seats with a tear in his eye and you thought: "God, he couldn't have done more, could he?"

Dave Mackay: My biggest disappointment is all the foreigners coming in. There's too many. As soon as somebody gets injured or hurt – a famous player – they bring in another. I was in Kuwait. I went there in 1978 and I was there for eight years and they had a similar problem. They didn't start football till 1960. The best teams in that area were in Egypt, so all of a sudden, all the Egyptian players, the good ones, were coming to play in Kuwaiti teams. So you're not getting any young players coming through from Kuwaitis. So they said: "Hey, the maximum is two foreign players. Two Egyptians, two anything, but you'll only get two."

Kuwaiti football went up from there. I think here it's getting worse and worse, and I don't see any real future for the youngsters being allowed to come through. The great players are not coming through from Scotland anymore.

Willie Carlin: The Premiership I think, sadly, is going to finish up with half a dozen of your top teams every year. You're going to have the same six every year and there'll be a hell of a gap.

Roy Christian: I'm afraid the Premiership is becoming like the Scottish League; Rangers and Celtic dominating everything. I suppose we've almost got to that position now, with Arsenal, Manchester United and Chelsea. Clubs with the money will dominate it, but there is still just a chance for one of the lesser cities to get in. Derby are not doing too badly, even though we must be the smallest centre of population, with the exception of Wimbledon, who don't have any spectators at all. And, of course, they got relegated last season. I don't understand them. Gates, of course, no longer matter any more, whereas at one time, teams like Hartlepools depended on a good Cup run.

Dave Mackay: I went to see my cousin. He played for East Fife, which is in the Second, Third Division in Scotland. I went there and there were 1,400 people or something like that, and they've got four or five foreign players, and four and five foreign players who are bad players, not good players. I mean, at that grade, you can't be a good player anyway because you'd be out as quick as anything, but these guys are bad players. You may as well have local bad players as foreign bad players.

Squad rotation

Brian Clough: The game's changed, but I don't believe in that. I didn't believe in it when I was in management. I'd got what I wanted and they played every match, every week, three times, whatever. They knew that because I told them. I don't mean to be sounding conceited, but I told them: "You've got to play twice a week. You're going to have to play." I played my son at right-back in the Reserves because he hadn't had a game or he was injured or whatever. If I can do it to my own son, I could do it to anyone else.

Brian Flint: Once you're financially secure and safe, the hunger, sometimes, can't be there. Too many players in this day and age – in my opinion – miss too many matches. Putting your best players on the bench and then playing them for five minutes? That's too clever for me, that one.

Kevin Hector: I was always wanting to play. We all did, Wednesday and Saturday. I'd rather play than train. I wouldn't have liked being changed around all the time. Managers should know their best team and stick to it.

Wages and pressure

Brian Flint: I think the wages are ridiculous. Somebody came on Radio Derby – I'm not sure if it wasn't Eric Steele – and said: "They earn this big money – not just Derby County players, but footballers in general – because they are entertainers. They are in the entertainment business and entertainers get big money." I agree with that, so isn't it time they began to entertain a little bit more? If you go to see Ken Dodd and he makes you laugh, when he comes again, you go again. If, all of a sudden, you sit all night and you don't laugh, next time he comes you think perhaps he had an off-night, so you give him the benefit of the doubt. If you don't laugh again the third time he comes, you don't go again. If football is bracketed with entertainment, then they've got to come up with the goods all the time because in no other profession do you hand over the money first, under the bracket of entertainment. No, it's a business. I think there's too much at stake to call it entertainment. The pressure is there to win.

Gordon Hughes: When we played, our pressure was playing well to keep in the side because our wages went down to £4 win bonus. Pressure? If I'm on £10,000, £20,000, certain people on £40,000, I wouldn't mind that sort of pressure. I cannot understand that there's too much pressure. All right, there's more pressure from the media, but I could stand that. There's always a certain amount of pressure, isn't there? They play, what, 30 odd games now? All right, they play a few more cup competitions, but they're 'jaded', they're 'tired' and they're going to get 'burn out'. Even Jim – from the press reports – is saying it, and I can't agree with that – I cannot agree with that at all.

Ted McMinn: Well the money has to stop soon. Even the big clubs need to sell 23-24,000 season tickets just to pay these guys' wages because these wages now are getting to a joke. How anybody can get stress by earning £40,000 a week? I'm sure I could buy a tablet to get rid of that stress, but there's some players that are having stress. I just wish I had that problem.

Gordon Hughes: As you know, it's the best feeling in the world, going and performing and doing well – and showing off really. You get your bad games as you know, but there's nothing better than having 30,000 or even 60,000, shouting your name, and getting the acclaim. That's what it's all about. I could stand that pressure. All right, they're more in the spotlight and the media is watching every move, but it's always been like that to some extent. No. I can't agree with all the talk about pressure.

Roger Davies: I'm not one of them who says: "I wish I was still doing it." I loved every minute of the time I had and I can live with that. I do have reservations about the game, the way it's going. I really do, because of the business in it. I wonder whether, in what's happening, the hunger is going out of some of these players because of the money. I mean, good luck to them if somebody's going to pay them that, but I wonder whether they've still got the hunger. Personally, whether I got 50p or £50,000 a week, it's a game of football to be won. Wages and money is nothing, once you cross the white line. It's a game of football between two teams and whether you were playing on a park pitch or here at Pride Park, it's a game of football that's got to be won. That's the main aim and if someone wants to pay you for winning a game of football, all the better.

Brian Flint: Players should be concerned with their own performance, not being entertainers. Willie Carlin told me that, the other week, outside the ground. He was saying how different it was when he played. He said: "If we'd lost, the wife got the children to bed, quick." If they'd lost, there was a chance he wouldn't be picked the following week and he'd lose money. He got paid a basic wage, win bonus and goals bonus. He said: "There were 11 players in the opposition trying to put my livelihood at risk. They were trying to get me dropped."

Eric Steele: Different now? Yes, very much so. I think they're different in the respect that they look upon it differently now. If you take what I call the good pro, that comes in, wants to train, then we don't have too many in terms of accepting that it's a job of work. You look at them now and it's like the motor show when you see the car park. They are given an awful lot too early. The footballers of yesteryear had to earn it the hard way.

Steve Sutton: It was a boyhood dream to play for Derby County. All my friends were Derby fans. I went to school in Ashbourne. Perhaps it was the expectations of the lad coming home, and I wanted so much for the club to get back to the top division, the Premier League, that my form went down a little bit and I played with injuries, and maybe at another club I would have said: "I'm injured. I've a cracked ankle. I can't play." But with everyone at the club, and Arthur like he was, and everyone wanting to do well and play in every game, I played when I shouldn't have played. I know that now to my cost, but yes, I think it was pressure, and as homegrown talent, you feel it. When you lose, you go away thinking: "It's my fault." You take it more personally, perhaps, than players who come from far away.

Eric Steele: We sometimes say: "Why is it? Why can't you just come in, train, play and enjoy, go home and look forward to coming in the next day?" They always seem to be looking for another agenda." Why are we...?" They always seem to be questioning. It used to be a joy to come in, train and you looked forward to it. Now you're back to good pros, you see. We have to work hard, and it's hard with different cultures to get spirit etc., but they do get things very early. They know now, three-year contracts, they're a millionaire by the time they're 30, and I don't care what anyone says; that money has had a great impact on it and I think it softens attitudes in people to strive, to be even better players.

Outside the ground today

John O'Hare: Going back to when I was a lad, we used to walk to the game and you had away supporters walk to the game as well. Maybe from the station or whatever. That's an impossibility now.

Brian Flint: I don't think it's the same now. I suppose we get older and things come along to change things, but there isn't the atmosphere, not outside the ground. I suppose if there was a little street with a tea bar opposite, a hot dog stand near and then your rosette man... You never see a man selling rosettes anymore. Probably the club wouldn't allow it because they've got to sell a rosette, not a street seller. All these things add up.

Keith Loring: The little cars for bringing people down from the South car park? The idea was mine. What's great is that the board let me do it.

Moving on

Michael Dunford: The position was advertised in the *Daily Telegraph*. Funnily enough, a national journalist rang me up and said: "Eh, have you seen this advert?" Now this was at a time when Derby were just going into the Play-offs, and I was 40. I think unless you're very close to what you are wanting to achieve, by the age of 40 you're very unlikely to achieve it. I'd had 25 happy years at Derby but I didn't like the political situation that was developing. Maybe had I not applied for the Everton job then I would not have stayed at Derby much longer anyway. But the chance to come to what I considered to be one of the top six clubs in the country was too good to turn down. I'd always said professionally, maybe Arsenal was the one club I'd have liked. They've always done everything correctly. But Everton had a good reputation, so when the opportunity arose to apply for the job, I did that and I've often been asked the question: "What would you have done had Derby County been promoted via the Play-offs?" I'd have still gone. I think it was right at my time of life and I think, sometimes, you can outstay your welcome. When you've been somewhere for 25 years, people tend to think you're part of the furniture. You tend to think your ways are the only ways it can be done and it's not true. It's not true at all. I don't regret moving.

Keith Loring: I'm still a Londoner, from the point of view of the Derby people, but the stupid thing is, I went back to London to work at Brentford. I was at Cambridge for 20 odd years and left London as a 21-year-old to bring my children up out of London. All I can say to you is this: "I can't see us moving." I could get the sack tomorrow – and by the time you've written this, who knows? The one thing I like about Derbyshire is that in two minutes, you are in peace. You can drive out, five minutes, ten minutes, whatever. I mean, we just love living here. The people, to Lesley and myself, have been magnificent. They could not have been more helpful. I'm not talking about people who want the chief executive to go to dinner and don't care about who he is. Someone asked me the other day: "If you left Derby, where would you go?" I've had three offers to leave since I've been here. One was a major Premier League club that didn't do particularly well this year, but is still a very big club. Another was one of the two Scottish clubs, one of the two. It's all very well saying: "I'm going to work with this club, but look who the chairman is." You think: "How the hell am I going to get on with him?" The chairman relationship is a very important point at this club. Jim Smith, Lionel Pickering, Keith Loring, that trio relationship. I'm not saying other relationships aren't important, but that has to be right. The most important one is Jim and the chairman. I'm not saying mine is as important as them, but that relationship has to be right. You look at clubs where it's not right. You hear about it.

Peter Gadsby: My word, hasn't there been some changes in football? And I don't think it's a change I welcome. Once you have a situation where Mr Murdoch has got control, and the present board hasn't got control, then you're talking about a multi-national tycoon, who will view Manchester United like the Atlanta Braves, whatever team he's got. I think history is being rewritten.

Michael Dunford: Differences? The size of the club. This is a massive club and the passion of the people in Merseyside, well. The first six months I came into Merseyside, the job wasn't too much of a problem, but coming to terms with the people was because they're so sharp upstairs, football-wise. Very friendly people, but God, they're different to Derby people. I would call Derby people 'moderates'. Up here, they're a different breed, very much so.

Lionel Pickering: We talk about all this Sky money, but you get more Sky money the higher you are up the table, and that's what the big bunfight is all about...I don't think the players realise that. Yes, I do think it's the players' business, of course I do. Our wage bill has rocketed over the past three or four years. That money's obviously going to the players and they've got, in my view, a commitment to the fans and to the club. They can't just go strolling around...They still get their money, if they're injured or if they're suspended. I can think of one person who made only a few Premiership appearances but still got his bonuses if we won. So there's something wrong somewhere. It's a bit different from your day, absolutely. You might have been lucky to get £20 in your day. Now, if they don't get £200,000, they're underpaid.

Brian Flint: I think if they keep putting the prices up, that'll be the biggest problem. The big wages separate the players so far from the supporters. I've never personally booed or shouted at players. It doesn't help anybody; it doesn't help me, but I can, perhaps, understand it. They're that far apart and I think resentment can come: "If you're on that much a week, I'm not on that much a year." That does come into it, but I don't think it's that that will stop people going, it's the prices.

Keith Loring: No, not at all. Let's just split these. First of all you've got your corporate, who's a completely different conversation to a three-year season ticket holder. Your corporate is going to be there and pay somewhere around about £100 a head. Remember quite a few of those are local people who have done good, who've supported the club from the terraces in the old days. Not all of them, but there are quite a few of those people, and what's the difference if I've got a 28,000 capacity and no corporate or a 30,000 capacity and corporate? It doesn't matter. It doesn't offend anybody. It's not a problem. Some people get wound up about it, but it's bringing revenue into the club, and if the revenue comes into the club, the bottom line's more and there's more to spend on the team, and back goes the circle. It's just one big circle. Lionel's not having any money out. Okay, you might agree that the franchise is worth more money, but Lionel is not trying to sell it. He sold 25 per cent of the company; he didn't sell it for himself, he sold it to put money back into the club. He didn't take a ha'penny.

Keith Loring: So you then go to 28,000 supporters, and so let's say a couple of thousand of those have a three-year ticket, you're down to 26,000. The number speaks for itself. You can't afford to price those people out of the market. They are your core business. They bring in more money than what the commercial people do. They may turnover £10 million, but they don't keep £10 million. On the other hand, all the ticket money that comes in, I don't keep any of that because it just goes in one place. It goes back through the system and straight into the players. You have to accept that the price of the tickets will reflect the price of the team because otherwise, what's the point of making a great big profit, if you don't spend it on the team?

Bobby Davison: They need to keep the prices down. It costs a fortune to watch football now. I don't think we'll have a European League. I think that will be too difficult to get started. I think we've got hooligans out of our football, to a certain extent, but if you look abroad, it's still there. Germany, France, Italy – there's still a lot of problems, so I think if we went European, that would start problems again. We're fine the way it's going at the moment.

Jim Fearn: I don't know when something is going to really happen to change things because it's market forces. Let's be fair, I suppose Derby County is following on the example, as far as the commercial world is concerned because we have Pride Park Stadium now and Pride Park is a seven-days-a-week operation. So we're taking advantage of all the things, not just football, but everything that's happening in Derby. We've now got probably the best venue for a banquet, for a conference in the area. I can't see that it is taking anything away from football. We've done it in a sensible way... any given Wednesday, you might have a regional WI meeting here, a luncheon. These are women – I'm not against women in football at all, we're trying to get families back – but these are women who wouldn't normally come to a football match, a cricket match or anything, but they're coming to Derby County's ground and spending money and enjoying the surroundings. That's good and we've been quite clever in that and I don't think anybody can criticise us. I think there was probably a little bit of a feeling a couple of years back, from the fans of Derby, one or two rumblings that, you know: "Don't get away from the fans." The way I see it now, you've got a three-way split. You've got a third of your money coming in from television, a third from the fans and a third coming from the corporate facilities here. I don't think the fans can really complain that a third of the money comes from outside, without really affecting them at all.

Roy McFarland: I just like playing football. I think football is timeless. Yes, it's changed and people are saying: "Has it changed for the better?" Of course it's changed for the better. You know, people talk about it and although lifestyles have changed, areas have changed. Before we were talking about the slums and the areas where footballers came from. We're still producing footballers, they just come from a different mould. Clubs have become more professional. We now have kids. We even have kids at Cambridge at nine years of age and we try to teach them the fundamental things, which they've been doing in Europe for years, and maybe we were blind to that.

At the end of the day

Gordon Hughes: Retirement? Oh, it's the prime thing in your mind or at least once you reach the 30 age. I think you're in your prime 28-30, but after that you feel yourself that things aren't happening the way they should, and it's because it's a young man's game. It's a very physical game. For the last three years of my career, that was virtually all my wife and myself talked about. Because in those days we hadn't earned enough, and it does come down to it. If they're sensible these days and look after the money they are getting, they won't have that problem will they? Isn't that a great change? It takes the uncertainty away, doesn't it?

Tommy Powell: Well, I finished in 1961. I finished because I went to Fred Walters, the chairman, and said: "I think I'll pack up because I don't want to feel that, as I'm 37 now, I don't want to feel that they're 'carrying' me." So I said: "I think I might as well call it a day." Which I did and I went working with a mate of mine. I was helping him run a bookie's and at that time, Heanor and Ilkeston and all them were getting good gates. Then Ivor Cox, from Heanor, came over and said: "Will you come and play for us." I said: "Well, I'm working." He said: "I'll tell you what, I can give you probably as much as you're getting at Derby. If you come and play on a Saturday, we'll pick you up at dinnertime and drop you off after." So my mate said: "You go. I'll get someone to cover you." Well, I was still retained, you see. So I went to see Fred Walters and he said: "You'd better have a word with Harry." When I went to see Harry and told him of the offer he said: " If you can play for them, you can bloody well play for me." So I said: "No. I've told you why." And he said: "I'll tell you what. Come and play in the Reserves – with the young lads – and I'll give you the same as the first team." It must have gone up to £25 by then. I said: "Is that a promise?" "Yes," he said and so I started off in the Reserves. That only lasted four or five weeks and then there were one or two injuries and I was back in the first team. Then I did my knee – against Portsmouth – and that was it. So if I hadn't have gone back, I wouldn't have had this twisted knee. Even so, I don't regret anything. Nothing at all.

Roy McFarland: We had some wonderful nights and performances, obviously because we won the League in 1972 and it was nice. Whether Derby County, in the future, will ever win that top championship? I doubt whether they will ever do it...We won it in a era when football was a little bit more open, and they're the memories you'll always take with you. The best thing is meeting up again with Alan Hinton, Alan Durban, Roger Davies, Jeff Bourne, Willie Carlin, Richie Barker and all them. Nice memories.

Dave Mackay: To me I've had three different clubs and they've all been fantastic clubs. Heart of Midlothian, Tottenham Hotspur and Derby County, fantastic.

Roger Davies: I loved every minute, playing. As you know, I run the ex-Rams side. I wish I was still playing. I'm not one of those players having sour grapes at what they're doing now. People say: "Do you miss it?" or: "Do you wish you were still doing it?" I don't miss it, no. I wish I was still doing it, but I don't miss it because all my memories are good and I can look back.

John O'Hare: My football days were the most enjoyable of my life. Derby was a football town. They were an average Second Division side and things happened so quickly, but it was still a

A Changing Game

football town. They'd had the history. The Carters and the Dohertys and people. When I first came, just in the town walking round Derby, even before we did as well as we did, it just seemed to be a football place. I came to live in Ockbrook straight away when I came here, and most of the people – not all of them of course – went to the matches. A lot went to the games and it always seemed to be a football place. It always will be.

Ted McMinn: High points? Winning Player of the Year. I think that was probably my high point. I always got a buzz just playing for Derby County, really. That was a high, for me.

Peter Newbery: Did I enjoy my days at Derby? Oh, very much so. The fact that one can still keep in touch with people and we have the annual reunion of former players is great. I had great times, great memories.

Willie Carlin: I could go in The Woodlands. Roy Mac would come in, Eddie Thomas, Phil Waller, Kevin Hector. They were just ordinary people and we mixed with them. Remember Harry Bedford? He used to drink in there. So you weren't aloof; you weren't away from them. It was a community thing. The wages were right. We weren't on much more than the ordinary fella in the street. In fact, I think Royce's were on more, if I'm not mistaken, basic wage. They were great days. When I was in Majorca and I said I was going home, people said to me: "To Liverpool?" No, I said: "To Derby. It's a lovely place."

Dave Mackay: I'd love playing now. Everything's in midfield anyway. It'd be a piece of cake. I'd love it.

Roy McFarland: I would love to play football today. I don't think it's changed that much that I couldn't play it. I don't mean to be big-headed about myself but I think good players can play football in any era. You think about Matthews playing in present-day football, he'd have got through. He'd have survived. You think in terms of Finney. He'd have survived, no problem. Nat Lofthouse, he would still be a handful.

Steve Powell: It's difficult to say. You can only play as well as you can at the time and I had, certainly during the Seventies, some great times and great memories and they can't take those away from you. I was just happy to have got paid for something I enjoyed doing.

Roy McFarland: Football is timeless. The people change because we always need new heroes. We always remember and it's nice to have a past, and I'll be, in a sense, part of Derby County's history. I said to my wife, Linda: "When I die, I want my ashes put on the Baseball Ground." She said: "They're not going there. That's the last place in the world they're going." I said: "No, love, I would like my ashes, when I die, I'd like them to go on the Baseball Ground, and if it's not going to be the Baseball Ground, then I don't mind it being at Pride Park, but I'd love it to be somewhere with Derby County because, without doubt, they were my happiest days."

Roger Davies: When you think, to get paid for playing football is such a privilege, and I wonder whether some people, some players playing now, really appreciate that. That's not being nasty, but to get paid for playing football – for what you'd do anyway – is such a privilege. It's an enjoyment and what a living. It's your paid hobby and I enjoyed every minute of my time at Derby County.

Brian Flint: The worst times had to be the Tommy Docherty time. Colin Addison tried his hardest, but there was such a nothingness then. It was hard. The best times have to be Cloughie's times and up to Dave Mackay going. They were the best times of all.

Alan Hinton: This is the best club in the country for taking care of its older players, and you've got a film star owner in Lionel Pickering, and I wish they'd knight him and call it Pickering

255

Stadium. It's always particularly nice for me, who lives in Seattle now, to come back, and people are so nice about the old days, and I'm just proud to have been a part of the two championships this club won in over 100 years in business.

Lionel Pickering: Peter Doherty was an entertainer, and he took the best penalty you've ever seen. It barely reached the goal. It just trickled, and probably just nudged the post, just went over the line, with the goalie diving hopelessly the wrong way because he used to do like a body swerve and a feint and you didn't know which foot he was going to kick it with. I used to copy it, as a kid. It was pure magic, actually. Those were the great days and it was a pity when Cloughie came on the scene and took down the pictures of those days. You don't want to forget them. I mean, we don't want to forget Cloughie and we don't want to forget Dave Mackay either and their great teams. That's going to be there for ever more, but don't take those other magic memories away from kids. I'm sure some of the kids who come today, some of these players they've seen now, they'll remember them for the rest of their lives.

Football in the future

Lionel Pickering: Well it seems to me that it is going to continue to prosper and develop. It'll change, for the worse maybe. I'm sure this pay-per-view is going to come in, as sure as eggs are eggs. People are putting in these new TVs aren't they? I see Murdoch is giving away these little boxes now so more people will convert to his way of things. That means, as with boxing for instance, you can switch something to just one television. Not the whole of Derby, just one television, for £15, £10 or whatever. That's going to happen, and a lot of people are going to watch these matches. Every Derby County match will be on the television, on the box, within two or three years. That's going to affect gates, surely. It may mean that it will become cheaper to come and watch football. Mind you, we shall get the benefit. We'll get paid for this, as we are getting paid from Sky. We're talking as if we're still in the Premier League, by the way.

Steve Powell: I hope things do stay. It would be horrible if there was some sort of collapse in the whole football system, but I think because there's so many television companies involved now, I can't really see that, certainly the Premier League folding or anything happening major there, but you worry for teams lower down the level.

Graham Richards: It's going away from what I love. I think we are in a golden era and it will be looked back as that. It's fashionable and I'm not comfortable with that. I love football too much for it to be followed by people who don't love it. It's a silly, introspective point of view, but once things become fashionable, they, in turn, become unfashionable. Maybe I will welcome that. I think the future is fairly secure for the Premiership. What is not at all pleasing is outside, where the First, Second and Third Divisions struggle and are likely to, and the top of the pyramid outside the League is struggling greatly, and the amateur game, where everybody starts and you have some of your most important experiences, is in a state of ruination as far as I can see. I've nothing to do with it these days, but I just pass pitches every day everywhere in England, that are just not being used.

Stuart Webb: Then there is the issue of pay-for-view, which people are hoping to try in the next year. The Nationwide have tried it. Man City have been on a couple of times. That's big bucks if that comes in. So, with all this surrounding the game, I think it's important that administrators and directors do not lose sight of the fact that it is a spectator sport. You're only as good as the environment in the stadium and, if pay-for-view comes in, and we drive people away on a wet winter Saturday, to stay at home on a Saturday and watch it on pay-for-view, then you're destroying the fabric of the game, which is now so successful. So you have to ensure the balance between a healthy stadium, a healthy atmosphere, coupled with extra cash coming in from pay-for-view or television, but you mustn't lose sight of the fact of a packed stadium.

Jim Fearn: The internet's a big thing. There have been a lot of people into the internet for a long time. A lot of people, for instance, in Norway. We have a massive supporters branch in Norway, who have been waiting for it to happen from Derby County's point of view. As a club, we're very much at the top of the tree. We're the only club that does an interactive matchday commentary, which means that wherever you are in the world, you can e-mail us. That was the case when we did the games in America. We had fans in the UK – the games kicked off at one o'clock in the morning – they said: "We're staying up, it's half-time now, but we're staying up." When we're here, somebody will e-mail from the beach in Florida and say: "It's 90 degrees here, how's somebody playing today? Is so-and-so in the team? We've just logged on, can you go through the teams?" It's a wonderful interactive way of doing things.

Lionel Pickering: I would like to see the Premier League develop into two leagues as well, Division One and Two because it's such a traumatic thing for teams to be relegated, it really is. There's such a big gap between the Premier League and the First Division, and the First Division is so tough to get out of as well. It's a hell of a rat race and yet, when you get into the Premier League, you suddenly realise what it's all about. You've gone up a gear.

Gerald Mortimer: A lot of major games worry me about the direction they're going because I see the wrong people running them. Decisions by FIFA and UEFA and people always looking for money. I think the single factor that would worry me most now, would be the way they're burning out players. You go back to Brian who always said: "The most important thing a footballer does is rest." When do they rest now? When Jacob Laursen put his cards on the table and said he didn't want to be considered for Denmark last June because he wanted a rest, I said to him: "You haven't had a summer rest since I've known you." He said: "No, the last one, proper one, was when I was 16." And always in June they've a couple of qualifiers. Three or four weeks later, they're reporting back again. It's the same in cricket. They say there is more cricket played, but the only increase in cricket – and it's the same in football – is in internationals. Thoughts of having World Cups every two years? One of the reasons people look forward to World Cups is because it isn't every two years. Things have a rarity value.

Keith Loring: When you think of putting moving pictures down the internet, and wherever you are in the world you can watch a game. Whether you do it or don't do it, it's going to be possible. Sooner or later, I actually believe the paying spectators may win; the people who are prepared to come because they will be part of that occasion. I can't tell you how it's going to go, but to be fair, we didn't put our prices up – and that's all I can tell you! We didn't put our prices up, and other clubs are doing.

Stuart Webb: The other fear that I have is that the commercialism that has come into football – and I was one of the leading lights in driving that early on – doesn't destroy what we've got because with television and commercialism, you've got corporate people coming now and spending huge amounts in boxes and entertainment – which is great. Pride Park is probably a leading example of what happens when a stadium functions every day – brilliant – but these are corporate people spending money, and if it's £20 a ticket, £25 a ticket, for a family to go it might cost them £100. When we talked about the Baseball Ground, you could get in for 2s 6d. All right, it is relative, but my point is, I went to my first football match with my father, my grandfather, it was tradition. If the new generation coming through, the new young kid, doesn't go to Pride Park because he can see it on pay-for-view, sitting in his Derby County kit, great. Sat in front of the fire at night before he goes to bed – but he's never been to Pride Park, so he's not got the habit. Then the corporate guys decide enough's enough and they'll move to rugby or something else, when football takes a dip. There could be a huge gap in that founder support, that bedrock of football as we know it, of kids not coming up and the corporates have gone. What's in the middle? That's the big worry.

Jim Fearn: I think now Derby County is more than aware of the fans that have always been awaiting that internet service because a lot of people have actually made a phone call to England and actually had the Radio Derby commentary held to the receiver. That's the way they've done it. We're making that easier now, but it's also breaking through in the States because we use somebody called Broadcast.com who are based in Texas and they actually stream the audio out for us, so it means that we are on the home page on a matchday on a top American site. They've just been taken over by Yahoo.com, which is a massive internet company and so we've got a good profile out there and I think what we'd aim to do is to become a lot of people's 'second' club. We can't stop people wanting to follow Arsenal and Manchester United because they've heard of them, but if we're providing a service week in week out, which we are doing, we find people are latching on. Again, an experience in the States was a guy from Cincinnati, who's never seen Derby County play, never been to England, who was there to see his favourite club now, for the first time. His name is Mike Sanger. It was great to welcome him to one of the training grounds, the Moody Bible Institute in Chicago, and for him to watch the team play. You feel there must be probably more Mike Sanger's out there and the more we can do to cultivate that, the better. It's a free service. You have to say, there's another line to that because we do want people to buy the merchandise. We're making that easier, you can do that on the internet now. We have a secure on-line merchandising thing where you can put you credit card in, in full safety. So we hope there is a spin off. There are other clubs in the Premiership that take a more cynical view. They charge people and you have to pay a subscription to actually listen to the commentary. We'd rather be out there, free, you know: "Come and listen to us." We hope to grab more people because of that.

Keith Loring: I think you have to accept that the Premier League decisions are not made by anybody other than Premier League chairmen, and you need a 75 per cent majority to change anything, so that protects you a little bit. The guys who run it on behalf of the Premier League can't make decisions without the chairmen of the clubs. The same thing happens with the Football League. But I'm not a part of that anymore, but that's how it used to happen. The FA, I believe, has got to change. I believe there's got to be a different set of rules for the amateur game and a different set of rules for the professional game. I think trying to mix the two means you get nothing. You get the best of nothing.

Gerald Mortimer: Athletes playing football. Probably two of the least remarked, if you like, but significant changes in my lifetime are states of pitches and weight of ball, and the effect of those is huge. You wonder about the future of football. I just think: "I wonder about the future of football, I wonder about the future of cricket." In the end I think they are both good enough games to survive the people who run them.

Lionel Pickering: Maybe, who knows, Premier League Divisions One, Two and Three because there are lot of clubs who were great – Preston North End, West Brom, Portsmouth – they've all had their days and now we've got Blackburn Rovers. They've been up, now they're going down again. Man City, they've actually been into the Second Division, although they're back now. You'd never leave Man City out of it, would you?

A Changing Game

Graham Richards: I think of the Birmingham that I knew, where I started to play football in a park, and it was very difficult to get a pitch for our team. We were a youth club team and it was impossible to get a pitch. We had to go from our homes in west Birmingham right over to east Birmingham to get a pitch. It was a journey of nearly 13 miles. That was a vast distance in the Fifties, but if we wanted a pitch for our youth club to play, we had to go to the other side of the city. There wasn't anything free. Now it's odd that I was working at Warwick a few weeks ago and I went over, back home through Birmingham, and I deviated to go to the playing field where I played my very first games in organised football. It was a sunny evening in late April and the field is still there, which surprised me. It must be 25 acres minimum and there was no one there. A man walking a dog and a couple of lovers walking along. The field was empty. That's mirrored on Saturday afternoons and Sunday afternoons. There were three pitches on the whole of this acreage. In my day, there might have been 15 to 20. There were three pitches, with no goal nets and no great sign of wear, I may say. Somehow, I think, that's going to have a long-term effect on the game. The two leagues in Birmingham where I played a lot of football as a teenager don't exist anymore. They've just gone. The Birmingham Youth Committee and the Birmingham Works League, which was very powerful in my day, very powerful and through which I got a very brief introduction into a better part of football, they don't exist any longer. I think people play with computers or mess around, rather than playing football, and a lot of that is due to this commercialism at the top of the game that's atrophying the grass roots of the game, with youngsters.

Lionel Pickering: I'd like to see 16 teams in the Premier League, 16 teams in the Second Division and 16 teams in the Third Division – of the Premier League. That means you could start your football in September and if you wanted a break midway through – they're talking about doing it in Scotland – you could finish at the end of April, with the Cup Final first week in May, as it used to be. Then we could have a decent cricket season. I like watching cricket and I'm looking forward to the cricket season, but before you blink too much, you're back on to football again, aren't you? They're coming back in July, for training. 19 August it starts again. It's all too soon. It is a different game.

Bibliography

Mortimer, Gerald *The Who's Who of Derby County* (Breedon Books 1992)

Rippon, Anton & Ward, Andrew *The Derby County Story* (Breedon Books Third Ed. 1998)

Hugman, Barry J. *Football Players' Records 1946-1984* (Newnes Books 1984)

Heath, John & Christian, Roy *Yesterdays Town* (Barracuda Books 1985)

Index

Index

Index